The Kingdom of God in Africa

The Kingdom of God in Africa

A Short History
of African Christianity

Mark R. Shaw

A • BGC • MONOGRAPH

Baker Books

A Division of Baker Book House Co
Grand Rapids, Michigan 49516

©1996 by Billy Graham Center

Published by Baker Books
a division of Baker Book House Company
P.O. Box 6287, Grand Rapids, MI 49516-6287

and

Billy Graham Center
Wheaton College
Wheaton, IL 60187-5593

Printed in the United States of America

Library of Congress Cataloging-in-Publication Data

Shaw, Mark, 1949–
    The kingdom of God in Africa : a short history of African Christianity / Mark R. Shaw.
      p. cm.
    Includes bibliographical references and index.
    ISBN 0-8010-2096-4 (pbk.)
    1. Africa—Church history. 2. Evangelicalism—Africa—History. I. Title.
BR1360.S475   1996
276dc20   96-35523

Billy Graham Center ISBN: 1-879089-20-3

For information about academic books, resources for Christian leaders, and all new releases available from Baker Book House, visit our web site:
http://www.bakerbooks.com/

Contents

92725

Preface

Books, like trees, begin from small seeds. The first seeds of this book were planted in the chalkdust of classroom teaching. Patient and perceptive students at Scott Theological College and Nairobi Evangelical Graduate School of Theology watched the first seeds fall into the ground and germinate. This book is dedicated to these brothers and sisters and the love for the African Christian story that they shared with me.

But seedlings need care to grow to maturity. That care was given through the kindness of the Billy Graham Center at Wheaton College in Illinois and the grant they gave to me as their 1994–95 Missionary Scholar in Residence. The advisory committee appointed by the BGC proved to be valuable in watering new ideas. James Kraakevik, Charles Weber, Mark Noll, Timothy Phillips, Scott Moreau, Mel Lorentzen, Dotsey Welliver, and Jane Nelson brooded with me over the book as it sprouted branches and leaves. Without their encouragement and advice the defects of *The Kingdom of God in Africa* would be greater. I am particularly indebted to Dotsey Welliver and Maria den Boer, who painstakingly edited this manuscript.

Libraries, like greenhouses, are ideal environments to grow things like books. In addition to several libraries in Kenya, the Wheaton College Libraries (Buswell, the BGC Library, and the BGC Archives) were crucial in the production of this volume. Ferne Weimer, Ken Gill, and Bob Schuster were ever helpful. The Day Mission's Library of Yale Divinity School under the able leadership of Martha Smalley filled in some of the resource gaps for me during two short but valuable visits.

The deepest roots of this book explore the concept of the kingdom of God and the ways in which African Christianity witnessed to that reality. I argued the relative merits of this approach before an expert assembly of mission historians from several different continents who had assembled for the 1995 Yale–Edinburgh conference on the history of Christian expansion. I appreciate the encouraging response I received from that gathering. To the gracious hosts of the conference, Andrew Walls and Lamin Sanneh, I express both my admiration and appreciation. Professor Sanneh's willingness to read the chapter on West Africa was greatly appreciated. Thanks also are due to Yale Divinity School and the Overseas Ministry Study Center in New Haven,

Connecticut, for co-sponsoring the conference and providing hospitality to its participants. Thanks are also due to Adrian Hastings whose stimulating conversations at the OMSC in 1995 made a deep impression.

I am grateful to Baker Book House and their academic editor, Jim Weaver, for their enthusiasm for this project and their willingness to join with the Billy Graham Center in publishing the book. Additionally I owe thanks to the administrations of Scott Theological College and Africa Inland Mission International, respectively, for granting the necessary study leave. Particular thanks go to my colleagues at Scott who bore a heavier load in my absence.

My wife, Lois, despite a very busy time completing her master's degree at Wheaton Graduate School, daily encouraged her easily discouraged husband. Her love for Africa and for me stands behind every page. My children, Anne and Jonathan, agreed to be dragged halfway across the world in order to permit their father to write this book.

Regarding terminology: I have not applied Bantu prefixes (Buganda for place, Baganda for people, Luganda for the language) with any consistency, preferring to use what I considered to be the most familiar designations for tribes, places, and people. Frequently that meant dropping prefixes altogether (Kamba rather than Wakamba for the tribe; Swahili for the language rather than the more correct term, Kiswahili). I have also tended (with a few exceptions) to use the modern name for an area (Ethiopia rather than Abyssinia; Zaire rather than Congo; Kenya rather than British East Africa, etc.) to minimize reader confusion.

This book is intended to be used as a text for college and seminary students in Africa as well as for people in the West interested in the fascinating story of African Christianity. Because of its approach the reader will notice that some areas of Africa have been neglected. For instance, the important story of Christianity in Madagascar has not been covered. Because I have chosen not to write an institutional history of African Christianity, a number of denominations and agencies also have been neglected. Many familiar missionary names have been left out in an attempt to include more African contributions to the story. And little attention is given to Christianity in Muslim countries in Africa in the twentieth century. But for all its limitations *The Kingdom of God in Africa* was written with the hope that, however far its branches reach, readers will discover the truth spoken by the ancient Greeks that "out of Africa, there are always surprises."

Part I

The Imperial Rule of God

Early African Christianity (100–600)

Wrestling with the Kingdom

Approaches to African Church History

Wrestling is one of Africa's oldest sports. Back when the pharaohs built the pyramids, the lanky Sudanese men of ancient Nubia wrestled along the banks of the Nile. They wrestle there still today. Chinua Achebe's prize-winning novel, *Things Fall Apart*, tells the story of Okonkwo, who gained fame in the surrounding villages for defeating Amalinze the Cat, so-called because for seven years he was an unbeaten wrestler whose "back would never touch the earth." Okonkwo's fame remained undiminished for twenty years, but it was the coming of Christianity that won a spiritual wrestling match with Okonkwo from which he never recovered.[1]

Like Achebe, I think wrestling is an apt metaphor for the story of African Christianity. For the Okonkwos of Africa, grappling with the person of Jesus Christ has been a long and absorbing contest. When Christ broke into human history in the first century, "no single mind could encompass the whole, no single hand could draw the definitive portrait of him."[2] That is still true for many Africans today. Wrestling with Jesus is a major part of the African story.

This is a book about the African church's long struggle to be an effective witness to the One they worship as risen from the dead. And a struggle it has been. One truth about the African church that will surface many times in the following chapters is that no single church, individual, or movement "could draw the definitive portrait of him." Just as Jacob wrestled through the night with the Angel of the Lord, so Africa has wrestled for centuries with rival concepts of Christ and his kingdom. Throughout this long struggle African Christians have discovered that reflecting the rule of Christ and his kingdom is often an elusive ideal never perfectly achieved by any of the real-world in-

---

1. Chinua Achebe, *Things Fall Apart* (London: Heinemann, 1959).
2. Stephen Neill, *Jesus Through Many Eyes* (Philadelphia: Fortress, 1976), 4.

stitutions that bear his name. Though the church's real-life imitation of and obedience to Christ their King is always flawed and often unfaithful, she continues to wrestle on. As you read through this book you may even find that the tussle between kingdom ideals and African church realities is the most interesting and important part of the story.

But before we look at this theme of the kingdom of God in Africa, another wrestling match deserves our attention: the struggle that engages writers of African church history. We need to look for a few moments at this preliminary contest over the values and ideas that shape the way one tells the story.

Wrestling with Church History: Current Questions in Writing African Church History

The subjective side of history. Voltaire once defined history as "a trick we play on the dead." His cynical definition points to an important truth. History is not just a factual study of the past, but is also often a highly subjective interpretation of the past. Most of us learn history through secondary sources—books about the past written by trained historians. What we sometimes fail to notice when we read these books are the values that shape the way historians think and write. Historians do see the objective facts of the past, but "what they see is colored by the tint of the glasses they wear."[3] While we must avoid the extreme opinion that the subjective element precludes accurate historical knowledge, we must at the same time recognize it as a part of the history books we read. How do these values affect historians? Roy Swanstrom explains:

> A historian from a developing country such as Kenya, anticipating a future dominated by the so-called Third World, will naturally look at the world and its historical past from a perspective different from that of an Englishman whose memory is filled with the glories of an empire almost gone. Historians identified with the radical left will differ in their perspective from historians identified with the moderate middle or the radical right.[4]

Because we all "look at the world and its historical past" from different perspectives, it is important to find out as much as we can about the values and perspectives of authors when we read their work. The study of how historians think and write about history is called *historiography*.

Missionary historiography. In the recent writing of African church history two major perspectives have emerged. One can be called *missionary his-*

---

3. Roy Swanstrom, *History in the Making* (Downers Grove, Ill.: InterVarsity, 1978), 29.
4. Ibid.

toriography; the other, *nationalist historiography*. Missionary historiography tries to tell the whole story of the African church, but tends to emphasize the role of the expatriate missionary as a church planter or discipler. African rejection of Western Christianity is either judged harshly or minimized in the story. The role of the missionary or the "native" who cooperated with the missionary is the main story line.

Examples of missionary historiography are Peter Falk's *Growth of the Church in Africa* and C. P. Groves' four-volume *The Planting of the Church in Africa*. Both studies are valuable and tell the story of African contributions to the establishment of Christianity in Africa, yet their emphasis is on the role of the missionary or the national who emulated the missionary.

Ogbu Kalu, a Nigerian historian, writes that though this approach was often noble and unselfish as it sought to tell the story of the triumph of the gospel, it "was bound to be *propagandist*" because such books were often "designed to boost morale and material aid." Even when this propagandist element is missing, "European writers still tend to study the history of Christianity in Africa by focusing predominantly on what missionaries did or did not do."

Why? Kalu feels that the reasons for neglecting the African perspective "were *race* and *written sources*."[5] Western historians until fairly recently assumed that Africa had "no history beyond the history of European activity in the continent."[6]

Nationalist historiography. Nationalist historiography reacts against this Eurocentric approach and seeks to give new emphasis to "indigenous" or independent expressions of Christianity in Africa. Kalu describes their goal:

> In the nationalist and critical writings of modern Africans, the old goals and methods have been discarded. It is recognized that the goal of church history in Africa now is to study how communities which had their own religions and viable instruments of social order came into contact with a new religious form, namely, Christianity and the variety of ways in which they reacted to this external agent of change.[7]

A striking example of this approach is A. J. Temu's *British Protestant Missions*.[8] Temu argues that missionaries were agents of colonialism in Kenya. The real story of African Christianity in Kenya is the Kikuyu revolt against colonial missionaries and the establishment of independent churches

5. Ogbu Kalu, ed., *The History of Christianity in West Africa* (London: Longman, 1980), 2.
6. Ibid.
7. Ibid.
8. A. J. Temu, *British Protestant Missions* (London: Longman, 1972).

and schools that acted as nurseries of nationalism.[9] This approach has been a useful corrective to the missionary approach, but its reactionary character makes one wonder if it, too, is a form of propaganda as ideologically driven as the missionary approach. Such a perspective can distort the story of African church history as badly as the approach it seeks to replace.

There seems, therefore, to be an impasse. Is there another vantage point that could break this deadlock? Some African historians have called for the use of an *ecumenical historiography* in recounting the past. This is an improvement over the two previous perspectives. One can see this approach in Catholic church historian John Baur's *2000 Years of African Christianity*.[10] One strength of this approach is that the contribution of different churches, Christian movements, and races can be brought out with a minimum of favoritism.

But an ecumenical perspective also has its weaknesses. Such an approach tends to be too uncritical of the kinds of Christianity it surveys. The ecumenical historian is obligated to present on equal footing any movement professing to be Christian and having a large enough membership to be taken seriously. An ecumenical perspective provides no solid ground for value judgments. And history without value judgments is sterile and of questionable value for the church.

Additionally an ecumenical approach may be just as propagandist as the other approaches, using church history to push forward some ecumenical agenda. Somewhat surprisingly, those churches and movements that have not joined the ecumenical movement or are critical of the ecumenical movement (such as fundamentalist and conservative evangelical groups) are not always treated fairly by ecumenical historians.

But other options exist. We need to find an alternative approach that has a higher reference point than church growth, ecumenism, nationalism, or cultural authenticity. We need an approach that can tell the whole story in a way that does justice to missionary contributions, nationalistic responses, and ecumenical fairness, but then moves beyond the limitations of vision that cling to these approaches.

One suggestion is the use of the concept of the kingdom of God. This theme has provided a motif that opens up the story of the church in other lands in surprising ways.

In 1980 E. A. Adeolu called for a new church history that went beyond Marxism and capitalistic analysis and did "for our time what Augustine did

9. Other examples of this nationalist approach can be found in vol. 7 of the UNESCO *General History of Africa, Africa under Colonial Domination (1880–1935)*, as well as in articles by E. A. Udo ("The Missionary Scramble for Spheres of Influence in Southeastern Nigeria 1900–1952," in Kalu, *West Africa*, 159ff.) and W. O. Ajayi ("Christian Involvement in the Ijaye War," in Kalu, *West Africa*, 200ff.).

10. John Baur, *2000 Years of Christianity in Africa* (Nairobi: Paulines, 1994).

for his: discern the mysterious intermingling of the City of God with the earthly city."[11] More recently, Nigerian theologian Ukuchuwu Chris Manus called for a new kingdom emphasis in African Christianity in order to promote social justice. "The reality of the kingdom of God," writes Manus, "provides men and women of all ages the vista to judge this world and to renew it through their total commitment to peace, justice, freedom."[12] Justice is served by a kingdom consciousness.

So also is ecumenicity. The need for a viable ecumenical perspective has led African church historians like Ogbu Kalu toward a kingdom framework for African Christianity. Kalu called for a rediscovery of this framework in order to move beyond the parochialism of institutional church history. "The basic assumption of Church history is that the Kingdom of God is here among men, providing enormous opportunities for renewal and reshaping of individual and communal lives."[13] While we must avoid the triumphalism that such an approach suggests, Kalu feels that a kingdom perspective would actually lift the story above local and denominational biases and illumine "the ways in which the community sees herself and the intruding presence of the Kingdom."[14]

One of the pioneers of this approach, H. Richard Niebuhr, found in the changing concepts of the sovereignty of God an interpretive key to American church history.[15] Niebuhr recognized that the biblical concept of the kingdom had three distinct but interconnected elements: God's sovereign rule, which is tied to the doctrine of providence; Christ's redemptive reign over hearts, which is tied to the doctrine of salvation; and the coming kingdom as an earthly utopia, which is tied to eschatology and ethics.

> The Christian faith in the Kingdom of God is a threefold thing. Its first element is confidence in the divine sovereignty which, however hidden, is still the reality behind and in all realities. A second element is the conviction that in Jesus Christ the hidden kingdom was not only revealed in a convincing fashion but also began a special and new career among men, who had rebelled against the true law of their nature. The third element is the direction of life to the coming of the kingdom in power.[16]

What was most striking about Niebuhr's model was the suggestion that the church during different periods of history tends to put more emphasis on one

---

11. Dr. E. A. Adeolu, "*A Research Proposal,*" *The Ecumenical Review* 32, no. 2 (April 1980): 127.

12. Ukuchukwu Chris Manus, *Christ the African King* (Frankfurt: Peter Lang, 1993), 164.

13. Ogbu Kalu, "Doing Church History," unpublished lecture, Yale Divinity School Archives, n.d., 2.

14. Ibid., 12.

15. H. R. Niebuhr, *The Kingdom of God in America* (New York: Harper and Row, 1937).

16. Ibid., 88.

of these three aspects of the kingdom to the relative neglect of the others. Niebuhr gave some examples.

The seventeenth-century New England Puritans emphasized the kingdom as the sovereign rule of God over all of life and attempted to witness to that reality by building a theocracy (or, more accurately, a theonomy) where the Word of God ruled every sphere or institution of society. The very success of their witness led to a rigid institutionalizing of the theocracy, which was unable to withstand the forces of change that occurred in the eighteenth and nineteenth centuries. In response to the demands of changing America, the church then moved from the old witness to bear fresh witness to the kingdom by emphasizing the redemptive reign of Christ over hearts.

The awakenings and revivals of the eighteenth and nineteenth centuries created an evangelical movement that emphasized converting individuals instead of building theocracies. But the changes brought about by the late nineteenth and early twentieth centuries (urbanization, immigration, religious pluralism, secularization) led to the social gospel, which interpreted the kingdom as an earthly utopia brought about by the steady advance of human progress. The institutionalizing of this liberal vision of the kingdom has likewise led to discontent and restlessness in the church, for the kingdom can never be equated with any human institution or structure.

Niebuhr was critical of this broken witness to the kingdom and called for the restoration of the whole gospel of the kingdom because "the three notes of faith in the sovereignty, the experience of the love of Christ and hope of ultimate redemption are inseparable."[17] Niebuhr was particularly critical of liberal Christianity, with its focus on the earthly kingdom to the neglect of the cross of Christ. "There was no way," argued Niebuhr, "toward the coming kingdom save the way taken by a sovereign God through the reign of Jesus Christ."[18]

Another American historian, William McGloughlin, has built on this model of Niebuhr and has shown how all American history may be related to the core values of the kingdom:

> From its first settlements, not only in Pilgrim Plymouth but in almost every colony, America has been a utopian experiment in achieving the kingdom of God on earth. Our Revolution was justified on these terms in 1776. Our history has been essentially the history of one long millenarian movement. Americans, in their cultural mythology, are God's chosen, leading the world to perfection. Every awakening has revived, revitalized, and redefined that culture core.[19]

17. Ibid., 127.
18. Ibid., 27.
19. W. McGloughlin, *Revivals, Awakenings and Reform* (Chicago: University of Chicago Press, 1978), 19.

What is remarkable about this statement is how easily it can be applied, with just a few word changes, to Ethiopian, Afrikaner, Zionist, or African charismatic forms of Christianity.

More recently, evangelical historian Ronald Wells has attempted to broaden this kingdom approach by using it as a framework for understanding all of Western civilization.[20] For Wells, "the story of humanity in the West is a story of trying to bring together what St. Augustine called the two cities, of God and of 'Man.'"[21] He calls this way of seeing history "the kingdom vision" and sees the basic plot of Western history as the gap between kingdom ideals and human realities. When this gap becomes too great, civilization is thrown into a crisis between its beliefs and its behavior. This kingdom perspective helps us see history as in ongoing tension between the "already and the not yet," between the provisional nature of today and the final reality when the kingdom of God will be consummated.

But does this perspective apply to Africa? John de Gruchy has tried to use the kingdom of God concept in understanding South African Christianity.[22] De Gruchy has used Niebuhr's categories to illumine the meaning of church history in that region of the continent:

> As the struggle of the church in North America was the struggle for the kingdom of God, so, too, the struggle of the church in South Africa is for the kingdom of God in another segment of world history. Indeed, as we look back on the history of South Africa, and the theologies that have shaped and interpreted that history, the cruciality of the kingdom emerges strongly and resembles in an almost uncanny way the story of the kingdom of God in America.[23]

I would like to follow up on the ideas of Niebuhr, McGloughlin, Wells, and de Gruchy by suggesting that African church history, not just American, Western, or South African history, "resembles in an almost uncanny way the story of the kingdom of God in America."

I believe the concept of the rule of God can open up the story of African Christianity fruitfully and overcome the historiographical bottleneck between mission-oriented approaches and nationalist approaches. I'd like to show exactly how this kingdom framework does that by beginning with a brief survey of the biblical teaching on the kingdom.

20. Ronald Wells, *History Through the Eyes of Faith: Western Civilization and the Kingdom of God* (San Francisco: Harper and Row, 1989).

21. Ibid., 27.

22. John de Gruchy, *The Church Struggle in South Africa* (Grand Rapids: Eerdmans, 1979).

23. Ibid., 199.

Wrestling with the Scriptures:
Understanding the Biblical Teaching about the Kingdom

In Acts 1:8 the risen Christ promised his followers that they would be his witnesses. Through the empowering of the Spirit, the church on earth would mirror the truth that Christ was Lord and that his rule or kingdom was the ultimate force in history. So important is this witness to the kingdom of God that Wolfhart Pannenberg can write that "the kingdom must be the central concern of the Church if the Church is to remain faithful to the message of Jesus."[24] But witnessing to the kingdom of God in Christ is not a simple matter. A complex of ideas makes up the biblical picture of the kingdom. We want to underscore three important parts of that complex.

The Kingdom of God

The kingdom as the providential and theocratic rule of God. First, Scripture teaches that the kingdom is God accomplishing his sovereign will through whatever comes to pass. The Old Testament in general and the story of Israel in particular presents this view of the kingdom (especially in the Psalms, such as 47, 93, 96, 97, and 99).

Herman Ridderbos sees the Old Testament witness to the kingdom consisting in "the universal divine kingship over the whole world, for the good of his [God's] people and for the overthrow of any power that opposes his rule."[25]

When the kingdom is seen as a theocratic rule over all things, the church on earth often tries to mirror this by building centralized political, theological, and ecclesiastical structures such as the Holy Roman Empire, medieval scholastic theology, or Byzantium. Holy wars with rival religious or political systems are seen as part of the faithful witness to the kingdom. When we encounter eighth-century Christian Berbers fighting against Muslim invaders, or sixteenth-century Ethiopian kings going to war under the banner of the cross, or twentieth-century Reformed theologians in South Africa attempting to construct a comprehensive reformational worldview for Africa, we are seeing forms of African Christianity that seek to witness to the kingdom as the theocratic rule of God.

The kingdom as the redemptive rule of Christ. Second, the Scriptures teach that the kingdom is God in Christ conquering sin through the cross and the worldwide spread of his gospel. The New Testament stresses this aspect of the kingdom which, like a small seed, will grow into a mighty tree (Matt. 13:31–32).

24. Wolfhart Pannenberg, *Theology and the Kingdom of God* (Philadelphia: Westminster, 1969), 259.
25. Herman Ridderbos, *The Coming of the Kingdom* (Phillipsburg, N.J.: Presbyterian & Reformed, 1962), 8.

Chris Manus writes of this radically new understanding of the kingdom introduced by Jesus Christ: "Though the Jewish mind understood the dawn of the new age in terms of God's display of his omnipotence, Jesus proclaimed the Reign of God which breaks in as divine intervention."[26]

Ridderbos states that "the preaching of God's gracious remission of guilt is the center and the basis of the gospel of the kingdom, especially because it is constantly contrasted by Jesus to the Jewish soteriology. The parables and stories in which this gospel of forgiveness finds its sublimest expression have often been rightly considered as the culmination-points of the whole gospel."[27] Ridderbos mentions the parables of the prodigal son (Luke 15:11–32) and the Pharisee and the publican (Luke 18:9–14), as well as the stories of the repentant sinner (Luke 7:36–50), the adulterous woman (John 8:1–11), and Zacchaeus (Luke 19:1–10) as evidence of this gospel of the kingdom.

What comes out strongly from these stories is that the kingdom is a spiritual reality involving the conquest of hearts. When the church emphasizes this reign of Christ over hearts in its witness to the kingdom, the activities of evangelism and church planting are stressed the most. The nineteenth-century missionary movement, the East African Revival, and the modern charismatic movement in Africa seem to be examples of the church's witness to the kingdom as a spiritual and personal redemptive rule of Christ.

The kingdom as the promotion of justice. "Thy kingdom come, thy will be done on earth as it is in heaven" is part of the Lord's Prayer and indicates the hope that God's rule would be visible in human life and society. The Book of Revelation paints the most vivid picture of this third aspect of the kingdom as a future world utopia brought in by the return of Christ, when all tears will be wiped away (Rev. 21–22).

This eschatological aspect of the kingdom when God transforms all things through his Spirit makes the church "dissatisfied with anything less than God's righteousness, justice, and peace in the world. The message of the kingdom makes us restless with things as they are."[28] Adds Chris Manus, "The reality of the kingdom of God provides men and women of all ages the vista to judge this world and to renew it through their total commitment to peace, justice, freedom."[29]

When the church gets caught up in this vision of the coming kingdom and seeks to witness to it in the present, acts of social justice and economic deliverance are often stressed. The church becomes a counterculture opposing the status quo and working for radical change.

26. Manus, *Christ the African King*, 164.
27. Ridderbos, *Coming*, 228.
28. De Gruchy, *Church Struggle*, 199.
29. Manus, *Christ the African King*, 164.

When we see a Desmond Tutu struggling against South African apartheid or a Julius Nyerere attempting to impose Christian socialism on Tanzania in the 1970s, we are seeing examples of churchmen attempting to bear witness to this aspect of the kingdom as an earthly utopia. The same could be said about the Coptic Christians of sixth- and seventh-century Egypt or the Donatist separatists of fourth-century North Africa. The kingdom as a future reality of justice and righteousness on earth can produce churches of protest that witness to the kingdom by fighting the structures of poverty and injustice.

Wrestling with the African Story: Using the Kingdom Framework

These three components of the Christian concept of the rule of God are each dynamic and have been difficult for the church in the West and in Africa to keep together. This is the great wrestling match in which the African church has been engaged for nearly twenty centuries. In light of the above discussion, my thesis about the way forward in the study of African church history is this: *God's raising up of witnesses to the theocratic, redemptive, and utopian aspects of his kingdom is the key to understanding the variety of churches and religious movements that have made up the story of African Christianity.*

As we study African church history we need to ask "kingdom" questions. How did the words and deeds of individuals, institutions, and movements spotlight one or more of these concepts of the kingdom? In what ways did the church fall short of witnessing to this kingdom vision? How did God graciously raise up witnesses for himself in spite of the church's failures?

We began this chapter by pointing to an impasse in the study of African church history between missionary historiography and nationalist historiography. A kingdom framework offers hope of finding a higher reference point than either church growth or African independence.

What will emerge from using the kingdom framework is a story that begins in the first fifteen hundred years with the church witnessing primarily to the theocratic rule of God. The sixteenth through nineteenth centuries will show a change in the witness to the kingdom, when the new emphasis becomes the rule of Christ over hearts. In the late nineteenth century and throughout most of the twentieth century, the third aspect of the kingdom becomes a bold emphasis of the churches.

One of the mysteries of the story in every period, however, is the struggle of the church to bear a balanced witness to the fullness of the kingdom. Just as the Okonkwos of African tradition once wrestled with Christianity, so now the African church must recognize that its own story is one of wrestling with the kingdom.

The Kingdom along the Nile

Christianity in Egypt

The story of Egypt is, in many ways, the story of a river. For thousands of years the River Nile and its wide flood plain fought back the desert and created the possibility of Egypt. The pharaohs, priests, farmers, and bricklayers that lined the banks of Egypt's three-thousand-year-old civilization were as much gifts from the river as were the crops that sprang annually from the dark soil. Yet those who knew the river best were aware of its dual personality. The Nile was, in fact, not one river but two.

The first, the White Nile, flowed from the Great Lakes of East Africa. Like a grand queen she marched through the African landscape heedless of drought or climatic change. The second river was different. The Blue Nile began in the highlands of Ethiopia during the summer rains and gathered to a muddy rage before bolting from the mountains like an exiled king bent on reconquest. Every year the Blue Nile flooded the banks of the Nile Valley in its wild fury. Yet the fertile soil that covered the flood plain after the waters receded gave life to the people. The angry king was really a benevolent savior.

This yearly drama inspired ancient Egyptians in many ways. Their religious myths reveled in the paradox of death and destruction leading to new life and triumph. Even their political dreams were shaped by the timeless struggle between chaos and order.

While Abraham was making his way from Ur, the Egyptian prophet-priest Neferty mourned over an Egypt full of chaos and calamity. Yet in his dark hour the spirit of prophecy came. From the moil of disorder a king would emerge, he predicted, and "right *(ma'at)* shall come again to its place, and iniquity/chaos" shall be "cast out."[1] Though many pharaohs and foreign conquerors partially fulfilled Neferty's prophecy, chaos always returned.

---

1. *Cambridge History of Africa*, ed. J. D. Clark, vol. 1 (Cambridge: Cambridge University Press, 1982), 662.

Yet not all in Egypt were left disappointed by the prophecy. For a young Egyptian living some twenty-three centuries after Neferty's vision, a king did come who brought lasting peace, not after a period of chaos, but within the midst of surrounding chaos. Antony (d. 356) of Egypt saw regal visions of his own in the caves of the mountains rimming the Red Sea. He wrestled with the demons of chaos in his mountain cave. One night the forces of evil in the form of wild animals invaded. "The place immediately was filled with the appearances of lions, bears, leopards, bulls, and serpents, asps, scorpions, and wolves and their raging was fierce."[2]

Antony was attacked by these hellish beasts but survived. While lying on the ground in pain, he rebuked the beasts in the name of Christ. At the name of the Heavenly King, a light broke through the darkness. The demons vanished. Antony addressed the light, pleading, "Where were you? Why didn't you appear in the beginning so that you could stop my distresses?"

The voice from the light replied, "I was here, Antony, but I waited to watch your struggle. And now, since you persevered and were not defeated, I will be your helper forever, and I will make you famous everywhere." With these words Antony's strength was restored.[3]

Though the enemy came in like a flood, the King of heaven would turn the struggles of soul into a harvest of righteousness and peace. The kingdom that Neferty only longed for, Antony experienced in the midst of his soul's dark night. The angry king was really a benevolent savior.

The story of Egyptian Christianity lies between the earthly social and political utopia envisioned by Neferty and the inward rule of Christ over sin and the demonic dramatized by the life of Antony. We want to follow this winding story through four stages. Following centuries of preparation for the coming of Christianity, Egypt saw the emergence of Jewish Christianity in the second century. This was followed by the hellenization of Jewish Christianity which occurred between A.D. 200 and 313. Finally Egyptian Christianity reached maturity in the years after the legalization of Christianity in A.D. 313. From the last period until the Muslim invasion of the seventh century, Egyptian Christianity became the Coptic church and a massive indigenization occurred, rooting the faith in a way that would prepare it for the coming storms.

The Period of Preparation: Egypt before Christ

Egypt as an African country. It is easy to forget that Egypt belongs to Africa. Egypt is a bridge that links the Mediterranean world to the rest of Af-

---

2. *Athanasius: Life of Antony and the Letter to Marcellinus*, trans. Robert C. Gregg (New York: Paulist, 1980), 38.
3. Ibid., 39.

rica. Over that bridge went a heavy two-way traffic of ivory, ebony, and ideas.[4]

We cannot tell the story here of the thirty-one dynasties of Egypt, of its conquest by Alexander the Great in the fourth century and by Rome in the first century before Christ when Cleopatra VII's charms and intrigues failed to stop the armies of Octavian. Our concern is with the ways in which Egypt was prepared for the reception of the gospel—a reception that triggered a religious revolution in the country by the fourth century of the Christian era.

The obvious influences should not be overlooked. Judaism was a strong force in urban Egypt at the time of Christ. Philo, a hellenized Jew of Alexandria, estimated that a million Jews lived in Egypt during this time (out of a total population of approximately 8 million). Many of them lived in Alexandria, where they dominated two quarters of the city. Jewish Scriptures, synagogues, monotheism, and messianic prophecies undoubtedly played a central role in the early reception of Christianity in Egypt.

Nor can we overlook the political and economic turmoil of Alexandrian Egypt. Taxation that alienated key ethnic groups such as the Jews and native Egyptians, pogroms and banishment after a bloody Jewish uprising, and a host of other destabilizing developments had their role in renewing the longing for order and peace that Neferty had dreamed of two thousand years before. As Henry Green has written, "If Christian missionaries were active in Egypt, this disenfranchised Jewish minority group would have been extremely receptive."[5]

The cult of death   There were a number of other influences in addition to the socioeconomic preparation for the gospel in Egypt. Although Egyptian culture offered many barriers to the gospel, three features in particular seem to have acted as bridges.

First was the Egyptian obsession with death and the afterlife. Though Egyptians lived by a river that was a source of life for their six-hundred-mile oasis kingdom, death was their great obsession. "If we were called upon to sum up Egyptian civilization in terms of a single monument," writes one historian, "a tomb would be the inevitable choice."[6] Their greatest architectural

---

4. Cf. C. A. Diops' opening chapter on the "Origin of the Ancient Egyptians" and the annex report immediately following in G. Mokhtar, ed., *Ancient Civilizations in Africa,* vol. 2 of *General History of Africa* (Paris: UNESCO, 1990), 15–61. Mokhtar points to the presence of ivory, obsidian, and ebony in Egyptian archaeological sites as indication of an active and regular contact between Egypt and Africa south of the Sahara.

5. Henry Green, "The Socio-Economic Background of Christianity in Egypt," in Pearson and Goering, eds., *The Roots of Egyptian Christianity* (Philadelphia: Fortress, 1986), 111.

6. Sabatino Moscati, *The Face of the Ancient Orient* (Garden City, N.Y.: Doubleday, 1962), 125.

achievement, the Great Pyramid, is an elaborate grave. One of their most revered gods, Anubis, was the god of embalmment. Egypt gave to the historical
lexicon the necropolis—a city of the dead.

What are we to make of this fixation with death?

It would be wrong of us to interpret this in modern terms as an existential
despair over the transience of life. The ancient Egyptian discovered life's purpose in preparing for the afterlife. No sooner had a pharaoh been crowned
than work would begin on his tomb.

What was the afterlife like? The world of the dead was a world that in-
tersected our own. The god Osiris was the lord and judge of this under-
world, where the spiritual elements of man (soul, spirit, and *ra* [the life
force]) wandered aimlessly but had the power to return to the lifeless body
from time to time. Embalming was necessary in order to preserve the body
for such moments in the future when it would house, if only for an instant,
the eternal spirit.

To think that this view of the afterlife only applied to the pharaoh or the
royal family is a mistake. Over time Egyptian views of eternal life changed,
with even the most humble given hope for a future of eternal bliss.

Christianity, with its promise of eternal life and its lord who conquered
death and who promised to prepare a dwelling place in eternity for his followers, found a receptive audience among people who for several millennia
regarded the next life as the proper contemplation for those found in the
present one. We should not be surprised that monasticism, with its denial of
this world for greater rewards in the next, spread so extensively in the land
of the Nile.

The religion of ancient Egypt. Underlying the obsession with death was a re-
ligious mythology that promoted longings for immortality. Though the
Egyptian pantheon included many gods, a family of three—Isis, Osiris, and
Horus—dominated the myths.

The main story starts with the divine king Osiris, a popular and just
ruler, and the undying love of his devoted wife, the winged goddess, Isis. Set
(or Seth) was Osiris' jealous brother whose evil heart moved him to fratri-
cide. The dismembered body of Osiris was discovered by Isis. As her tears
fell upon her dead husband and her wings stirred the air, Osiris rose from
the dead.

Their renewed love brought forth a son—Horus, the falcon god—who
battled the evil Seth and avenged his father. Osiris became lord of the afterlife; Horus, the sun god who guided departed souls to his father's eternal
kingdom.[7]

7. For a summary of the main story, see Jill Kamil, *Coptic Egypt* (Cairo: American University Press, 1987), 30.

By the time of Christianity the names of the divine family had changed to Isis, Serapis, and Harpocrates, and their popularity had spread throughout the Roman Empire. "By the first century," writes one historian, "people everywhere were invoking Serapis and Isis as saviours."[8] The temple of Isis at Philae remained a center of the cult until closed by Justinian in the sixth century.

When Eusebius wrote that "beyond all peoples, the work of His [Christ's] gospel teaching grew in strength among the Egyptians," he probably did not have in mind the preparation for the gospel provided by Egyptian religion and its mythology. In many ways the cult of Isis was a barrier to the gospel. But at the same time, traditional religion insured that the new faith would not seem entirely foreign to the Egyptian mind.

Beyond the crude parallels with the Christian doctrine of the Trinity are the more pointed analogies between Christ and Osiris. The concept of a divine king who rises from the dead and is made lord of the world to come was readily understood by those still in touch with Egyptian traditional religion. What made Christianity so attractive was the fact that the resurrected and ascended Lord was not a mythical symbol but a historical person.

Divine kingship. A final significant preparation for the coming of the gospel to Egypt was the tradition of divine kingship. Though Roland Oliver has called the concept of divine kingship "Egypt's eventual legacy to so much of the rest of the continent,"[9] inner Africa may have provided the roots for the idea. From the rainmakers who controlled the rains and floods grew the idea of a semidivine chief/king who stood halfway between God and man. However much the Egyptian model of kingship borrowed from the heart of Africa, it gave back more than it took.

During much of Egyptian history the divine status of the pharaoh (from *per-ao,* meaning the "great house" of the prince and his court) was tied to the belief that he was the incarnation of Horus and thus the son in the flesh of Isis and Osiris.[10] Some ancient texts even equate the pharaoh with the supreme god Ra.[11]

The treatment of this divine king became highly ritualized. His names and titles were regarded as sacred. Great pomp accompanied his appearances. The women surrounding the pharaoh were given special status, with the wife receiving the title "wife of Amon," another name for the supreme god.[12]

The divine king was judged by a standard of justice called *ma'at,* which carried the connotations of cosmic order, peace, and prosperity analogous to the Hebrew concept of *shalom.* After the pharaoh's death the tomb became

8. Mokhtar, *Ancient Civilizations,* 120.
9. R. Oliver and J. Fage, *A Short History of Africa,* 6th ed. (London: Penguin, 1988), 54.
10. Clark, *Cambridge History of Africa,* vol. 1, 659.
11. Ibid.
12. Mokhtar, *Ancient Civilizations,* 84.

a sacred place and the deceased pharaoh's divine status increased. Through the gateway of Nubia the concept of divine kingship would spread throughout the continent to reshape much of African politics and religion. It also played a role in providing the categories in which to understand the person and work of Christ as a divine king who promised a kingdom of *shalom* that would never end.

The Stage of Introduction: Jewish Christianity (to A.D. 200)

First-century contact with the gospel. "Mark, they also say, being the first that was sent to Egypt, proclaimed the gospel there which he had written, and first established churches at the city of Alexandria."[13] His first convert was a shoemaker named Annanias, who later became the second bishop of Alexandria. So says Eusebius, the early church historian who in another work dated Mark's arrival in Alexandria as "the third year of Claudius" (A.D. 43). The Coptic church regards Mark's founding of the church as beyond dispute. Visitors to Egypt can see the site of St. Mark's tomb in Boukolou.

But how reliable is this tradition? Judging from the context of his statement, Eusebius is quoting from a document written by Clement of Alexandria. Until this century the document in question was lost.

In 1973 historian Morton Smith published a rediscovered fragment of what might have been this lost work of Clement. Clement claimed that Mark came to Alexandria in the early 60s after the death of Peter in Rome and produced a second version of his famous gospel that was more "spiritual."[14] This is some twenty years after the date referred to by Eusebius.

Further complicating the story is the so-called *Acts of Mark,* which tells of his martyrdom in Alexandria, probably in A.D. 66, during a pogrom against the Jews conducted by the Roman government. The *Acts* tell of Mark's bold preaching in Boukolou against the feast of Serapis, which aroused such rage in the crowd that "he was dragged through the town with a rope tied around his neck and finally killed."[15]

To reconcile the chronology of these accounts is difficult, though not impossible. Some historians discount the value of the tradition completely. Adolf Harnack is unwilling to recognize any bishops in Egypt prior to Demetrius.[16] Until more evidence is produced, we should neither rule out St. Mark's role in Egyptian Christianity nor endorse the tradition as it stands.

13. Eusebius, *Ecclesiastical History* (Grand Rapids: Baker, 1955), 65.
14. Morton Smith, *Clement of Alexandria and a Secret Gospel of Mark* (Cambridge, Mass.: Harvard University Press, 1973).
15. Ibrahim Noshy, *The Coptic Church* (Washington: Sloan Associates, 1955), 6.
16. Adolf Harnack, *The Expansion of Christianity in the First Three Centuries,* vol. 2 (New York: G. P. Putnam, 1905), 90.

The words of C. P. Groves are well taken: "The luminous haze of legend is scarcely favourable to the recovery of historic fact."[17]

What we do know is that by the late second century Christianity was thriving in Egypt. Bishop Demetrius (189–231) makes an abrupt appearance on the historical stage as the supervisor of a number of churches and subordinates as well as the patron of a rising theological school. The star of Egyptian Christianity shone almost as brightly as in Rome. The church of Demetrius must have begun some years earlier.

The thesis that Christianity made its entry as a sect within Judaism seems reasonable given the large Jewish community in Alexandria and the proximity to Jerusalem. Eusebius was convinced that the great numbers of early converts were drawn from Judaism, and modern scholars have generally agreed.[18] Judaism and Christianity coexisted for decades within the synagogue. The Jewish revolt of A.D. 115 and the terrible purge following that nearly exterminated Judaism from Alexandria probably triggered a separation between Christianity and Judaism.

What was the character of this early Jewish Christianity? Three features may be noted.

First, early Egyptian Christianity may have had ascetic tendencies. What we know of first-century Judaism from Philo of Alexandria and Eusebius may shed some light. The latter, quoting Philo, described early Alexandrian Christianity as "a great multitude of believers" who lived in "extreme philosophical discipline and austerity."[19] Whereas Philo may have only been describing a certain segment of Alexandrian Judaism, Eusebius is probably right in supposing that Christianity developed in similar ways.

Second, Christianity seemed to appeal to the poor. The comments of a second-century pagan critic of Christianity, Celsus, exposes a movement that found its greatest appeal among the poor and disenfranchised. Origen, the third-century Alexandrian Christian theologian, quotes Celsus' criticisms: "Far from us, say the Christians, be any man possessed of any culture or wisdom or judgment; their [the Christian's] aim is to convince only worthless and contemptible people, idiots, slaves, poor women, and children. . . . We see wool-carders, cobblers, washermen, people of the utmost ignorance and lack of education."[20] Though Celsus sees Christianity's appeal to the poor as

---

17. C. P. Groves, *The Planting of Christianity in Africa*, vol. 1 (London: Lutterworth, 1948–58), 35.

18. Cf. Birger Pearson, "Earliest Christianity in Egypt," in Pearson and Goering, eds., *Roots of Egyptian Christianity*, 134.

19. Though Eusebius has probably wrongly appropriated Philo's description of Alexandrian Judaism for the Christian movement, he is probably correct to think that early Egyptian Christianity took much the same shape as Egyptian Judaism. See Eusebius, *Ecclesiastical History*, 65.

20. Quoted in Stephen Neill, *A History of Christian Missions*, 2nd ed. (London: Penguin, 1986), 40.

an argument against the faith, his comments go a long way in explaining the early rootedness of Christianity among the masses.

Third, Jewish Christianity during this first stage gave rise to sects. Clement of Alexandria refers to the *Gospel of Egyptians,* which describes this hellenized, ascetic, and legalistic piety. *The Gospel of Hebrews* appears to be an Alexandrian product. Judaized expressions of Christianity such as *The Shepherd of Hermas* and the *Gospel of Thomas* were circulating in Egypt during the second century.[21] The Platonism of a hellenized Jew like Philo may well have influenced some of these sects. This feature of early Egyptian Christianity partially accounts for one of its most fascinating forms—Gnosticism.

Gnosticism. We have noted the obscurity that surrounds early Christianity in Egypt. Only after the appearance of Bishop Demetrius does the fog begin to lift. One of the most controversial explanations for this obscurity has been offered by Walter Baur.[22] Baur argued that the original Christianity in Egypt was "heretical." Since orthodox Christianity eventually triumphed, the story of this earlier Christianity was suppressed.

Recent historical scholarship led by Colin Roberts has corrected Baur by demonstrating the Jewish nature of early Christianity.[23] Yet what this debate about early-second-century Egyptian Christianity has underscored is the importance of understanding Gnostic Christianity and its place in the story of the developing African church. The 1945 discovery of the Nag Hammadi papyri in Egypt containing forty-nine Gnostic treatises written in Coptic has further heightened interest in this movement.

The Christian Gnosticism of Basilides, Isidore, and Valentinus. The tale of Gnosticism in Egypt begins about A.D. 130, when a father-and-son team developed and taught a new understanding of the Christian faith that promised to liberate it from its Jewish roots. Basilides (fl. 125–155) and his son and disciple, Isidore, wrote their new theology down in a number of works, which included twenty-four books of scriptural exegesis.

Basilides hated Judaism and its view of God as a creator. He began his new version of the faith with a different view of God. God created thought *(nous)* and reason *(logos),* followed by the lesser virtues of prudence, wisdom, and power. From these primal virtues came all the heavenly beings. By some cosmic accident one of these heavenly beings *(Yahweh)* brought into existence the material world, which imprisoned some of the spiritual beings in human bodies.

---

21. W. H. C. Frend, *The Rise of Christianity* (Philadelphia: Fortress, 1984), 130.

22. W. Baur, *Orthodoxy and Heresy in Earliest Christianity,* trans. and ed. R. A. Kraft (Philadelphia: Fortress, 1977), 44–53.

23. Colin Roberts, *Manuscript, Society, and Belief in Early Christian Egypt* (London: Oxford University Press, 1979).

Basilides was convinced that evil was to be equated with the material world and the evil god, Yahweh of the Jews, who had made it. Sin was equated with ignorance of the true origins of the soul and of the material world. Jesus Christ was Thought, an emanation of the supreme God, who came to earth to enlighten imprisoned spirits about their true origin. This secret truth about the spiritual origins of humanity is the *gnosis* that saves from the sin of ignorance. Basilides eloquently argued that true Christians must reject both the Old Testament and the crucified Christ and embrace this spiritual Christ found in the new teaching.

More successful in promoting this new brand of the faith was the gifted teacher Valentinus (fl. 140–65), who probably came from Egypt and lived and worked for a time in Alexandria. Younger than Basilides, he made a deep impression on those who came under his teaching. Even his later critic, Jerome, not known for his kindness to those with whom he disagreed, admitted that "no one can bring heresy into being unless he is possessed by nature of an outstanding intellect, and has gifts provided by God. Such a person was Valentinus."[24]

Four of the Nag Hammadi works *(Gospel of Truth, Gospel of Philip, Exegesis on the Soul,* and *Treatise on Resurrection to Rheginus)* have been associated with his school of thought. Like Basilides' works, his theology began with speculation about the otherness of God and the many spiritual emanations *(aeons)* that move from the purely spiritual to the dangerously material.

The source of evil in the world is the creator god, called the demiurge, an *archon* or evil god and an offspring of the spiritual being Sophia. The demiurge seeks to destroy the spiritual by the creation of the material, but secretly Sophia implants pure spirit into some of the creatures made by the demiurge. These *pneumatics* were capable of salvation and even destined for salvation through learning the secret knowledge of their origins.

Once individuals are aware that they are truly divine and spiritual, they can begin the long journey back to pure spirit. Such soul travelers are the *pneumatics,* the truly spiritual ones who make up the top class in the Gnostic church. The lower spiritual classes such as the matter-loving hylics and the double-minded psychics do not have as much hope for true salvation as do the pneumatics.

The *Gospel of Truth* seems to regard Christ's death as in some way real and valuable; yet the true redemption of our souls according to Valentinian theology comes from Christ, the teacher of the secret *gnosis,* and not the Lamb of God who takes away the sins of the world.[25] The moral implications of this theology were important. The Gnostic was not only free from creation

---

24. Quoted in Frend, *Rise of Christianity,* 207.
25. See the discussion of this point in Hans Jonas, *The Gnostic Religion,* 2nd ed. (Boston: Beacon, 1963), 195.

but also free from law. In fact, breaking the laws found in the Old Testament, such as the Ten Commandments, was a liberating thing to do. Since these norms come from the demiurge, the evil creator God of the Old Testament, "the pneumatic thwarts the design of the archons and paradoxically contributes to the work of salvation."[26]

Gnosticism stands in sharp contrast to orthodox Christianity. Its theology and morality are in many ways the opposite of that which Jewish Christianity espoused. Yet on a deeper level Gnosticism represented a longing in Egyptian religion shared by figures as diverse as the pagan prophet Neferty and the Catholic monastic Antony.

Gnosticism was yet another expression of the Egyptian longing for an inner *ma'at*, a cosmic state of peace and order that included the soul's *shalom*. The Gnostic witnessed to Christ as the spiritual King who would restore the true spiritual order of the universe. Some Gnostics such as "Eugnostis" taught that Jesus was "the name of the Divinity and the Lordship and Kingship" and the repetition of his name could release his regal power to transform the cosmos and produce peace.[27]

Gnosticism is a longing for the kingdom of God within. Its speculative theology was the wrong path along which to pursue that longing, but the restless spirit it displayed in the second century continued to haunt even the most orthodox within the church. Though the threat of Gnosticism faded in the third century through the patient work of orthodox pastors, bishops, and theologians (particularly Ireneus of Lyons), the spiritual hunger it expressed did not. The quest for a kingdom of peace flowed down the Nile into the history of the continent.

The Stage of Maturation: Hellenistic Christianity (200–313)

Persecution and martyrdom. Just as the battle with Gnosticism seemed to be won, another battle broke out that tested the churches in extreme ways—the struggle between church and state. In the second century the Jewish character of earliest Christianity was fading. Christianity was at last understood by the outside world as something distinct from Judaism. This liberated Christianity could no longer enjoy the religious privileges that Judaism had enjoyed, such as exemption from emperor worship. As Egyptians sought to live in the world without being of it, a new stage of spiritual warfare began.

Persecution under Severus, Decian, and Valerian. In March 203 two women, Perpetua and Felicitas, were brutally martyred in the amphitheater of

26. Ibid., 46.
27. See "Jewish and Platonic Speculations in Early Alexandrian Theology: Eugnostus, Philo, Valentinus, and Origen," in *Roots of Egyptian Christianity*, 193.

Carthage. The crime that inspired this public death was simply their profession to be Christians. In that same year Clement of Alexandria fled from the theological school that he administrated due to a wave of "roastings, impalings, and beheadings" of Christians. Thus began the persecution under Septimus Severus that lasted until about 212. Origen's father was killed in this pogrom against the Christians, as were many of Clement's students and young converts. The faith of many was shaken, but after the fury passed, church life seemed to return to normal.

By 250 a new persecution began under the emperor Decian. The imperial edict that all must sacrifice to the emperor and the traditional gods of Rome caught the Alexandrian church off guard. Bishop Dionysius wrote with disgust how Christians who feared for their lives "ran eagerly towards the altars, affirming by their forwardness that they had not been Christians even formerly." Even those who at first held out for the faith eventually gave in to pressure. Dionysius fled for his life and wrote from exile that the clergy who had remained faithful numbered about six besides himself. Just as Egyptian Christianity reached the edge of collapse, Decian died in battle. By the end of 250 the church was back on its feet and the complicated process of restoration and reconciliation was well underway.

Seven years of peace under the new emperor Valerian were broken with an edict in 257 that initiated new police action against the church. Dionysius was forced back into exile and hundreds of Christians were killed. Many saw the intervention of God on behalf of his church when in 260 Valerian was captured by the Persians. His son called off the persecution. Christianity had passed the test.

By the time of the final major persecution under Diocletian in 303, the strength of the church in Egypt and elsewhere was too great to be uprooted by the sword. By that time the cult of martyrdom had become so developed that Eusebius could write as an eyewitness of the persecutions in Thebes in a way dramatically different from Dionysius' description some fifty years before. "We also, being on the spot ourselves, have observed large crowds in one day; some suffering decapitation, others tortured by fire" but what was amazing to Eusebius was that "As soon as sentence was pronounced against the first, one after another rushed to the judgment seat and confessed themselves Christians."[28] When peace came to the hellenized Christianity of Egypt (and the rest of the empire) in 313, the era of intense religious persecution ended.

What is important to remember about the era of martyrs in Egypt is the witness to the kingdom. Christians who resisted the demands to sacrifice to the cult of the emperor did so because of the politics of the kingdom. Christ, not Caesar, was lord. Because Christians saw their religion as involving an

28. Eusebius, *Ecclesiastical History*, 328.

ultimate patriotism (loyalty to the kingdom) they consequently opposed the "blending of religion and patriotism" on any other level.

For the many Christians who submitted to the pressures of the imperial edict this kingdom witness was obscure. But for those who endured martyrdom or loss of property, the idea of the church as a countercultural witness to the transcendent kingdom of Christ was strong. After 313 this same kingdom patriotism that galvanized the martyr would also promote the monastic movement in Egypt to oppose the externalization of the kingdom of God in the Christianized Roman Empire.

The theological maturing of the church. During the long century that began with Bishop Demetrius guarding the flock from the wolves of Gnosticism and traditional religion all the way through the storms of persecution mentioned by Bishop Dionysius, the catechetical school of Alexandria helped the church face difficult intellectual challenges. It soon became the center for Christian scholarship in the Roman Empire. The distinguished names of Pantaenus (d. 180), Clement (c. 150–215), Origen (185–254), Dionysius (d. 264), and Theognostus (d. c. 282) are associated with this school. Little is known about the founder Pantaenus, but much has been written by and about Clement and Origen.

Clement and Origen. The legacy Clement and Origen left to African Christianity is an important part of our story. The two men were different in a number of ways. Clement lived in relative peace with the Alexandrian church leadership throughout his years at the catechetical school, whereas Origen was in constant conflict with the bishops. Clement had a positive view of creation and culture in general; Origen had such a radical aversion to the physical that he made himself a eunuch for the sake of the kingdom.

Clement, the somewhat stuffy and eccentric author of *Miscellanies*, was an inferior thinker compared to the brilliant Origen. The latter labored for forty years on his famous *Hexapla,* a work of impressive biblical scholarship in which parallel translations of the Old Testament were printed side by side for scholarly comparison. His stunning speculative reasoning in *First Principles* earned him the title of the first Christian systematic theologian.

What binds these two men together is a passion to make Christian theology understandable to people of a particular culture. In the case of Clement and Origen their target audience was composed of Greco-Roman intellectuals whose minds were marinated in Platonism and Gnostic ways of thinking. The world of metaphysics was alive to the Alexandrian addressed by Origen in his *First Principles* and Clement in *Miscellanies*. Origen especially has been criticized for making theology too abstract.

Many of the major theological controversies of the next few centuries, including the Trinity, millennialism, and allegorical exegesis, owe much, for both good and ill, to the mind and writings of Origen. The consciousness that biblical ideas must be translated into the thought patterns of Gentile cultures as surely as biblical texts need to be translated into the languages of Gentile tribes is a legacy that began with St. Paul. However, it finds powerful early expression in the catechetical school of Alexandria.

Antony and monasticism. Third-century Egyptian Christianity was not simply a Christianity of the school and of the city. The life of St. Antony (d. 356) is a testimony to the penetration of Christianity into rural Egypt. Because of Antony, the greatest legacy of Christian Egypt would be a kind of piety forever associated with the name of monasticism.

Antony was not the most likely candidate for spiritual sainthood. He was born in southern Egypt to Christian parents. He spoke no Greek but felt most comfortable with the emerging dialect of rural Egypt that would eventually be given the name "Coptic" (from the Arabic word for Egypt). He dropped out of school while young and became something of a recluse at home.

The turning point in his life came after the death of his parents, when Antony and his sister inherited their wealth. He heard the words of Matthew 19:21, "If you would be perfect, go, sell what you possess and give to the poor, and you will have treasure in heaven," and could not get them out of his mind until he acted on them. His personal application of this command of Christ drove him to sell all he possessed and move to the edge of the village. He spent much time wandering in the desert and seeking the heavenly treasure in solitude. Wherever he went Antony met men like himself whose brushes with spiritual despair, economic disaster, or the Roman police during the Decian and Valerian persecutions had driven them into the wilderness to look for the kingdom of God.[29]

After a number of years he yearned for even greater solitude and climbed into the Arabian mountains on the east side of the Nile. During the time he spent in the mountains Antony underwent a series of temptations. The demons of lust, fear, and pain tormented him so severely that at times he lost consciousness. But always he emerged victorious. On the night when he was attacked by demons in the guise of wild beasts, the voice of the heavenly King confirmed that his spiritual disciplines and warfare was the approved path to the kingdom of God.[30]

Antony emerged from the mountains a changed man and became the counselor of bishops and emperors. Only one spiritual goal evaded him—to die a martyr's death. He had outlived the age of persecution. However, his followers credited him with a bloodless martyrdom when he died in 356, be-

---

29. Gregg, *Athanasius*, 30–33.
30. Ibid., 39.

cause he had so died daily to sin and the flesh that he was regarded as more of a martyr than any martyrs who had died but once.

One of Antony's enduring legacies is a particular vision of the kingdom. In explaining Antony's impact on the monastic movement, his friend and biographer Athanasius writes that because of Antony's example "there were monasteries in the mountains and the desert was made a city by monks, who left their own people and registered themselves for the citizenship in the heavens."[31]

Athanasius also writes that Antony's life is a testimony to the truth that Jesus Christ "leads those who serve him to the end into the kingdom of heaven."[32] For Antony, if Athanasius is to be trusted, the kingdom of God is not to be equated with earthly structures. In fact, a repudiation of earthly power and prestige is the mark of the kingdom. Antony strikes a note about the kingdom that will be struck again and again in the centuries to follow— witnessing to the kingdom means acting as a counterculture in the world.

Pachomius and cenobitic monasticism. The popularity of Antony greatly promoted the monastic movement in Egypt. But if the monastic movement was to survive over time, organization needed to be added to inspiration.

This was the great achievement of Pachomius (or Pachom in Coptic). Born in Egypt in 292, Pachomius converted to Christianity in 312–313, just as the faith's legal status was changing in the Roman Empire. His longing for more spiritual reality led first to the hermit Palamon and then to a life of solitude in Tabnessi on the Nile in 323. In 324 younger disciples began gathering around Pachomius in such numbers that soon a number of monastic foundations were started. These recognized Pachomius as their head and his rule as their pattern of life. By the time of his death in 346 the Pachomian *koinonia* numbered nine monasteries and two nunneries involving several thousand individuals.[33] After his death the movement continued to grow, both numerically and geographically.

Over the centuries monasticism became a central fixture of Coptic Christianity. In what way did monasticism meet the spiritual longings of its members?

At the heart of Egyptian monasticism lies a certain understanding of the kingdom already seen in Antony. Armand Veilleux believes that "the ultimate end of monastic life is the Kingdom of God," which was understood to mean "contemplative union with God in prayer."[34] The conversion of the heart and the disciplining of the mind and body through ascetic practice were the means to reach that end.

31. Ibid., 42–43.
32. Ibid., 99.
33. Armand Veilleux, "Monasticism and Gnosis in Egypt," in *Roots of Egyptian Christianity,* 273–75.
34. Ibid., 304.

The Stage of Indigenization: Coptic Christianity (313–600)

The two churches of Egypt. By the year 300 the church of Egypt was really two churches. In cities like Alexandria the hellenized Christianity pioneered by Clement and Origen continued. In rural Egypt a different kind of Christianity was developing. The size of this rural Christianity was significant. In 303 Athanasius writes of more than one hundred bishops scattered about Egypt. Harnack estimated a fourth-century Egyptian church of "a million strong" with many of that number found in towns and villages along the Nile.[35]

The growth among non-Greek-speaking segments of the population created a strong market for Bible translations in the vernacular. Beginning in the late third century and continuing well into the eighth century a periodic stream of translations in the major Coptic languages (Sahidic, Bohairic, and Bashmuric) were produced. With vernacular translations and the multiplication of local churches, the roots of the faith began to sink deeper into Egyptian soil.

Driving both church growth and Bible translation was a hungry church full of longings for a kingdom within, for a *ma'at* of the soul. Without theological guidance such spiritual longings could lead a soul in heterodox directions. Coptic Christianity in the fourth century tended to mingle the gospel of the resurrected Savior with the local legend of Osiris.[36]

Adolf Harnack observes that "if the Egyptians were for the most part Christians by the middle of the fourth century, then they had created a sort of national religion by grafting on the latter to the cravings and remnant of the old."[37]

Archaeological evidence supports this picture of a general syncretism. Burial practices mingle old and new religion with food offerings, mummification, and symbols of both Isis and the cross found at gravesites. It is significant that Antony, though citing reasons of humility, left strict instructions to his followers not to allow his body to be mummified and put on display in local homes.[38]

The continuing presence of syncretistic Christianity is further evidenced by the Nag Hammadi papyri. The name of the papyri comes from the upper Egyptian village where the works were discovered. The letters found in the collection indicate a fourth-century date. The mingling of Eastern, old Egyptian, Jewish, Platonic, and Christian ideas in the fifty-some writings is syncretism of the highest order. The presence of a Christian monastery (associ-

---

35. Harnack, *Expansion*, vol. 2, 321.
36. Groves, *Planting*, vol. 1, 37.
37. Harnack, *Expansion*, vol. 2, 320–21.
38. Gregg, *Athanasius*, 96.

ated with the great monastic leader Pachomius) near the site has raised questions about the involvement of monks in the practice of syncretistic Christianity.[39]

Though Harnack paints a picture of a fourth-century paganism on the verge of collapse, the spread of orthodoxy was by no means easy or automatic. What was needed in rural Egypt, at least in the eyes of church leaders, was a theological purification in order to prevent rural Christianity from boiling over into heresy. Few would have expected that the heretical spill would take place not in the village but in the city and that the urbane Arius and not some syncretistic monk would be the fomenter.

Athanasius and theological controversy in the fourth century. Athanasius of Alexandria (296–373) was just the man to disciple the mind of Coptic Christianity. Probably of Egyptian origin (he spoke Coptic like a native), Athanasius was uniquely positioned to bridge the gap between the church of the city and the church of the countryside, for he felt at home in both worlds.[40] For several years he served as secretary to Bishop Alexander, who was the enemy of a new heresy called Arianism (which argued that Christ was a created being and not fully God). Then Athanasius took up the banner of orthodoxy after becoming the bishop of Alexandria upon Alexander's death.

The important Council of Nicea in 325 declared the Arian position to be heretical. Athanasius fought to enforce this decision in Egypt (aided by his spiritual mentor Antony, about whom he wrote an influential biography). The changing theological loyalties of a succession of emperors made his job more difficult, but after a long struggle marked by numerous exiles Athanasius and the Christian doctrine of the Trinity triumphed. The orthodox position from that time was that Christ was "very God of very God," "begotten and not made," who "for our sins and our salvation" became incarnate.

In one of his most important works, *On the Incarnation of the Word*, Athanasius argued that the salvation of fallen humankind depended on a mediator who was both truly God and truly man. Exactly how that incarnate nature related to the true deity was left undefined and would lead to the major division in Egyptian Christianity in the next century. Athanasius is also remembered for his contribution to the closing of the canon of Scripture and the promotion of monasticism throughout the Roman world. By the time of his death in 373 Athanasius had helped purge the church of much of its syncretism. But other efforts beyond his would be needed.

39. See the article on Nag Hammadi in Ferguson, McHugh, and Norris, eds., *Encyclopedia of Early Christianity* (New York: Garland, 1990).

40. On the ethnicity of Athanasius, see Kamil, *Coptic Egypt*, 45.

Shenoute and Chalcedon. In the fifth century, monasticism continued to grow throughout Egypt. Old temples and abandoned military fortresses were taken over by the movement. So popular was monasticism (which carried with it an exemption from military duty) in the late fourth and early fifth centuries that the government had difficulty finding enough able-bodied men to staff its army. As a compromise, a number of strategically located monasteries became guardians of the borders of the empire.

The most famous of these fortress-monasteries was the White Monastery (founded 440), located near the Libyan foothills in upper Egypt. Leading the 1,800 nuns and several thousand monks affiliated with the White Monastery was the great Coptic leader, Shenoute (d. c. 466).[41] For over twenty years he ruled his order with a rigor and discipline that made the Pachomian rule seem lax.

Through his writings (which helped shape the Coptic language and literary tradition), the syncretism of popular Egyptian Christianity was opposed and even purged. In a way that was as significant as either Antony's or Athanasius' efforts, Shenoute helped shape Coptic Christianity. He was a violent preacher who believed that traditional Egyptian gods were demons, and he incited mobs to attack pagan temples.

Shenoute was also a fiery opponent of theological innovation such as the one proposed by Nestorius, bishop of Constantinople, around 430. When Shenoute heard that Nestorius was arguing that Christ's divine and human natures were in some ways separable (so that, for example, Mary should not be called *theotokos*, or mother of God, for she only bore the human side of Christ), he was outraged. His last years were spent winning the condemnation of Nestorius (achieved at Ephesus in 431) and defending what he believed was the Athanasian formula of Christ as an undivided divine being assuming human flesh. This latter position argued by Egyptian theologians and church leaders more sophisticated than Shenoute became known as Monophysitism—Christ had only one nature, not two.

When Leo of Rome gathered the bishops in Chalcedon in 451 to produce a final statement on the problem of the two natures of Christ, both Nestorianism and Monophysitism were condemned. Shenoute and most of the monastic community of Egypt were outraged. They rejected the creed of Chalcedon.

A deep and lasting rift appeared in Egyptian Christianity. The Melkites, Egyptian churches who accepted Chalcedon, were strongest in Alexandria. The Jacobites, stronger in the rural areas, rejected Chalcedon and took the

---

41. The dates of Shenoute's life and work used here are at variance with many of the standard historical dictionaries and follow the chronology presented by Janet Timbie in "The State of Research on the Career of Shenoute of Atripe," in *Roots of Egyptian Christianity,* 260–61.

Monophysite position. After Shenoute's death the Jacobite branch of Egyptian Christianity grew while the Melkite branch became weaker. It appeared that Chalcedonian Christianity was dead. But the triumph of Monophysitism in Egypt was blocked by the imposing figure of the Byzantine emperor, Justinian I (483–565).

Sixth-century developments. Justinian became Roman emperor in 527 and immediately inaugurated two campaigns. The first was a series of military campaigns to reclaim sections of the empire overrun by barbarian tribes. The second was a series of theological campaigns to reclaim sections of the church overrun by heresy.

Egypt was one of the targets of his second campaign. Through coercion, imprisonment of leaders, and bullying at the negotiating table, Justinian tried to bring Egyptian Christianity in line with the rest of the Mediterranean church. Justinian's vision of a kingdom witness on earth demanded that a monolithic church and a monolithic state act in concert to mirror the sovereignty of God in all of life. Egyptian Christians had different ideas about the kingdom. They insisted that an effective kingdom witness could be launched by a protesting church, such as the Coptic church was becoming.

In the midst of this clash of kingdom witnesses, the Coptic church received a surprising ally in the person of Justinian's wife, Theodora. Theodora I (500–547) had been crowned as co-ruler of the empire in 527 when her husband became emperor. She took her power seriously, especially when it came to church affairs. Her theological convictions were Monophysite. So her sympathies in Egypt lay with the Coptics, who had become synonymous with the Jacobite or Monophysite position. Her support was sorely needed in the year 535 when Timothy IV, bishop of Alexandria (still the most powerful position in the church of Egypt), died.

Theodora sent her personal representative to Alexandria. That agent maneuvered the church to name the Monophysite deacon Theodosius as the new bishop of Alexandria. This imperial interference aroused a strong nationalist reaction and the Chalcedonian party put forward another candidate, the monk Gaianus. For over one hundred days the fanatical followers of both parties battled for the appointment. Imperial troops were sent, and Theodora and the Coptic party won the day. But the victory was in many ways a hollow one. The imperial control over ecclesiastical life (which often reversed theological allegiances), coupled with the political and economic stranglehold of the Byzantine administration ruling the country, had a deadening effect on Egyptian church life.

The seventh century. In the early seventh century Egyptian Christianity was roused from its slumbers by an invasion of the Sassanid king, Chosroes II. In 615 his Persian armies occupied the Nile Delta, liberating Egypt from Byzantine political and ecclesiastical rule. Monophysite Coptic Christianity came to life once again. For several years it enjoyed a new status as the only official church of the country.

This period of relative independence came to an end in 629, when Byzantine armies under Heraclius regained colonial control. The next thirteen years were full of anarchy and terror as the Melkite bishop of Alexandria sought to impose his own strange theology, which was neither Monophysite nor Chalcedonian. The period of confusion ended in 642 with the invasion of Egypt by a new power that had risen in the east—Islam.[42]

Conclusion

Like the White and Blue Niles, the story of Egyptian Christianity is the story of a steady flow of spiritual longing combined with less predictable periods of turbulent religious change. From Neferty the pagan prophet through Gnostic dreamers like Valentinus, from demon wrestlers like Antony to fiery fundamentalists like Athanasius and Shenoute, religion in Egypt witnessed to this pattern of continuity and change.

Whether Orthodox or Coptic, hellenized or indigenous, the churches of Egypt bore witness to the kingdom of Christ in a variety of ways.

Most notable is the witness to the kingdom *as an inner spiritual experience*. Gnostics like Basilides, Valentinus, and Eugnostus pointed to the deep inwardness of the kingdom in ways that were ultimately unbalanced. For most Gnostics the inner kingdom collapsed into the kingdom of the self, in which the spiritual capacities of the individual were magnified to the point where the soul became synonymous with God. But the monastic tradition, purified from the theological confusion of the Gnostics, carried on this important witness in healthier form. Howard Snyder describes this witness to the kingdom:

> Generally this is a highly individualistic conception of the kingdom. God reigns over all, but above all in the invisible, spiritual realm. To see and experience the Kingdom requires spiritual sight, for the Kingdom is not visible in society. Fully entering into the Kingdom is an ineffable experience that cannot really be shared with another human being. In this model of the Kingdom, fully to experience the Kingdom is to be lost in God.[43]

This emphasis on the kingdom as communion with God was not entirely individualistic. The quest for the kingdom in the life of an Antony or a Shen-

---

42. For a convenient summary of this period, see *Ancient Civilizations in Africa*, vol. 2, *General History of Africa* (Paris: UNESCO, 1990), 139–40.

43. Howard Snyder, "Models of the Kingdom," *Transformation* 10, no. 1 (January–April 1993): 1.

oute had a communal aspect. The rule of Christ over hearts can also be seen *as the mystical communion of saints centered in the Eucharist.* This second witness to the kingdom involves "a spiritual communion with all believers—with those on earth and with those who had gone before."[44]

The moment when this communion occurred was usually at the celebration of the Eucharist, a sacrament receiving consistent stress from Athanasius to Shenoute and beyond. The moment of communion around the table became a prelude to the ultimate kingdom experience of stepping into the fellowship of heaven itself. While Eastern spirituality in general emphasized this witness to the kingdom, Egyptian Christianity in the earliest centuries was a vivid expression of this understanding.

A third witness to the kingdom can be seen *in the rejection of the world* by martyr and monk. The martyrs of Thebes and monks like Antony, Pachomius, and Shenoute remind the church that the kingdom is not of this world. This is *the countercultural witness to the kingdom,* in which the church challenges the norms of society and turns its back on comfort and power to point to a reality greater than worldly wealth or political potency—the coming kingdom of God.

Though the world renouncing Christianity was riddled with the distortions of dualism and extremism, an authentically biblical note is struck when the transcendent otherness of Christ's kingdom is brought to the fore. This radical antithesis between the kingdom of God and the kingdoms of men would be a theme taken up in North Africa by a gifted theologian named Augustine.

44. Ibid.

The City of God

Christianity in North Africa

To a Roman of the first century, Africa was more a colony than a continent. When an Italian in the age of Caesar imagined the lands that made up Roman North Africa—Africa proper, Numidia, and Mauritania (basically modern Tunisia, Algeria, and Morocco)—she would have pictured mile after mile of farms gilded with maize and grain. So rich was African soil that the city of Rome depended on her produce for eight months' supply of food per year.[1]

The faces of Roman Africa that would have appeared in our imaginary Italian's mind would belong to three distinct groups of people. First, she would picture people who looked a lot like herself, Italian immigrants who had made Africa their home and had brought Latin language and culture to the cities and towns that dotted these fertile lands between the desert and the sea.

The second kind of face that would have appeared in her mind's eye would belong to the Punic segment of the population. These were the descendants of the Phoenicians, who had colonized these lands in the ninth century B.C. and had lost a brutal and costly war to Rome in the second century. Yet though their empire was gone, Punic language and culture remained. Even Punic religion, best preserved in the Saturn cult with its dreaded human and animal sacrifices, continued well into the Roman era.[2]

The last face that our Italian daydreamer would have imagined would be a dark one. This face belonged to the aboriginal people of North Africa, the Libyan or Berber race that composed the third strata of African society. Though dominated by Latin and Punic language and rule, the Berbers survived in towns and rural areas, generally aloof and suspicious, scrutinizing the foreigners.

1. G. Mokhtar, *General History of Africa*, vol. 2 (Paris: UNESCO, 1990), 274.
2. Cf. W. H. C. Frend, *The Rise of Christianity* (Philadelphia: Fortress, 1984).

Two visions of Carthage. These three faces of Africa confronted each other in Carthage. With the possible exception of Alexandria, Carthage was the greatest city of the southern Roman Empire and one of the leading seaports in all of the Mediterranean. If ever a city had risen from the dead it was Carthage. Invaded by the Roman legions in 146 B.C. the city had been burned, buildings leveled, and salt sown in the soil to make it barren. Yet by 44 B.C. Carthage had risen again, settled by veterans of the Roman army. Soon it became the capital of the colony. In resurrected Carthage, tree-lined avenues led from the heights of the city, the Byrsa, down to the busy port, which sent the grain and olive oil of Africa to the rest of the Roman world.[3] Marble buildings devoted to the theater, entertainment, politics, and public baths were everywhere.

But behind the outer appearance of Carthage lay hidden a city with a divided soul. One side of the Carthage soul was obsessed by man and his dark side. The other side was filled with religious longings, represented by a rising Christian movement. The first city, the young Augustine confronted when at sixteen he was lured by her lights and his lusts. He would later describe Carthage as a "caldron of unholy loves—seething and bubbling all around me."[4] This was the city of Apuleius, the writer whose bawdy tales contained in *The Golden Ass* show little concern with morality.

The second city was the home of Tertullian and Cyprian and growing churches. The first city swallowed souls. The second city saved them. For those who knew Carthage best the warfare between these two inner cities was fierce.

The kingdom witness. The church that flourished in Carthage and spilled over into the towns and villages of Africa was a church sensitive to the struggle between these two cities. Until the demise of North African Christianity in the eighth century, the church bore eloquent but anguished witness, particularly in the writings of her most famous son, Augustine, to the paradoxes of the kingdom. The story of that anguished witness is the concern of this chapter. It is a story that begins with a dozen deaths.

The Second and Third Centuries: The Age of Tertullian and Cyprian

First soundings. Like the city of Carthage, Christianity in North Africa rose from death. While the Jewish presence may well have prepared the way, the

---

3. A vivid description of Carthage and its history is given in Peter Hinchliff, *Cyprian of Carthage* (London: Geoffrey Chapman, 1974), 10–11.

4. Albert Outler, ed., Augustine's *Confessions*, Library of Christian Classics, vol. 7 (Philadelphia: Westminster, 1955), 61.

first evidence of Christianity in the province is in A.D. 180. Seven men and five women from the village of Scilli (on the outskirts of Carthage) gave up their lives in martyrdom.

Their crime as announced by the proconsul Saturninus was simply that they were practicing Christians. Speratus, the spokesperson of the twelve martyrs, gives us some insight into the seriousness of the charge. When the proconsul hinted at a possible reprieve if they would but "swear by the genius of the emperor" and "offer prayers for his health," Speratus refused. Defiantly he rejected allegiance to "the empire of this world" and reasserted his loyalty to the one who "is the emperor of kings and of all nations."[5] With these words the twelve were killed. The first to die, Namphano, bore a Punic name.[6]

Two decades later, during one of the sporadic persecutions that took place between 195 and 212,[7] the noblewoman Perpetua (d. 203) and her African slave girl, Felicitas (who was responsible for introducing her mistress to the Christian faith), gave similar witness to the hostility that existed between representatives of the two African societies that Augustine later characterized as the City of God and the City of Man. Christianity was clearly "adopting the stance of an opposition movement."[8] It is important to note not only that North African Christianity saw its witness in kingdom terms but also that Christianity appealed to the Punic-speaking portion of the population, raising hopes that an indigenous Christianity might take root in North Africa as it had done in Egypt.[9]

Growth and persecution in the third century. Nothing is known of the Greek-speaking Christianity that must have preceded the Latin Christianity flourishing by the time of Tertullian (c. 160–225).[10] As in Alexandria, a strong Jewish Christian community may well have been the first expression of Christianity, but again no evidence exists to support this supposition.[11] What we do know is that Tertullian, writing in 197 to his non-Christian opponents, could say, "Day by day you groan over the ever-increasing number of Christians."[12]

The growing numbers of Christians in the rank and file of the church were paralleled by the growth of clergy. "The Church of North Africa,"

5. Frend, *Rise of Christianity,* 290.

6. Adolf Harnack, *The Expansion of Christianity in the First Three Centuries,* vol. 2 (New York: G. P. Putnam's Sons, 1905), 415.

7. Frend, *Rise of Christianity,* 293.

8. Mokhtar, *General History of Africa,* vol. 2, 279.

9. Harnack, *Expansion,* 414–15.

10. Ibid., 413.

11. Frend summarizes the few indicators of an earlier Jewish Christianity in his *Rise of Christianity* (1984), 347.

12. Quoted in Frend, *Rise of Christianity,* 290.

writes Stephen Neill, "was a Church of Bishops."[13] Harnack points to the existence of at least seventy African and Numidian bishops at a synod in Carthage early in the third century. Ninety bishops attended a synod at Lambaesa sometime before A.D. 240.

This increase in clergy confirms the overall growth of the Christian movement in the late second and early third centuries. But beneath the numbers is an alarming characteristic of early North African Christianity. For every martyr and hero, there were many who compromised with the imperial cult or fled in terror when rumor of a new police action circulated. This Christianity of compromise stood in sharp contrast to the Christianity of the martyrs. Both holiness and half-heartedness could be found within the church of Africa. For this reason, a number of early leaders saw holiness as important to address as heresy. The holiness campaigns of two of these leaders deserve particular attention.

Tertullian and Cyprian

Tertullian. Quintius Septimus Florens Tertullian (d. c. 225) was born into a prosperous pagan home. Though his father may have been a centurion, Tertullian trained for the law. The early historian, Eusebius, claimed that Tertullian's skill in law made him "especially distinguished in Rome."[14] Jerome, writing a century after Tertullian, described him as possessing a "sharp and violent talent."[15] He became a bold and original apologist and theologian in Africa.

Tertullian showed in his writings not only how different Athens was from Jerusalem, but also how different Alexandria was from Carthage. As the founder of the Carthaginian "school" of theology, he pioneered lines of thought and approaches far removed from the Christian Gnosticism of Clement and Origen. For example, he employed paradox to arrest the attention of his hearers. The gospel of a crucified God was "certain because it is impossible." He also employed the element of surprise in confronting his ideological adversaries.

His most original apologetic work was probably his *Praescriptione Haereticorum* in which he defended the faith against heretics by refusing their right to use the only authority that can command belief—the Scriptures. He defended the unity of the Old and New Testaments in his polemical writing against the Marcionites, and gave the church a new word, "Trinity," in his attacks on modalism.

13. Stephen Neill, *History of Christian Missions*, 2nd ed. (London: Penguin, 1986), 34.
14. Eusebius, *Ecclesiastical History, Nicene and Post-Nicene Fathers*, 2nd series, vol. 1 (Grand Rapids: Baker, 1955), ii.2.4.
15. Quoted in Frend, *Rise of Christianity*, 348.

But as different as he was from Alexandria on most points, he shared with the Christianity of that sister city a tendency toward asceticism that never left him. He used his "violent talent" to attack what he regarded as the lax state of the African church. When the leadership failed to respond in the way he thought they should, Tertullian left and joined the ranks of an ascetic and prophetic movement known as Montanism. When he died in 225 he died as a critic of Catholic Christianity and an unflinching champion of a rigorous holiness.

It was as a champion of holiness that Tertullian made his most lasting impact on African Christianity. Tertullian was a puritan who declared war against spiritual mediocrity in the church. In his book, *Modesty*, Tertullian declared that since the church was "the bride of Christ" without "spot nor wrinkle," the impure and unrepentant sinner should be purged from her presence.

The primary focus of his campaign to purify the church centered around the issue of idolatry. To the question of how the church can live in the world, Tertullian's answer was "to make as clean a break as possible."[16] Since the world around the church is so saturated with idolatry, the Christian must live a separated life.

Christians, argued Tertullian, should not become magistrates, soldiers, or schoolmasters, for this would involve them in idolatrous associations. Craftsmen must not work for temples. Carpentry and farming have so many pagan and idolatrous associations that Christians should avoid these professions. To those who would accuse him of extremism, Tertullian had a ready answer. Since idolatry is the root of all sin, avoiding it is the key to holiness.

> The principal charge against the human race, the world's deepest guilt, the all-inclusive cause of judgment, is idolatry. Although each particular fault keeps its own characteristic features and will certainly be condemned under its own name, it is listed under the count of idolatry. Forget the terms on the charge-sheet and look at what they do. An idolater is also a murderer. You ask who he has killed? No stranger, no enemy, but—if it adds at all to the scope of the indictment—himself. By what inducement? His own error. What weapon? God's wrath. How many blows? One for every act of idolatry. . . . After offense so fatal and destructive of salvation, any others, as we go down the list, are seen to be essentially present in idolatry in one way or another.[17]

Tertullian's great legacy to African Christianity was his passion for a spiritual church distinct from the world and its idolatry. But driving this passion

16. S. L. Greenslade, ed., *Early Latin Theology*, Library of Christian Classics, vol. 5 (Philadelphia: Westminster, 1956), 79.

17. Ibid., 83.

for holiness was an obsession with the imminence of the coming kingdom. The fact that "Christ might return at any moment to claim his own" made central the question, "Who would then be found worthy to reign with him in the Kingdom of God?"[18] Tertullian's kingdom eschatology, a vision of the city of God to come, was the factor "more than any other which pushed Tertullian into a position where he had to embrace perfectionism as the only solution to the pressing demands of sanctification."[19] This double commitment to holiness and eschatology explains Tertullian's attraction to Montanism.

Though he died as a member of a heretical church, Tertullian influenced mainstream Christianity in Africa as well as in the West in a profound way. Africa's long search for a sanctified and charismatic Christianity alive with the sense of the coming kingdom began with this apologist from Carthage. "Thanks to Tertullian the North African church was and remained a gathered church concerned with the maintenance of its integrity."[20] Tertullian passed on to Cyprian the task of maintaining the purity of the church and fostering its charismatic character.

Cyprian (d. 258). The two cities of Carthage, the pagan and the Christian, were both well known to Cyprian. As a pagan rhetorician he knew firsthand about the city of human vanity filled with the values of Apuleius. But in a dramatic turn dated about the year 246, Cyprian became a citizen of that second Carthage, the society of men like Tertullian for whom holiness and expectation of a higher kingdom was the controlling passion.

As a non-Christian he was afraid of the power of evil and demons. He had trusted the gods to protect him from "black magic." "After he became a Christian he put his trust in the power of the Lord of all things" to conquer the kingdom of darkness.[21] The change in his life was immediately noticed. Two years after his conversion he was made bishop of Carthage and soon found, like Tertullian before him, that life in the city of God was not always tranquil. In 249 the Decian persecution erupted and unsettled life in the second city. Cyprian was forced to flee Carthage for his life. When he returned in 251 he found a divided church.

The issue that most disturbed the church concerned what to do with the "lapsed"—those who had sacrificed to the emperor or had purchased certificates *(libelli pacis)* claiming they had done so. Such an act was regarded as so disloyal to the imperial claims of Christ that some within the church wanted permanently to bar the lapsed from fellowship. Cyprian disagreed and made provision for the repentance and restoration of the lapsed.

18. Gerald Bray, *Holiness and the Will of God: Perspectives on the Theology of Tertullian* (Atlanta: John Knox, 1979), 155.
19. Ibid.
20. Frend, *Rise of Christianity,* 350.
21. Hinchliff, *Cyprian of Carthage,* 25.

This action by Cyprian outraged the rigorists. Their protests, so in keeping with the spirit of Tertullian, reached across the Mediterranean to Rome, where they found an advocate in Novation, a rival bishop of Rome opposing Bishop Cornelius. Novation insisted that the purity of the church could only be maintained by purging from her midst traitors and compromisers. Under the influence of his teaching the rigorist party broke away and formed Novationist churches.

Cyprian resented Novation's unwelcome interference in Africa and disagreed with the separatist party. In Cyprian's judgment, schism was worse than lapsing. This angry bishop of Carthage poured out his full fury against the Novations in his most famous work, *On the Unity of the Church*, condemning separatism and elevating the role of the bishop as the key to the purity and unity of the church.

Cyprian was the clear winner of this showdown. Soon the church was back to full strength. When barbarian raiders dragged off Carthaginians and demanded ransom, Cyprian helped raise one hundred thousand sesterces to ransom the captives. Pagans were impressed and soon Cyprian wrote of the church filling with "a new population of believers."[22]

On the surface, Cyprian, who saw himself as a disciple of Tertullian, seemed to have betrayed his Master by lowering the standards of holiness. Was this the case? Probably not. Cyprian was not so much lowering the standards as shifting the burden of holiness from people to priest. Cyprian accepted Tertullian's eschatology and lived and worked under the lengthening shadow of the second coming. But in this fallen and hostile world, a militant church—not individual martyrs—was the best way to witness to the kingdom.

Where was the Spirit in all of this? What had happened to the charismatic power that Tertullian longed to see in the bride of Christ?

The office of bishop became the locus of the Spirit. The church as a hierarchical institution bore witness to the kingdom by her unity, holiness, and order, centered in the office of the bishop, for "the church was in the bishop." The church was holy because she was led by holy leaders.[23] The bishop, for Cyprian, was not a bureaucrat but a charismatic.

Cyprian believed in dreams, "allowing himself," says his biographer, "to be guided by them and regarding them as portents and prophecies of what was to come."[24] He believed that the bishop was called to do battle with evil spirits. All rivals who claimed to belong to the true church were liars and schismatics doomed to destruction because, in Cyprian's words, "outside the church there is no salvation." Cyprian developed Tertullian's theology of the kingdom by institutionalizing it.

22. Quoted in Frend, *Rise of Christianity*, 324.
23. On this development in Cyprian's theology, see Frend, *Rise of Christianity*, 408–9.
24. Hinchliff, *Cyprian of Carthage*, 25.

Cyprian's essential agreement with Tertullian was illustrated by his debate with Bishop Stephen, Cornelius' successor in Rome. Two Spanish bishops who had betrayed the faith during the Decian persecution appealed to the bishop of Rome for reinstatement. Stephen was agreeable to this petition, but he met stiff opposition from the African bishops led by Cyprian. The voice of the bishop of Carthage who had been so moderate about lapsed laity became extreme when it came to the separate issue of lapsed clergy. The sacraments had no efficacy if offered by an unworthy minister, argued Cyprian. The best unholy clergy could hope for was to be restored to the laity of the church. To be reinstated as a leader was impossible.

Of lapsed leaders Cyprian wrote: "Their speech is a cancer, their conversation is a contagion, their persuasion more deadly and poisonous than the persecution itself."[25]

Why such harshness? Cyprian reveals the legacy of Tertullian, insisting on a Spirit-controlled church separated from the world. For Tertullian this call to holiness was to all Christians. For Cyprian the call was primarily to the clergy. By exalting the position of the clergy in the church, Cyprian also intensified the standards that leaders must meet. For all his clericalism, Cyprian still advocated "Spirit" churches, where the lifestyle of the kingdom was visible in the leadership of the congregations.

The outcome of Cyprian's struggle with Stephen was cut short by the latter's death in 257. The African churches were now free to follow the path of Tertullian and Cyprian. But Cyprian's death precluded his enjoyment of victory. When he was martyred in 258, surrounded by weeping followers, a new way to witness to the kingdom had become entrenched. Clericalism, not martyrdom, was the new way. Strong and godly leaders would build a militant and impregnable church that would declare to the world the reality of the coming kingdom of God. Throughout the history of African Christianity this legacy of Cyprian would remain.

The Diocletian persecution. Cyprian's theology of holiness was severely tested in 303. Diocletian issued an edict in that year against the Christian faith for the crime of "undoing tradition."[26] He declared that no blood should be shed and no sacrifices to the gods be demanded, but that clergy should be harassed, Christian public officials deposed, and Christian property seized and destroyed.

By 304 Diocletian was a dying man and actual decision making in the empire fell to his colleague, Galerius. Galerius joined with a co-ruler, Maximian, and immediately issued a new edict calling for mandatory sacrifices to the gods on pain of death.

25. Quoted in Frend, *Rise of Christianity*, 325.
26. Cf. Frend, *Rise of Christianity*, 457.

Eusebius surveyed the terror that the church endured throughout the empire but commented that the African church "suffered the war of persecution during less than two years," being "deemed worthy of a speedier divine visitation and peace."[27] But peace is a relative term. During those two years of trouble a number of Christian laity and clergy compromised their testimony to the kingdom by collaborating with the police and handing over the Scriptures to be destroyed, thus becoming traitors (from *traditor*, one who handed over the "traditions"; i.e., Scriptures and liturgical books). When the Christian emperor Constantine finally brought an end to hostilities, divisions surfaced in North Africa between the saints who resisted and the lapsed who had not.

Crisis in the Fourth Century: Donatism and Augustine

The Donatist split. The trouble began with an ordination service. In 311 a clergyman named Caecilian was elected bishop of Carthage. Officiating at his installation service was Bishop Felix. Rumors circulated that Felix had been a "traitor." If this were true then his authority to baptize, offer communion (which by this time was regarded in almost magical terms), or ordain clergy would be invalid. The Holy Spirit would simply not indwell an unholy or unworthy cleric—so the tradition of the church of Africa had taught.

A council of bishops who met in 312 condemned Caecilian and appointed a rival bishop. The two parties within the church quickly polarized, with the "puritan" party taking the name of one of their early champions, Donatus. The Donatists, acting according to Cyprianic principles, required those who had lapsed and desired to rejoin the true church of "saints and martyrs" to be rebaptized.

This action outraged the Caecilianists, who took the matter to the authorities. A series of petitions to the government resulted in a victory for Caecilian and the "Catholic" party. From 316 to 321 the government sought to destroy the Donatist movement without success. Both the Catholics and the state had underestimated the power of Donatus and his followers.

Much of the movement's survival must be credited to its leader. Donatus was a strong, uncompromising man whose authority was respected even by his enemies. When a Roman prefect tried to repress his movement, Donatus wrote to the prefect, calling him "the pollution of the senate and the disgrace of the prefecture."[28] Historians report that the prefect backed down. By 330 Donatus was the acknowledged leader of some three hundred bishops, and the movement was growing.

27. Eusebius, *Ecclesiastical History*, 13.13.12.
28. Quoted in W. H. C. Frend, *The Donatist Church* (Oxford: Clarendon, 1952), 166.

The theology that fueled his movement was straightforward. Frend gives a summary: "The Christian Church was a small body of the saved surrounded by the unregenerate. Its progress had been described in the Parable of the Tares. The field was the world, the tares the false Christ, and the wheat the elect. The tares had increased, and it was necessary for the true Christians to separate themselves from them."[29] Donatism, for Harnack, was a protest "against the secularization that was imposed upon [the church] by the removal of the attribute of holiness—from *persons to institutions.*"[30]

Though Cyprian had moved the burden of holiness from laity to clergy, to move the burden from clergy to corporation was going too far. This was against the tradition of Cyprian and Tertullian in which holiness was still to be modeled by either laity or leaders. Donatus was determined to fight to keep the convictions of African spirituality alive.

Radical Donatism: The Circumcellions. After the death of Donatus, the movement continued to spread throughout North Africa. "The Donatists," wrote one historian, "swept in like a forest fire."[31] Over the last half of the fourth century Donatism threatened to become the majority faith of Africa. With aggressive expansion came aggressive action. Catholic churches were plundered. Nuns were raped. Catholic eucharistic bread was fed to dogs. Buildings were seized and reconsecrated. Tertullian had been described as a "sharp and violent talent." The Donatist genius for survival was worthy of the same adjectives.

This mixture of violent tactics and separatist passion was the special brew of the Circumcellions. The movement represented the radical fringe of Donatism. Their name came from their habit of encircling Catholic settlements before attacking *(circum cellas).* Their own preferred label was *agonistici,* soldiers of Christ, who rushed into battle shouting *laudes Deo* (praises to God). The economic and social injustices of colonialism fueled the Circumcellions, who "represented at bottom the social and racial revolt of a repressed peasantry."[32]

The kingdom eschatology of Tertullian boiled over in the worldview of the Circumcellions. Their pamphlets declared that the emperor's commissioners were "forerunners of Antichrist" and that the emperor's court was "an abode of Satan."[33] The Circumcellions saw themselves involved in a relentless warfare between the kingdom of God, for which they fought, and the kingdom of Satan, chiefly represented by the Roman government and the

29. Ibid., 166–67.
30. Adolf Harnack, *History of Dogma*, vol. 5 (Boston: Roberts, 1896–99), 40.
31. Frend, *Donatist Church*, 603.
32. C. P. Groves, *The Planting of Christianity in Africa*, vol. 1 (London: Lutterworth, 1948–58), 64.
33. Frend, *Rise of Christianity*, 574.

Catholic Church. "Their personal goal was martyrdom, attained by uncompromising opposition to all aspects of contemporary life that could be associated with Satan's kingdom and its allies, the pagans and Catholics."[34]

Many of those who did not die in battle threw themselves from cliffs in a suicidal martyrdom that would win for them entrance into the eternal kingdom. Though they were hunted by the Roman army and weakened by their own suicidal fanaticism, the *agonistici* survived into the fifth century. They became "the first Christian group to aim openly at the overthrow of the existing social order and a complete reversal of its values."[35] They would not be the last. They introduced into the story of African church history the kind of violent witness to the kingdom of God that would resurface in a later century in Black liberation theology and its attendant movements of revolution.

Meanwhile mainstream Donatism was fighting its case in the courts. In 412 they faced their stiffest legal battle and lost. A new government edict proscribed the movement, and imperial troops (blessed by the saintly Augustine) sought to exterminate them. But Donatism survived. Bearers of a witness to the kingdom as old as Tertullian, they continued on into the eighth century only to be swept into oblivion by Islam.

Augustine: conversion and ministry. One of Donatism's greatest foes was also one of Africa's greatest sons.[36] Augustine (354–430), bishop of Hippo and native of Numidia, shaped the theology of the worldwide church. In the course of building a legacy for all subsequent Christianity, he bequeathed to Africa a profound vision of church and kingdom.

Before Augustine could write about the kingdom he had to enter it. His conversion in 386 was a dramatic one. Born to a saintly Berber mother and an irritable pagan father, the young Augustine pursued a career in rhetoric that eventually brought him to the city of Carthage, that "caldron of unholy loves."

Augustine had drifted through periods of nominal Catholicism, half-hearted Manichaeism, and full-blown hedonism, all the while testifying to a restlessness of heart that could not be quenched. "My soul was unhealthy and full of sores," he wrote in his *Confessions*, "itching to be scratched by scraping on the things of the senses."[37]

His restlessness led him to Italy. There he encountered Bishop Ambrose of Milan, whose mild Christian Platonism and fervent evangelical preaching

---

34. Ibid.

35. Ibid., 573.

36. Among the many biographies of Augustine, two helpful ones are Peter Brown, *Augustine of Hippo* (London: Faber, 1967), and Henry Chadwick, *Augustine* (Oxford: Oxford University Press, 1986).

37. Augustine's *Confessions*, LCC, vol. 7 (1955), 61.

pierced the young hedonist's heart. The end of his search for peace came in a quiet Italian garden upon reading the command of Romans 13:13–14 to "behave decently, as in the daytime—not in sexual immorality and debauchery" but instead by clothing "yourselves with the Lord Jesus Christ" and not thinking about how "to gratify the desires of the sinful nature." His mother Monica (a Berber name) was overjoyed at her prodigal son's conversion and died in peace soon after.

Augustine returned to Africa after his conversion and in 395 was elected bishop of Hippo. Seeming to believe that the pen was as powerful as the pulpit, Augustine gave himself to the production of a brilliant polemical theology that sought to refute the major threats to the African church of his day. He disputed effectively against Manichaeism (a Gnostic, dualistic religion from the East), Pelagianism (which emphasized human effort and free will in salvation), and Donatism (with its rigid Puritanism and divisive separatism). Augustine won most of these debates (he was least successful against Donatism) and led a revival of African Christianity that affected the wider church.

But a more serious threat to the church was paganism. Augustine's last and arguably greatest work, *The City of God*, was directed against that old foe.

The two cities of Africa: Augustine's vision of the kingdom. Augustine wrote *The City of God* in response to the fall of Rome in 410 to Alaric and his Goths. Furious pagans blamed Christians for this outrage. Many Christians were too shocked by the event to respond adequately to the charges. "The whole world perished in one city," mourned Jerome from his monastery in Bethlehem.[38] Pagan critics claimed that Christianity made Christians so loyal to the otherworldly kingdom that they neglected their duty to defend their human kingdom on earth. Additionally, pagans claimed that the fall of Rome was a sign of the gods' anger over being abandoned by those who had joined the Christian faith.

Augustine's response to the fall of Rome was different from that of either angry pagans or anxious Christians. Augustine took the two principal pagan arguments and turned them against paganism itself. Regarding the second criticism, Augustine blamed continuing Roman paganism, corruption, and sin for the fall of the capital of the empire—not Christianity's rejection of pagan religion. God's wrath on Rome was deserved.

To the first criticism—that the Christians were too mindful of the heavenly kingdom to be very useful in the earthly one—Augustine responded by tracing the history of the kingdom of God and the kingdoms of man, which he described as two cities. He contended that hope for the future lay not with

---

38. Roy Battenhouse, ed., *A Companion to the Study of Augustine* (Grand Rapids: Baker, 1955), 259.

propping up the worn and doomed City of Man but in concentrating energies on the coming City of God, a society of peace and justice. What did Augustine understand by the City of God?

The City of God is the church of Christ in heaven and on earth. First, Augustine saw two contrasting societies as he surveyed his times. The first was the City of God, the fellowship of holy angels and departed saints along with believers who are struggling to bear witness to the heavenly city on earth. The characteristic features of this society are a concern for peace and justice. The church and Christian civilization are the visible (though imperfect) expressions of this heavenly city. Their concern is for the poor and the destitute.

The City of Man is pagan society doomed to destruction. In contrast to the society of peace and justice stands the second society, the City of Man. This is the city of Cain, who murdered the citizen of the City of God, his brother Abel, and rebelled against his Maker. This city is founded by the devil and has spread its evil throughout history. It will reach its appointed end when "the sentences of destiny and doom are passed by our Lord Jesus Christ, the Judge of the living and the dead."[39]

The rival value systems of the two cities. Third, the value systems of the two cities fight for the control of individuals and institutions. The love of the City of Man is self-love. This destructive self-love of the City of Man sunders a relationship with God and slowly undermines the bonds of society. The fall of Rome was thus the bitter fruit born of the internal growth of self-love within Roman society. God-centered love, in contrast, leads to eternal life and earthly happiness. It is agape as opposed to eros.[40] Thus, wherever God-centered love is shown, there the witness to the true kingdom is born. Conversely, wherever selfishness and sin are shown (presumably even in the church), the witness of the kingdom is obscured.

The struggle of the two cities is the story of history. Fourth, the story of Africa and the world is the story of these two loves and the two societies they form. By envisioning history as a moral and spiritual struggle on the level of ultimate values, Augustine continued and expanded the holiness tradition of Cyprian and Tertullian.

Tertullian saw the struggle for holiness largely in individual terms. Cyprian saw the struggle in clerical terms. Augustine saw it in historical terms. Each agreed, however, that the struggle to reflect the values of the kingdom was the central issue in holiness.

---

39. Augustine, *The City of God* (Garden City, N.Y.: Doubleday, 1958), 495.
40. For a critique of Augustine's view of love, see Andyrs Nygren, *Agape and Eros* (Chicago: University of Chicago Press, 1982).

But Augustine did not see this struggle for holiness in purely black-and-white terms, with the church as the "angel" and the nonchurched as the "devil." He recognized that the church could be corrupted by self-love and that some pagans in the City of Man were filled with virtue and were moving toward the City of God. Like the divided soul of Carthage, the struggle of the two cities raged within each institution, and though the victory of divine love is assured, no human institutional expression adequately captured the fullness of that agapic rule.

Augustine further refused to equate the City of God with the Christianized Roman Empire. He had seen enough by his old age to know that self-love can invade the most revered institutions. He even envisioned that a world of nation-states might be a more adequate earthly ally for witnessing to the kingdom.[41] Chadwick describes Augustine's ambiguities about the eternal kingdom and its time-bound witnesses:

> In the *City of God* there are places where Rome is symbolic head of the earthly community in the grip of satanic forces, while the church is at least an anticipation of God's city. . . . But there are also texts where Rome is given a positive significance in God's purpose for his world, whereas the empirical Church is seen as failing to realize divine intentions because of compromises with the secular world.[42]

For Augustine, the citizens of the kingdom of God are like the biblical Abraham, without permanent habitation on earth, wandering "as on a pilgrimage through time looking for the kingdom of eternity."[43] Yet the outcome of the story is never uncertain, for the City of God will triumph in the end.

Augustine's *City of God* thus represented the highest expression of an African theology of the kingdom. Antony of Egypt had seen holiness as wrestling with the demonic. Tertullian had seen the struggle in separating from the visible idolatry of pagan culture. Cyprian had seen the holiness of the church as clerical heroism.

In ways that corrected Antony, Tertullian, and Cyprian, Augustine placed the witness to the kingdom in every human heart, where self-love and love for God wrestle for control. This struggle is not only the most individual of struggles but, according to Augustine, is also social, political, and economic. Witnessing to the kingdom for Augustine required at bottom regeneration of the heart by grace. Though Augustine rejected the Donatist emphasis on a pure church, the vision of a truly evangelical understanding of church and kingdom ruled by transformed hearts began its long journey through African history with *The City of God*.

41. Chadwick, *Augustine*, 101.
42. Ibid., 104.
43. Augustine, *The City of God*, 325.

The City of God was the last great act of Augustine's life. When he lay down his pen in 430 the forces of barbarism were invading his beloved Africa. Augustine's biographer described the scenes of warfare between representatives of the two cities that passed before the great man's dying eyes: "The man of God saw whole cities sacked, villas razed, their owners scattered as refugees, the churches deprived of their bishops and clergy, and the holy virgins dishonored and dispersed, some tortured to death, some killed outright."[44]

A new era had begun.

Fifth-Century Captivity: Vandals and Catholics

Gaiseric and Huneric. With the fall of Rome and the subsequent invasion of Spain and Africa, the Vandals stabbed the heart of Christian civilization and the Roman world recoiled with pain. By 439 the Vandal leader Gaiseric had captured Carthage. In 442 Gaiseric was recognized by the Byzantine Empire as an independent ruler. Gaiseric and his successor Huneric were ardent Arians, and in their zeal for the faith they proceeded to seize the property of the Catholics while demanding that the clergy turn Arian. Soon an Arian bishop ruled in Carthage. Huneric's untimely death (484) eased matters for the Catholics, but it was not until early in the sixth century that Catholic fortunes began to change.

Thrasamund and Fulgentius. A key figure in the renewal of African Catholicism in the Vandal era is the monk Fulgentius (c. 462–527). Fulgentius had grown up in wealth and privilege in Vandal-dominated Africa. In spite of his Catholic faith he had risen to a high position in the government bureaucracy. Yet his soul was restless.

In 483 Fulgentius joined a monastery and sought the kingdom of God. He was eventually made bishop of the coastal town of Ruspe. Just as further opportunities seemed to be opening up, the new Vandal emperor, Thrasamund, sent the Catholic clergy of Africa (including Fulgentius) into exile.

For thirteen years the exiled monk meditated on the state of the church and its need for renewal. How much he appreciated the actual state of affairs is not fully known. In hindsight, the most glaring omission of Catholic Christianity was the failure to disciple the indigenous Berbers. Though there were Berber Christians, there were no Berber Bible translations, no ordained Berber clergy, and no Berber sermons. A profound silence reigned on the Berber level of Africa.

The middle level of African Christianity was slightly better. Preaching in Punic was common, but few Punic-speaking clergy could be found and no Punic Bible translations are known. Christianity in Africa was the Christian-

---

44. Frend, *Rise of Christianity*, 683.

ity of the colonial culture, with its Latin sermons, Latin Bibles, and Latin-educated clergy. It was to this last level of Christianity that Fulgentius devoted his efforts at renewal and reform, apparently blind to the faith's crumbling cultural and linguistic foundations.

Fulgentius studied and wrote as though only Latin Christianity mattered, honing his arguments against Arianism, Pelagianism, and Donatism. The works of Fulgentius, though not of the quality of Augustine's, stirred African theology and worship to life. Eventually his books caught Thrasamund's attention, and Fulgentius was summoned to an audience with the king in 515.

For two years the monarch and the monk crossed theological swords until the weary Thrasamund sent Fulgentius back to Sardinia. Yet Fulgentius had the last word. In 523 Thrasamund died and his successor Hilderich (523–530) granted freedom to the Catholics. Fulgentius returned from exile and witnessed the reorganizing and resurgence of the church before his own death in 527. The resurgence of Catholic Christianity hastened the decline of Vandal rule, which was formally ended by the armies of Byzantium.

Sixth-Century Liberation: Byzantine Reconquest

The reconquest. By the sixth century the Vandal Empire was collapsing. Nomadic tribes chipped away at its boundaries even as a resurgent Catholicism eroded its Arian faith. Hilderich was overthrown by the anti-Catholic Gelimer. His renewed persecution of the church aroused the wrath of Justinian, emperor of the East, who had pledged to reconquer the West and reunite the ancient empire. In 533 he sent his general, Belisarius, at the helm of a great fleet. Carthage was recaptured and by 534 the kingdom of Gelimer collapsed. Catholicism was fully restored. A difficult century of captivity had ended. An equally difficult century of Byzantine misrule had begun.

Justinian and the Berbers. The rule of Justinian meant a new wave of heavy taxation, persecution, and repression for Donatists, Jews, pagans, and Arians. With these groups, repression seemed to work quite well. But the new rulers soon realized that Berber insubordination was a more serious threat to their continued control. Repression and military action did not seem to work. Justinian adopted a new policy to deal with them. He granted special privileges to Berber leaders who converted to the Catholic faith (a policy extended to leaders of other dissident groups as well). Berber chiefs and Arian warlords made liberal use of this policy, which was in effect until the Arab invasions more than a century later.

The kingdom vision of Justinian. Driving Justinian's program of reconquest was a powerful vision of the kingdom of Christ. This vision is captured well in a mosaic found in the church of San Vitale in Ravenna, Italy. The central mosaic depicts Christ the emperor serenely ruling the world, surrounded by his court of angels and saints. On one side of the empire of heaven is Justinian, outfitted as a Persian king of kings. His court stands around him. Opposite Justinian and on the other side of Christ is Theodora, bedecked with jewels and surrounded by her admirers. "Here is a potent association of imperial power and religious devotion expressed by an iconography that fuses sacred and imperial powers and serves to sanctify the imperial ideology."[45]

Justinian pictured himself as lord on earth, just as the risen and ascended Christ was Lord in heaven. Earthly power was thus a mirror and witness to the heavenly. The City of God was being realized through the building of a truly Christian empire. Justinian codified law and persecuted heretics in order to purify his earthly replica of the kingdom of God. With the reconquest of Africa his dream was coming true—the will of God was being done on earth as it was in heaven.

Yet there was another side to Justinian not depicted in the mosaic in Ravenna. The palace historian, Procopius, exalted the role of the Christian emperor in his *History of the Wars*. But while he sang Justinian's praises by day, by night he composed a private history of Justinian, the *Secret History*. Procopius described a man whom power had corrupted, a man who was insane, murderous, and filled with treachery and duplicity. "This Justinian is a demon who stalked the imperial palace by night, his severed head tucked under his arm, and a monster who extorted taxes to hand out as bribes to barbarians."[46]

Procopius had his own reasons for hating Justinian, but his *Secret History* is a reminder of Augustine's two cities. Even the follower of Christ can become corrupted by the self-love of the City of Man and compromise his or her witness. Justinian's theocratic witness to the kingdom of God, which ended the pre-Islamic era of North African history, combines the strengths and the contradictions of the two cities.

Conclusion: The Two Cities

When Speratus, the second-century martyr from Scilli, defiantly rejected allegiance to "the empire of this world" and reasserted his loyalty to the one who "is the emperor of kings and of all nations," he declared a theme running throughout North African Christianity. From the kingdom visions of Tertullian and Cyprian through the violent kingdom consciousness of Cir-

45. Emily Albu Hanawalt, "The Christian Empire and the Early Middle Ages," in Howard Clark Kee et al., *Christianity: A Social and Cultural History* (New York: Macmillan, 1991), 179.
46. Ibid., 180.

cumcellions, from Augustine's concept of the two cities to the theocratic empire of Justinian, the rule of Christ was a central concern of African Christianity. Carthage, with its inner cultures of darkness and light fighting for survival and supremacy, however, was a symbolic reminder that the story of the church's witness to the kingdom is a story of partial victories and mixed messages. Yet in spite of such ambiguities, a rich witness to the kingdom emanates from the story of North African Christianity.

The kingdom as the rule of Christ in hearts. The first point to be noted is the spiritual nature of the kingdom pointed to by martyr and convert. Beginning in the second century with the Scillian martyrs and reaching its high point in Augustine's *Confessions,* the kingdom of Christ is a transcendent reality that breaks into this fallen world as a power that regenerates hearts and redirects loyalties from earthly things to eternal things. Christ, not Caesar, was the "emperor of kings and of all nations." Tertullian and Cyprian witness to this otherworldly kingdom with their emphasis on holiness and separation from the world. This evangelical impulse with its emphasis on Christ's rule over hearts through regeneration and sanctification is a powerful current in African history. Though submerged for centuries, this impulse was never entirely lost.

The kingdom as justice: Circumcellions, Donatism, and Augustine's City of God. Equally as striking as the evangelical emphasis on the spiritual rule of the kingdom is the political witness to the kingdom as justice on earth. Circumcellions witnessed to the kingdom in ways that anticipate liberation movements in the twentieth century. What must not be lost, however, is the sincere if violent theology of the kingdom that motivated "the first Christian group to aim openly at the overthrow of the existing social order and a complete reversal of its values." Augustine's *City of God* looks ahead to the time when the values of the City of God, including peace and justice, transform the kingdoms of this world. Such a vision in a fallen world is not soon forgotten and many who would not recognize Augustine's name would share his dream.

The kingdom as the sovereignty of God. Justinian's concept of empire is the clearest testimony to this third witness to the kingdom, though many a Roman official or Berber warlord doubtless held cruder versions of the same kingdom theology. When the Sudanic kingdoms of Nubia and Ethiopia embraced the gospel, Justinian's vision appealed the most to newly converted rulers grasping for a politically relevant witness to the kingdom of Christ. The idea of the messianic empire—a political system that will usher in the blessings and *shalom* of the kingdom of God—was born in the bosom of Byzantium, only to become a recurring vision in later centuries.

The paradox of the kingdom. Augustine's second city, the city of self-love, was a reminder that human sin corrupts all witnesses to the kingdom. Tertullian's extremist piety, Cyprian's exaggerated clericalism, Augustine's approval of government coercion of Donatism, Donatism's spiritual pride and separatism, Fulgentius' Latin bias, the Circumcellions' use of violence—all remind the African church history student of this fact.

The spiritual witness of the evangelical convert can become the privatistic and self-obsessed witness of the spiritual narcissist. The political witness of the Christian revolutionary or reformer can degenerate into carnal grasping after vengeance and power. The theocratic witness can become a suffocating totalitarianism that kills spiritual and social vitality. North African Christianity reminds us that no single witness to the kingdom, however well-crafted, is either full or final.

Kings of Glory

Christianity in Ethiopia and Nubia

The Nile corridor stretches from the shores of the Mediterranean to the Great Lakes of East Africa. The Nile kingdom of Nubia (part of modern Sudan) was the gateway between the colonial coast and the African heartlands. Comprising a kingdom that enjoyed its independence from the empire of Rome, Nubia still acted as a bridge between Rome and the mysterious continent to its south. We should not be surprised that a bust of Augustus Caesar, dating to the first century, was found just over a hundred miles from Khartoum.

The guardians of this gateway were the great kings of Nubia. They had defeated their enemies to the north and west time and again and inscribed their victories on steles that can still be seen today. The mounds and pyramids where they were buried also remind us of their majesty. Their remains were placed on litters by which they could be carried to the next world. Surrounding the dead king were his wives, servants, and even horses. Exquisite jewels, pottery, and furniture inlaid with ivory were buried with the king and his entourage. Statues of the gods stared down at the dead king as though envious of his earthly power and glory.

The royal tombs cover many centuries of Nubia's glory, but from the sixth century on the mounds disappear. Did Nubian civilization decline after that century?

The testimony of history is surprising. Nubia reached some of its greatest heights after that time. Why the disappearance of the royal burial mounds? Other material artifacts of Nubia in the period after the year 600 give us a clue. In the words of William Adams, "The king whose glory was celebrated in the art, architecture, and literature of the Middle Ages was a heavenly rather than an earthly one."[1] The rule of Jesus Christ became the theme of Nubian art,

1. William Adams, *Nubia: Corridor to Africa* (Princeton: Princeton University Press, 1977), 436.

eclipsing the glory of earthly kings. Just as Nubia was the link between Africa's northern shore and its vast interior, so Christ was declared by Nubian art, to be the royal bridge between the empire of Nubia and the heartland of heaven. His position was thus greater than an earthly monarch's could ever be.

Nothing less than a religious revolution can explain how the entombed glory of Nubian royalty was swept away to be replaced by the exaltation of a heavenly King. How this revolution in Nubia and in the rival kingdom of Ethiopia happened is the subject of this chapter. The story begins in Ethiopia.

Religious Revolution in Ethiopia

The kingdom of Axum.[2] In the northern corner of the Ethiopian highlands a new kingdom emerged sometime in the first century. By the third century the imperial capital, Axum, was ranked among the greatest cities in the world.[3] It was a "city of splendid stone monuments—including palaces, temples, and carved stone obelisks."[4] Through the port city of Adulis, eight days' journey by foot from Axum, trade in ivory, rhinoceros horn, tortoise shell, and obsidian was carried on with the Mediterranean world.[5] This trade with the Greek-speaking world to the north made learning Greek a desire of Axum's kings. Ella Amida, the king of Axum in the early fourth century, was particularly desirous that his bright heir to the throne, Ezana, acquire the new knowledge. Teachers, however, were lacking.

Frumentius and Aedesius. Providence soon remedied the situation. The fifth-century historians Rufinus (who claimed to have interviewed an eyewitness) and Socrates Scholasticus (who gives Rufinus' account almost word for word) recorded the coming of Christianity (and the new learning) to Ethiopia. Ethiopian written tradition tells much the same story.[6]

A Syrian philosopher named Meropius, accompanied by two young relatives, Frumentius and Aedesius, embarked on a journey to India, which on maps of the ancient geographers was connected to Africa. Putting into port on the Axumite coast (Adulis?), the tourists and crew were seized by hostile locals angered by a recently violated treaty with Rome. All were killed except the two youth, who were then sent to the capitol.

The king was so "pleased with the personal appearance of the youths," writes Socrates, that he "constituted one of them, whose name was Edesius,

---

2. Axum sometimes appears as Aksum. I have adopted the spelling that is used in UNESCO's *General History of Africa.*
3. Cf. G. Mokhtar, ed., *General History of Africa,* vol. 2 (Paris: UNESCO, 1990), 204.
4. R. Oliver and J. Fage, *A Short History of Africa* (London: Penguin, 1988), 29.
5. Mokhtar, *General History of Africa,* vol. 2, 204.
6. Particularly the history of the kings, Tarike Neguest.

cup-bearer at his table; the other, named Frumentius, he entrusted with the care of the royal records."[7] This arrangement, however, was short-lived. The king died unexpectedly and his distressed widow turned to the two young men for help. Since her son Ezana was still in his infancy, they offered their services as regents.

Frumentius became the virtual ruler of the realm and used his position to locate Christian merchants within Ethiopia and encourage them to begin local churches. When Ezana came of age, the grateful monarch granted Frumentius and Aedesius their freedom to return home. Frumentius decided to visit the newly installed patriarch of Alexandria, Athanasius, to describe the spiritual needs of the Ethiopians. Athanasius, moved by Frumentius' zeal, immediately consecrated the latter as bishop and commissioned him to return as a missionary to the place of his former captivity. By 350 Frumentius was back in Axum and found that Ezana, the boy king, had grown up.

The conversion of Ezana. Ezana, in Frumentius' absence, had become a successful warrior king. Sometime in the 340s he embarked on a series of military campaigns designed to solidify his authority. The memorial inscriptions of these campaigns contain the typical boasts of a victorious king as well as praises to Astar and other gods of the Axumite pantheon. But in 350 something changed.[8]

Ezana's successful invasion of the neighboring kingdom of Meroe was celebrated with a memorial stele found in the ruins of Axum. On this stele no reference is made to the traditional gods. Instead ten references are made to the "Lord of All," "Lord of Heaven," and "Lord of Earth," referring in context to the same deity. In another inscription of about the same time the king declares, "I believe in your son Jesus Christ who has saved me," confirming that Ezana had converted to the Christian faith.[9] Coinage appears during his reign bearing the symbol of the cross.[10] A sincere conversion seems to have occurred in Ezana's life that would change the future of Ethiopia and much of Africa in ways comparable to the impact of Constantine's conversion in the West.

Though details are lacking, Frumentius must have played a key role in this religious revolution. The loyalty that Ezana showed to him bears this out. When the Roman emperor Constantius, an Arian sympathizer and

7. Socrates Scholasticus, *Ecclesiastical History, Nicene and Post-Nicene Fathers*, vol. 2, 2nd series, ed. Schaff and Wace (Grand Rapids: Eerdmans, 1978), 1.19.

8. Steven Kaplan, "Ezana's Conversion Reconsidered," *Journal of Religion in Africa* 13, no. 2 (1982): 102.

9. Ibid., 103.

10. C. P. Groves, *The Planting of Christianity in Africa*, vol. 1 (London: Lutterworth, 1948), 52.

enemy of Athanasius, wrote to Ezana and his brother insisting that Frumentius be sent back to Alexandria for investigation by the Arian patriarch, Ezana apparently refused. Every indication we have is that Frumentius lived out his days at the court of his king, convert, and friend. "Christianity had become the court religion," writes P. L. Shinnie, and from that time "there began the close connection between Christianity and what was to become the Ethiopian nation."[11] Yet beyond the conversion of the court lay the challenge of the countryside.

The Nine Saints. For the century after the death of Ezana (c. 400) Christianity was confined to "a narrow corridor between Adulis and Axum along the main caravan routes."[12] The successors of Ezana, such as Kaleb and Gabre Maskal, were sincere Christians who puzzled over how to bring the Good News of the kingdom to the masses.

An answer came in the form of a new missionary force entering the country. Beginning in the fifth century Syrian monks of mildly Monophysite persuasion filtered into Ethiopia, possibly to escape persecution from the pro-Chalcedonian Byzantine emperor. Ethiopian church tradition identifies a select group of these missionary refugees as the *tesseatou Kidoussan* (the Nine Saints). These nine monks (Abba Aregawi, Abba Guerima, Abba Aftse, Penteleon, Likanos, Alef, Tsihma, Ym'ata, and Gouba) learned the local languages, translated Scriptures into Ge'ez, preached, planted monasteries and churches, and traveled extensively throughout the Axumite lands. Abba Aregawi was the most revered. His greatest legacy was the founding of monasticism in Ethiopia, which emanated from his center, Dabra Damo.[13]

Although other missionaries like the *Sadqan* and Abba Libanos were significant in the spread of the faith in Ethiopia, the Nine Saints are given the primary credit for rooting Christianity among the people.[14] For centuries after, the stories and church murals of the Nine Saints would be a significant part of Ethiopian tradition.

The coming of the Syrian monks and their introduction of the rule of St. Pachomius changed the character of Ethiopian Christianity. Monasteries more than churches became the bases from which Christianity was established and extended in the kingdom. It was to the monasteries, says Roland Oliver, that "the faithful repaired at great festivals and in times of personal

---

11. P. L. Shinnie in *Cambridge History of Africa*, vol. 2, ed. J. D. Fage (Cambridge: Cambridge University Press, 1978), 265.

12. Quoted in Steven Kaplan, *The Monastic Holy Man and the Christianization of Early Solomonic Ethiopia* (Wiesbaden: Franz Steiner Verlag, 1984), 16.

13. For a discussion of the nine saints, see UNESCO's *General History of Africa*, vol. 2, 229.

14. Kaplan, *Monastic Holy Man*, 17.

need."[15] When King Gabre Maskal granted land to Abba Aregawi, a tradition was established that would eventually make "the Church the largest landowner in the country."[16]

Yet the work of the monks and their successors was not without flaws. To their credit they did present an apolitical Christianity that clearly distinguished the acceptance of Christ as King from submission to the king sitting in Axum.

However, the conversion process used by the monks had unintended side effects. The new missionaries of the fifth century and their successors established a ritual for conversion that involved a profession of faith, the experience of baptism, and the assigning of a new name. Little teaching or training was given. This meant that "many new Christians had only a minimal commitment to their new faith."[17] Combined with the lack of trained clergy, such converts frequently slipped into syncretism or eventual apostasy. Belief in sacred groves and trees persisted within the community of the church into modern times. Beneath the numeric successes of the monastic missionaries lay a deeper failure to bring converts beyond the "threshold of Christianity" to the point of "an irreversible commitment."[18]

Linked with Egyptian Coptic Christianity (the *abun* or chief bishop of the church continued to be an Egyptian) and armed with vernacular Scriptures, Christian kings, and great numbers of local churches, the church of Ethiopia entered the Middle Ages where, in Gibbon's exaggerated phrase, they "slept near a thousand years, forgetful of the world, by whom they were forgotten."[19]

Nubia

New light on Nubian Christianity. In 1960 UNESCO sent out an appeal to scholars around the world to explore the area along the Nile that would be flooded by the Aswan Dam. About forty separate archaeological expeditions answered the appeal.

The most important discovery was made by a Polish expedition under Michalowski. This was the unearthing of the cathedral of Faras, capital of Nobatia, the northern kingdom of Nubia. Careful digging revealed a Nubian church containing 160 frescoes and 400 wall inscriptions in Greek, Coptic, and Old Nubian. Among the inscriptions were lists of bishops of

15. Roland Oliver, *The African Experience* (San Francisco: HarperCollins, 1991), 82.
16. John Baur, *2000 Years of Christianity in Africa* (Nairobi: Paulines, 1994), 36.
17. Ibid., 132.
18. Ibid.
19. Quoted in Eike Haberland, *Altes Christentum in Süd Äthiopien* (Wiesbaden: Franz Steiner Verlag, 1976), 1.

the Faras cathedral from 707 to 1169. Other archaeological work confirmed the existence of Christianity in Nubia prior to the previous date of 542.[20]

What picture of Nubia in general and the early years of Nubian Christianity in particular emerges from these recent explorations?

The Three River Kingdoms of Nubia: Nobatia, Makuria, and Alwa. Before there was a Nubia, there was a Meroe. And before there was a Meroe, there was a Kush. The kingdom of Kush was known in Old Testament times. Its successor kingdom, Meroe, was represented in the New Testament by the eunuch of Acts 8.[21] By the third century the kingdom of Meroe was in ruins (probably due to Ezana's raids). A warrior tribe of fleet horsemen skilled with the sword and the bow (known as the "X-Group" to historians) overran the dying kingdom of Meroe.

Upon the ruins of the old kingdom the conquerors built the three kingdoms of Nubia: Nobatia to the north with its capital at Faras, Makuria in the middle with its capital of Dongola, and Alwa to the south with its capital of Soba.[22] Though the rural folk of these three kingdoms survived by farming and fishing, a ruling elite amassed riches through traffic in gold and slaves. At the top of this ruling elite was the king.

Kingship in Nubia. Nubian kingship carried on the royal traditions of Meroe. The king was regarded as semidivine. Though sacred in his own person he was also seen as a servant of the gods. Before 250 B.C. this fact had led to the practice of royal suicide. The priests would claim to receive a message from the gods that the king must die. They would report this to the reigning monarch, who was then expected to take his life in compliance with the will of the gods. Ergamenos brought an abrupt and lasting end to this tradition when he killed the priests who brought him the divine summons of suicide. This assertion of the right of kings even over the will of the gods represented a heightened status for the king.

Next to the king in power and status was the queen mother, the *kandake* or candace. She played a pivotal role in the election and coronation of the king. In the years before Christ, the candace often ruled as king, taking upon

20. A useful summary of literature on Nubia is found in Paul Bowers, "Nubian Christianity: The Neglected Heritage," *East Africa Journal of Evangelical Theology* [now the *Africa Journal of Evangelical Theology*] 4, no. 1 (1985): 3–23.

21. The term "Ethiopia" to the first-century world meant the lands of the Blacks south of Egypt, particularly the lands along the Nile. The royal title "candace" (from *kandake*) is unique to the royal system of Nubia. We have no reliable historical evidence that the eunuch ever returned to Nubia, although in the third century Origen speculated that he was the first evangelist of "Ethiopia." Similarly the tradition that the apostle Matthew came to Ethiopia and Nubia in the first century is based on a confusion in first-century geography in which India was felt to be connected to Africa south of the Sahara.

22. See the discussion of this point in UNESCO's *General History of Africa*, vol. 2, 170.

herself the titles of "Son of Amon" and "Lord of the two lands."[23] Nubia preserved many of these institutions and helped pass them along to Africa. Nubia
with its precursor kingdoms of Kush and Meroe was a "strongly original civilization which, beneath an Egyptian style veneer—remained profoundly African."[24] This deep reverence for a king who mediated between God and man
may help explain the successful reception of the gospel of the kingdom.

The coming of Christianity in the fifth century. By the fifth century the kings
of Nubia were confronted by a strange invader. A new religion made its way
into the river kingdoms south of Egypt. Evidence for this is strong. The Polish
excavations that uncovered the great cathedral of Faras also unearthed the
remains of an early Christian church beneath the ruins of a royal palace. A
late-fifth-century date has been given to this find. Additionally, Christian
graves and artifacts were found in "X-Group" cemeteries. Rufinus records
that monks had penetrated Nubia by the early fifth century.[25] In sharp contrast to its reception in Ethiopia, Christianity in Nubia spread among the
poor but avoided the palace. That pattern would change in the sixth century.

The mission of Julian, 543. It is hard to say what kind of marriage Justinian
and Theodora, the emperor and empress of Byzantium, enjoyed but it seems
safe to say that it was competitive. They clashed in Alexandria over the appointment of the patriarch. They clashed again over Nubia.

After becoming emperor in 527 Justinian married the lovely but controversial Theodora. Her earlier life offered little hint of future greatness. She had
been a prostitute in Alexandria. Monophysite monks brought her to the Christian faith. Her ascent to the throne as wife of Justinian was an almost unthink-
able reversal of her fortunes. She never forgot the debt she owed to the Syrian
monks, heretics though they might have been in the eyes of her husband.

Justinian was concerned about growing religious disunity in his empire.
In Alexandria alone there were twenty different rival denominations in
500.[26] He therefore opposed Monophysitism (as well as paganism) and
sought to promote the Chalcedonian Christology of two natures united in
one person. When Justinian closed the temple to Isis in Philae in the border-
lands between Egypt and Nubia, a religious vacuum was created that affected Nubians and prompted King Silko of Nubia to write to Justinian requesting missionaries.[27] Justinian was eager to do so. He gathered a group of

---

23. Ibid., 174.
24. Ibid., 170.
25. Giovanni Vantini, *Christianity in the Sudan* (Bologna: EMI, 1981), 36.
26. Ibid.
27. Although Adams points out that an attempted closing of the temple a century earlier
had aroused armed revolt, no such reaction occurred this time—a testimony perhaps to the
spread of Christianity in the fifth century. Cf. Adams, *Nubia*, 440.

ambassadors, loaded them with gifts and baptismal robes, and then dispatched them to Nobatia by way of the governor of upper Egypt (headquartered in Thebes).

Theodora found out and acted quickly. She already knew whom she would send as her representative. Earlier in 543 a priest named Julian had approached Theodora to express his desire to be a missionary to the people of Nubia. Julian was part of the entourage of Theodosius, the deposed Monophysite patriarch of Alexandria, whom Theodora was sheltering at court. She dispatched Julian and his party immediately with instructions to beat the ambassadors to the governor first and then beat them to Nobatia.

Julian arrived in Thebes just ahead of the unsuspecting ambassadors of Justinian. He handed the governor a letter from the empress that threatened a beheading if he did not detain Justinian's group and speed Julian on his way. The governor found Theodora's letter persuasive and did as she commanded. Julian was given the headstart he needed. As he neared the borders of Nobatia a "whole army was sent to meet them," according to John of Ephesus (d. 686), a Monophysite historian. John describes what happened next:

> They received Julian's expedition with joy and introduced them to their king, and the latter also received them gladly. Then [Julian] produced the letters of the queen. They were read and their content was understood. They accepted also the great gifts and the numerous baptismal garments, everything in plenty. They soon offered themselves to be instructed, renouncing the errors of their forefathers and confessing the God of the Christians, saying "This is the one true God, and there is no other beside Him."[28]

No sooner had the king dried off from the waters of baptism than he was informed that ambassadors of the emperor Justinian had arrived. Being warned of the rival faith the imperial delegation brought with them, Silko prepared himself. When the ambassadors were ushered into the king's presence, Silko listened, received the presents that were brought, and then refused to accept "the wicked faith professed by the King [Justinian]."[29] The Orthodox mission was expelled. Regrouping from this shock, they paddled downstream to Makuria, where they received a kinder reception.[30]

Julian stayed in Nobatia for two years until the heat finally became unbearable. For those two years, we are told by the partisan John of Ephesus, Julian spent seven hours each day in caves sitting naked (or nearly naked) in puddles of water in order to stay cool. Julian carried on his evangelism from these puddled caves, but one wonders how effective such evangelism could

28. Quoted in Vantini, *Christianity in Sudan,* 39.
29. Ibid.
30. Oliver, *African Experience,* 82–83.

be. Though Julian introduced Christianity to the Nubian elite, others were needed to disciple the nation.

The First Mission of Longinus, 568. Theodoros, bishop of Philae, was Julian's immediate replacement in Nobatia, but it was Longinus of Byzantium who had the greatest impact. Longinus was from Alexandria but found himself in Byzantium as a representative for a Monophysite church in Antioch. While Longinus was there Justinian died (565). Theodora had died in 547. Longinus was selected by the overjoyed Monophysite leaders to resume the mission to Nobatia. It was hoped that the new emperor, Justin, would be more sympathetic than his father. They were wrong.

As Longinus prepared to sail for Nubia, he was arrested and imprisoned. Three years later, in 568, Longinus escaped from jail and made his way to the kingdom of Nobatia. "When he arrived," wrote John of Ephesus, "he was received with great rejoicing."[31] Longinus was successful in building churches, training and ordaining clergy, and reforming worship.[32] Years later the Nubian ambassador to Byzantium told Emperor Justin (much to his annoyance) that "though we were Christians in name, yet we did not really know what Christianity was until Longinus came to us."[33]

The second mission of Longinus: The kingdom of Alwa. In 575 the mission of Longinus in Nobatia was interrupted by messengers from Alexandria urging him to return immediately to help in the election of a new Monophysite patriarch. Emperor Justin had died and the new emperor Tiberius was known to be a friend of the anti-Chalcedonian party. The time seemed right to restore a Monophysite patriarch to Egypt. Longinus was torn. Only a little while before, the king of Alwa, the southernmost kingdom of Nubia, had written requesting missionaries to come and evangelize that land. Longinus decided to heed the call of Alexandria. Intrigue followed him in Alexandria, and it was only with difficulty that he was able to return to Nobatia, where he prepared for his crusade in Alwa.

Barring the way to Alwa was the middle kingdom of Makuria. Not only was this kingdom orthodox in its religion; it was also politically hostile to the two sister kingdoms of Nubia. Passage down the Nile would be impossible given Makuria's opposition. An arduous route by land was chosen. The heat was unbearable. Seventeen camels died. The spies of the Makurian king were everywhere. Yet, according to John of Ephesus, "God blinded the eyes of those who wanted to hold him" and Longinus arrived in Alwa in 580.[34]

The reception in Alwa was dramatic.

31. Quoted in Vantini, *Christianity in Sudan*, 44.
32. Groves, *Planting*, vol. 1, 50.
33. Quoted in ibid., 50–51.
34. Quoted in ibid., 51.

Immediately upon his arrival he spake unto the king and to all his nobles the word of God and they opened their understanding, and listened with joy to what he said; and after a few days' instruction, both the king himself was baptized and all his nobles; and subsequently in the process of time, his people also.[35]

The depth of Nubian Christianity. With the conversion of Alwa the story of Christian beginnings in Nubia is complete. Yet two questions need to be addressed. How deep was the impact of Christianity on Nubia and its culture? What kind of Christianity took hold—Monophysitism or Orthodoxy?

The evidence we have suggests that Orthodox Christianity took hold in Nubia. When Christianity began trickling into Nubia in the fifth century, it encountered a religious people. The most important god in the Nubian pantheon was the lion god, Amon, lord of fertility. Next to him in importance was the sun god Mandulis. Horus, the hunter god, and Musawwarat es-safra, the elephant god, were also venerated. The role of these gods was to bless the worshiper in this life and in the next.[36]

By the fifth century the longing for eternal life and for deliverance from suffering and want was as strong as ever in Nubia if the size and number of the traditional temples are any indication. But almost overnight after 550 this traditional religion is swept away. Burial practices are transformed, royal buildings are converted into churches, and the art that had glorified kings and gods is now focused on Christ as the King of kings.[37] In light of this evidence of a rapid and widespread change in culture Adams writes that "the advent of Christianity wrought an ideological transformation unparalleled since the introduction of civilization itself."[38]

No Roman emperor imposed Christianity upon her from above and no philosophy eroded the old gods of Nubia as in Rome. Christianity took root, and deep root at that, because it met the deepest longings of the Nubian heart for eternal life enjoyed under the sovereignty of an eternal King. The burden of mortality, more than the pragmatism of politics, best accounts for the enthusiastic embrace of the new religion.

More surprising is the kind of Christianity that was eventually embraced. In spite of the scheming of Theodora and the heroics of Julian and Longinus, Orthodox Christianity seems to have gradually triumphed in Nubia. Orthodox forms of prayer and Byzantine formulas of worship have been found in inscriptions not only in Makuria but also in Nobatia.[39] In the Middle Ages a Melkite bishop ruled over the northern kingdom. Monneret de Villard ob-

---

35. Vantini, *Christianity in Sudan,* 47.
36. Cf. Vantini's useful discussion of Nubian traditional religion, 26–27.
37. *Cambridge History of Africa,* vol. 2, 564.
38. Adams, *Nubia,* 435.
39. Vantini, *Christianity in Sudan,* 41.

served that "the earliest hierarchical organization in Nubia, the names used by the Nubians, the names of the Saints to whom there was great devotion in Nubia, all these show a much closer connection with the Byzantine church than with the Coptic church in Egypt."[40]

One explanation for the comeback of Orthodoxy after the early lead of Monophysitism may lie in Nubia's independence. A patriotism that burned against colonial intrusion fueled the Monophysitism of Egypt. But no such colonialism existed in Nubia. A religious consumerism, uncomplicated by such political concerns, was freer to choose among the available "products." The consumers seem to have chosen Orthodoxy. But these conclusions must be tentative. The sands of Nubia have not spoken their final word.

Conclusion: Kingdom Witness in Ethiopia and Nubia

Just as Nubia was the link between Africa's northern shore and its vast interior, so Christ was declared by Nubian art to be the royal bridge between the empire of Nubia and the heartland of heaven. Only recognition of the lordship of Christ over all of life can explain how the entombed glory of Nubian royalty was swept away to be replaced by the exaltation of a heavenly King. This chapter has attempted to explain how this revolution in Nubia and in the rival kingdom of Ethiopia occurred.

Though Nubia and Ethiopia were not part of the Byzantine Empire, their model of the kingdom bore striking parallels to the model of Byzantium. Church and state, while distinct in many ways, formed a whole—a total life witness to the rule of Christ over all things. At the top of this earthly pyramid of witness was the king, his stature altered by Christian faith and the exaltation of Christ as King. Under the king were the monks and the priests, seeking to save their own souls through deprivations and the souls of the masses through the Eucharist and baptism. At the bottom of the pyramid were the people themselves, embracing the new faith but separated from the heavenly King Jesus by the spiritual and political classes above them.

This theocratic witness to the kingdom kept alive an awareness of the providential rule of God much as Israel's theocracy did in the Old Testament. It also projected a certain vision of God. He alone was the true King of kings, more potent than the greatest monarch of Egypt or of Ethiopia. He alone was seated upon history and the heavens as upon a throne. Since "God is king, not an elected official," the earthly structures of church and state are "not to be organized democratically." Instead "righteous ones rule in the name of

---

40. Quoted in Vantini, *Christianity in Sudan*, 41.

God and unrighteousness is not tolerated."[41] This model tends to see the kingdom "as more a kingdom of law than of grace."[42]

Behind the glory of such a theocratic witness lies a danger. The evangelical impulse, the kingdom as the redemptive rule of Christ, can be eclipsed by the "power" model of the theocratic kingdom. Christ as Pantocrator (ruler of the universe) can overshadow Christ the suffering Savior. Additionally, the vision of the coming kingdom of justice and peace of which all earthly constructs are but pale shadows can be crushed beneath the weight of the institutional status quo. The idea of the kingdom as counterculture so earnestly pursued by Coptic Christianity never found the same resonance in Nubia or Ethiopia. Augustine's reminder that the selfish values of the City of Man are never far from any witness to the City of God is relevant.

The churches of Africa entered the Middle Ages armed largely with a theocratic witness to the kingdom of God. From 600 to 1600 they would confront rival kingdoms that would provide their most severe test to date.

41. Howard Snyder, "Models of the Kingdom," *Transformation* 10, no. 1 (January 1993): 4.
42. Ibid.

Part 2

The Clash of Kingdoms

Medieval African Christianity (600–1700)

The Kingdoms of Allah and Mungu

Islam and African Religion in the Middle Ages

Africa is a continent with a triple heritage.[1] For thousands of years she has been the meeting ground of Western, indigenous, and Semitic cultures. This triple heritage is particularly evident in the area of religion. Islam, Christianity, and African traditional religion are all deeply rooted in the African past. Yet the true story of these three great religions and their complex relationships in Africa is obscured by a number of widely held myths. Four come to mind.

The first myth refers to Islam. The story of Islam in the African Middle Ages has been hampered by the myth of forced conversions. The picture of Muslim zealots on horseback demanding submission to Allah at the point of the sword is widely believed but far from historical fact. The reality is that forced conversions were the exception rather than the rule. The nomad and merchant rather than the soldier and swordsman were the real missionaries of Islam in Africa.

The second myth concerns Christianity. Popular belief holds that Christianity in Africa was extinguished by the rise and spread of Islam. A corollary to this is that with the disappearance of this early Christianity from Africa, the missionary Christianity of the eighteenth and nineteenth centuries was a foreign and culturally destructive force that should be rejected by contemporary Africans.

The reality is quite different. Christianity in the African Middle Ages survived the rise of Islam in three of its four early centers. In at least two African kingdoms Christianity reached its peak of influence during the Muslim centuries. The spirit of this surviving African Christianity created a culture force

---

1. See the discussion of this point in Ali Mazrui, *The Africans* (Boston: Little, Brown, 1986).

known as "Ethiopianism," which not only tempered the Christianity brought by the missionary but also played a major part in the political, cultural, and religious renewal of Africa in the twentieth century.

The third myth concerns African traditional religion (ATR) and history. Africa in the Middle Ages (roughly 600–1600) really had no history according to this myth. African political systems were crude and "uncivilized" and African religion was backward and polytheistic. The reality is that African kingdoms reached unprecedented heights in the Middle Ages under the leadership of powerful kings revered as divine mediators. African traditional religion and African concepts of kingship converge to create a period of splendor and achievement throughout the continent.

A fourth myth stresses the rivalry among these three great African religions to the exclusion of their common interests. The mutual exclusiveness of Islam, Christianity, and ATR has been exaggerated and the mutual influences have been ignored. The reality is that both ATR and Islam cultivated a widespread longing for the kingdom of God and for a sacred king that eventually led millions of Africans to seek their fulfillment in the redemptive reign of Christ.

This chapter seeks to explode some of these myths. The story of Allah and Mungu (Swahili for God) in the African Middle Ages is a story of profound changes and great achievements that serve to prepare the continent for the coming kingdom of Christ.

The Kingdom of Allah: Early Expansion of Islam, 600–1000

Islam's beginnings. The life of Muhammad[2] the prophet of Allah—his message of monotheism, his flight from Mecca in 622, his conversion of Medina, and his triumphant return to Mecca before his death in 632—is a story that has often been told. Less familiar is the story of his successors and the impact they had upon Africa in the thousand years from the seventh century to the seventeenth. It is a story of wide expansion and deep division.

The four caliphs and the succession struggle. The story begins with the first four successors of Muhammad: Abu Bakr, Umar, Uthman, and Ali. In Allah's name these Islamic leaders engaged in a holy war *(jihad)* that took their armies deep into the recesses of the Persian Empire and the Middle East. By 650 Islam had become entrenched in these ancient lands. But other areas beckoned. Across the Red Sea lay Egypt's rich farmlands and prosperous cities. By 640 Amr ibn al Ac had added a compliant Egypt to the expanding

2. I have adopted the spelling of the prophet's name used in UNESCO's *General History of Africa.*

kingdom of Allah.[3] In the early 700s North Africa became another link in the Islamic chain.

Yet beneath the surface of Islamic unity, dissension lurked. The deepest divisions involved the issue of succession. After the third caliph, Uthman, was murdered, Ali, husband of Muhammad's daughter Fatimah, was declared the fourth caliph. No sooner had he begun his rule than a struggle for power occurred with the Syrian governor Mu'awiya, who was the sworn avenger for the blood of Uthman. Mu'awiya won the ensuing struggle and established the dominant dynasty of Islam in the seventh and eighth centuries—the Umayyad dynasty.

But a cloud hung over the Umayyad rulers. Many felt that Ali's son (also called Ali) was the only rightful heir to Islamic headship. The assassination of Ali the Younger split Islam into those who favored the Umayyads (the Sunnis) and those who did not (the Shi'ites and the Kharijites). The Sunnis enjoyed official favor. The Shi'ites, loyal to the line of Ali from which a messiah would come, remained in the area of the former Persian Empire that eventually became Iran. The Kharijites came to Africa.

The Kharijites were the militant puritans of Islam. They held that personal righteousness alone qualified someone to rule and taught that even a Negro slave who was pure in heart could become caliph. Their insistence on personal integrity had even led to disillusionment with the elder Ali, whose negotiations with Mu'awiya were seen as a compromise.

As the Kharijites migrated west through Africa they encountered the newly conquered Berbers, who shared a similar hatred of the Umayyad rulers. Early contacts between Muslim soldiers and Berber leaders like Kusaila and Kahina (the Berber Joan of Arc) were violent, but ultimately the witness of the Kharijites won the respect and devotion of the Berber tribes of the Mahgrib (Arabic for "west" and applied to all of the lands formerly under Roman rule in North Africa). It is not surprising that the Kharijites were able to impart their brand of rigorous holiness to the heirs of Tertullian and Cyprian.[4]

When the Umayyad dynasty was overthrown in 750, the Kharijites and their Berber converts rejoiced. The new dynasty, the Abbasids, was unable to establish control of the Mahgrib. Independent Kharijite and Berber kingdoms took their turns holding the reins of power.[5]

Oral and written Islam. One achievement of the Umayyads, little appreciated by the radical sects of Islam at the time, was the establishment of a written Islam to supplant the oral Islam of the seventh century. The Islam of

---

3. See the discussion of the Muslim invasion in Falk, *Growth of the Church in Africa* (Grand Rapids: Zondervan, 1979), 63, and in *Cambridge History of Africa*, vol. 2, 496–99.

4. Kharijite Islam under the name Ibadi or Abadis can still be found today in small enclaves of North Africa and Zanzibar according to A. Guillaume, *Islam* (London: Penguin, 1956), 112–13.

5. *General History of Africa*, vol. 3, 26.

the 600s was the Islam of the *jihad,* a military movement that did little to spread the faith among the subject people. It was the religion of the soldier and warlord.

The written Islam of the eighth and ninth centuries was the product of Greek and Persian scholars, who codified customs and legal traditions in the Middle East and rationalized them with the oral tradition attributed to Muhammad.[6] This written Islam of the Hadith (acts and deeds of Mohammad) and Quran produced a truly missionary religion, which turned from the sword to the sermon as the weapon of conversion.

From the ninth century on "no picture could be more false than that which long prevailed in western Christendom of a creed imposed upon the subjected at the point of a sword."[7] The fact that Christians could be found in the town of Tozeur in Islamic North Africa as late as the eighteenth century is striking evidence to dispel the myth of widespread forced conversions.[8]

Muslim missions in the ninth and tenth centuries. With a newly clarified and written theology, Islam as a religion was ready for missions. The deepening of Islamic faith among the Kharijite Ibadis of North Africa (principally in the tenth century and later)[9] was significant for later African history. Ibadi merchants accompanied Berber camel caravans that traversed the Sahara. Trade with West Africa commenced. Along the trade routes passed a new faith that would assure Islam a role in the African kingdoms rising along the Niger.

Islam in the High Middle Ages, 1000–1600

Slaves and messiahs in the High Middle Ages. As the trade with sub-Saharan Africa grew, slaves became one of the principal commodities sought by the Ibadi merchants. It was also, according to Roland Oliver, the "key to the politics of medieval North Africa."[10] Slaves made it possible for local governors to assemble sizable armies and build semiautonomous kingdoms. The Aghlabids illustrate this process. After absorbing a number of Berber tribes, the Aghlabid warlords added Black slaves from West Africa to their growing army. They soon achieved wide hegemony over North Africa. Other Muslim leaders began to copy this pattern.

6. Cf. Michael Brett's discussion of the evidence in *Cambridge History of Africa,* vol. 2, 491–92.

7. Oliver, *African Experience,* 84.

8. *General History of Africa,* vol. 3, 34.

9. For a discussion of the Islamization of the Berbers, see J. Spencer Trimingham, *The Influence of Islam upon Africa,* 2nd ed.(London: Longman, 1980), 8.

10. Oliver, *African Experience,* 86.

The Aghlabid success was eventually matched and then surpassed by the Fatimid dynasty (909–1171). The slave-laden armies of the Fatimids swept over North Africa and Egypt. Their founder, the mystic 'Ubayd Allah, declared himself to be the longed-for messiah and bade his followers to establish the kingdom of Allah on the sands of Africa. The messianic kingdom they set up in Egypt was an unmistakable testimony to the African kings passing through Egypt to Mecca on religious pilgrimage that a theocratic monarchy claiming to be the kingdom of God on earth could succeed. That testimony would not be forgotten.

Islamic expansion into West Africa in the eleventh century. The Fatimids were not the only group that turned religious revival into political power. The Almoravid movement of the eleventh century followed a similar pattern. A leader of the Lamtuna Sanhaja, a small branch of the Berber tribe on the southwestern corner of the Sahara, became concerned that the southern Bantu kingdom of the Soninkes was expanding northward and threatening their survival. He was unable to unite the various segments of the Berbers to take up arms.

Hoping that religious zeal might provide the necessary unity, the Berber leader requested a Muslim missionary to revive the flagging faith of his people. Abdallah ibn Yasin was sent to examine the state of the Muslim faith among this Berber group. He was shocked to find a crude syncretism bearing little resemblance to orthodox Islam. Abdallah went into seclusion but slowly gathered a group of loyal disciples that called themselves the Almoravids *(al-Murabitun)*.

In time Abdallah and his disciples went forth to preach. They found a receptive audience among the Lamtuna Sanhaja. The Almoravid preachers called for a return to orthodox Islam and a *jihad* against the infidels (in this case the Soninke of Ghana). The subsequent crusades of the next few decades extended the Muslim kingdom of the Almoravids deep within West Africa, forcing the retreat of the Soninke kingdom. Even as they shrank back from Almoravid swords, the Soninke embraced this revivalistic version of Islam. Soninke merchants took the faith to the Mande-speaking people south of Ghana. Islam grew.

By 1100 the Almoravids were in decline and a new Islamic renewal movement, the Almohads, arose, spreading among the African kingdoms along the Niger. The Almohads brought literacy and the study of the Quran to the African kingdoms of the South.[11] As Muslim communities multiplied, the numbers of Muslim clerics did as well. Serious study of the Quran spread.

---

11. See the summary of these events in Shillington, *A History of Africa* (London: Macmillan, 1989), 90–93.

Even as a more studious Islam increased, an older folk Islam, stressing spirits, faith-healing, dreams, and divination, thrived as well. African traditional religion was not obliterated by Islam but was altered by it. The impact was mutual. Elements of ATR slipped into Islam. Beyond the external submission to the five pillars (confession of Allah, daily prayers, fasting, alms, and pilgrimage), Islam tolerated a wide diversity of traditional beliefs and practices. At first Islam was only the religion of the king; the people were permitted to continue in their traditional beliefs. As time went on, the faith trickled down and mingled with popular beliefs.[12] This syncretistic tendency of Islam was widespread throughout the Sudanic states of West and Central Africa.[13]

Islam and East Africa. In contrast to West Africa, where it penetrated the interior, Islamic contact with East Africa was limited to the coast. Ethiopia and Nubia were barriers to the spread of the faith down the Nile.

The Indian Ocean was a more congenial highway. Muslim traders plying their wares south of the Horn of Africa wrote home about a group they called the "Zanj," who inhabited the coast and traded in ivory. Though there was no visible religious law practiced by the Zanj, they did have kings.[14]

By the eleventh century the "land of Zanj" was overrun with a new group of people called the "Shirazi," who set up their trading communities along the coast and soon mingled with the local customs sufficiently to create the Swahili culture still visible in the coastal towns of Lamu and Mombasa. Mosques proliferated on the coastal trading islands of Pemba, the Comores, Zanzibar, and Kilwa. Yet this growing presence of Islam did not spread inland. Unlike West Africa, interior trade routes were undeveloped before the European period. The mosques cut from the coral that dotted the coast remained a testimony to a foreign presence and not an indigenous faith.[15]

The survival of African Christianity. As Islam expanded, African Christianity contracted. In Egypt Christianity did survive but not without losses. Caliph Umar had forbidden new churches or monasteries, but under the Umayyads (661–750) this law was not enforced.[16] Other forms of pressure were put on the Christian community. When in 744 the Muslim governor of

12. Rene Bravmann, *Islam and Tribal Art in West Africa* (Cambridge: Cambridge University Press, 1974), 29.

13. *General History of Africa*, vol. 3, 39.

14. Shillington, *History of Africa*, 127–28.

15. For a discussion of this restricted spread of Islam, see J. Spencer Trimingham, *Islam in East Africa* (Oxford: Clarendon, 1964), 10ff.; and I. M. Lewis' introduction to his edited study, *Islam in Tropical Africa*, 2nd ed. (International African Institute and Indiana State University, 1980), 10–13.

16. Falk, *Church in Africa*, 64.

Egypt offered tax exemption for Christians who converted to Islam, 24,000 responded.

After 750, when the Abbasids were in power, restrictions against Christians were renewed. A series of Coptic revolts against the government brought even harsher repression. Coptic Christianity declined under the Fatimid dynasty of the tenth century and their Mamluk successors. Though deeply indigenized, the Coptic church suffered from a lack of trained leadership, discriminatory laws, and a stagnant ritualism.[17] This decline continued to the end of the African Middle Ages, when Ottoman rule replaced that of the Mamluks. Though Egypt at first was "a Christian enclave under Arab Muslim domination," it eventually became "a country of dual religious cultures."[18]

North African Christianity was harder hit than Egyptian Christianity. Donatist Berbers eventually converted and the Roman segment of the population evacuated to other parts of the empire. Although Christian merchants were active in North African towns throughout the Middle Ages, the decline of the faith was nearly total by the sixteenth century though some Christian communities survived until the eighteenth century.[19] Attempts by the Fourth Crusade to liberate North Africa politically and by Franciscan missionaries to revive it spiritually, ended in failure. A faith only lightly rooted in the culture faded into mere memory.[20]

African Christianity was by no means in universal retreat. Nubian Christianity grew for much of the middle period until its demise in the fifteenth century. Ethiopian Christianity underwent several cycles of renewal and emerged from the Middle Ages as the most vital of all the expressions of African Christianity. The next chapter deals with these two Christian kingdoms, but enough has been said here to dispel the myth that African Christianity disappeared by the end of the Middle Ages.

Theocratic and messianic longings. By the fifteenth century Islam in North Africa, Egypt, and the Middle East was once again unified into a single empire under the Ottomans. Looking back over the previous thousand years the Ottoman rulers may well have praised Allah for what they erroneously thought was the almost complete destruction of the Christian witness to the kingdom of God. Even from a Christian perspective one might be justified to speak, as does one church historian, of the African Middle Ages as "a millennium of darkness."[21] Yet for all its opposition to Christian churches and Christian theology, Islam carried deep into sub-Saharan African kingdoms a

17. Ibid., 70.
18. Trimingham (1980), 7.
19. Falk, *Church in Africa,* 71.
20. For a recent treatment of North African Christianity's decline and death, see Robin Daniel, *Holy Seed* (Harpendon, Eng.: Tamarisk, 1992), 408–32.
21. Falk, *Church in Africa,* 61.

message spoken beforehand by Jews and Christians. This was the message of messianic hope.

The political ideal of Islam is theocracy. The king, who derived his authority from God, was not only the ruler of the state but also the ruler of the mosque. When the faithful gathered on Friday, the *khutba* or sermon was given not only in the presence of the prince but in his name and by his authority.[22] The great Islamic political theorist, Ibn Khaldun, taught that the ideal government was an absolute monarchy committed to the institutions of divine law.[23] He also taught that this ideal monarchy could not be sustained for more than a few generations. The state's decline and ruin were inevitable.

Yet Ibn Khaldun's pessimism about the fate of earthly theocracies was tempered by another strain within Islamic theology—the teaching about the messiah. Shi'ism was consumed by the question of legitimate theocratic rule. It taught that true political authority belonged to the *imams*, the righteous rulers and teachers of Islam. Recognizing, however, that each human *imam* was both mortal and imperfect, it also taught that a day would come when the "hidden" *imam* would reveal himself as the true *mahdi* or messiah who would destroy the Antichrist and "restore peace and justice to the world."[24]

Throughout the Middle Ages and into the modern era in Africa, self-professed *mahdis* emerged to renew this hope of heaven on earth. Though originally a teaching associated with the minority Shi'ites, the teaching about the Messiah also spread to the Sunni branch.[25] Though the role of the prophet *Isa* (Jesus) in this theology of the *mahdi* was unclear, this messianic impulse so crucial to the proper understanding of both Jewish and Christian faith was spread throughout much of sub-Saharan Africa by Islam.

African Kingdoms in West and Central Africa

The pattern of the great king. African traditional religion said little about a messiah from heaven, but it had a great deal to say about a mediator between heaven and earth—the sacred king. All over Africa in the Middle Ages one finds kingdoms built around the central figure of the sacred chief or king. This royal tradition has been called "Sudanic" due to the similarities found all over the continent with the kingship tradition of Nubia. Yet more was involved in the rise of kingship than mere imitation. Reaching back to the phar-

---

22. *Cambridge History,* vol. 2, 544.

23. See the discussion of Ibn Khaldun's views in Abdul Malik Al-Sayid, *Social Ethics of Islam* (New York: Vantage, 1982), 94ff.

24. Hrbek, UNESCO's *General History of Africa,* vol. 3, 23.

25. Ibid.

aonic tradition of ancient Egypt and borrowing heavily from the Nubian pattern, African kingship was also shaped by local factors such as ancestor veneration and rainmaker mythology.[26]

How extensive was Sudanic kingship? John Mbiti insists that "not all African peoples have had traditional rulers in the form of kings, queens or chiefs," but admits that the pattern of sacred kingship was nonetheless widespread.[27] Adrian Hastings adds that though most Africans lived in stateless societies by "1500 in a good many areas, west and east, stateless units were being slowly integrated into kingdoms of a certain size, with a capital and a royal dynasty."[28]

African cities in the Middle Ages. Urban settlements in West Africa date back to before the time of Christ. While East Africa could boast impressive coastal cities like Mombasa and Kilwa, they could not match the urban development that occurred in the West African interior along the banks of the Senegal and Niger Rivers. Even before the coming of Islam, Jenne Jeno, a Mali city along the Niger, had an estimated population of between five thousand and ten thousand people, making it approximately the size of ancient Athens during its golden age. These ancient cities, often walled, were called *kafu*. The *kafu* was ruled by a traditional leader called the *mansa* or king. The primary function of the *mansa* was to handle family and lineage disputes and manage the captives that were taken through trade or conquest.[29] From such modest beginnings a much more powerful office evolved.

Early kingdom building: Ghana. Exploration around Lake Chad has uncovered several medieval towns in close proximity. These towns were the distinctive seeds of the first West African city-states. As clusters of *kafus* linked together, urban areas developed. The trans-Saharan trade increased the size and wealth of many of these city-states. With greater centralization came kingship. Such was the beginning of the early kingdom of Ghana.[30]

King Tenkaminen and the Soninke Kingdom of Ghana (900–1100). Al Bekri of Cordoba reported on the conditions in Ghana in 1067. The name "Ghana" originally meant king and eventually became the name for the

---

26. Ibid., 375.

27. John Mbiti, *African Religions and Philosophy* (London: SPCK, 1969), 238. Basil Davidson has been particularly critical of the idea of a widespread Sudanic pattern of kingship. Note his criticisms in *Africa in History*, rev. ed. (London: Granada, 1984), 113–19.

28. Adrian Hastings, *The Church in Africa: 1450–1950* (Oxford: Clarendon Press, 1994), 48.

29. Oliver, *African Experience*, 93.

30. Basil Davidson, *The African Past* (Boston: Little, Brown, 1964), 70–71. Davidson's book is a useful collection of the principal primary sources covering a wide period of Africa's history.

kingdom itself. The great king that Al Bekri encountered in Ghana was Tenkaminen, "master of a large empire and a formidable power."[31]

According to Al Bekri, the king had at his command two hundred thousand warriors, including forty thousand archers.[32] Tenkaminen held court in a large pavilion in his capital city of Kumbi, surrounded by his ministers and the princes with their gold-plated hair. Tenkaminen's kingdom dripped with gold. Even the dogs that guarded his gates wore collars of gold. The hills of Tenkaminen's empire were riddled with gold mines. By royal decree all gold belonged to the king, although the gold dust could be kept by the people.

Kumbi soon became a major destination for Muslim traders and became heavily muslimized. Twelve mosques rose above the streets of the city, breaking up the monotony of the clay and thatch constructions that otherwise dominated the scene. Despite his patronage of Islam, Tenkaminen was a traditionalist and not a Muslim. Six miles from Kumbi was a kind of parallel capital, called El Ghaba, freed from foreign influence where the royal tombs, the temple with its priests, and the sacred groves could be frequented by worshipers without interruption. By 1076 the Almoravid Berbers captured the Ghana capital and hastened the decline of this splendid early African kingdom. The victory of the Almoravids also insured that the kings of West Africa would increasingly profess to be Muslims.

The kingdom of Mali (1200–1400). In 1240 the king of the Mandingo, Sundiata (fl. 1250–55), defeated the king of the Sosso.[33] With this victory the kingdom of Mali was born. Sundiata was a follower of African traditional religion early in his reign, but eventually converted to Islam. Sundiata's son and successor, Mansa Uli, was the first of a long line of Mali leaders to make the pilgrimage to Mecca.

The most famous pilgrimage of a Malian king took place in the fourteenth century, when Mansa Musa (1312–37) ascended the throne. He spent so much gold in Cairo en route to Mecca that the value of gold in Egypt plummeted and remained depressed for several years.[34] Musa patronized scholarship and his principal cities of Timbuktu and Jenne were filled with libraries and schools of law and theology. The kingdom grew in power and size until one Arab historian wrote with obvious wonder (and exaggeration) that it took four months of travel to get from the northern borders of the empire to the southern borders.[35] So famous was Mali even in Europe that a

31. Quoted in Davidson, *African Past*, 72.

32. Most historians dispute these figures as gross exaggerations. Ten thousand has been suggested as a more probable number for Tenkaminen's standing army.

33. An account of this victory is given in Davidson, *African Past*, 73. On Mali in general, see Davidson's discussion in *Africa in History*, 105–7.

34. Reported by the fourteenth-century Arab historian Al Omari. His account of the pilgrimage of Mansa Musa is found in Davidson, *African Past*, 75–76.

35. Davidson, *Africa in History*, 105.

1375 Spanish map of the African continent featured a painting of an enthroned Mali king dominating the continent.

The kingdom of Songhay (1400–1600). As Mali declined in the late fourteenth century the empire of Songhay rose to take its place. Sonni Ali, a religious traditionalist hostile to Islam, conquered Timbuktu and founded a new empire. He organized his kingdom into provinces which he ruled through appointed civil servants supported by his standing army. After his death in 1492, his successor was overthrown by one of his Muslim generals, Muhammad Ture (1493–1528). Ture became known as the caliph of Islam in the western Sudan. He expanded the boundaries of the empire in all directions until he was deposed in 1528. By 1591, under pressure from Moroccan invaders, Songhay began its long decline.

The central Sudanic kingdoms. Upon the ashes of these earlier empires was built the kingdom of Kanem-Bornu. Arising in the sixteenth century, Kanem-Bornu was a loose confederation of three Hausa kingdoms. The great mastermind of this empire building was Idris Alooma. His horsemen united the grassland country of the central Sudan. His capital at Kano evolved into a great city, and his ambassadors were welcomed with respect in Tripoli and Cairo. His gifts were warmly received by the sultan of the Ottoman Empire in Istanbul. He was simply "the most successful West African monarch of his day."[36] When European explorers traversed the West African interior in the early nineteenth century, the vestiges of this great kingdom were still visible.[37]

Kingdoms on the coast: Oyo and Benin. The Sudanic pattern of sacred kingship spread to the delta of the Niger. The kingdom of Oyo among the Yoruba and the kingdom of Benin among the Edo are two examples. When a Dutch observer visited Benin in 1602 he was astounded by what he saw at court. "The King's court is very great," he wrote, "within it having many four square plains." By his estimate "the King had many soldiers; he has also many gentlemen who when they come to court ride upon horses."[38] African royalty seemed to live in a style similar to their European counterparts. When the Portuguese arrived in Africa in the fifteenth century, they found African kingship almost everywhere they looked.

The City-States of East and Southern Africa

Merchant kingdoms on the coast. In the thirteenth century the politics of the eastern coast of Africa were changed by the arrival of the "Shirazi." Shirazi

36. Ibid., 102.
37. Ibid.
38. Quoted in Oliver and Fage, *Short History of Africa*, 90.

culture was tribal, with upper-class clans ruled by a council of *wazee* (Swahili word for "elders"). Though the full pattern of sacred kingship seemed to be absent from Shirazi culture, some of the elements appear. At the head of the council of elders would often be a *shaikh* or headman who was invested with the power of a chief or king in times of crisis.[39] The chief was formally enthroned in an elaborate ritual and given the *kiti cha ezi* or "chair of power."

Zanzibar is an indicator of this movement toward sacred kingship in Shirazi culture. This island kingdom, which would in the nineteenth century become the center of a vast trading empire, by the sixteenth century was ruled by a *Mwinyi Mkuu* or "Great Master." This leader "was surrounded by the sanctity of a divine chief" and was invested with the symbols of sacred wooden horns and drums.[40] While insufficient detail exists to match up Zanzibarian kingship with royal traditions in Nubia and West Africa, it seems safe to say that coastal culture in the late Middle Ages was heading toward a fuller pattern of kingship.

Inland kingdoms. The ruins of Engaruka in Tanzania, like the stone enclosure of Great Zimbabwe to the south, provide an intriguing but inconclusive testimony to kingdom building in the East Africa interior. Whatever early kings ruled the Rift Valley and its highlands were eclipsed by the migration of the proto-Luo, Kalenjin, and Maasai groups. Around Lake Victoria, however, the kingship tradition seems to have taken hold, and by the early nineteenth century European explorers looking for the source of the Nile wrote home about a strong Gandan kingdom ruled by a powerful *kabaka* (king).[41]

Great Zimbabwe and Shona kingdoms. Visible today at the head of the Sabi river valley in Zimbabwe are the ruins of a walled enclosure known as Great Zimbabwe ("stone buildings"). The walled city is a testimony to the existence of an early Shona kingdom. The thirty-foot mortarless walls were built with such precision that their like has not been found elsewhere in sub-Saharan Africa. These ruins, dated between 1200 and 1400, were probably built "to emphasize and enhance the mystery, power, and prestige of the king."[42] Like the kingdom of Ghana, the Zimbabwe economic basis was the gold trade. The gold of Zimbabwe was brought to Kilwa. From Kilwa it went to the rest of the world.

But gold alone could not keep the ancient kingdom of Great Zimbabwe intact. By the fifteenth century the palace of Great Zimbabwe was abandoned, probably due to the ravages of overgrazing and the depletion of local

39. Trimingham, *Islam in East Africa*, 14–15.
40. Ibid., 16.
41. Davidson, *Africa in History*, 152.
42. Shillington, *History of Africa*, 150.

salt deposits. King Mutota of the Shona moved the kingdom north near the Zambezi River, conquering tribes along the way. Under Mutota and his son Matope the kingdom flourished through renewed trade. These kings and their successors took the title *munhumutapa* (conqueror) and extended their kingdom widely through warfare. The great kings of this Shona Empire were the dominant power in southeastern Africa until the sixteenth century, when Portugal presented a new challenge.

Zulu Kingdoms. By the nineteenth century the southern tip of Africa bore witness to a similar pattern of kingship that had transformed ancient Egypt and Nubia as well as the medieval realms of West and Central Africa. In the eighteenth century subgroups of the Nguni tribe of southern Africa had formed into distinctive groups. One of these groups became the Zulu, who under the leadership of powerful kings such as Shaka, Dingane, and Mpande forged an empire that reached impressive heights by the nineteenth century. The birthplace of the Zulu nation was the *Makosini* valley ("valley of the kings"). The formation of a powerful sacral kingship pattern was the prelude to Zulu empire building.

The office of *nkosi* bound the Zulu into a single nation. The king's titles were numerous. To his people he was "the lion of the heavens," "the bird who eats all birds," and "the awe inspiring one."[43] The king was "the personification of the law," the "representative of the tribal ancestors, and the centre of ritual."[44] Though kingship cannot be found everywhere in the continent before the advent of European expansion into Africa, it was a general phenomenon that shaped African history in the Middle Ages.[45]

The Internal Kingdom: Kingdom Worship in ATR

Kinship and kingship. How much do we know about the actual pattern of sacred kingship? African traditional religion and culture rested upon the twin pillars of kinship and kingship. Kinship is foundational and pervasive in African culture. According to John Mbiti, "the deep sense of kinship, with all it implies, has been one of the strongest forces in Traditional life." At heart this sense of kinship meant that "the individual does not and cannot exist alone except corporately—He is simply part of the whole."[46] The idea that identity was found only in community became the frame of reference for in-

---

43. Ukuchukwu Chris Manus, *Christ, the African King* (Frankfurt: Peter Lang, 1993), 110.

44. Ibid., 111.

45. Chris Manus's statement seems justified that "the tradition of ritual kingship, in precontact times, prevailed throughout the length and breadth of Africa" (ibid., 116).

46. John Mbiti, *African Religions,* 104, 108.

terpreting all of reality. God himself was seen as an ancestor of the tribe. "Among the Zulu God is *Unkulu-unkulu*, the Great Ancestor," the original source of the tribe and the ultimate power that sustains its life.[47]

Because kinship ties were hierarchical and generational, the African traditional value system venerated the dead ancestors as the leaders of the family and tribe. These ancestral leaders continued to impact the tribe, even from the spirit world. The forces of nature were a reflection of the mood of the ancestral spirits.[48] Kinship ties thus connected the living individual with all of nature, including the world of the spirits. Because the departed kin exercised such a powerful role over the living, the issue of mediators between heaven and earth became critical for kinship cultures. A host of traditional medicine men and diviners attempted to bridge this gap, but the office of king was regarded as the most successful solution.[49]

Priestly role of king. African kings were not chosen for their talent or ability but rather for their influence with the spirit world, for "their office is the link between human rule and spiritual government."[50] Because of this role as mediators between heaven and earth, the African kings were "divine or sacral rulers, the shadow or reflection of God's rule in the universe."[51]

Among the Malinke of West Africa the king, or *mansa*, was the "direct link with the 'spirits of the land'" upon whom a successful harvest depended.[52] This priestly role of the monarch was expressed in the traditional Zulu coronation ritual. The new king, after visiting the national temple to pray to the ancestors, proceeded to the graves of his grandfather and father, where bullocks were sacrificed in order to "wash the king clean."[53] After his coronation, the Zulu king "was the only one who could approach the ancestral spirits for their blessing on the tribe."[54] A true king in proper relation-

47. Manus, *African King*, 44. On the vexing question of monotheism in African traditional religion, see Emefie Ikenga-Metuh, "Religious Concepts in West African Cosmogonies," *Journal of Religion in Africa* 13, no. 1 (1982): 11–23. He concludes that monotheism is in fact a prevalent concept of God in West African societies and that it can logically coexist with a lower-level polytheism.

48. For a discussion of the importance of the concept of ancestors to traditional religion and Christian theology, see Charles Nyamiti, *Christ as Our Ancestor* (Gweru, Zimbabwe: Mambo Press, 1984). For an informed missiological perspective, see Richard Gehman, *African Traditional Religion in Biblical Perspective* (Kijabe: Kesho, 1989).

49. On the emergence of kingship from kinship among the Ibo, see Richard Henderson, *The King in Every Man: Evolutionary Trends in Onitsha Ibo Society and Culture* (New Haven: Yale University Press, 1972).

50. Mbiti, *African Religions*, 238.

51. Ibid.

52. Shillington, *History of Africa*, 96.

53. Manus, *African King*, 113.

54. Ibid., 114.

ship with his spiritual ancestors was expected to be a source of protection and benevolence for his people.[55]

Divine character of the king. Because of his role as the crucial middleman between the spirits and the people, the king was regarded as a semidivine being. He was a superhuman figure "to whom divine honours were paid and to whom divine powers were attributed."[56]

Among the Yoruba, kings were in some way divine for they were the descendants of the creator God Oduduwa, who became the first king of Ife.[57] Rulers generally had "shrines, temples, sacred groves, personal priests and diviners in or near their palace."[58] Because of his semidivine status the king was usually not permitted to die a natural death. His demise was "often hastened by poison or ritual suffocation."[59] A cult of the royal tomb grew up around the departed king, with worshipers fingering relics of the king's hair or fingernails as fetishes. The spirit of a departed king had to be propitiated and consulted in order for the tribe to be blessed. The *mansa* of the Malinke lived in isolation from his people, who approached him on their knees. According to Mbiti,[60] "some rulers must not be seen in ordinary life—they wear a veil, take meals alone (e.g., Shilluk, Baganda, and Shona), their eating and sleeping must not be mentioned."

The respect for the special status of the king was such that "in some societies (like Luna, Nyamwezi, and Baganda) the king must not touch the ground with his feet, and has either to be carried or walk on a special mat."[61] While it is probably best to avoid the term "divine kingship," the supernatural status of the king, similar to that originally visible in pharaonic Egypt, is clearly indicated.

The role of the king was thus unique in African society in the Middle Ages and early modern periods. In the king was invested the tribal hope of overcoming evil and suffering and ushering in a future of peace and prosperity, what the ancient Egyptian ancestors had called *ma'at*. The evil against which the king was to contend was not merely law breaking or social injustice. The evil that traditional culture feared was the power that "destroys life."[62] Evil in this sense was "illness, infertility, pestilence, famine, and sudden or inexplicable death."[63] The sacral kingship was formed out of a longing to over-

---

55. Ibid., 220.
56. Oliver, *Short History of Africa*, 31.
57. Ikenga-Metuh, "West African Cosmogonies," 16.
58. Mbiti, *African Religions*, 239.
59. Oliver, *Short History of Africa*, 31.
60. Ibid.
61. Ibid.
62. Richard Gray, *Black Christians and White Missionaries* (New Haven: Yale University Press, 1990), 101.
63. Ibid.

come this kind of evil but as each kingdom soon discovered, no earthly king could fulfill such expectations. African kings raised hopes but produced disappointing results.

Conclusions: Islam, ATR, and the Kingdom of Christ

Myths about Islam, ATR, and Christianity in the Middle Ages continue to cloud the true story of Africa between 600 and 1600. Did Islam spread primarily by the sword? The historical reality says no. Did Christianity disappear from Africa after the spread of Islam? Christianity, in fact, survived and in a few instances even flourished during the Muslim centuries. Did Africa languish in a Stone Age prehistory of stateless societies during the Middle Ages? On the contrary, African history entered a brilliant period of kingdom building that attracted the interest of the world.

But what of the myth that Christianity, Islam, and African traditional religion are antithetical religious systems without significant common ground? Beyond the easy example of monotheism, this chapter has pointed to at least one other shared value: a longing for the kingdom of God. Whether the Islamic passion for correct succession and the coming *mahdi*, the African veneration of king and kin, or the Christian concern for redemption and eternal life, each of the major religions of Africa share a longing for the kingdom of God on earth. The hope of a perfect theocracy visible on earth was a hope shared by medieval rulers, whether in Baghdad, Byzantium, or Benin.

It was a scandal to the Muslim and a surprise to the African traditionalist that the Christian answer to the dream of earthly utopia was a rejected king of the Jews who lived in humility and died in weakness. Yet, declared the Christian message, for those who by faith accept the paradox of the kingdom, Christ "ushers in the Reign of God and assumes the challenging tasks of healing the sick—raising the dead and expelling the demons."[64] Such a witness to the kingdom, with its paradox of weakness and strength, would require more clarification. The experiences of the Christian kingdoms of Nubia and Ethiopia provided further opportunities to explore these paradoxes of the kingdom.

---

64. Manus, *African King*, 234.

Crumbling Kingdoms

Nubian Collapse and Ethiopian Survival

Near the city of Adefa in the highlands of Ethiopia lie the ruins of the new Jerusalem. Built in the thirteenth century by Emperor Lalibela, the heavenly city was hewn from solid rock. The origins of the city are shrouded in legend. According to tradition, the emperor was supernaturally transported to the old Jerusalem. There Lalibela encountered the risen Christ, who told him that the kingdom of God was about to be consummated on earth and that its capital would be in the African highlands of Ethiopia. Lalibela returned to his African kingdom and obeyed the heavenly vision. He constructed a new City of God.

Today the remains of the eleven rock churches that made up the new Jerusalem (now named Lalibela after its founder) bear testimony to the emperor's belief that Ethiopia was to be the center of the kingdom of God on earth.[1]

Though Islamic kingdoms multiplied in North and West Africa during the medieval era, surprising things were happening south of the first cataract of the Nile and in the highlands to the southeast. Two Christian kingdoms reached their peaks of greatness in these middle centuries. For one of the Christian kingdoms, Nubia, the moment of greatness was like the flash of a comet across the night sky.

For the second Christian kingdom, Ethiopia, the religious nationalism forged between the seventh and sixteenth centuries was more enduring. Ethiopia not only survived the threats to its sovereignty but also entered the ranks of legend. Ethiopia became more than an empire. Under the leadership of emperors like Lalibela, she became a myth that would inspire many African religious, cultural, and political movements in the twentieth century.

1. Tadesse Tamrat, "Ethiopia, the Red Sea and the Horn," in Roland Oliver, ed., *Cambridge History of Africa*, vol. 3 (Cambridge: Cambridge University Press, 1977), 115.

"Ethiopianism" is the name given to this cultural phenomenon inspired by Ethiopia's history. Adrian Hastings defines it as "the assertion across the name of the continent's most famous kingdom . . . of the values of authentic African culture and history over and against indiscriminate Europeanisation."[2] For thousands of African independent churches, millions of Rastafarians, and scores of Black nationalist movements before 1960, Ethiopia has been an inspiring symbol of African authenticity and independence.

What is sometimes overlooked when Ethiopianism is discussed is the role of Christianity in shaping Ethiopia and contributing to its survival. Ethiopia in the Middle Ages bears eloquent testimony to the fact that Christianity is deeply rooted in African history and culture. Through the Ethiopianism movement of the twentieth century, this Africanized Christianity of Ethiopia helped take the Western Christianity of the White missionary and indigenize it in significant ways, ways that we make clear in later chapters.

This chapter surveys the historical developments that contributed to Ethiopianism and its mythology. The fall of Nubia made the survival of Ethiopia all the more spectacular. What should not be lost in this story of Nubia and Ethiopia in the Middle Ages is their witness to the kingdom. For centuries each Christian kingdom sought to create a Christian civilization in which the City of God would be embodied in the principal institutions of society. The ideal was better than the reality. Beneath the surface of the Christian cultures of Nubia and Ethiopia were the superficialities and hypocrisies so characteristic of Augustine's second city, the City of Man. Yet for all the failures of these African Christian kingdoms, they bear enduring testimony, like Lalibela's churches of rock, to the power that comes from a kingdom vision.

The Rise and Fall of Nubian Christianity

Nubia from the sixth through the eighth centuries. Nubia's entry into the African Middle Ages began with two momentous events. The first was the Christian revolution of the sixth century when almost overnight 2,500 years of cultural and religious tradition "were discarded in favour of . . . new can-

2. Adrian Hastings, *A History of African Christianity 1950–1975* (Cambridge: Cambridge University Press, 1979), 40. Some scholars have minimized the connection between Ethiopia and "Ethiopianism," contending that the movement uses the term in its Greco-Roman sense to refer to Black Africa in general. For this understanding, see J. Mutero Chirenje, *Ethiopianism and Afro-Americans in Southern Africa, 1883–1916* (Baton Rouge: Louisiana State University, 1987), 1–2. More accurate in this writer's opinion is G. C. Oosthuizen, who argues that the term is "referring to the only remaining black African independent state after Africa was cut up and distributed among western colonial powers at the Berlin Convention of 1884–5. Ethiopia became the symbol of liberation" (*The Healer-Prophet in Afro-Christian Churches* [Leiden: E. J. Brill, 1992], 2–3).

ons of faith, of art and of literature."[3] The second was the rise of Islam a century later. The combined impact of these two events was to produce a profound inwardness in Nubian civilization that intensified Christian faith and created longings for eternal kingdoms. "So dominant," writes William Adams, "is the heavenly king in the medieval Nubian ideology that it is hard to find much information about earthly kings and their doings."[4]

These centuries of religious intensity also witnessed profound political developments in Nubia. The first was one of political consolidation. Makuria and Nobatia, two of the three traditional component kingdoms of Nubia, merged in 704.[5] King Mercurios of Makuria (697–710) led in this union. Makuria became the seat of political power with its capital of Old Dongola. Nobatia became the religious capital of the combined empire with its capital of Faras. The southern kingdom of Alwa, about which we know little, seems to have maintained its independence from the two northerly kingdoms until sometime later.[6]

The second development was that of the *baqt*. After the Islamic conquest of Egypt in 642, the armies of Allah invaded Nubia. By 710 Nubia had successfully repelled the invaders and negotiated a treaty (*baqt*, literally "tribute") that obligated Nubia to provide slaves for Muslim Egypt (about four hundred a year) in exchange for a variety of goods. This arrangement endured more or less intact for six hundred years and gave Nubia many centuries of peace and prosperity.[7]

The apex of Nubian civilization: eighth to eleventh centuries. With the *baqt* signed and its borders stabilized, Nubia reached new heights between 750 and 1100. "Church building flourished," writes Basil Davidson, "and fine arts were practiced."[8] Not only was Nubia able to enforce the *baqt* whenever border skirmishes threatened to scuttle the arrangement, but she was also willing to go on the offensive when needed. In 737 Nubian troops marched to Alexandria to rescue the Coptic patriarch.[9] In 836 emissaries from Nubia traveled to Baghdad to negotiate new terms of agreement.[10] The caliph listened and granted their requests. In 962 Nubia invaded Fatimid Egypt and occupied the south for a short period of time. Nubia's foreign influence made it a useful mediator between Egypt and Ethiopia, especially in church affairs.[11]

---

3. William Adams, *Nubia: Corridor to Africa* (Princeton: Princeton University Press, 1977), 506.

4. Ibid.

5. Vantini, *Christianity in the Sudan* (Bologna: EMI, 1981), 273.

6. Baur, *2000 Years of Christianity in Africa* (Nairobi: Paulines, 1994), 32.

7. Ibid., 507.

8. Davidson, *Africa in History*, 125.

9. Baur, *Christianity in Africa*, 32.

10. Adams discusses the details of this mission in *Nubia*, 455.

11. Hrbek, "Egypt and Nubia," in Oliver, ed., *Cambridge History of Africa*, vol. 3, 71.

This new assertiveness abroad was joined with a new energy at home. The crude capitals of united Nubia (Faras in the north, Old Dongola in the middle kingdom, and Soba in the south) became great cities. The cathedral of Faras with its granite columns and 169 mural paintings is one symbol of this early medieval greatness. The ruins of Old Dongola, the royal city of the high kings of Nubia, is another. Covering hundreds of square acres, this urban center was settled after the Christian era. The remains of the palace (formerly thought to have been a church) bear the marks of high civilization. Even Soba in the southern kingdom of Alwa underwent a face lift. "Fine buildings," wrote a visitor to the southern capital, "roomy houses, churches with much gold and with gardens lie in this city." Added the visitor: "This land is more fruitful and bigger than Makuria."[12]

More than just buildings flourished during this golden age of Christian Nubia. The rule of bishop and king also prospered. While the details about specific kings are lacking for these centuries, some broad features about early medieval kingship seem clear. The Nubian king was an absolute monarch. In an empire that had as many as thirteen vassal kings he was regarded as a king of kings.[13] His subjects were legally his slaves. All land belonged to him. No governing council could oppose his will. He was the great priest who "could enter the sanctuary area of the church and celebrate the liturgy like any [other] priest."[14]

Frequently Nubian kings resigned their thrones in old age and joined a monastery. The pictures we have of confident emperors bedecked with embroidered gowns and jewel-encrusted crowns carrying the ceremonial parasol as a scepter accurately reflect the reality of Nubian kingship.[15]

While we might be tempted to see in this unfettered monarchy a mere continuation of the sacred kingship pattern, new factors were present that altered the pattern. The king daily contended with the growing power of the church and its bishops. Though the king could celebrate the liturgy, this privilege could be revoked "if he had shed innocent blood."[16] He could not appoint bishops, this being the prerogative of the patriarch of Alexandria, who stood above the king in matters of religion. Though the king in many ways reflected the glory of the risen Christ, the church was a constant reminder that all human witnesses to the kingdom had limits.

The bishops of Nubia made sure this lesson was taught at court. Like North Africa centuries before, the church of Nubia was a church of bishops. The remains of the cathedral at Faras give the names of twenty-seven bishops.

12. Davidson, *Africa in History,* 125.
13. Adams, *Nubia,* 464.
14. Ibid., 463.
15. Ibid.
16. Ibid.

One of the most significant names is that of Abba Paulos (d. 720), a contemporary of King Mercurios who was the unifier of Nubia. Paulos led the expansion of the cathedral from three to five aisles. It was during the reign of this monk/bishop that the official allegiance of the Faras cathedral was transferred to the Coptic patriarch of Alexandria, thus indicating that the earlier advances of Chalcedonian Christianity had at last failed.

The decoration of the cathedral, whether undertaken under Paulos or one of his successors, is dominated by biblical scenes, particularly the three young men in the fiery furnace (a scene found in almost all the churches of Nubia) as well as scenes from the passion of Christ. In the Faras cathedral the largest mural is of Christ as the risen ruler of the universe. But alongside the murals of kingly glory is the more subtle symbolism of the cross. Even when the Trinity is depicted in the wall murals the faces of three persons of the Trinity are the faces of Christ, and three crosses appear to symbolize the cooperation of the Trinity in the work of redemption.

Within the majestic environs of the cathedral and surrounded by the symbols of the cross, the act of public worship was performed. The liturgy of the churches over which the bishops presided was that of the Coptic church and both Coptic and Nubian languages were used. Once again the cross dominates. The *Encomium* or "praise of the cross" played a large role in Nubian worship. Samples of this litany in Greek and Nubian have been found in various parts of Nubia. Forty-six sentences speak of the excellencies of the cross ("the staff of the lame," "the resurrection of the dead," "guidance of the blind," "the dignity of kings," etc.).[17] The cross was both a symbol of suffering and a celebration of victory over death and sin. This litany of the cross had few equals in Western liturgy.

The twelfth-century turning point. The churches of Nubia would learn much about the sufferings of the cross in the twelfth century. In 1172 Turkish cavalry under the Saracen general, Shams ed-Dawla, attacked northern Nubia. This attack was successfully repulsed, but the testimony of archaeology is that Nubian confidence was shaken by this event. The year of this cavalry attack marked the beginning of Mamluk rule in Egypt.

Under the legendary Saladin and his successors, the Mamluk Turks were more hostile to Christianity than their Fatimid predecessors had been. Saladin's private plan was to annex Nubia as his own personal property in case he was overthrown in Egypt.[18]

Nubia seemed to sense Saladin's designs. Castles and fortified houses began to appear on the landscape, testimony to a new feudal spirit. This feudalism represented a loss of faith in the central government and a decision to

17. Vantini, *Sudan*, 152.
18. Ibid., 159.

take military matters into local hands. A siege mentality replaced the old confidence and Christianity was slowly replaced "by the secular and militaristic spirit of the feudal age."[19] To the casual observer Nubia was flexing its military muscles through new fortifications. Yet the deeper truth was that Nubia was turning inward, its confidence in its earthly and heavenly kings shaken by invasion and fear. Nubia was losing its nerve.

Decline and extinction: 1250–1550. The visible glory of the Nubian kings began its long descent in the thirteenth century. In 1272 the Nubian king, David al-Maqurra, raided a Mamluk port city. Babyars I (d. 1277), the Mamluk sultan and empire builder of Cairo, sent his army into northern Nubia as a reprisal. Faras was captured, Old Dongola was sacked, and the Nubian army was defeated. The Mamluks became the rulers of Nubia though puppet kings continued on the throne.

In 1315 when the Mamluks installed as king a Nubian prince who had converted to Islam, the end was in sight. Though Christianity remained the official faith of the kingdom throughout the fourteenth century, the organization of the church began to unravel. Cathedrals were turned into mosques. The priestly ranks dwindled. Surprisingly, Christianity was described as still strong by Arab observers writing about 1360. Yet all documentary evidence about the church in Makuria stops shortly after this time, when the newly appointed bishop Timotheos died a violent death.[20]

The kingdom of Alwa with its capital, Soba, survived until 1504 when it was overthrown by the Fung sultans of Sennar (a Muslim kingdom south of Alwa along the Blue Nile). In 1524 Alwa sent a delegation to Ethiopia to request a bishop because they had no more priests. Ethiopia refused, explaining that they, too, were in short supply of bishops and relied upon Egypt for most of their clergy.[21] This is the final word we hear about Nubian Christianity.

Davidson provides the obituary for this fallen Christian kingdom: "The inheritance of the Christian kings and monks of Nubia disappears rapidly from the inner lands of Africa where they had conserved it for so long. The engulfment was strangely complete. . . . The Nubian kingdoms vanished from the scene, unhonoured and unsung, or almost so, until the twentieth century."[22]

Reasons for the failure of Christianity in Nubia. The collapse of a Christian government does not necessarily mean the collapse of the Christian church. The churches of North Africa weathered the government persecutions of the

19. Adams, *Nubia*, 510.
20. Baur, *Christianity in Africa*, 33.
21. Ibid., 34.
22. Davidson, *Africa in History*, 125–27.

first three centuries very successfully. Did not Tertullian say that the blood of martyrs was seed? Even after the rise of Islam, Coptic Christianity had been able to survive within an antagonistic political system. Why was the church in Nubia unable to follow the pattern of more successful sister churches? A number of contributing factors can be suggested.

The first cause of Nubian Christianity's demise was simply lack of evangelism. While there is archaeological evidence around Lake Chad that the Nubian church attempted to expand westward, there is no evidence of missionary campaigns to convert either the Arab nomads wandering down from the north or the Fungs to the south. Both of these groups rose up at the end of the Middle Ages and in the name of Allah joined with the Mamluks in destroying Nubian Christendom.

What would have happened if Nubian bishops had supported aggressive evangelism? There is little doubt that Nubia's traffic in slaves (hundreds each year had to be sent to Egypt as part of Nubia's treaty obligations) made her the hated enemy of her near neighbors and rendered effective evangelism all but impossible. This is a lesson that Portuguese Christianity would learn in a later generation.[23]

Isolation was a second factor contributing to the demise of Nubian Christianity. The rise of the Mamluk Turks and their conquest of Egypt in the late twelfth century led to a decline in the vigor of Coptic Christianity. In the next century Nubian Christianity needed help from Egypt just as lines of communication were being severed by hostile forces and the resources of Egyptian Christianity were at a low ebb. Additionally, the spirit of feudalism led to a withdrawal of the Nubian church from more active cooperation with other national churches. Only in desperation do we see later Nubian Christianity reaching out to sister churches in Africa. Such "last gasp" efforts were too little and too late.

Third, Nubian Christianity failed due to a lack of leaders. Monasticism in Nubia, while never as strong as in Egypt or Ethiopia, had been a source for priests and teachers. Their apparent decline in the feudal period that followed the Mamluk invasion deprived Nubia of an important source of able leadership. The Nubian church was too dependent on Egypt and the Nubian monarchy for their leadership. This lack of control of their internal affairs greatly weakened the Nubian church in the late Middle Ages.[24] More dramatically, Nubia's "dependency on external arrangements for leadership preparation proved fatal."[25]

23. Cf. Peter Falk, *The Growth of the Church in Africa* (Grand Rapids: Zondervan, 1979), 73.

24. Adams, *Nubia*, 541.

25. Paul Bowers, "Nubian Christianity," *Africa Journal of Evangelical Theology* 4, no. 1 (1985): 18.

A fourth contributing cause to the decline of Nubian Christianity was clericalism. Clerical monopoly of worship and church affairs weakened the hold of Christianity on the laity. Though leadership is crucial the failure of the laity to be more meaningfully involved in the worship and practice of the church was an error. Since clergy often served in secular capacities by royal appointment, the double duties of the priest made the sharing of ministry with laity all the more necessary. This clericalism was spiritually suffocating and contributed to a widespread lack of religious vitality among the masses.[26] The degree of clerical domination can be seen in the changing architecture of Nubian churches. According to Vantini the original church structures had space for the people within the sanctuary, whereas later church buildings were reserved only for the priests with the people standing outside.[27]

A fifth cause of Nubian Christianity's decline involved its theology of the kingdom. The theocratic nature of Nubian Christianity meant that the prospects of the church were tied to the fate of the state. "When the political structures collapsed, the church was inevitably entangled in the ruin."[28]

Justinian's model of church and kingdom had served Nubia well for centuries but in the hour of political disaster she needed to learn from the older kingdom models of St. Antony or the North African martyr Speratus, who rejected earthly kings and declared his loyalty to the one who "is the emperor of kings and of all nations."[29] While the Nubian theocratic witness to the kingdom was dying, Ethiopia's kingdom witness was being reborn.

The Renewal of Ethiopian Christianity

The early Middle Ages in Ethiopia: seventh through ninth centuries. The three-hundred-year period from the rise of Islam in 640 to the "pagan crisis" of the 940s is an obscure period in Ethiopian history.[30] Despite the lack of detailed evidence, enough is known to contradict the traditional picture of an eighth-century Ethiopia encircled by an aggressive Islam. While it is true that the old empire of Axum was forced to move south, deeper into the Ethiopian highlands due to the encroachment of Muslim groups in Eritrea and along the Red Sea coast, relations with their Muslim neighbors to the north were remarkably cordial.

26. Ibid.

27. Vantini, *Sudan*, 147–48. Vantini adds that this is still the practice of the Ethiopian church today.

28. Bowers, "Nubian Christianity," 17.

29. W. H. C. Frend, *The Rise of Christianity* (Philadelphia: Fortress, 1984), 290.

30. Cf. C. P. Groves, *The Planting of Christianity in Africa*, vol. 1 (London: Lutterworth, 1948), 109.

"Throughout the Middle Ages," write Oliver and Fage, "Ethiopian bishops were consecrated in Cairo, and Ethiopian pilgrims, thousands at a time, marched through Egypt on visits to the Holy Land, with drums beating and flags flying, and with regular halts for the celebration of Christian worship."[31] Though the eighth century was a time of migration and change, by the ninth century Ethiopia had navigated these changes successfully.[32]

The pagan crisis of the tenth century. When the peace of the Christian kingdom of Ethiopia was finally disturbed, it was at the hands not of zealous Muslims from the north but aggressive pagans from the south. A small African kingdom belonging to the Agau people of Damot that had once lain sleepily along the elbow of the Blue Nile now arose with a surprising ferocity and invaded Ethiopia in the mid-tenth century. A powerful queen had arisen and launched a highly effective resistance movement to Ethiopia's southward expansion.[33] The Christian kingdom went into a decline as a result of these wars which lasted even into the eleventh century when the tightening Muslim control of the Red Sea trade further constricted the Ethiopian economy.

The monks and bishops of the church observed this decline of the kingdom with alarm. They blamed the defeats in battle and in business on the kings who had broken ties with the patriarch of Alexandria. A seventy-year period without a presiding bishop had led to a depletion in the number of priests, which in turn led to a dearth of spiritual ministry among the people.[34]

The message of the church to the king was clear. The Ethiopian nation was part of the chosen people of Israel. Was not the ark of the covenant brought to Ethiopia?[35] Did not Solomon and Sheba begin the royal dynasty of Ethiopia? Had not Emperor Ezana ushered the nation into the blessings of Christ? Ethiopia was in fact the true Israel because unlike the first Israel they had accepted the Messiah Jesus as their King.[36]

Like biblical prophets the clergy of Ethiopia implored the nation and its leadership to repent and return both to the Lord and to the patriarch of Alexandria. So strong was the fervor of the church for national renewal that when the Egyptian-born metropolitan of Ethiopia, Sawiros, was found to be in league with the Muslim leaders of Cairo he incurred the wrath of the nation and was imprisoned. The treachery of Sawiros inspired more clerical warnings of additional judgment to come. The nation longed for a king who

31. Roland Oliver and J. Fage, eds., *A Short History of Africa,* 6th ed. (London: Penguin, 1988), 76.
32. Tamrat, "Ethiopia," 98.
33. Ibid., 103.
34. Ibid., 102.
35. Ibid., 110.
36. Ibid., 108.

would deliver this new Israel from the wrath of God and Cairo. A line of kings rose up in the late twelfth century who seemed to be the answer.

The Zagwe Dynasty (c. 1137–1270). The origins of the Zagwe dynasty are obscure. From the ranks of the Christianized Agau came a group of local chiefs who were able to seize power and form a new royal house. They reopened the links with Palestine and soon a steady stream of pilgrims from the new Israel were making their way annually to the old one.[37] They began an era of expansion, extending the empire to the west and south. They presided over a revival of Christian literature and art. Yet their rule was not welcomed by all.

The Tigrean clergy of the north remained opposed to this new line, whom they regarded as usurpers, but with the ascension of Lalibela the criticisms died down for a time. Lalibela ruled Ethiopia from his native Lasta sometime between 1200 and 1250.

In an effort to blunt the criticisms of the Axumite faction who questioned his legitimacy as king, Lalibela built a new capital in the highlands near Adefu. Helped by "Angels of God" who, according to the official tradition, served as "masons and ordinary laborers," Lalibela built the new Jerusalem. Eleven churches with names derived from the Holy Land were hewn, as in Nubia, from the living rock. The main river was renamed the Jordan. The heights of the city were called Calvary. To many it seemed that judgment had lifted and the blessings of the kingdom of God were descending.

Restoration of the Solomonic line by Yekunno-Amlak (1270–85). Despite the success of Lalibela's reign the critics of the Zagwe rulers persisted in their complaint that the nation was ruled by usurpers. Until a member of the Solomonic dynasty was restored to power the church could not rest. Their fear of God's judgment upon the nation seemed to be realized when the sons of Lalibela brought the kingdom to the brink of civil war with their rival claims for power. The critics were also helped in their cause by the arrival of an important book on the national scene. The *Kebra-Nagast* (History of the Kings), which appeared in approximately 1225, was an extended piece of anti-Zagwe propaganda that played into the hands not only of the church critics but also a new political rival—Yekunno-Amlak.[38]

Yekunno-Amlak rose to power in 1270, claiming to be a descendant of the ancient kings of Axum. Whether his claims of Solomonic lineage were true or not, he had gathered the military might needed to overthrow the unpopular Zagwe rulers and "restore" (at least in the minds of his subjects) the line of Solomon.[39] Yekunno-Amlak inaugurated a new era of expansion, in-

37. Kevin Shillington, *A History of Africa* (London: Macmillan, 1989), 108.
38. Tamrat, "Ethiopia," 124.
39. Taddesse Tamrat, *Church and State in Ethiopia: 1270–1527* (Oxford: Clarendon, 1972), 67.

cluding the conquest of former Muslim areas. A later king, Amda-Siyon, led his armies in victory over the rival Muslim kingdom of Ifat in the east.

These rulers also inaugurated a new style of kingship. The new emperors were men of the battlefield, kings who ruled from their portable capitals with their tented palaces as they migrated around their expanding kingdom. The brand of Christianity that flourished under their rule was equally spartan. The key figure in the religious revival under the new dynasty was the monk and missionary Tekla-Haymanot.

Religious revival under Tekla-Haymanot (d. 1312). Tekla-Haymanot was born about 1215 in Shoa, the southernmost region of the Ethiopian kingdom at that time. Small Christian communities had trickled into Shoa over time, and churches had been established. But a new danger arose while Tekla-Haymanot was still a boy. The pagan king Motalami of Damot launched a series of attacks against the Christians of Shoa. Christian homes were destroyed and churches were burned down. Christianity was threatened with extinction.

Against this background of spiritual decline, Tekla-Haymanot matured into manhood. At thirty years of age he became a disciple of the saintly Iyasus-Moa and joined his monastic community at Dabra Hayq. After a period of discipleship he moved north to Tigre in search of assurance of salvation and settled in a new monastic community. The intensity of his own quest for salvation soon attracted disciples.[40]

After resolving his own spiritual crisis and inspired perhaps by the word of the restoration of the Solomonic line by Yekunno-Amlak, Tekla-Haymanot turned his attention to the spiritual needs of his homeland to the south. He and his disciples relocated to Shoa and formed a new monastic community, Dabra Asbo (later called Dabra Libanos), one of the first new monastic orders since the work of the Nine Saints in the seventh century. Though much of his work was directed at reviving the flagging faith of Shoan Christians, Tekla-Haymanot also directed enormous energy at the evangelization of the pagan population. If Tekla-Haymanot and his followers were expecting a warm welcome from the pagans of Shoa, they were soon disappointed.

The mission began with a dramatic confrontation. Tekla-Haymanot and his men marched into the pagan stronghold of Damot, where the witch doctors and their cult of devil worship was concentrated.[41] In this same stronghold (called Bilat) dwelt the evil king Motalimi, who was worshiped as a god, following the pattern of sacred kingship that was spreading throughout Africa.[42]

40. Ibid., 160–63.
41. Ibid., 179.
42. Ibid.

Tekla-Haymanot's life was threatened by the pagan priests, but he countered their threats with a challenge. Hearing that King Motalimi lay sick and dying, the missionary monk derided the witch doctors for not healing their king and shamed them into a fresh attempt. When they were unable to heal Motalimi they blamed their failure on the superior "magic" of Tekla-Haymanot. Reading his cue, the saintly monk moved to the king's bedside. He offered a brief prayer in Christ's name and then touched the sick king. The king was healed, to the amazement of all.

According to traditional sources, the restored king was so shaken by this demonstration of the power of Christ that he proposed an ordeal by fire to decide the religious loyalties of his people. A great fire was built. Tekla-Haymanot and the witch doctors were told to stand in the middle of the flames and pray for deliverance. The traditional priests prayed to their gods while the monk prayed to the Trinity. The pagan priests "were burnt up and became like ashes."[43] Tekla-Haymanot emerged from the flames unscathed. Through stories such as this the faith spread.

After Tekla-Haymanot's death, his disciples, further inspired by the missionary zeal of the new *abun*, Bishop Yaiqob, carried on the evangelistic work of their master. By the end of the fourteenth century Christianity had moved south of the Awash River and past Lake Abaya. The military conquests of the Ethiopian emperors like Emperor Dawit (d. 1412) opened up new areas for missionary work. After centuries of stagnation and even decline, Ethiopian Christianity was back on the move, witnessing to the kingdom of the sovereign God and his law.

With this renewed witness to the transcendent kingdom, the Ethiopian church ran into conflict with the kingdom on earth. As the influence of Tekla-Haymanot's order grew, tensions with the state mounted. Under the rule of Abbot Fillippos (1314–41) matters reached a point of crisis. Fillippos and the Ethiopian bishop Yaiqob (d. 1344) criticized the emperor, Amda-Siyon (1314–44), for his polygamy, a traditional practice of the Ethiopian kings. Fillippos was flogged and exiled for daring to challenge the sovereignty of the emperor, though the abbot could have argued that his challenge was in the name of the higher sovereignty of God. The disgrace of Fillippos and his exile actually led to the strengthening of Ethiopian Christianity in Shoa and other regions to the south.[44]

Rival monastic groups arose, some with a very legalistic bent, to add further chaos to the religious scene in fourteenth-century Ethiopia. By the beginning of the fifteenth century the church of Ethiopia was divided by two rival monastic groups, the followers of Tekla-Haymanot and the followers

---

43. Steven Kaplan, *The Monastic Holy Man and the Christianization of Early Solomonic Ethiopia* (Wiesbaden: Franz Steiner Verlag, 1984), 114.
44. Tamrat, "Ethiopia," 161.

of the more legalistic Abba Ewostatewos who emphasized Sabbatarianism (the recognition of Saturday as a Sabbath day for Christians). Reform and reunification were needed once again. The stage was set for the climax of the Ethiopian Empire under the legendary Zara-Yaqob.

The reign of Zara-Yaqob (1434–68). Zara-Yaqob was crowned king of Ethiopia in 1434. His coronation was held in ancient Axum, suitably renamed Axum-Siyon (Zion). In the young king's mind the true Jerusalem was in Ethiopia, home of the ark and of the true soldiers of the cross who had fought successfully against Islam for centuries. Zara-Yaqob was seen as the new David who would lead his people against the new Philistines of paganism and Islam. His glory was acknowledged not only in Ethiopia but even in Europe, where his ambassadors sought technical aid. Zara-Yaqob set high goals for his reign. To reach these goals he needed to marshall the resources of the nation and redirect them toward his kingdom visions. One of the resources he desired most was that of a united church.

In 1450 Zara-Yaqob convened a church council at court. The purpose of this council was to reconcile the divided factions of the church, divided primarily over the question of the Sabbath. Like a new Constantine, Zara-Yaqob sought to reunite the church in order to strengthen the empire.

With a little arm twisting Zara-Yaqob was able to forge an agreement between the rival factions in which both Saturday and Sunday would be recognized as holy days. With the church now at peace the emperor reorganized the monasteries and churches, generously endowing selected ones, and prodded the church to disciple the nation as effectively and as quickly as possible. Islam was held at bay. New efforts were made to establish contact with Rome and the West. Under Zara-Yaqob's reforms "the Ethiopian church reached the pinnacle of its cultural, literary and spiritual attainments."[45]

Zara-Yaqob came by his religious zeal honestly. One tradition tells that Zara-Yaqob as a young prince was forced to flee from his jealous brothers at court due to a prophecy that he and not they would be king. Raised in hiding in a remote monastery, Zara-Yaqob became a scholar and ascetic. When the throne finally came to him he continued to practice many of the disciplines of his monastic years (with the notable exception of chastity).[46]

There was, however, a ruthless side to this African Constantine. His zeal for the faith produced a violent reaction against paganism. Throughout the realm, African traditional religion had infiltrated the church. Many church members consulted traditional witch doctors in secret. Zara-Yaqob regarded such practices as "devil worship" and made them punishable by death. The "Chronicle" of his reign described the result of this policy:

45. Ibid., 163.
46. Tamrat, *Church and State*, 220.

> In the reign of our king Zara Yaqob, there was great terror and great fear in all the people of Ethiopia, on account of the severity of his justice and of his authoritarian rule and above all because of the denunciations of those who, after having confessed that they had worshipped Dasak and the devil, caused to perish many innocent people by accusing them falsely of having worshipped thus together with them.[47]

Yet after the purges died down the chronicler concluded that "during the reign of Zara Yaqob, there was in the whole land of Ethiopia a great peace and a great tranquility, for the king taught justice and faith."[48] The witness to the kingdom through a highly patriotic religious nationalism became the hallmark of these remarkable years under Zara-Yaqob.

The theocratic version of the kingdom promoted by Zara-Yaqob did not go unchallenged. The Stefanite movement offered to Christian Ethiopia in the fifteenth century an alternative model of the kingdom. The movement took its name from the founder, Estifanos, born in Tigre around 1400. Estifanos began a new monastic movement around 1430 that had as its major distinctive a new vision of the kingdom of God. Mount Zion was not the nation of Ethiopia, proclaimed Estifanos. Rather it was a spiritual kingdom "for those who purify their heart and bear the yoke of Christ's gospel."[49] When the emperor imposed the cult of the Cross and of Mary on his subjects, Estifanos protested that "I worship the Father, the Son and the Holy Ghost and I prostrate before this. I shall not add to this . . . for the love of the rulers of the world."[50] The Stefanites were savagely persecuted by the emperor but survived. Their minority witness that the kingdom could not be identified with any earthly political system or ideology is a testimony to the diversity and vigor of Ethiopian Christianity in the Middle Ages.

The conquest of Ethiopia by Ahmad bin Ibrahim, 1529. After the death of Zara-Yaqob in 1468, the fortunes of Ethiopia took a downward turn. While Rome quietly filed the correspondence received from the Emperor Zara-Yaqob, events were spinning out of control on Ethiopia's eastern border.

The Muslim kingdom of Adel was growing in the East under a new leader. Ahmad bin Ibrahim, variously known as Ahmad Gragn ("left-handed") or Imam Ahmad, had seized power in Adel with the full support of the religious leaders who saw him as a quasi-messianic figure deserving the title of *imam* or supreme teacher-ruler.[51]

47. Quoted in the collection of primary sources by Basil Davidson, *The African Past: Chronicles from Antiquity to Modern Times* (Boston: Little, Brown, 1964), 118.
48. Ibid.
49. Adrian Hastings, *The Church in Africa: 1450–1950* (Oxford: Clarendon, 1994), 38.
50. Ibid., 39.
51. Tamrat, "Ethiopia," 182.

In 1529 in the battle of Shimbra-Kure, Imam Ahmad defeated the Ethiopian army and became the virtual ruler of Ethiopia, driving the emperor into exile. Churches were destroyed. Monasteries were burned. Towns were leveled. The devastation of Imam Ahmad's reign of terror was everywhere.

The Ethiopian emperor who fled before the armies of Imam Ahmad was Lebna-Dengal (1508–40). Portuguese diplomats had resided at court since 1520, and to them Lebna-Dengel now turned. Ahmad was having trouble governing his newly conquered kingdom and revolts were widespread. While Ahmad was off balance, the time was ripe for a major Ethiopian offensive.

In 1543 at a place called Woina-Dega, a large contingent of musket-bearing Portuguese soldiers combined with the remnants of the Ethiopian army to provide just such an offensive. Imam Ahmad was killed, the Muslim army crushed, and Christian rule of Ethiopia regained. But the damage had been done. Though Ethiopia had survived and regained its independence, thus entering the ranks of legend, the glory of the kingdom as it had been under Zara-Yaqob would never be the same.

Conclusion: Legacy of Nubia and Ethiopia

With the fall of Nubia and the weakening of the Ethiopian Empire in the aftermath of 1543, the great centuries of African theocratic witness to the kingdom of God came to an end. Beginning in the age of Constantine and reaching a climax in the High Middle Ages, the era of large-scale theocratic witness in Africa lasted over a millennium. In their passion to bring all of life under the rule of Christian state and Christian church these earthly miniatures of the heavenly rule of Christ left an impressive legacy of witness to the greatness of the kingdom. In the case of Ethiopia, its witness to the kingdom in the phenomenon known as "Ethiopianism" has been rediscovered with force in the twentieth century.

What was not always clear in the theocratic witness was the redemptive and utopian aspects of the kingdom. The rule of Christ over hearts often gave way to a religious ritualism and outward conformity that left conversions shallow and hearts unchanged.[52] Additionally, the political status quo of both Nubia and Ethiopia institutionalized a number of injustices that stood in contradiction to the future kingdom of God on earth as foretold by the Christian Scriptures, Scriptures that both Nubian and Ethiopian leaders vowed to uphold.

52. Cf. Kaplan's discussion of this point in *Monastic Holy Man*, 117. See also a similar point made by Ulrich Braukämper, "Aspects of Religious Syncretism in Southern Ethiopia," *Journal of Religion in Africa* 22, fasc. 3 (August 1992): 197.

These inconsistencies in the witness of Nubia and Ethiopia do not take away from what they actually achieved in their attempts to do the divine will on earth "as it is in heaven." What the inconsistencies do suggest, however, is that partial witnesses to the kingdom cannot last. In the fall of Nubia and the weakening of Ethiopia we have a reminder that the glory of all finite, human witnesses to the kingdom must fade before the eternal glory of the transcendent kingdom of God. That was a lesson yet to be learned by Christian kingdoms from Europe that entered the African story just as Nubia lay dying and Ethiopia mourned its fading glory.

The Kingdoms of Christendom 1

The European Discovery of Africa, 1500–1700

During the decades in which Emperor Zara-Yaqob sought to build a new Israel in Ethiopia, a young king in the faraway land of Portugal sought to do the same. Henry of Portugal (1394–1460), known to history as Henry the Navigator, had much in common with Zara-Yaqob. Both kings recognized that the greatest enemy of their respective kingdoms was Islam. Both devoted their lives to destroying this rival kingdom. Both saw the greatest resources for their kingdom mission as the forging of a strong internal Christian nationalism coupled with a strong international partnership with the larger world of Christendom.

Both men sought to make connections with the other. Henry pursued the elusive "Prester John," as the emperor of Ethiopia was known in Europe. Zara-Yaqob had sent ambassadors bearing urgent letters to Rome in quest of a Christian king who could send technical aid to his embattled empire. Both accomplished great things in their lifetimes, but both died without ever seeing their ultimate dream of a world-dominating Christian kingdom realized. The major difference between the two was that Henry of Portugal came close.

Henry began to spin his grand design as a young man. At twenty-one years of age he fought the Muslim Moors on North African soil and won. The victory was hollow, however, because the Muslim Empire, though checked for a time, remained real and sinister. This experience shaped his future life.

What was needed was not a single victory but a systematic destruction of Islam economically, geographically, and militarily. A trading empire that bypassed the Muslim trade routes would choke off the Ottomans and rejuvenate Christian Europe. Henry had learned from Arab geographers that Africa was surrounded by sea and was connected to India, the land of the fabled

107

Prester John ("prester" an old English word for priest, and "John" from "Gian," an Ethiopian word for king).

To the medieval mind "India" included Ethiopia, and Prester John was not an embattled African king, but a wealthy monarch with innumerable armies and great cities whose streets were paved with gold.[1] To join forces with him in a vast economic and military crusade against the Muslim threat would remove the greatest enemy of the kingdom of God and usher in a golden age in which the rule of Christ would be realized on earth.[2] Additionally Henry hoped to discover new lands and new people groups "to make increase in the faith of our Lord Jesus Christ and to bring to him all the souls that should be saved."[3]

The pope approved of Henry's plans. As early as 1418, Martin V had authorized an African crusade. Henry had been appointed master of the Knight's Templar, a Christian military organization that had as its main purpose the military defeat of Islam. In 1452 Pope Nicholas V granted Henry renewed rights for a *conquista,* the conquering of Muslim and pagan lands in Africa in order to "reduce Muslims, pagans and other enemies of Christ to perpetual servitude."[4]

An earlier papal decree had approved trading in African slaves, a practice that the Portuguese, following the Muslim precedent, began in 1441. "Papal reasoning," writes John Baur, "proceeded from the crusading spirit of the Church Militant, which considered the use of arms proper for the establishment of the kingdom of God on earth."[5] The pope also authorized the use of missionary-priests under the policy of *padroado* (or royal patronage) whereby the missionary was directly responsible to the royal government. The visible symbol of the *padroado* was the *padrao,* the stone cross the Portuguese explorers used along the coasts of Africa to mark the land they claimed for their earthly king.[6]

To advance this *conquista,* Portuguese sailors began to sail down the west coast of Africa. Cape Bojador was an early milestone but Henry wanted to push his explorers farther. His seamen complained about the dangers that lurked in the waters beyond Bojador, about the satanic hand that would rise up out of the water and destroy a ship.[7] Such fears were paralyzing and Henry needed new ways to motivate his shaken sailors.

1. John Baur, *2000 Years of African Christianity* (Nairobi: Paulines, 1994), 43.
2. Bailey Diffie and George Winius, *Foundations of the Portuguese Empire, 1450–1580* (Minneapolis: University of Minnesota Press, 1977), 76.
3. Quoted in Baur, *2000 Years,* 46.
4. Ibid., 47.
5. Ibid.
6. Ibid., 49.
7. C. P. Groves, *The Planting of Christianity in Africa,* vol. 1 (London: Lutterworth, 1948), 121.

Just when an added incentive was needed Ethiopia came calling. In 1441 Ethiopian monks from a cloister in Jerusalem came to Rome and promised to bring word to the emperor of Ethiopia, Zara-Yaqob, of Christendom's desire for a new crusade. In that very year Henry's ships landed on the coast of Mauretania and inaugurated the European discovery of Africa. A new chapter of the kingdom of God in Africa had begun.

Changing concepts of the kingdom. The late Middle Ages introduced a concept of the kingdom already encountered in the Byzantium of Justinian the Great and to a lesser degree in the Ethiopia of Zara-Yaqob. This new concept of the kingdom was called Christendom.

At the heart of the concept of Christendom was the vision of the rule of Christ over all of life through a partnership of church and state. To its proponents Christendom was "the conscious elaboration of a programme which was to bring mankind under the law of Christ."[8] To its critics, "Christendom was a provincial, western, and insular parody of the great civilized Roman empire."[9] Whatever its merits, this ideal of the kingdom of God embodied in the institutions of the Western church (under the authoritarian leadership of the pope) and Western states (under the nominal leadership of the Holy Roman Emperor) dominated Portuguese missions.

Between 1500 and 1700 the theocratic rule of Christ brought enormous changes to Africa. In the kingdom of Congo the concept of Christendom destroyed for a time the traditions of sacred kingship and replaced them with a more Ethiopian vision of a Christian king ruling over a national expression of God's kingdom on earth. In Cape Town, Dutch Protestant nationalism, having broken from the traditional concept of Christendom during the sixteenth-century Protestant Reformation, forged a covenantal vision of the kingdom of God. Christ's rule in heaven was seen best in his chosen people, the elect, whose task was to construct Christian commonwealths to oppose Catholicism on the one hand and paganism on the other.

The common thread running through these competing kingdom concepts was that of the sovereignty of God over all of life. What was sometimes lost in this accent on the kingdom as providential rule were the equally significant themes of personal redemption and public justice. The failure to find balance among these three aspects of the kingdom spelled trouble for Portuguese missionaries, African kings, and Dutch settlers alike. We begin with the troubles of the missionaries.

8. John McManners, ed., *The Oxford Illustrated History of Christianity* (Oxford: Oxford University Press, 1990), 199.
9. Ibid.

The Portuguese Discovery of Africa

The discoverers. After the death of Henry the Navigator in 1460 the pace of discovery quickened, aided no doubt by the tragic fall of Constantinople, the capital of Byzantium, to the armies of the Ottomans in 1453. The search for Prester John and the launching of a crusade from Africa became more imperative. In the year of Henry's death the Cape Verde Islands were discovered.[10] By 1472 the kingdom of Benin appears to have been reached.[11] In 1471 the equator was crossed.

In 1485 Diogo Cão reached the Congo and made contact with King Nzinga Nkuwu. Bartholomew Diaz reached the Cape of Good Hope (called by his embattled sailors, the Cape of Torments) in 1486. In 1493 Pope Alexander V fueled the fires of exploration by granting to Portugal the right to colonize all of Africa as well as Brazil in South America. The need for slaves to aid in the taming of the land also increased.

The climax of this spectacular century of Portuguese exploration was reached in 1498 when Vasco da Gama made maritime history with the European discovery of the Zambezi, Mombasa, Malindi, and finally, the grand prize, India. In the wake of the discoverers came the soldiers, the merchants, and, above all, the missionaries.

Missionary efforts on Cape Verde, São Tomé and Príncipé Islands. The first missionary conquests in the newly discovered lands of Africa took place on the islands of her western shore. The Cape Verde Islands after 1460 became an important base for African slaves and African priests. The former were on their way to the New World. The latter had been educated in Lisbon and brought to the islands to establish Christianity among the owners and slave labor of the new plantations. The church of Cape Verde was envisioned as the launching pad for Christian expansion on the mainland. Though great success was achieved by the African clergy in building a strong church among the settlers and slaves of the islands, the continent never felt the impact.[12] One of the many ironies of West African Christianity is that the future missionary force that would later transform West Africa would come from the slaves who had been sent from Africa and not the Lisbon-trained clergy sent to Africa.[13]

São Tomé and Príncipé Islands far to the south of Cape Verde developed a thriving church among the settler community. Over time the mulatto

---

10. I am, of course, referring to the European discovery of these places throughout this chapter. The African discovery and sometimes the Muslim discovery of key geographic areas had occurred centuries earlier.

11. Lamin Sanneh, *West African Christianity: The Religious Impact* (Maryknoll, N.Y.: Orbis, 1983), 36.

12. Ibid., 19.

13. Ibid.

clergy refused to cooperate with the African clergy, even attempting at one point to block their ordination. There are also reports that Africans refused to take communion from their own African priests and insisted on being ministered to by Whites.[14] In spite of such attitudes Portuguese missionaries and their African colleagues established a church that endured into the twentieth century.[15]

Missionary efforts on the West African Coast. In 1457 Diogo Gomez reached the edges of the fabled kingdom of Mali, where he sought to convert one of the vassal kings, Nomimansa, to the Christian faith. A Muslim sheik debated with Gomez in the presence of the king. The king converted to the Christian faith, and the religious aspect of the Portuguese *conquista* was launched.[16]

In Ghana, Christianity was introduced in 1482, when Diogo da Azambuja celebrated Mass in the coastal village of Elmina. Azambuja and his chaplain tried without success to convert the local king Nana Caramansa, who was astute enough to understand that conversion meant political subjugation to European Christendom in general and Portuguese Christian nationalism in particular.[17] The church that was eventually included in the Castle of St. George, constructed by the Portuguese soon after Azambuja's initial landing, came to symbolize not only a foreign presence but a hostile one as well.

More successful was the witness to the nearby king of Efutu, who converted in 1503. Three hundred of the palace elite followed in the footsteps of the king. Political and economic factors weighed heavily in these conversions, for within ten years the king and his elite had lapsed in their faith.[18] Though the ensuing centuries saw waves of Augustinians, Capuchins, and Dominicans attempt to build a lasting work, their efforts ended in failure. Thus began a pattern of initial success followed by eventual collapse that would characterize Portuguese missions in Africa.

In Benin this pattern developed an interesting twist and pointed to the more bitter side of mission—conflict between the Christian church and the culture of Christendom. In 1655 Spanish Jesuits baptized the king of Benin. The entire kingdom was opening up to the Catholic faith. To the dismay of the missionaries, the Portuguese military invaded Benin and ordered the missionaries to leave. The policy of *padroado* insured that the work of the gospel would play a secondary role to the advance of the kingdom of politics. Centuries later when archaeologists uncovered a rich treasury of Benin bronze

14. Ibid., 36.
15. Ibid., 49.
16. Groves, *Planting*, vol. 1, 126.
17. Sanneh, *West African Christianity,* 24.
18. Ibid., 25.

and ivory carvings from these centuries it was the symbolism of the Portuguese soldier and not the symbols of the gospel that reoccur.[19]

The bitter words of the Dominican missionary, Fr. Loyer, as he left Africa aboard a Portuguese slave ship in 1703, summarized the frustration of more than two hundred years of Catholic labors in West Africa. "I can say without exaggeration," wrote Fr. Loyer, "that of all the peoples of the earth, the most malignant, the most thievish and the most ungrateful are the Negroes."[20] Farther down the western shore of Africa, in the kingdom of Congo, more promising prospects for extending Christendom were found.

The Congo mission. On May 3, 1491, before Columbus discovered the New World, Afonso I discovered a new faith. He was baptized by Portuguese missionaries on that day along with his father and so many others that "the arms of the missionaries became tired."[21]

Afonso, formerly Mvemba Nzinga, was elated about the new discovery. "The grace of the Holy Spirit enlightened us," the king later wrote, "by a unique and special favour, given to us by the Holy Spirit—We received the Christian doctrine so well that by God's mercy, it was from hour to hour and from day to day better implanted in our heart." So powerful was the gospel's impact that "We definitely renounced all errors and idolatries which our ancestors thus far had believed in."[22]

After his ascension to the throne in 1506 Afonso demonstrated his zeal for his new faith. He launched a campaign to destroy the traditional temple in the capital city, Mbanza Kongo. Popular opposition followed, but Afonso remained undaunted and triumphed in the ensuing struggle. To commemorate his victory over paganism, Afonso built a church dedicated to "Our Savior." Mbanza Kongo was renamed São Salvador.

But there was another side to Afonso. It is true that during Afonso's reign the Catholic Church was planted in every locality in the kingdom. Yet the true picture of the coming rule of Christ was not as sunny a picture as Afonso painted. Afonso's father, Nzinga Nkuwu (given the baptismal name of Joao), had requested missionaries after early contact with European explorers (who were looking for Prester John). Though baptized, Joao never gave up his traditional kingship role and reverted to polygamy and traditional religion within a short time.

Afonso himself, for all his spiritual sincerity, used the new religion in pragmatic ways. At the death of Nzinga Nkuwu, the rightful heir to the throne was not Afonso but his brother and hated rival, Mpanzu a Kitima, who re-

19. Groves, *Planting*, vol. 1, 127.
20. Quoted in ibid., 34.
21. Baur, *2000 Years*, 57.
22. Letter 13 written in 1512, translated by J. Baur and quoted in *2000 Years*, 57.

jected Christianity and called for a return to the traditional ways. Afonso, supported by the Catholic priests, seized the throne in 1506 and defeated his brother in a decisive battle. Like Lalibela and the Zagwe dynasty in medieval Ethiopia, Christianity gave legitimacy to an otherwise tainted crown.[23]

To consolidate his power Afonso needed to establish the new religion upon which his legitimacy depended. He called for large numbers of missionaries from Portugal and also sent his own sons and grandsons to Lisbon for theological training. Soon the kingdom of Congo was filled with missionaries and priests. To the great distress of Afonso and his subjects the priests from Europe plunged into open immorality. The priests even joined with the slave-trading Portuguese settlers to oppose Afonso. The Congo king wrote to King Manuel of Portugal, "Today our Lord is crucified anew by the very ministers of his body and blood."[24]

Afonso's hope that an African clergy trained in Europe would remedy the problem did not seem to materialize. Afonso's own son Henrique (d. 1531) was ordained bishop in 1521 by Leo X (who was having his own problems with a German priest named Martin Luther). Henrique returned to serve in a religious-political role but seemed to make very little impact. Three years before Afonso's death in 1540 a priest named Alvaro plotted an unsuccessful assassination attempt against him. Though he died in the faith, Afonso complained to the end about the uncontrolled slave trade[25] and unworthy missionaries.[26]

Catholic Christianity continued in Congo under the descendants of Afonso, who pleaded with Lisbon and Rome for "zealous, not business-minded priests." After a century of frustration the kings of Congo were finally granted their request with the arrival of the Capuchins. This Italian order eventually sent some 440 missionaries between the years 1645 and 1835, making it "the greatest missionary enterprise in Africa before the modern period."[27]

Between 1645 and 1700 the Capuchins in Congo and Angola (a distinct Portuguese colony to the south) baptized an estimated six hundred thousand people (mostly children). They started numerous schools, each averaging about six hundred pupils. The success indicated by their numbers obscures the constant struggle to root the Christian faith among the people.

---

23. I am siding with the interpretation of Anne Hilton in her *Kingdom of Kongo* (Oxford: Clarendon, 1985), 64, in opposition to Baur, *2000 Years of African Christianity*, 57, who calls Mpanzu a Kitima the "usurping brother."

24. Quoted in Baur, *2000 Years*, 59.

25. See the text of Afonso's July 1526 letter to Joao III in Basil Davidson, *The African Past* (Boston: Little, Brown, 1964), 192, where he strongly condemns the slave trade and calls for the Portuguese king's help in bringing it to an end. His words went unheeded.

26. Baur, *2000 Years*, 60.

27. Ibid., 63.

The missionaries viewed African traditional religion with horror. Operating with an exaggerated Augustinian view of the kingdom, they saw their work in Africa as part of the age-old struggle of the kingdom of Satan with the kingdom of God. All that was not part of the Christian church (equated with the kingdom of God) was therefore to be regarded as belonging to the kingdom of Satan. Such a stark kingdom vision empowered Capuchin missionaries like Cherubino da Savona (fl. 1758–74) to embark on numerous evangelistic journeys and baptize thousands.[28] At the same time such sharp polarities could also inspire reactions among the local people.

Matters became complicated when, after a period of protest by African catechumens that baptismal requirements were too rigid, the Propoganda (a Roman Catholic mission governing body) permitted the policy of *in fides ecclesiae* ("in the faith of the church"). This policy permitted missionaries to baptize anyone, using their own discretion, who they felt was incapable of properly understanding Christian beliefs. They could be baptized because they put their faith in whatever the church believed, however deficient their own understanding may have been.

Though the Capuchins were very conscientious, a policy like *in fides ecclesiae* did not encourage "a very high ideal of missionary work."[29] The combination of missionary hostility against African traditional belief, an uncompromising view of the two kingdoms, and occasional laxity in instructing converts encouraged the rise of syncretistic expressions of Christian faith.

One such syncretistic expression was led by an African prophetess named Beatrix Kimpa Vita. Distressed by a civil war that had three claimants fighting for the throne and that had left the Congo Capital, São Salvador, deserted, this young African girl claimed to be the voice of St. Antony of Egypt who had wrestled with demons in another part of Africa. She claimed to have died but had been raised by the spirit of St. Antony at the moment of death. She asserted that the kingdom of Congo was not just an earthly kingdom but that it was the kingdom of God. Jesus and Mary were in fact Congo ancestors and therefore Christ was a Mukongo. São Salvador was Bethlehem. Beatrix moved into the ruins of the new "Bethlehem" and proclaimed the restoration of the kingdom. Since Christendom had failed to bring in the kingdom, African attempts were needed. Her miracles and healings attracted a wide following. The Capuchins and King Pedro IV had her arrested and executed as a witch in 1706.

The syncretism symbolized by Beatrix continued into the eighteenth and nineteenth centuries. When a European traveler visited the Congo capital in 1879 all signs of vital Christianity were gone: "King and people were wholly

28. Stephen Neill, *A History of Christian Missions,* rev. ed. (London: Penguin, 1986), 168.
29. Ibid.

given to fetishism and all the superstitions and cruelties of the Dark Continent. Some ruined walls of the cathedral remained, the chancel arch and part of a chapel. The sad relics of a failure."[30]

The Jesuit mission in Angola. To the south of the kingdom of Congo lay the kingdom of Ndongo with its center in Luanda. The kingdom was ruled by a powerful *ngola,* or king, who eventually gave his title to the country. In 1575 the Portuguese began a colony in Luanda.

Jesuits joined other orders in laboring among the population of Luanda and its environs, which consisted mostly of Portuguese settlers and African slaves. One of the most notable achievements of the Jesuits was the experiment with Christian villages under the leadership of Fr. Pero Ravares. Tracts of land were granted for the purpose of establishing African Christian communities using the village model. Fr. Pero traveled tirelessly among the many villages, instructing the estimated twenty thousand catechumens.[31] When the Dutch launched a series of invasions against Luanda (1641–47), much of the work was destroyed.

By the time David Livingstone arrived in Angola in 1854 little evidence of Christianity remained. "All speak well of the Jesuits and other missionaries," wrote Livingstone, but they "were supplanted by priests, concerning whom no regret is expressed that they were allowed to die out."[32]

Missions along the Southeast Coast. Gold and the ghost of Prester John continued to lure the Portuguese farther around the coast of Africa. In their quest they sailed past the Cape of Good Hope (though Cabral did construct a chapel at Mossel Bay) and continued on to the eastern shore, establishing bases in Kilwa, Sofala, and Mombasa to name the principal sites. In these settlements along Africa's east coast, Portugal encountered the kingdoms of Allah. The naval victory of the Portuguese in 1509 over a Muslim fleet insured a century of European domination of the Indian Ocean. Missionaries followed the triumphal march of the soldiers along the coast. Churches and chapels were built in the major settlements. Heroic missions were attempted. One of the most heroic efforts took place along the Zambezi.

The Jesuit mission to the empire of Mwene Mutapa. In March 1498, on his first voyage along Africa's eastern shore, Vasco da Gama discovered the island of Mozambique. The great explorer wrote excitedly in his log book about a conversation with some Muslim traders. "We were told, moreover, that Prester John resided not far from this place; that he held many cities

30. Groves, *Planting,* vol. 1, 131.
31. Baur, *2000 Years,* 74.
32. Groves, *Planting,* vol. 1, 131.

along the coast and that the inhabitants of those cities were great merchants and owned big ships."

After the Portuguese explorer pressed the Moors for details, he was told that "the residence of Prester John" was actually "far in the interior, and could be reached only on the back of camels." Rather than being discouraged by this change in their story, da Gama and his crew were elated. "This information . . . rendered us so happy," he wrote as his ship rolled gently on the waves of the Indian Ocean, "that we cried with joy, and prayed God to grant us health, so that we might behold what we so much desired."[33] The great quest to locate the kingdom of God in Africa and its illustrious Black king seemed to be nearing its end.

After a century of fruitless search, it was clear that da Gama's elation was premature. Though the Portuguese had built a fort and a church in 1507 on the island of Mozambique, no African Christian kingdom had been found. The Portuguese were given a consolation prize, however. They had made contact with "the Emperor of Gold," whom the Portuguese called Monomotapa (Mwene Mutapa) and who ruled from a place called Zimbabwe.

News of this emperor fired the imagination of a Jesuit missionary who had worked first in India and then among the Tonga south of Mozambique. Fr. Gonsalo da Silveira (1521–61) traveled up the Zambezi to the court of Mwene Mutapa, arriving at Christmas 1560. His initial audience with the king was a great success. The Mwene Mutapa had never met a Portuguese man who had not demanded women and gold. Silveira's ascetic piety greatly impressed the monarch, who granted him a hut near the palace. After a series of visions of the Virgin Mary, the king converted to Christianity. Silveira baptized the king and his court on January 20, 1561. The priest became an instant hero to the populace. For Silveira the kingdom of Zimbabwe seemed to be at the threshold of a Christian revolution to rival that which had taken place in the Congo.

At this hopeful moment, Muslim traders arrived at court. They convinced the king that Silveira was a sorcerer and a spy of the Portuguese. The local witch doctor joined in the chorus of accusation. On March 16, 1561 the king pronounced the death sentence on the saintly missionary. Silveira refused to flee. He forgave the king and spent his final day preaching and baptizing. That night while he slept, the ardent Jesuit was strangled.

The immediate military reprisals that followed the death of Silveira triggered a century of Portuguese conquest and repression of the kingdom of Mwene Mutapa. Though Christian baptism of each new king continued, it was little more than a hollow ritual. The ravages of the slave trade combined with the injustices of Portuguese traders, colonial governors, and settlers de-

33. Davidson, *African Past*, 125.

stroyed the credibility of Christianity in the region. Once again a mission begun with great promise collapsed in failure.

Mission efforts in East Africa. Though the quest for Prester John had failed in the Congo and Mozambique, the Portuguese continued their *conquista* up the coast to East Africa and its offshore islands. This was the site of the Zanj Empire with its city-states like Kilwa, Mombasa, Malindi, and Lamu.

In 1498 Vasco da Gama planted the *padrao* pillar on the coast near Malindi. When the legendary Jesuit, Francis Xavier, stopped in Malindi in 1542 on his way to India he exulted at "the might of the cross, seen standing so lonely and so victorious in the midst of the vast land of the Moors."[34] Yet Xavier's words were premature. The victories of the gospel were hard to see in the midst of the sixteenth century. Missionary efforts were lacking and the construction of Fort Jesus in 1595 in Mombasa made the gospel seem more like a threat to flee than a treasure to seek.

This cold witness to the gospel by stone pillar and armed fortress was transformed in 1597 when da Gama's grandson, Francisco, became viceroy of India. He ordered missionaries to plant the faith along the East African coast. The Augustinian Hermits (OESA) responded to the governor's call, and Mombasa became a center of their work. Within a year the Augustinians reported six hundred converts in that ancient city. Significant work was also done in the Lamu archipelago to the north and on the island of Zanzibar to the south. So cooperative was the sultan of Zanzibar that the missionaries called the island the "most fruitful mission centre"[35] of the entire region.

In general the prospects of a triumphant Christian church in East Africa looked promising. Optimism exuded from Urban VII, the Roman pontiff, who wrote to the "King of Mombasa and Malindi" describing him as a "Son much beloved in Christ." The pope was particularly glad that "the blessed Augustine himself—the bright light of your Africa and the whole Church—makes his voice thrill through your ears by means of the Augustinian missionaries."[36]

How deep the faith was being planted must be questioned given the Augustinian policy of providing rice to new converts to entice them to remain faithful to Christ.[37] Yet despite these small signs to the contrary it appeared that the City of God was about to triumph among the alabaster cities of the western rim of the Indian Ocean.

In the eyes of the missionaries this triumph seemed to be doubly assured by the conversion of Yusuf bin Hasan, who was installed as sultan of Mom-

34. Quoted in Baur, *2000 Years*, 88.
35. Ibid., 89.
36. Quoted in Groves, *Planting*, vol. 1, 137–38.
37. Justus Strandes, *The Portuguese Period in East Africa* (Nairobi: East African Literature Bureau, 1968, orig. 1899), 153.

basa in 1625. His enthusiasm for the faith seemed deep and genuine. "I am obeyed by my Moorish vassals with every courtesy and submission and in two years I have converted more than one hundred to the faith of Christ."[38] But conflict with the Portuguese captain at Fort Jesus soon soured the young sultan. He silently converted back to Islam. On August 16, 1631 Yusuf bin Hasan attacked Fort Jesus, killing the captain and his guard. He then launched a campaign of terror against the Christian community, threatening Portuguese and African alike with death unless they converted to Islam. Three hundred refused and were killed for their faith, including three Augustinian fathers.

Though the Portuguese regained power soon after, the cause of Catholic Christendom began to wane in East Africa. By the end of the seventeenth century the Portuguese and their brand of Christian faith were a fading memory in the city-states of the coast. A dubious pattern had now been established by the policy of *padroado,* where Portuguese soldiers in the name of the king often undid what Portuguese missionaries achieved in the name of God. Ethiopia would slightly contradict that pattern for there the failure of Catholic Christianity was due to the man with the Bible rather than the man with the musket.

The Jesuit mission to Ethiopia. The relentless quest for Prester John finally resulted in success when European contact was established with the kingdom of Ethiopia. The story of the visit of Francisco Alvarez (1520–26) and the Portuguese intervention on Ethiopia's behalf against Imam Ahmad was recounted in the previous chapter. The establishment of diplomatic and military ties led to the cautious forging of religious ties during the time of King Galawdewos. After an earlier openness Galawdewos changed and began to oppose the Catholic version of Christianity. He was a learned monarch and became an able defender of Alexandrian Christology and other distinctives of Coptic Christianity.

Following his death the Jesuits launched another attempt to convert the nation. In 1603 Pedro Paez arrived in Ethiopia and within twelve months had learned to read, write, and speak Ge'ez. His brilliance and godliness were a marvel to all. Paez's witness soon exerted a powerful influence on two emperors, Za-Deingil (d. 1607) and his successor Susenyos (d. 1632). In spite of resistance and even armed rebellion the Latin liturgy was imposed and a reunion with the Roman Church was proclaimed in 1626.

At this key moment Paez died and was succeeded by the Spanish Jesuit Mendez. It was the wrong choice. His policies and practices alienated just about every section of Ethiopian society from prince to people. Mendez insisted that all Coptic clergy be reordained, all Ethiopian Christians be rebaptized (in contradiction to the Catholic policy against rebaptisms established

38. See Baur, *2000 Years,* 89.

during the time of Donatism in North Africa), and all churches be reconsecrated. Susenyos's son, Fasiladas (d. 1635), could take no more of Mendez and his extremist views. Fearing civil war unless he acted decisively, Fasiladas expelled the Jesuits in 1632 and restored the Ethiopian Coptic church.

Henry's Prester John, after two centuries of searching, proved to be a disappointing ally for European Christendom. While Rome regretted this final failure in Africa, the new Protestant nation of the United Netherlands rejoiced. The Dutch had their own dreams of Africa, which included neither Prester John nor the Catholic Church.

The Dutch Discovery of Africa

The founding of Cape Town in 1652. Though the history of South Africa begins with the coming of Khoisan (the combined name for two related groups, the Khoikhoi and the San tribes) and Bantu groups to the region, the history of European settlement begins with the founding of a refreshment station by the Dutch East India Company (DEIC) at Cape Town in 1652. The farflung holdings of the DEIC extended from Holland to Batavia in the Pacific including numerous sites in West Africa. The Cape of Good Hope was a logical place for a waystation for ships navigating such a long voyage.

The Council of Seventeen (who directed the work of the DEIC) chose Jan van Riebeeck to establish this waystation at the foot of Table Mountain. Neither a missionary like Silveira nor a nobleman like Henry the Navigator, van Riebeeck was a businessman and a loyal employee of the DEIC, one of the world's largest companies. Landing at the Cape in 1652 with over one hundred employees, van Riebeeck built a hedge around the company's property and then a fort within the hedge. The fort and the hedge symbolically stated that the rest of Africa was not welcome in this outpost of Europe at Africa's southern tip.

Van Riebeeck was a strict man who ruled himself and others with "a rod of iron" and insisted upon regular Sunday worship for all. His rod of iron also extended over his relations with the Khoisan. Van Riebeeck depended on the local Khoisan cattle for meat and on Khoisan land for fresh fruit and vegetables. These two items became sources of severe conflict.

The local people had actually had over a century of contact with Europeans prior to the coming of van Riebeeck and his group. The Portuguese and earlier Dutch visits had given the Khoisan enough contact to be wary of Europeans in general but lulled them into thinking that Whites were transients with no intention of permanent settlement.[39]

39. Richard Elphick, *KhoiKhoi and the Founding of White South Africa* (Johannesburg: Ravan Press, 1985), 86–87.

The Khoisan were willing to sell their surplus cattle to the Dutch but the latter demanded more. When van Riebeeck released some of his soldiers from their contracts so that they could start farms to provide fresh produce they settled on Khoisan grazing land. This led to war in 1659. After several unsuccessful attempts to take the fort the Khoisan alliance fell apart and they were forced to seek a negotiated settlement. Van Riebeeck proved intransigent in the ensuing talks and simply informed the Khoisan leaders that they had lost their land in war and it now belonged to the settlers by "right of conquest."[40] Later wars between Khoisan and the settlers, soon called "Boers" (Dutch for farmer), reduced the Khoisan to servitude.

Behind van Riebeeck's harsh dealings with the Khoisan were certain attitudes about race and the kingdom of God. Unlike other Dutch who had early contact with the Khoisan (such as Leendert Janssen, who held them in high regard), van Riebeeck regarded the local people as "by no means to be trusted, being a brutal people living without conscience."[41] Later he wrote that the Khoisan were "dull, stupid, and odious" and therefore to be regarded as "black stinking dogs."[42] Van Riebeeck was convinced that the Khoisan were without a conscience and probably without a soul.[43]

These early racist attitudes, not uncommon in Europe in the seventeenth century, had a slightly religious twist for in the Holland from which van Riebeeck came, the Dutch thought of themselves as a New Israel. Though van Riebeeck was no theologian it did not take him long to recognize who the new Canaanites were.

The Golden Age of the Netherlands. Where did this Dutch mythology come from that influenced businessmen and farmers from the earliest days of the Cape colony and became a fixture of Afrikaner civil religion in subsequent generations? The members of van Riebeeck's original community were not religious idealists like the New England Puritans or even the French Huguenots who came later to South Africa. Half of van Riebeeck's group were unable to read or write.[44]

Some contemporary South African historians question whether anything like a "chosen people" mentality existed in South Africa before the nineteenth century.[45] What can be reasonably held, however, is that these earliest Dutch settlers came from a Netherlands that was developing a distinct national folklore in the age of Rembrandt and that all ranks of society were touched in some way by this folklore.

40. Kevin Shillington, *History of Africa* (London: Macmillan, 1989), 216.
41. Quoted in Allister Sparks, *The Mind of South Africa* (London: Mandarin, 1990), 29.
42. Ibid., 29–30.
43. Ibid., 29.
44. Ibid., 28.
45. See the discussion of André du Toit's ideas in ibid., 28–29.

What was the nature of the national folklore? Historian Simon Schama has explored the roots of this patriotic mythology in seventeenth-century Holland.[46] Dutch self-understanding was built around the twin ordeals of trial by water and trial by fire. The ordeal by water involved the struggle against the sea. The sea was a friend to Dutch sailors but an enemy to Dutch farmers and burghers who had fought against its inundations in their low-land landscape. Their elaborate system of dikes and canals enabled them to overcome this physical tyrant and pass the test of trial by water. As the story of Noah reminds us, the successful survival of the ordeal by water is a sign of divine election and favor.[47]

The trial by fire was the David and Goliath struggle of the low countries against the political tyranny of Spain. William of Orange had led them in their successful struggle for independence and union in 1574. This winning of the war against Spain was also seen as an additional sign that God had chosen the Netherlands for some significant purpose.[48]

To interpret these two trials and their successful passage through them, the Calvinistic Christians of the Netherlands turned to the Bible and partic-ularly to the Old Testament. "From their tribulations," writes Schama, "vic-tories, captivities, peregrinations and prophecies—related through the printed word of the Bible, the oral culture of the pulpit, the narrative drama-tizations of historical theater and the compelling imagery of the print—the Dutch were able to answer those questions about their identity."[49]

After the Dutch defeated England in 1688 Jacobus Lydius wrote, "When men ask how the Netherlanders, with such little power, could overcome their enemies on land and destroy them at sea—we can only say that this could only have come about through the eternal covenant made between God and his children below."[50] The Dutch "were reborn Hebrews, children of the Covenant."[51]

Though van Riebeeck's pilgrims were unlearned they were not immune to the influence of these cultural myths. Their tiny nation was in some way central to the witness of God's rule in the world. What they needed was a conscious Christian community that could allow these subtle seeds of folk beliefs to mature and bear fruit. Just such a Christian community was found within the Dutch Reformed Church (DRC).

The beginnings of Christianity in South Africa. From 1652 to 1656 the spir-itual needs of the Dutch community were served by William Wylant, a "sick

---

46. Simon Schama, *The Embarrassment of Riches: An Interpretation of Dutch Culture in the Golden Age* (New York: Knopf, 1988).
47. Ibid., 35.
48. Ibid., 42.
49. Ibid., 68.
50. Quoted in Sparks, *Mind of South Africa,* 26.
51. Schama, *Embarrassment,* 68.

comforter," a kind of lay minister who was granted many of the powers of an ordained clergyman. A series of sick comforters followed in his footsteps until the arrival in 1665 of Johan van Arckel, the first ordained DRC clergyman. In that same year the first congregation was formally constituted under the Amsterdam classis.

In 1687 a second congregation was established at nearby Stellenbosch. By 1745 five congregations existed and formal ties were established between the local churches. The same mythology that shaped Dutch nationalism influenced the DRC. They saw themselves as part of a second reformation, who as the chosen of God needed to aspire to holiness and keep unspotted from the world. They emphasized the importance of the new birth and experiential religion even while respecting the sacraments and forms of order and worship found in their denomination.[52]

Joining the Dutch in building the kingdom in South Africa were French Huguenots. They arrived at the Cape in 1688. When the French king revoked the Edict of Nantes in 1685 the Protestant Huguenots lost their right to freedom of worship in Catholic France. Many moved to the Netherlands and signed on with the DEIC when the company issued a call for settlers for their new colony at Cape Town. By 1700 nearly two hundred had arrived and soon blended into the Dutch Reformed congregations. By the late eighteenth century Lutherans (1778) and Moravians (1738) were added to the religious scene.

Developments in missions. As early as 1662 converts from the Khoisan had been baptized, but only sporadic attempts were made to evangelize the tribe. The first European missionary to work among the Khoisan was a Moravian, George Schmidt.[53]

Schmidt arrived in Cape Town in 1738 and immediately formed a non-denominational community at Genadendal, one hundred miles east of Cape Town, with the specific purpose of evangelism among the indigenous people. It did not take long for Schmidt to run into trouble with the settler community. He was called a "hypocrite and sham" for praying in public. His theology of universal grace was regarded as heretical. In turn, Schmidt responded that "the impiety is very great in this country, a real devil of drinking reigns."[54] He added that "most people mock at me, but I take no heed, they do not know what they are doing."[55] Schmidt chided the DRC for their lack of zeal in the conversion of the Khoisan. In 1748 the Dutch authorities forced

52. J. W. Hofmeyr and G. J. Pillay, eds., *A History of Christianity in South Africa*, vol. 1 (Haum Tertiary, 1994), 13.

53. John W. de Gruchy, *The Church Struggle in South Africa* (Grand Rapids: Eerdmans, 1979), 2.

54. Hofmeyr and Pillay, eds., *History*, vol. 1, 22.

55. Ibid.

Schmidt to stop his mission work. This was the beginning of a long history of conflict between "mission church" and "settler church."[56]

Though his own efforts were not successful, Schmidt's presence signaled a dramatic change in the history of African Christianity. Schmidt was the harbinger of a new kind of witness to the kingdom—the spiritual rule of Christ in hearts. By the early eighteenth century the forces of the European Enlightenment, a movement of rationalism and radical humanism that denied the supernatural and miraculous, were destroying the old medieval synthesis in which all of life was governed by Christian church and Christian state. A sharp distinction was made between the secular and the sacred areas of life. As a result of the Enlightenment, religion was relegated increasingly to the private and personal sphere.

In response to the dualism and rationalism of the Enlightenment, an evangelical awakening began in Britain just as Schmidt arrived in Cape Town. This awakening would emphasize personal conversion and private citizenship in heaven rather than Christendom or Christian nationalism. Schmidt was a prophetic voice of these changes. His new view of the kingdom would come in like a flood in the next century.

Conclusion: The Kingdom in Transition

In the course of building their African empires the Portuguese and the Dutch witnessed to the kingdom of God. Despite many theological differences, their witness to the kingdom between 1500 and 1700 had something in common—the emphasis on the kingdom as a theocracy. Christendom was the name given to the model of the kingdom inherited by Portugal in the Middle Ages. The Dutch version of this kingdom witness was Protestant nationalism. In each case Christianity was more than just a faith to believe. Christianity was a way of life, a way of civilization that must be institutionalized and imposed on all. The kingdom was equated with the national project of building Christian civilization.

Such views of the heavenly kingdom produced a lot of earthly trouble. Under the policy of *padroado,* the Portuguese missionary was the servant not only of God but also the Portuguese king. "They were continuously in danger," noted one Catholic historian, "of confusing the interests of God with those of the king."[57] Portugal was called by her representatives, *il Reyno,* which simply means "the kingdom." The *conquista* was seen by African and European alike as the conquest of paganism and Islam for the glory of God and Portugal, and not always in that order. This identification of the divine

56. De Gruchy, *Church Struggle,* 2.
57. Baur, *2000 Years,* 93.

kingdom with a finite human kingdom was a serious deficiency of Catholic missions during the early modern period. This false equation led to a serious undermining of the credibility of the gospel in the eyes of many Africans.

With the coming of the Dutch to Cape Town little changed in terms of the witness to the kingdom. Though in Dutch eyes Catholic Christendom was no longer the model of the kingdom on earth, Protestant nationalism took its place and continued the same attitude of domination that had marked the Portuguese *conquista*.

When the kingdom is understood as the providential rule of God through church and state, and earthly political systems are equated with the kingdom, the biblical concept of God's rule becomes distorted. The significant themes of personal redemption and public justice can get lost beneath the attempts to impose Christian institutions on new lands in the name of Christ. Additionally, the sacramentalism of Catholic missions often obscured the evangelical emphasis on the personal experience of redemption. The racism and national mythology of the Dutch violated the witness to the kingdom as social justice.

Of all the inconsistencies of the theocratic model of the kingdom none was more scandalous than the slave trade. For many Africans who had contacts with Europeans it appeared that Christians evangelized the people one day and sold them into slavery the next. Indeed, by the early nineteenth century even Rome recognized that "the greatest hindrance of missions is the slave trade, operated by the Christians of Angola. It renders our religion odious to the Africans who keep in mind their chains instead of seeing the freedom brought to them in Christ."[58] The Dutch involvement in the slave trade was equally troubling.

The next generation of African Christianity sought to address these deficiencies. With the coming of Schmidt a new witness to the kingdom appeared in reaction to Protestant nationalism and Catholic Christendom. This new witness presented Christ as the liberator of hearts from sin and hands from chains. The new witness sought to combine evangelical fervor for souls with an eschatological passion for justice. The point at which this fervor for souls and passion for justice met was slavery. The concept of the kingdom as Christ's justice on earth and Christ's renewal of hearts would change Africa in ways that Prince Henry or van Riebeeck never imagined. Beatrix, however, would not have been surprised.

---

58. The secretary of the Propoganda Fide to the Portuguese ambassador. Quoted in ibid., 95.

Part 3

The Reign of Christ

African Christianity in the Eighteenth and Nineteenth Centuries

The Liberating Kingdom

The Crusade Against the Slave Trade

For Europeans living between 1600 and 1800, sugar was king and slavery was its handmaid. Attempts to sever the link between sugar and slavery seemed doomed to failure. Even kings appeared powerless. In 1609 Philip II of Portugal declared that all Amerindians in Brazil, Portugal's largest colony, were free. No longer could they be enslaved and forced to work in the cane fields.

Plantation owners were outraged. They supplied sugar for the demanding European market and had used Native American labor for decades. The demand for labor was so great that Black slaves from Africa had begun appearing in Brazil in the 1580s to supplement the indigenous workforce. By 1611 the king was forced to rescind these antislavery laws, so powerful was the sugar lobby in Lisbon. Sugar was one of the most profitable of all Portuguese commercial enterprises, outstripping even the Asian spice trade.[1]

By the eighteenth century English colonies in the Caribbean joined the network of sugar plantations that dotted the islands of the new world. The 550 coffee and tea shops of London in 1740 pushed the demand for sugar to new heights.[2] Few Englishmen who smoked their tobacco or stirred sugar into their coffee realized that their little luxuries were purchased at the expense of African freedom. Britain's greatest source of sugar, Barbados, had a population of 250,000 slaves by 1810. Virginia tobacco planters sought to emulate the economic success of Barbados by importing slaves to work in the fields. Between 1690 and 1770 Virginia imported 100,000 African slaves.[3]

1. William Phillips Jr., *Slavery from Roman Times to the Early Transatlantic Trade* (Minneapolis: University of Minnesota Press, 1985), 182.
2. Cf. the discussion of this in James Walvin, *Black Ivory: A History of British Slavery* (London: Fontana, 1993), 1–4.
3. Ibid., 9.

The equation of sugar and slavery brought into existence yet another major industry—the Atlantic slave trade. The Portuguese had begun this trade back in the sixteenth century but England was the major player by 1700. Until the abolition of the trade in 1807 England dominated the trade and made it a central fixture of its economy. Liverpool became the great commercial center of slavery sending out, at the height of the trade, nearly 200 ships annually capable of carrying about 50,000 slaves.[4] In one ten-year period (1783–93), the merchants of Liverpool transported 303,737 slaves to the West Indies.[5]

So lucrative were the profits from the trade in slaves that it became "inseparably associated with the commerce and welfare, and even the national security of Great Britain."[6] The trade employed about 5500 sailors and was credited with directly or indirectly generating nearly £6,000,000 sterling.[7] Slavery was "legalized by charters (1631, 1633, and 1672), by an act of Parliament (1698), and by treaty (1713, 1725, and 1748)."[8]

Despite its economic success, the Atlantic slave trade was notoriously cruel. Beyond the torment of being taken from homeland and family, the African captive suffered the miseries of "mid-passage." As many as five hundred were crammed into the hold of a slave ship. They were placed on shelves with no more than two and a half feet of headroom and without proper sanitation. Beatings were frequent. Captains routinely lost 10 percent of their human cargo to disease and death. But these were the fortunes of trade, and most were willing to overlook the cruelties of so profitable an institution.

Though slavery entered the nineteenth century enjoying the support of both great and small, it was eliminated by law within a few decades. At great expense and against the protests of plantation owners and politicians, slavery was ended by a moral crusade led by a small group of highborn evangelical zealots. These evangelical crusaders not only brought an effective end to the African slave trade but also inaugurated a new era of Christian missions on the African continent.[9] This chapter seeks to explain these startling events. Though many factors contributed to the success of the evangelical cause, new

4. Frank Klingberg, *The Anti-Slavery Movement in England* (Hamden: Archon, 1968), 13.
5. Garth Lean, *God's Politician* (London: Darton, Longman & Todd, 1980), 3.
6. Ernest Howse, *Saints in Politics: The "Clapham Sect" and the Growth of Freedom* (Toronto: University of Toronto Press, 1952), 28.
7. Lean, *God's Politician*, 3
8. Ibid., 29.
9. It has been objected that the loss of the American colonies to the rebels after 1776 reduced the value of the West Indies to the British economy. Hence the crusade against slavery succeeded because its economic values had already eroded. James Walvin points out in contrast that the plantations of the West Indies were profitable as late as the 1820s. The antislavery campaign was thus an example of moral principle rising above the profit motive. See Walvin, *Black Ivory*, 303.

views of the kingdom played a prominent role. The story of this new eschatology begins with the evangelical revivals of the 1740s.

The Revival of Evangelicalism and New Views of the Kingdom

Evangelical revivals in the eighteenth century. The rise of the Enlightenment in the seventeenth century had a deadening effect on European Christianity. Man was believed to be perfectible. All problems could be solved by the application of reason and the scientific method. Man must be his own savior and not rely on supernatural help from above. Deism was one religious expression of such views and sought to accommodate Enlightenment viewpoints by rejecting miracles, the resurrection of Christ, and the divine inspiration of the Bible. Even where Deism was rejected, a cold, formal Christianity prevailed.

In reaction to this deadened Christianity a number of renewal movements appeared in the 1730s and 1740s that sought to return the church to the truths of human sin and divine grace in salvation that had characterized the Reformation. Those who emphasized such truths were sometimes known as "new lights" or Methodists, but the label that stuck over time was "evangelical."

In the American Great Awakening of the 1740s, leaders such as Jonathan Edwards, Gilbert Tennent, and George Whitefield helped forge a powerful evangelical movement that dramatically altered American church and political life.[10] The evangelical revival in England, Scotland, and Wales under Whitefield and the Wesleys was similarly widespread. "There are few or no counties in England or Wales where there is not a work begun," wrote John Syms, an associate of Whitefield, in 1743.[11]

The cross, the new birth, and the coming kingdom. At the heart of these evangelical revivals were three powerful convictions. The first was the centrality of the death of Christ for salvation. A second was the necessity of the new birth. The third was a new eschatology that envisioned the spread of Christianity around the world as a prelude to Christ's personal return. These convictions reshaped the Protestant understanding of the kingdom of God and rekindled interest in global missions.

10. Among the leading studies of the Great Awakening are Joseph Tracy, *The Great Awakening* (New York: Arno, 1967), Edwin Gaustad, *The Great Awakening in New England* (Gloucester, Mass.: Peter Smith, 1965), and the collection of source documents by Miller and Heimert, *The Great Awakening* (Indianapolis: Bobbs-Merrill, 1967). For the British dimension of the Awakening, see A. Skevington Wood, *The Inextinguishable Blaze* (Grand Rapids: Eerdmans, 1969). The widest perspective on the Awakening is given in W. R. Ward, *Protestant Evangelical Awakening* (Cambridge: Cambridge University Press, 1992).

11. Quoted in Iain Murray, *The Puritan Hope* (Edinburgh: Banner of Truth Trust, 1971), 120.

Awakened evangelicals countered the moralism and humanism of the Enlightenment by emphasizing the cross of Christ. "Evangelicals preached other doctrines than the atoning death of Christ," wrote Brian Stanley, "but the cross was the very heart and essence of their message."[12] John Wesley insisted that nothing "is of greater consequence than the doctrine of Atonement. It is properly the distinguishing point between Deism and Christianity."[13]

Deism looked upon humankind as ignorant and needing enlightenment, not from the Bible but from nature. Evangelicalism looked upon humankind as dead in sin and needing a substitutionary atonement in order to be cleansed from sin. Deism saw the religions of the world as more or less the same. Evangelicalism, in light of the cross, saw the world's religions as expressions of idolatry and self-righteousness from which humanity needed to be saved. Idolatry was "the master sin of Heathenism" and the gospel was the only remedy for this lethal disease of the soul.[14]

The second defining conviction of revived evangelicalism was the idea of the new birth. Evangelicals taught that in order to benefit from the atoning sacrifice of Christ, one needed to be born again. This was the subjective side of the doctrine of the cross. The new birth was the most personal of the truths that came to dominate the revival era.

Wesley believed that next to the doctrine of justification, no doctrine was more fundamental to evangelicalism than the new birth, defined as "the renewing of our fallen human nature at the time of conversion."[15] At the head of Joseph Milner's list of distinctive doctrines that were necessary to salvation stood the "divine light, inspiration or illumination" of conversion.[16]

The experience of the new birth separated true Christianity from nominal Christianity and made the difference between heaven and hell. Those who were not "twice-born" were doomed. Hudson Taylor founded China Inland Mission in 1865 largely on the basis of the conviction that "a million a month" were "dying without God," by which he meant, dying without the conscious and heartfelt trust in Christ characteristic of the born-again Christian.[17]

The emphasis on the cross as the foundational work of God in redeeming a fallen world shifted the understanding of the kingdom of God from his providential rule in creation and culture to the rule of Christ over hearts. "To be a member of this kingdom," wrote H. R. Niebuhr, "is to be one who sees

12. Brian Stanley, *The Bible and the Flag* (Leicester: Apollos, 1990), 62.
13. Quoted in David Bebbington, *Evangelicalism in Modern Britain* (London: Unwin Hyman, 1989), 14.
14. Cf. Stanley, *Bible and Flag*, 64ff.
15. Bebbington, *Evangelicalism*, 3.
16. Ibid.
17. Stanley, *Bible and Flag*, 67.

the excellency and the beauty of God in Christ, and so loves him with all his heart for his own sake alone."[18]

But the rule of Christ over hearts was not a quiet experience. To be born again was to be changed at the root of one's being into an activist for the coming kingdom. The twice-born lived in militant opposition to the kingdom of darkness and focused their efforts toward the realization of the transformation of the earth through the gospel.

This confidence in the coming kingdom constituted the third defining conviction of the evangelical movement. If the new birth was the personal center of evangelicalism, the belief in the postmillennial return of Christ was the all-encompassing vision of history's meaning and purpose.

As desperate as the evangelical conviction appeared that most of the world was dying without knowledge of Christ, the fact of the matter was that evangelicals in the nineteenth century were optimists, convinced that the world was on the verge of a massive turning to Christianity. Christ's personal return would be preceded by the glorious reign of the church on the earth in which Christian belief and Christian civilization would be universal.

Jonathan Edwards, the leading evangelical theologian of the eighteenth century, was convinced that the message of redemption in Christ and regeneration by the Spirit was about to sweep across the globe. "We are taught also by this happy event [of revival]," Edwards wrote in a preface to *A Faithful Narrative of Surprising Conversions,* "how easy it will be for our blessed Lord to make a full accomplishment of all his predictions concerning his kingdom, and to spread his dominion from sea to sea, through all the nations of the earth."[19] Edwards added that he felt the millennium would begin in America.

In 1747 Edwards enlarged on his views of the coming kingdom in his *An Humble Attempt to Promote Explicit Agreement and Visible Union of God's People in Extraordinary Prayer for the Revival of Religion and the Advancement of Christ's Kingdom on Earth.*[20] Developing Augustine's view of history as the warfare between the City of God and the City of Man, Edwards believed that concerted prayer would help usher in the coming kingdom.

As several of Edwards' ministerial friends wrote in the preface, through prayer and revival we can advance "this universal and happy reign" of Christ on earth.[21] William Carey was convinced by Edwards that the conversion of

18. H. R. Niebuhr, *The Kingdom of God in America* (New York: Harper and Row, 1937), 112.

19. Jonathan Edwards, *The Great Awakening,* vol. 4 of *The Works of Jonathan Edwards,* ed. C. C. Goen (New Haven: Yale University Press, 1972), 132.

20. The text can be found in Jonathan Edwards, *Apocalyptic Writings,* vol. 5 of *The Works of Jonathan Edwards* (New Haven: Yale University Press, 1977), 307ff.

21. Ibid., 309.

the nations was necessary for the ushering in of the millennial reign of Christ.[22] Thomas Chalmers spoke of "that universal reign of truth and of righteousness which is coming."[23] Though some evangelicals were skeptical, "the postmillennial theory was evidently widespread."[24]

This postmillennial view of the coming kingdom encouraged the rise of the nineteenth-century missionary movement. "The content of their hope," according to Brain Stanley, "was not merely a conglomerate of individual conversions but a comprehensive revolution in 'heathen' society in which every aspect of that society would be pried from the grip of satanic dominion and submitted to the liberating lordship of Christ."[25] One of the ironies of nineteenth-century evangelicalism was that its eschatology, shaped in reaction to the Enlightenment, became an unconscious ally of the latter's rosy optimism and somewhat uncritical belief in the benefits of Western civilization and imperialism.[26]

These three doctrinal convictions born of the evangelical revivals led to an activism at home and abroad. New agencies modeled after trading societies were established to promote missions. Prominent among the early agencies were the Baptist Missionary Society (1792), the London Missionary Society (1795), and the Church Missionary Society (1799). The challenge taken up by these societies was the conversion and civilizing of the nations through the advance of "Christianity and Commerce."

William Wilberforce saw this creed as the key to curing the greatest single stain on Christian civilization in the West and the greatest obstacle to missionary advance in Africa—slavery. The horizons of the coming kingdom of justice and the rule of Christ in hearts were merging. For Wilberforce and his colleagues, missions and the spread of the kingdom of Christ in hearts was the great end. To promote that great end, abolition became a necessary means.[27]

---

22. See Bebbington, *Evangelicalism,* 62.

23. Ibid.

24. Ibid., 62–63. Boyd Hilton in *The Age of Atonement: The Influence of Evangelicalism on Social and Economic Thought, 1795–1865* (Oxford: Clarendon, 1988) describes the "extreme" evangelicals who were premillennial and generally hostile to the antislavery cause. Moderate evangelicals before 1840, according to Hilton, had more public influence than did the extremists, and their views of missions, eschatology, and social justice prevailed.

25. Stanley, *Bible and Flag,* 75.

26. See Stanley's discussion of this in *Bible and Flag,* 68–71.

27. "I took a very active part," wrote Wilberforce, "in that greatest of all causes, for I really place it before the Abolition, in which blessed be God we gained the victory—that I mean of laying a ground for the communication to our Indian fellow-subjects of Christian light and moral improvement." Quoted in Ford K. Brown, *Fathers of the Victorians* (Cambridge: Cambridge University Press, 1961), 108.

The Antislavery Campaign

Granville Sharp (1735–1813) and the beginnings of the antislavery movement. Granville Sharp was an evangelical believer who quite early made abolition the goal of his life. Sharp, though a grandson of the archbishop of York, was an obscure government clerk when his interest in the question of slavery was aroused.

In 1767 Sharp met Jonathan Strong, a slave from Barbados who had been so savagely beaten by his master that he almost lost his eyesight.[28] When Strong's master sold him to another planter who was returning to the Caribbean, the slave appealed to Sharp for help. Granville was successful in winning Strong's freedom in the courts, but no clear precedent was set. Sharp studied the law on this question and began representing other slaves who wanted to be declared free on English soil. His goal was to find a case that would firmly establish this policy. Such a case presented itself in 1771.

Lord Mansfield and the cases of James Somerset and Joseph Knight. In 1771 James Somerset had been brought to England by his master Charles Stewart. Once in England he had run away but had been forcibly recaptured and was about to be shipped back to Virginia. Sharp got wind of the case and appealed to the courts for a ruling.

A series of hearings from December 1771 to June 1772 debated the legality of slavery in England. Lord Mansfield, though hesitant to offer a judgment that would threaten the legal foundations of slavery, was forced to issue a verdict in favor of the slave's rights because "no master ever was allowed here to take a slave by force to be sold abroad."[29] This judgment was widely perceived as an emancipation proclamation for slaves in England. If there was any doubt about the meaning of this verdict, a similar case in 1778 involving the slave Joseph Knight established the rule that once a slave arrived in England he could not be sent "out of the country against his consent."[30] Slavery became functionally illegal in Britain.

In spite of these earlier victories a new case in 1783 made it clear how much work was ahead for Granville Sharp and his allies. In March of that year Sharp was visited by one of the leaders of the Black community in London, Olaudah Equiano (also known as Gustavus Vassa). Equiano alerted Sharp to the *Zong* affair. For insurance purposes, the captain of the slave ship *Zong* had thrown sick slaves overboard (thus making the insurance company liable for damaged property) rather than have them die on the ship (which would have exempted the insurance company of liability).

---

28. Walvin, *Black Ivory*, 13.
29. See the discussion of this case in ibid., 15.
30. Quoted in Klingberg, *Anti-Slavery Movement*, 40.

Sharp wanted the captain and his crew tried for murder. The justices decided that since slaves were property and not human beings before the law, the captain was justified in his actions and the insurance company liable. Sharp was outraged by this decision and sought to turn public opinion against so savage a judgment.

The pivotal year of 1787. In the wake of the *Zong* case Granville Sharp and a growing host of supporters decided to widen the arena of action. Several major developments in 1787 enlarged the scope of the antislavery campaign.

The first was the formation of a freed slave colony in the West African country of Sierra Leone. Once again Granville Sharp was the practical visionary behind the Sierra Leone scheme. After the Somerset and Strong decisions, there were growing numbers of freed slaves in England without employment. Additionally, a number of loyalist Blacks in Nova Scotia were anxious to find a more suitable climate than Maritime Canada. Members of both Black communities would be crucial in the settling of the new colony.

Sharp and the Sierra Leone company saw as their purpose "to colonize a small part of the coast of Africa, to introduce civilization among the natives, and to cultivate the soil by means of free labour, at the same time abjuring all concerns whatever in the odious traffic of human bodies."[31] To realize this dream 411 settlers under Captain Thompson left England on February 22, 1787. Of the hardships they faced in translating Sharp's vision into reality more will be said in the next chapter.

The second action was the formation of an antislavery society. Quakers had protested slavery for nearly a century and leading social philosophers such as John Locke, Adam Smith, and the Baron de Montesquieu had condemned the practice but popular sentiment against the institution occurred only after evangelical Methodists joined the protest.[32]

Wesley had written against the trade in 1774 in a pamphlet entitled *Thoughts on Slavery.* Though the Methodists tended to repeat the arguments against slavery pioneered by others, they were able to bring their "institutional strength to bear, on both sides of the Atlantic, as a vocal, highly organized pressure group opposed to the slave trade and, later, to slavery itself."[33] Wesley remained vocal in his opposition to the very end of his life. Four days before his death in 1791, Wesley wrote to Wilberforce instructing him to "Go on, in the name of God, and in the power of his might, till even American slavery (the vilest that ever saw the sun) shall vanish away before it."[34]

31. Quoted in C. P. Groves, *The Planting of Christianity in Africa*, vol. 1 (London: Lutterworth, 1948), 48.

32. Klingberg surveys the role of Enlightenment thinkers in protesting slavery (ibid., 34ff.).

33. James Walvin, *England, Slaves and Freedom, 1776–1838* (Jackson: University Press of Mississippi, 1986), 103.

34. Quoted in Klingberg, *Anti-Slavery Movement*, 47.

Granville Sharp sought to focus the protests of humanists and evangelicals through the formation of an antislavery society. In May 1787 the Society for the Abolition of the Slave Trade was brought into existence with Sharp as its first chairman. William Wilberforce was an early member along with eight Quakers and three other non-Quakers.

The committee, overruling the desires of the chairman, chose to direct their attack on the evils of the slave trade rather than the more complicated issue of slavery itself. Speaking tours were arranged. Thomas Clarkson wrote powerful tracts that were widely distributed and read. Members of Parliament were lobbied. Josiah Wedgewood designed a striking plaque for the society depicting a slave holding up his chained arms in prayer and uttering the words, "Am I not a man and a brother?" England had never seen a publicity campaign quite like it.[35]

Consciousness raising by Cugoano and Equiano. A third key event of 1787 was the publication of a book by Ottobah Cugoano, a Fanti from Ghana. Cugoano wrote about his life as a slave and appealed to the British government to bring an end to this great evil. Cugoano hoped to return to Africa as a missionary, an aspiration that was shared by many liberated slaves.[36]

His colleague in the Black community of London, Olaudah Equiano, was an Ibo from Nigeria. In 1789 he published *The Interesting Narrative of the Life of Olaudah Equiano, or Gustavus Vassa, the African,* in which he depicted his early life in Nigeria but also the fated day in 1756 when he was captured and brought to the coast. There he saw fierce-looking White men. He was put on board a ship where he saw "a multitude of black people of every description chained together, every one of their countenances expressing dejection and sorrow." At that moment, wrote Equiano, "I no longer doubted of my fate."[37]

After a period as a slave in Virginia he was sold to a slave owner in England. In 1777 he purchased his freedom and became a leader in the antislavery movement. Like Cugoano he called on Christian England to make Africa safe for Christianity and commerce and to bring to an end the traffic in slaves.

William Wilberforce (1759–1833) and the Clapham Sect. The forces of protest against slavery found their most able spokesperson in William Wilberforce. In 1780 at only twenty-one years of age he was elected to Parliament

35. Howard Temperley, *British Antislavery: 1833–1870* (Columbia: University of South Carolina Press, 1972), 3.
36. Lamin Sanneh, *West African Christianity: The Religious Impact* (Maryknoll: Orbis, 1983), 56.
37. From an excerpt of Equiano's *Narrative* in Basil Davidson, *The African Past: Chronicles from Antiquity to Modern Times* (Boston: Atlantic, Little and Brown, 1964), 243.

from Hull. In 1784 he switched his seat to Yorkshire. Converted to evangelical Christianity in 1785, he joined the "Clapham sect," a group of wealthy
and influential evangelicals who gathered at the home of the banker, Henry
Thornton, in the Clapham section of London.

John Venn had become rector in Clapham in 1792 and soon inspired
Thornton and his friends such as Hannah More, Sir James Stephens,
Granville Sharp, Zachary Macaulay, and Charles Grant to a more activist
faith. But the one who was regarded as "the very sun of the Claphimic system" was Wilberforce. Through the influence of his friends in the Clapham
sect and evangelical advisors such as John Newton, Wilberforce came to believe that evangelical convictions required practical action for the liberation
of the oppressed. When he made these views public in a book, *A Practical
View of the Prevailing Religious System of Professed Christians*, published
in 1797, he found a responsive audience.

Early attempts to pass legislation against the slave trade in 1789 had
ended in failure. By 1807 the climate had changed and Wilberforce was able
to gain passage of a bill that made the slave trade illegal. In 1812 Wilberforce
moved from Yorkshire to a safe seat, which he occupied until his retirement
from Parliament in 1825. Even in retirement he worked vigorously for the
final defeat of slavery. Though the antislavery campaign had many heroes,
Wilberforce was the one remembered by freed slave and moral crusader
alike. As a Jamaican slave song of 1816 put it: "Oh me good friend, Mr. Wilberforce, make we free!"[38]

The victory of 1833. Upon Wilberforce's retirement the leadership of the antislavery campaign in Parliament fell to Thomas Buxton (1786–1845). In
1823 he helped found, along with his mentor Wilberforce, the British and
Foreign Antislavery Society to galvanize public opinion against slavery itself.
The harsh repression of a slave revolt in Jamaica led by the saintly Samuel
Sharpe aided the antislavery cause in England. Churches signed numerous abolitionist petitions in the early 1830s attacking an institution that was "highly
offensive in the sight of God, disgraceful to us, as a free and a Christian people."[39] In 1833 the Abolition of Slavery Bill declared that all slaves in British
dominions were to be freed on August 1, 1834. Though various schemes of
"apprenticeship" were used by slave owners to stall the implementation of the
law, the legislation of 1833 was the effective end of slaveholding in the empire. Wilberforce died knowing that his life cause had been realized.

Christianity and Commerce. With the defeat of slavery, evangelical energies
were redirected toward the twin tasks of missions and civilization in Africa.

38. Quoted in Walvin, *England*, 131.
39. Ibid., 154.

The dreaded trade was still being carried on by foreign governments (particularly Portugal), and Thomas Buxton sought to strike slavery at its root by transforming the economics of Africa.

In 1839 Buxton published *The Africa Slave Trade and Its Remedy* in which he offered the prescription for the glorious transformation of Africa through "encouraging commerce and Christianity" and "diffusing the blessings of Christianity."[40] Beyond founding settlements like Freetown in Sierra Leone, Buxton envisioned the formation of vast networks of trade to "effectually check the Slave Trade and produce a revolution in Africa."[41] Buxton's enthusiasm for capitalism is a reminder how closely evangelicals lined up with certain notions of the Enlightenment. The superiority of free enterprise, the belief in progress, and the providential right of imperialism were liberally mixed with the earlier convictions about the cross, the new birth, and the postmillennial reign of Christ.[42]

Acting on Buxton's advice the British government sent an expedition to the Niger River Delta in 1841. The expedition intended to lay the foundation for legitimate trade as well as to establish a base for missions in the area. Death and disease soon brought an end to this effort and the expedition was recalled. Buxton was shocked and disgraced by the failure of this project. He died a broken man in 1845 and a sad symbolic end to a glorious half century of evangelical achievement.

Conclusion

How should the modern reader view the antislavery campaign of the evangelicals from the 1780s to the 1830s? Some, like the late African historian Walter Rodney, have dismissed this campaign as motivated purely by economic self-interest. "The economic interpretation of [slavery]," argues Rodney, "suggests that changes in productivity, technology and patterns of exchange in Europe and the Americas made it necessary for the British to end their participation in the trade in 1807."[43] Rodney was supporting the earlier criticisms of Dr. Eric Williams, who argued in *Capitalism and Slavery* that overproduction of sugar during the Napoleonic wars rendered slavery unprofitable.

But these views represent the minority opinion. The historical consensus favors the judgment of Roger Anstey that slavery was still profitable in the

40. Thomas Buxton, *The Africa Slave Trade and Its Remedy* (London: Cass and Ltd, 1967, orig. 1839), 399.
41. Ibid.
42. See Stanley's discussion in *Bible and Flag*, 68–69.
43. Walter Rodney, "Africa in Europe and the Americas," in Richard Gray, ed., *Cambridge History of Africa*, vol. 4 (Cambridge: Cambridge University Press, 1975), 598.

early nineteenth century. Slavery was opposed and defeated because behind "the political activity of the religiously minded men who constituted the core of the abolitionist lobby was a theology of a profoundly dynamic kind and one which . . . had a profound significance on the development of a theology of antislavery and for future reform."[44] Wilberforce, Sharp, and the evangelicals who fought the injustices of slavery were fired not by economic self-interest but by new visions of the kingdom. "From the assurance that their sins were forgiven," wrote Dr. Anstey, "through the Grace of God in the redemptive work of Christ, they knew not only that they could overcome evil in their own hearts but also that they could conquer the evils in the world which they felt called to combat."[45]

Despite the failures of the expedition of 1841, the postmillennial visionaries of the kingdom were not daunted. Providence lent a hand where individual efforts seemed to fail. Though the British Navy did what they could to intercept slave ships and liberate the captives on the African shore, what "finally extinguished the slave trade" was "the cessation of the demand on the other side of the Atlantic." Ultimate success came only when "the victory of the North over the slave owning South of the United States in 1865 was rounded off by the final abolition of slavery in both Cuba and Brazil in the 1880s."[46]

The providential rule of God that had so inspired earlier theocratic witnesses to the kingdom seemed to be joining with the evangelical emphasis on the rule of Christ over hearts and the coming kingdom of justice. The three emphases, perhaps for the first time in history since the early church, were converging together on the continent of Africa. A glorious century was ahead in which the kingdom of God after many false starts throughout Africa's previous history would at last be realized.

Yet the evangelical vision of the kingdom contained an inner tension. By combining the new birth with postmillennial optimism and capitalistic enthusiasm, the ambiguous witness of Western evangelicalism to the kingdom of Christ was mingled with a confidence in the kingdoms of man. Augustine's theology of the two kingdoms in conflict gives insight into this inner tension, which would be imported into Africa by evangelical churchmen and missionaries and would intensify Africa's perennial wrestling with the complexities of the kingdom.

44. Quoted in Lean, *God's Politician*, 64.
45. Ibid.
46. Roland Oliver and J. D. Fage, *A Short History of Africa* (London: Penguin, 1988), 117.

Kingdom and Community in West Africa

In 1787, 411 settlers (mostly freed slaves from London) landed on the shore of Frenchman's Bay in Sierra Leone to begin an experiment in Christian community in Africa. A small microcosm of the reign of Christ was being set up on Africa's western coast. Hopes were high.

The settlers dreamed of land and commerce. What they found was hunger and disease. Within a year most of the settlers were dead. Granville Sharp and Zachary Macaulay, convinced that the kingdom was progressively unfolding around the earth and eager to strengthen their hand in the antislavery battles in England, fought to keep the kingdom community of Sierra Leone alive. Their prayers and efforts were answered in 1792 (the very year William Carey published his Enquiry urging apathetic British Christians to engage in global mission) when 1,200 former slaves arrived from Canada to join the visionary experiment of the Clapham sect. Their arrival was dramatic. As small boats brought the ex-slaves to shore they sang hymns to God. After landing they gathered in the open air to worship their liberating king with the words, "The day of jubilee is come, Return ye ransomed sinners home."[1]

Conscious that they, like the Puritans who went to New England, were building a city set on a hill, the new settlers renamed the settlement "Freetown," for it would be a community where the liberating power of the gospel to break the chains of sin and slavery would be demonstrated. Freetown was intended to be "a Christian settlement into which freed slaves would be concentrated and from which Christianity would emerge as an attractive religion."[2]

Enlightenment mythology, evangelical eschatology, and kingdom community. Freetown was an expression of an evangelical dream fueled by Enlightenment views of progress. A half century before Freetown's founding, Jonathan Edwards, the leading evangelical theologian of his generation, wrote of the day when the veil would be taken off the eyes of Africa.

1. Christopher Fyfe, *A History of Sierra Leone* (London: Oxford University Press, 1962), 36–37.
2. Lamin Sanneh, *West African Christianity: The Religious Impact* (Maryknoll: Orbis, 1983), 53.

Then all countries and nations, even those which are now most ignorant, shall be full of light and knowledge. Great knowledge shall prevail everywhere. It may be hoped that then many of the Negroes and Indians will be divines, and that excellent books will be published in Africa, in Ethiopia, in Tartary, and other now the most barbarous countries; and not only learned men, but others of more ordinary education, shall then be very knowing in religion.[3]

All this would be accomplished by revivals, declared Edwards. But for Edwards true revival was the revival not just of isolated individuals but of an entire believing community. So powerful was this theme of corporate renewal that one summary of his model of revival defines it as "an extraordinary work of God the Holy Spirit reinvigorating and propagating Christian piety in a *community*."[4]

The postmillennialism of Edwards and many of the evangelicals who labored in the antislavery crusade in England and America envisioned the liberation of Africa and the world through a widening circle of awakenings and an enthusiastic embrace of Western civilization by newly established Christian communities. Though the vision of the future that moved Western evangelicalism to engage in their African mission is drawn largely from the Bible, there is additionally a connection between the postmillennialism of the evangelicals and the idea of progress found in the Enlightenment. "It is only more recently," observes Brian Stanley, "that historians have come to recognize that Evangelicalism, even as it reacted against the Enlightenment, also borrowed a great deal from it."[5] The idea that the witness to the kingdom throughout the world would be steady and progressive seemed to be a working assumption.

Blyden's vision of kingdom community. One hears this mixture of humanistic optimism and evangelical eschatology in the voice of E. W. Blyden, a leading African American missionary, free thinker, and statesman of Liberia. As the nineteenth century progressed, the vision of a revived African Christian community transforming Africa from within through the gospel was kept alive, even in the face of crushing disillusionment. The movement retained a number of visionaries such as Blyden who, in 1887, eloquently repeated the persistent dream of a kingdom community in Africa.

In visions of the future, I behold those beautiful hills—the banks of those charming streams, the verdant plains and flowery fields, the salubrious highlands in primaeval innocence and glory, and those fertile districts watered

---

3. Jonathan Edwards, *The Works of Jonathan Edwards*, vol. 1 (Edinburgh: Banner of Truth, 1974), 609.

4. J. I. Packer, *A Quest for Godliness* (Wheaton: Crossway, 1990), 318.

5. Brian Stanley, *The Bible and the Flag* (Leicester: Apollos, 1990), 62.

everywhere as the garden of the Lord; I see them all taken possession of by the returning exiles from the West, trained for the work of rebuilding waste places under severe discipline and hard bondage. I see, too, their brethren hastening to welcome them from the slopes of the Niger, and from its lovely valleys—Mohammedans and Pagans, chiefs and people, all coming to catch something of the inspiration the exiles have brought—to share in the borrowed jewels they have imported, and to march back hand in hand with their returned brethren towards the sunrise for the regeneration of the continent. And under their united labours, I see the land rapidly reclaimed—raised from the slumber of ages and rescued from a stagnant barbarism; and then to the astonishment of the whole world, in a higher sense than has yet been witnessed, "Ethiopia shall suddenly stretch out her hands unto God."[6]

By the close of the nineteenth century this kingdom dream of a regenerated Africa where converts from Islam and traditional religion marched "hand in hand" with brethren from the West was in sad disarray. Because Freetown represented the beginning of the fulfillment of this postmillennial dream, its establishment and early progress held special meaning. Yet West African Christianity was destined to become deeply divided along lines of race and money.

Though postmillennial dreams of a heavenly community of saints on earth were not realized, Christianity in West Africa nevertheless attempted to witness to the kingdom by its message of personal salvation and the establishing of communities of transformed saints. Though they fell short of kingdom ideals, West African Christians, both White and Black, remind us that even failed attempts can be powerful witnesses to the kingdom.

The Founding of Kingdom Communities: Freetown, Badagry, and Abeokuta

Early contact with West Africa. As Portuguese influence waned in the late eighteenth century other European nations established contact with West Africa. The Netherlands, Denmark, and England all sent out ships to explore and initiate trade along the African coast. In the early eighteenth century English Christianity entered West Africa through Thomas Thomson who came to Cape Coast in 1752 as an SPG chaplain for English traders. His successor was Philip Quaque (d. 1916), a European educated missionary of African descent (as had been the case earlier with Jacobis Capitein of the Dutch Reformed Church). But it was really later in the century that a new era in West African Christianity truly dawned. By 1780 Britain had established a domi-

6. E. W. Blyden, *Christianity, Islam and the Negro Race* (Edinburgh: University Press, 1967, orig. 1887), 129.

nant interest in Sierra Leone, and it was there that the forces of antislavery first looked when they sought a solution to the problem of the "Black poor" in London.

Developments in Freetown. While the vision of Granville Sharp, Zachary Macaulay, and the Clapham sect was crucial in the founding of Sierra Leone in 1787, the practical realities of the first five years of settlement such as lack of land, food, trade, and hostile raids by the local chief (King Jimmy) nearly destroyed the holy experiment. The Nova Scotians, mostly Baptists, were the decisive element in the survival of the community.

Outstanding leaders such as David George and Thomas Peters established Baptist churches and worked alongside early governor John Clarkson to promote the colony in England. Moses Wilkinson sought to strengthen Christian community with his work on behalf of the Methodists. The Countess of Huntington's connection also worked in Freetown to help the experiment succeed. These groups worked in harmony alongside Anglican chaplains who serviced the spiritual needs of the original settlers. In a short period of time Maroons (ex-slaves from Jamaica) and missionaries from Europe enlarged the growing colony. In 1808 it was officially brought under the English Crown.[7]

The colony grew more through trade than through agriculture. It also grew through the founding of a number of schools. The best known, Fourah Bay College, was begun in 1827 by the Church Missionary Society (CMS) after a number of false starts. The purpose of the college was to train Africans as missionaries, pastors, catechists, and teachers. Just as Harvard was founded by New England Puritans in order to insure qualified spiritual leaders for their Bible commonwealths, so Fourah Bay College would serve to push forward the kingdom vision of a Christian community. In 1876 it began to award degrees from the University of Durham.

Samuel Onyeidu noted that most "African agents were trained on the job rather than in the missionary institutions."[8] The shortage of missionary agents would not be met primarily by Europeans, African Americans, or descendants of the Black poor from London. The majority of evangelists and missionaries to extend the kingdom community of Freetown throughout West Africa would be drawn from the ranks of the recaptives.

Recaptives. Even while Freetown was expanding as a model Christian community, the rest of West Africa continued to ply the slave trade. Through the work of Wilberforce and others, Britain decided in 1807 to ban the slave

7. Sanneh, *West African Christianity*, 59.

8. Samuel Onyeidu, "The African Lay Agents of the Church Missionary Society in West Africa: 1810–1850" (unpublished M.Litt. thesis, University of Aberdeen, 1978), 403.

trade from British territories. Soon the British Navy was patrolling the waters off the West African coast. Slave ships that were intercepted were forced to transfer their human cargo to the care of the British Navy.

Freetown became the primary destination for these "recaptives." In 1808 the settlement numbered about two thousand. Over the next decades seventy-four thousand recaptives would join them. Though many adopted English European dress and went to Freetown schools, not all the recaptives embraced Christianity. Most were of Yoruba origin and a percentage retained their Muslim religious heritage liberally mingled with elements of Yoruba folk religion.

Yet the majority of the recaptives accepted the gospel of Christianity and commerce. As one recaptive confessed, "We know that England and indeed Europe owes her prosperity, greatness, and security mainly to Christianity."[9] Whether Christian or Muslim or traditionalist, the recaptives built their own distinctive culture in Sierra Leone (called Creole) and shaped their own unique language, Krio, which like their culture was a mixture of indigenous and Western elements.

Out of this Creole subculture came the most famous of the recaptives—Samuel Ajayi Crowther (1806–91). Born in the Yoruba town of Osogon, Crowther spent a childhood interrupted by war. In 1821 his village was destroyed and Crowther became a domestic slave in Abeokuta. His fear of the shrines that lined the roads out of Abeokuta prevented attempts at escape.

Crowther was eventually sold to a slaver destined for the Portuguese colony of Brazil. His ship was intercepted by the British Navy and he found himself in Freetown. Crowther joined the newly opened Fourah Bay College in 1827 and upon graduation he became a teacher there. After participating in the Niger Expedition of 1841 he published his journals, which brought him wide recognition. Ordination in London followed in 1843, thereby making him Sierra Leone's first priest. He became Africa's first Anglican bishop in 1864.[10]

But Crowther was not destined for quiet pastoral work. He was restless for mission. Like St. Patrick of Ireland, his burden was to return to his former captors and share with them the liberation he had found in Christ. Crowther

9. Quoted in Elizabeth Isichei, *A History of Christianity in Africa* (Grand Rapids: Eerdmans, 1995), 163.

10. There appears to be no modern critical biography of Crowther. The only book-length biography of Crowther seems to be Jesse Page, *The Black Bishop* (1908), built upon an earlier life of Crowther written in 1888. Brief sketches of Crowther's life have been drawn by J. F. Ajayi in P. Curtin, ed., *Africa Remembered* (1967), and by J. Loiello in Elizabeth Isichei, ed., *Varieties of Christian Experience in Nigeria* (1982). P. McKenzie focused on a single aspect of Crowther's life and work in his 1976 study, *Inter-Religious Encounter in West Africa: Samuel Ajayi Crowther's Attitude to African Traditional Religion and Islam.* The best brief treatment is A. F. Walls' "Samuel Ajayi Crowther," in G. Anderson, ed., *Mission Legacies* (Maryknoll: Orbis, 1995).

would export the blessings of Freetown's Christian community to Nigeria's communities of fear and war.

Badagry and Abeokuta. The success of Freetown inspired attempts to establish other Christian communities. Between 1839 and 1842, while Crowther was sailing up the Niger, hundreds of recaptives returned to western Nigeria.

Badagry was the first destination for the returning exiles. It was hardly an ideal spot for the planting of a Christian commonwealth. Badagry was a slave mart on the Nigerian coast. The dream of a Christian community there had originally belonged to two Hausa men who, having been freed from slavery in Trinidad, had traveled through Freetown in 1837 on their way to Badagry. So much enthusiasm for their scheme was generated among the recaptives that a number of them contributed to the purchase of a ship, the *Queen Victoria*. In 1839 with sixty-seven passengers and a hull full of goods for trade, the *Queen Victoria* made a successful voyage to Badagry and back.

Thomas Will, a leader of the Creole community, sought government approval and backing for the establishment of a British colony in Badagry. The petition was rejected but permission was granted for a private venture. "Before long," writes Lamin Sanneh, "a stream of settlers started arriving there from Freetown, carried in ships owned by themselves and supported from their own funds."[11]

The new settlers in Badagry were joined by an English Methodist missionary of African descent, Thomas Birch Freeman, later to enjoy a distinguished missionary career in Ghana (Gold Coast). When Freeman arrived in 1842, he helped establish a church among the recaptives that would be the base for the christianization of a number of surrounding areas.

One of those surrounding areas that Freeman had his eye on was Abeokuta. He sent a message to Shodeke, the chief of Abeokuta, requesting permission to visit. The king responded warmly and sent an escort to accompany Freeman.[12] Within a short time the returned exiles numbered three thousand.[13] Among that number was Samuel Crowther, who had returned to the village of his captivity in 1844 to minister alongside CMS missionaries Henry Townsend and C. A. Gollmer. Crowther, after more than twenty years of separation, was reunited with his mother, Afala, and sisters. When Crowther's mother attempted to offer a sacrifice to the traditional gods she was stopped by her son, whose actions signaled that a new religious order had come.[14]

Though persecution of Christians broke out in Abeokuta in 1849 after Shodeke's death, the recaptives continued to come and their new faith was

---

11. Sanneh, *West African Christianity*, 81.
12. Peter Falk, *The Growth of the Church in Africa* (Grand Rapids: Zondervan, 1979), 124.
13. Isichei, *History of Christianity in Africa*, 170.
14. Falk, *Growth of the Church in Africa*, 125.

increasingly accepted. The conversion of three *babalawo* in the 1860s under the ministry of Samuel Pearse, an Egba from Sierra Leone, illustrates the powerful reception that Christianity enjoyed in Abeokuta. The *babalawo* were diviners of the cult of Ifa associated with Ife in Yorubaland. The dramatic and deep conversion of these three professional diviners came at great personal cost.[15]

The success of Christianity at centers such as Badagry and Abeokuta is unique in nineteenth-century West African missions. Christianity was brought to the Yoruba by other Yoruba, returning exiles who had suffered much but who had found the Christian God an unequaled help through their hardships. The foreignness of the gospel was thus minimal, and its incarnation in a Christian community composed of their own kin proved to be too powerful a witness for the Yoruba to resist long.[16] While Christianity spread to Calabar, Bonny, Lagos, and numerous centers along the Niger, it would seldom match the success it enjoyed in the homeland of the recaptives.

The missionaries—agents of Christian community. Badagry and Abeokuta remind us of the role of the African diaspora in the expansion of Christianity in Africa, a role that has been underplayed in the past. Yet the story of West African Christianity and to a large extent the whole of sub-Saharan Christianity is the story of African initiative. As Andrew Walls has written:

> There is something symbolic in the fact that the first church in tropical Africa in modern times was not a missionary creation at all. It arrived ready-made, a body of people of African birth or descent who had come to faith in Christ as plantation slaves or as soldiers in the British army during the American War of Independence, or as farmers or squatters in Nova Scotia after it.[17]

The contributions of men like Samuel Crowther, Samuel Lewis, David George, Samuel Pearse, and Thomas Birch Freeman to the success of the postmillennial vision of an expanding Christian civilization in Africa cannot be overestimated.

Alongside the missionaries of African descent worked a number of Europeans. They were but a trickle at the beginning of the nineteenth century. Few could foresee that they would be a flood by its end. There were a few signs early in the century that a foreign missionary movement was on the rise.

---

15. Adrian Hastings, *The Church in Africa: 1450–1950* (Oxford: Clarendon, 1994), 352–53.

16. Ibid., 341.

17. A. F. Walls, "The Significance of Christianity in Africa" (The St. Colm's Lecture, 1989, Edinburgh, unpublished), 5, quoted in Kwame Bediako, "Cry Jesus! Christian Theology and Presence in Modern Africa," *Vox Evangelica* 23 (1993): 11.

Religious revival, postmillennial eschatology, global exploration, and evangelical biblicism all pointed to a bright future for the missionary enterprise.

But the surest sign was the proliferation of mission agencies. The formation of the Baptist Missionary Society in 1792 was followed by a dizzying array of agencies in the next few decades: the nondenominational London Missionary Society in 1795; the Church Missionary Society in 1799; the American Board of Commissioners for Foreign Missions in 1810; the Wesleyan Methodists in England in 1813; and the Basel Mission Society in 1814 followed soon after by societies in Berlin, Paris, Leipzig, and Bremen. "What in 1780 existed in the Protestant world as at most the rather idiosyncratic concern of a handful of Moravians was by 1840 central almost to the very *raison d'être* of all the mainline churches as understood by their more lively and enthusiastic membership."[18]

A particularly striking factor about these new agencies was their independence from government control. Unlike during the Portuguese era, missionaries in the nineteenth century tended to be free of government funding or direction. The new agencies, following the model created by William Carey in 1792, were organized like trading companies with interested partners "buying shares" (making donations).

The missionaries sent out by these new agencies were simple men and women often with little formal education, "convinced that training, education, and theology were rather pointless."[19] Typical was Mary Slessor (d. 1915), who joined the Calabar Mission in 1876. Her childhood was spent as a mill worker in Dundee, Scotland. Her humble pedigree gave her a heart for the poor that won her the love of Africans and acclaim by the international community.

The early European missionary to West Africa was often nonordained. Ordination was sometimes given to those who stuck it out on the field even though they had few qualifications. They tended to be poor evangelists but quickly realized the value of the African convert as a key to successful evangelism.

The one area perhaps more than any other where the missionary from abroad shone brightest was in the area of language and translation. African missionaries like Crowther had engaged in linguistic and translation work. The expatriates, generally, devoted themselves to the study of African languages with an intensity that won the admiration of their African colleagues. Samuel Crowther's CMS associate on the Niger expedition, J. F. Schoen, mastered the Ibo and Hausa languages, writing a grammar for the latter. In 1877 Schoen was awarded the Volney prize by the French Institute for his linguistic work. Gustav Nyländer began his work in Sierra Leone in 1806. By

---

18. Hastings, *Church in Africa: 1450–1950*, 245.
19. Ibid., 258.

1812 he had mastered Bulom Sherbo and had translated Matthew's Gospel into that vernacular.

Johann Christaller, the son of a tailor and a baker's daughter, came to Ghana with the Basel Mission. He spent most of his life studying and translating Scripture into the Twi language. Christaller's Twi dictionary "gave the Akan an important instrument for cultural self-awareness in the context of the advancing machinery of colonial subjugation."[20]

S. W. Koelle, a CMS missionary who had trained at Basel, may have excelled all others with his *Polyglotta Africana*. Compiled from notes taken in interviews with the recaptives passing through Sierra Leone, the *Polyglotta* is a comparison of about 300 words and phrases in 150 African languages. It won its author several prestigious academic awards in Europe. Such language work not only laid a foundation for later language studies but, more important, "it welded the expression of . . . Christian worship to the native tongue."[21]

Missions in Sierra Leone. Missionaries did more than language study and translation. They frequently worked side by side with African pastors and catechists in evangelism, education, and church planting. Wesleyan Methodists such as Joseph Brown, George Warren, and William Davies were pioneers of their church in Sierra Leone but a rash of deaths depleted the missionary ranks and the work was carried on by their Creole counterparts.[22]

The Quakers were represented by Hannah Kilham. She came to Freetown permanently in 1830 (after two earlier visits) already having learned the Wolof and Mandinka languages. She started a school for recaptive girls in Charlotte Village near Freetown teaching in Mende and Aku (a Yoruba dialect). She held progressive views about the teaching of English as a second language.

The CMS sent their first two missionaries to Sierra Leone in 1804. Melchior Renner and Peter Hartwig were assigned to work among the Susu in the country. Their personal conflicts with one another ("great crowds used to gather outside their house to listen")[23] did not bode well for the future. Though Renner persisted, Hartwig eventually gave up missions and became a slave trader.

The CMS tried again in 1806 and sent out three more missionaries: Leopold Butscher, Johann Prasse, and Gustav Nyländer. Nyländer was extremely successful both in setting up schools and in language work. Prasse focused on the Susu. Butscher returned to Freetown, where he worked in industrial education at the Christian Institute (the forerunner of Fourah Bay

20. Lamin Sanneh, *Encountering the West: Christianity and the Global Cultural Process* (Maryknoll: Orbis, 1993), 83.

21. Quoted in Kwame Bediako, "Cry Jesus!" 9.

22. Sanneh, *West African Christianity,* 64.

23. Ibid., 60.

College). There Butscher developed his pioneering ideas about slavery and commerce—ideas that would later be picked up and given a wider audience by British antislavery crusader Thomas Buxton.

Roman Catholicism had been active in Sierra Leone as far back as 1605. In the late eighteenth century an African king, Signor Domingo, the Temne chief at Royema, not only embraced the Roman Catholic faith but had also sent a son to England for training. However, missionary efforts waned during the late eighteenth and early nineteenth centuries. After early failure, the Holy Ghost Fathers initiated work in Sierra Leone in 1864. Catholic growth was slow for much of the rest of the century.

Church, missions, and Christian community. By the middle of the century, Freetown, Badagry, and Abeokuta were shining examples of the kingdom of God in Africa—outposts of Christian faith and harmony where the benefits of the rule of Christ could be tangibly seen. Yet signs of discord threatened to wreck the holy experiment. Missionary infighting reached such a serious level that the CMS sent out Edward Bickerswith, a lawyer,[24] in 1816 to restore order. More ominous was the occasional conflict between African and missionary.

John Ezzidio was a recaptive who became a lay leader in the Methodist church in Freetown. He gave himself sacrificially to build up the work until soon there was a thriving congregation. The burden of pastoral care for the busy layman became so great that Ezzidio appealed to the English Methodists for missionary assistance. The man they sent was Benjamin Tregaskis.

Tregaskis was a troubled man who soon sowed discord in the Freetown church. He used his position as a foreign missionary to win a following for himself that only deepened divisions with the other members of the church. Ezzidio's efforts to reconcile were futile. Tregaskis attacked his former benefactor with open contempt and venom. When Ezzidio died, "Tregaskis was seen to rejoice openly at the graveside."[25] The missionary went on to rule the Methodist churches in Sierra Leone and Gambia in a dictatorial manner. The experiment in Christian community had suffered a blow but it was only a single incident, however prophetic it might be of the future.

One mission leader who reacted to the Tregaskis–Ezzidio affair was Henry Venn (1796–1873), the secretary of the CMS from 1841. Venn accepted Leopold Butscher's idea that Christianity and commerce was the best formula for the defeat of the slave trade and the liberation of the continent. But Venn went further than most missionary strategists (the American Rufus Anderson excepted) in drawing out the implications of an economically independent Africa for the building of the African church.

24. Ibid., 62.
25. Ibid., 65.

Venn was inspired by the classic text of the Great Commission in Matthew 28:19–20 with its emphasis on the full discipleship of "native" churches ("teaching them to observe all things that I have commanded you"). Based on this line of thought Venn developed the celebrated concept of a "three-self" church—self-supporting, self-propagating, and self-governing.

As Venn looked at the Sierra Leone situation and applied his theories he objected to expatriate pastors ruling the African churches on the grounds that it "would be too apt to create a feeble and dependent native Christian community."[26] To counter the possibility of foreign missionaries dominating the West African church Venn developed the idea of the native church pastorate. In 1861 the CMS placed nine parishes in the hands of national pastors. The CMS also withdrew support, arguing that finding local means of support was necessary to the maturing of the church.

Venn believed that the indigenization of the African church would promote a new unity in the church's witness to the kingdom. "Let a native church be organized as a national institution," Venn argued, because, "as the native church assumes a national character, it will ultimately supersede the denominational distinctions which are now introduced by Foreign Missionary Societies."[27]

Such thinking was supported by the postmillennial optimism of so many evangelicals. But not all missionaries shared Venn's progressive views. E. W. Blyden, who worked with the CMS for a short time, wrote appreciatively to Venn about his views and warned that "dark will be the day for Africa when the active influence of Henry Venn is taken from the African Church." Blyden's comment was prophetic. Venn's death in 1874 would severely test the Christian communities of West Africa and intensify the power struggle between expatriate and African for leadership of these new communities of Christ.

The Expansion of Kingdom Communities in West and Central Africa

Liberia. The experiment of Freetown was hailed as a glorious success by the antislavery forces in England and North America. In the United States, abolitionists were inspired to follow the Sierra Leone example. They sought a suitable location in West Africa where a Christian community for liberated slaves (numbering about 250,000 by 1820) could be built.[28]

26. Quoted in J. F. A. Ajayi, "Henry Venn and the Policy of Development," in Ogbu Kalu, ed., *The History of Christianity in West Africa* (London: Longman, 1980), 66.
27. Ibid.
28. Ibid., 90.

The American Colonization Society (ACS) was formed with the enthusiastic endorsement of thousands of African Americans. In 1820 the ACS sent out an expedition led by the Rev. Samuel Bacon numbering eighty-eight liberated slaves. Their purpose was to find and procure a large tract of land that could become a new nation peopled by liberated slaves from the New World. After a brief stop in Sierra Leone the party ventured down the coast to Sherbo, where the marsh and mud proved nearly disastrous. They retreated back to Freetown and regrouped.

Dr. Eli Ayers and a naval officer, Lieutenant Robert Stockton, were charged with finding a more suitable site. They sailed to the area around Cape Mesuardo immediately south of Sierra Leone. The coastlands of the Cape looked promising. Negotiations began with the local leader, King Peter. When the king attempted to drive a hard bargain, Lt. Stockton held a pistol to King Peter's head. The deal was closed. Millions of dollars worth of land was purchased at gun point for about $300 worth of trinkets, rum, and guns. The beginnings of a new kingdom community that would be a light to the nations of Africa was off to a rocky start.

The first settlement was to be named Christopolis, the City of Christ. Augustine would have been pleased. But in the end political loyalties rose above such pious gestures and the small community was named Monrovia after the American president, James Monroe.[29]

Fear of local hostilities consumed the young settlers. The threat of attack from an angry and unreconciled King Peter was constant. In August 1822 Jehudi Ashmun, a White agent of the ACS, was sent to act as Monrovia's governor and chief military officer. His major tasks were to organize the community's defense and deal with growing internal conflicts among the settlers. Ashmun found that dealing with African tribes was at times easier than managing Christian settlers. There were two revolts against his leadership, both involving Lott Carey, the settlement's health officer and Ashmun's second in command. The second revolt forced Ashmun to flee for his life. Soon after, a compromise was reached and normalcy was restored. But Ashmun knew his days were numbered, and citing health issues, returned to America in March 1828, leaving Lott Carey in command.

Lott Carey (1780–1829) proved to be a worthy successor to Ashmun. Fired by a missionary vision forged in the Second Great Awakening in America, Carey had come to Liberia not as a settler but as a missionary. Carey's sole purpose in Africa was to "found a Christian colony which might prove a blessed asylum."[30]

Carey was born in 1780 to slave parents bound to a Virginia farmer. In 1807 Carey became a Christian and five years later he purchased freedom for

29. Isichei, *History of Christianity in Africa*, 165.
30. Quoted in Sanneh, *West African Christianity*, 94.

himself and his two children. His zeal for the evangelization of Africa led him to join the African Baptist Mission Society, which underwrote his support. It was decided that he would cooperate with the American Board of Commissioners for Foreign Missions who were joining forces with the American Colonization Society in the Liberia venture, an alliance that Carey questioned from the beginning.[31] Carey served the new colony in many ways as missionary, doctor, governor, and soldier.

What kind of leadership he would have provided over time will never be known because his administration was cut short by his death in 1829. An accidental explosion occurred while Carey was organizing a rescue party for some captured colonists.[32] "To him," wrote a contemporary, "was the colony indebted more than to any other man, except Ashmun."[33]

Despite the loss of its early leaders Liberia survived. By 1866 the new colony numbered about 18,000, approximately a third of whom were recaptives. A new constitution had been formed in 1847 officially joining Monrovia and its various spinoff settlements into the Republic of Liberia with its motto "the love of liberty brought us here."[34] Like the New England Puritans before them, the colonizers confined liberty only to themselves and did not extend it to the indigenous people. The conflict that had commenced with Lt. Stockton's pistol grew greater as the decades wore on.

As the nation evolved, missions advanced. The Methodists built their first church in Monrovia in 1832. Baptists began work in 1833. Catholic work in Liberia began with a Philadelphia priest, Fr. Edward Barron, who arrived in 1842 as the newly appointed prefect apostolic of upper Guinea (consisting of Sierra Leone and Liberia).[35]

The Episcopalians in the United States chose a remarkably gifted African American representative, Alexander Crummell (b. 1819), to advance their cause in Liberia. Arriving in 1853, Crummell largely but not exclusively confined his ministry to the Americo-Liberians.[36] The Presbyterians established churches as early as 1834. Commencing in 1859 they worked among the Kroo people. Outstanding Presbyterian missionaries were Abraham Miller, James Amos, Thomas Amos, and an African agent, John Deputie.[37]

31. Carey correctly saw that the tasks of evangelization and colonization conflicted at many points. The Portuguese had discovered this earlier and South African Christianity was to discover this in the nineteenth century. For a discussion of this point in Carey's thinking, see Leroy Fitts, *Lott Carey: First Black Missionary to Africa* (Valley Forge: Judson, 1978), 34.

32. Ibid., 62.

33. Quoted in Sanneh, *West African Christianity*, 94.

34. Isichei, *History of Christianity in Africa*, 165.

35. Edmund Hogan, *Catholic Missionaries and Liberia: A Study of Christian Enterprise in West Africa, 1842–1950* (Cork: Cork University Press, 1981), 13.

36. The story of Crummell has been told by Luckson Ejofodomi, "The Missionary Career of Alexander Crummell in Liberia: 1853–1873" (unpublished Ph.D. diss., Boston University, 1974).

37. Ibid., 235–36.

Liberia's missionary ranks were filled with strong characters. But no missionary in nineteenth-century Liberia cut a more striking figure than E. W. Blyden. He was brilliant, irritable, prejudiced, and unstable. Above all, he was mercurial.

In 1864 he became a professor at Liberia College. From 1864 to 1867 he was Liberian secretary of state. Blyden served as an ambassador to England as well as a secretary of the interior. He ran for president in 1885 and lost. In the 1870s he went to Sierra Leone to serve with the CMS but was asked to resign after his reputation was sullied with charges of adultery. His marriage was a tragic failure and his later years were spent living with a mistress.

Yet for all of Blyden's changes and contradictions the consistent theme that runs through his life and work, most notably his *Christianity, Islam and the Negro Race* (1888), is the need for a Christian civilization in Africa that is not imposed from without but emerges from within. Blyden labored to cultivate a respect for African languages, cultures, and customs among Westerners in general and missionaries in particular. He was convinced that no true Christian community could survive in West Africa without a high level of mutual respect. What he detected in the attitude of the competing missionaries of various denominations was an unhealthy struggle for power. "All efforts here," he wrote, "seem to have been directed mainly to a solution of the question of who shall be uppermost."[38]

Though his theology drifted in later years toward a vague Christian Deism, Blyden's plea for an African Christianity that had cultural authenticity and transcended the church rivalries of the West was a valuable legacy that would inspire the generation of Leopold Senghor (president of Senegal). One of the ironies of Liberia where Blyden labored for most of his life is that the Americo-Liberian ruling party never seemed either willing or able to overcome the cultural arrogance against which Blyden warned.

Missionary advance in West and Central Africa. While men like Venn and Blyden were strategizing about Christianity in Africa, numerous efforts were taking place to extend the faith in West and Central Africa. In Ghana German mission societies, such as the Bremen Mission and the Basel Evangelical Mission Society, were hard at work opening stations, translating Scriptures, and employing African evangelists. Johann Zimmerman was a leading missionary with the Basel Society who planted churches in Ghana and Volta. J. G. Christaller was a colleague of Zimmerman, whose outstanding work in the Twi language was noted earlier.

Yet no group captured the heart of Ghana as deeply as the Methodists. Their success in Ghana was largely due to the labors of Thomas Birch Free-

---

38. Quoted in Hollis Lynch, "The Native Pastorate Controversy and Cultural Ethnocentrism in Sierra Leone 1871–4," in Kalu, ed., *History of Christianity in West Africa*, 277.

man, who arrived in the Gold Coast in 1838, three years after the original introduction of Methodism. Freeman's efforts at Badagry and Abeokuta have already been mentioned. Yet despite fruitful work across West Africa his greatest impact was in Ghana.

Freeman's African roots were appreciated by the people to whom he ministered but his tactics would hardly have met with the approval of men like Blyden. When a revival of the Naanman ancestor cult threatened the spread of the Christian faith, Freeman moved in, aggressively baptizing hundreds and building a Methodist chapel on the toppled sacred shrine.[39] Though willing to oppose traditional religion Freeman showed great respect for African kings and the sacred kingship tradition they represented. One key to his success in Ghana was his rapport with the king of the Ashanti.[40] Freeman worked for over fifty years in Ghana establishing churches and schools as well as raising up a mature African Methodist clergy. Though he never learned an African language, "his contribution, direct and indirect, to the Christian awakening in West Africa was enormous."[41]

Cameroon also experienced the beginnings of Christianity in the middle of the century. The evangelical war against slavery continued to rage in the early nineteenth century. Off the Cameroon coast, in the hidden coves of the island of Fernando Po, lurked British warships, waiting to capture slave ships making their way west. The liberated slaves were brought back to Fernando Po before being taken elsewhere.

In 1843 the Baptist Mission Society, deploying Jamaican missionaries, began to minister in Fernando Po and on the Cameroonian mainland. Outstanding leaders enabled the Baptist churches to gain a foothold in that Central African region. Alfred Slaker, a missionary linguist and translator, and his two African colleagues, Thomas Johnson and George Nkwe, were an effective team in the building of the Cameroonian church. Slaker's experience underlined the emerging principle of missions in Africa—to be effective, foreign missionaries "would have to rely to a great extent on African agents, or failing that, look to West Indian Christians."[42]

Senegal and Gabon were the arena of significant missionary activity in the precolonial decades of the nineteenth century. Roman Catholicism was active in extending a witness to the kingdom, though early attempts to gain a foothold met with failure. Ann-Marie Javouhey, founder of the sisters of St. Joseph, had worked in Sierra Leone but health problems forced her home in 1823.[43] Black Brazilians built a church in Benin. One recaptive from Brazil,

39. Sanneh, *West African Christianity*, 122.
40. Falk, *Growth of the Church in Africa*, 120.
41. Sanneh, *West African Christianity*, 122.
42. Ibid., 110.
43. Isichei, *History of Christianity in Africa*, 161.

Antonio, became the pastor of the Catholic community of Lagos, which numbered about six thousand members in 1868.[44]

It was to be the distinction of the Holy Ghost Fathers to exercise the most permanent impact on West African Catholic Christianity. Francis Libermann (1802–52) converted from Judaism to Catholic Christianity in his youth. In 1841 after his ordination he founded the Holy Ghost Fathers. Libermann stated that the purpose of this new society was "to announce His holy gospel and establish His Kingdom among the poor and most neglected in the Church of God." Through the work of Edward Barron and John Kelly, the Holy Ghost Fathers determined that Liberia, Senegal, and Gabon were "poor and neglected" enough to become sites where the kingdom could be established. Notable was the work of Jean Bessieux, who founded in 1844 St. Mary of Gabon, modern Catholicism's first permanent mission station in Africa.[45]

Zaire. Catholic Christianity in Zaire was still alive at the beginning of the nineteenth century during the reign of Garcia V. After his death in 1830, things deteriorated rapidly. Mission activity shifted to Angola in the south. Garcia's own son, Dom Pedro, left São Salvador for employment in Angola. In 1834 an anticlerical government came to power in Portugal and monastic orders were surpressed. The last capuchins, including African lay brothers, left the old Christian kingdom in 1835. The cathedral in São Salvador fell into ruins. Africa's most famous Christian kingdom after Ethiopia had apparently come to its end.

But one man's rubble is another man's foundation. In 1878 Thomas Comber and George Grenfell of the Livingstone Inland Mission arrived in São Salvador. They were welcomed by Pedro V. By 1882 Baptist missionaries from both the United States and Britain had built a church beside the ruins of the old cathedral. Some of the cathedral's stones were used in the construction. The Baptists played down the continuity between their evangelical faith and the earlier catholicism but for the Africans the connection was strong. Holman Bentley, a Baptist missionary who translated the Kikongo New Testament in 1893, recalled that sometimes after his sermons a member of the congregation would stand and exhort his fellow Africans to accept the message because it was the same as their ancestors had believed in the glory days of the kingdom of Congo.[46] The earlier Christianization of Congo prepared the soil for this later evangelism.

44. Ibid., 161.
45. John Baur, *2000 Years of African Christianity* (Nairobi: Paulines, 1994), 132–33. For a brief account of the revival of Catholic missions in the nineteenth century, see Hastings, *Church in Africa: 1450–1950*, 248–50.
46. Adrian Hastings, *The Church in Africa: 1450–1950* (Oxford: Clarendon Press, 1994), 386

Nigeria. While the story of nineteenth-century West Africa's bold witness to the kingdom through the building of radical Christian communities begins in Sierra Leone, it concludes in Nigeria. Nowhere did the Africanization of the missionary task achieve such heights. Nowhere was the apparent failure of Christian unity and community greater. The central figure in this story of climax and collapse is Samuel Crowther.

Venn's forward-looking policies regarding African leadership of the African church seemed to be vindicated by the rise of Samuel Crowther to leadership. In 1864 Crowther was ordained as Africa's first bishop. Venn placed him in charge of the Niger mission, an assignment that covered an impossibly vast area of tribal and geographic diversity from the delta regions of Brass and Bonny (where a great deal of evangelistic success occurred)[47] through the middle region of the Igbo all the way to the Muslim north of the Hausa people.[48] Crowther and his Yoruba associates established a strong center at Onitsha on the Niger in the 1860s but by the 1870s trouble was brewing.

Two new developments were unraveling the Christian experiment in the Niger mission. The first development was the failure of a few of Crowther's African missionary colleagues. One missionary was found guilty of manslaughter after beating to death a young girl who worked for him. Charges of misappropriation of funds were also brought against certain members of Crowther's missionary team. A report by CMS missionary J. B. Wood in 1879 recommended that African missionaries be replaced by White ones.[49] With Venn now dead (1873), a reaction against his policies began.

In 1881 Wood enlarged upon his accusations against African missionaries in general and Crowther in particular at the Madeira conference. A number of Bishop Crowther's African colleagues were dismissed from the Niger mission, and the financial control of the mission was taken out of the bishop's hands and given to a committee of White missionaries, who "became the executive organ of the CMS mission."[50] In 1883 the Niger mission had ground to an almost complete stop. Crowther was stripped of power and influence. When he died in 1891 he was replaced by a White missionary.

The second development was the way in which capitalism along the Niger was undermining Christianity. The British palm oil trade expanded along the Niger in the 1870s. Crowther's boat, the *Henry Venn*, not only was used to transport the missionaries but also played a small role in assisting the palm oil trade. The immorality of many of the traders was criticized by the

47. On the successes at Bonny, see the discussion in G. O. M. Tasie, *Christian Missionary Enterprise in the Niger Delta: 1864–1918* (Leiden: E. J. Brill, 1978), 26ff.

48. See Hastings' discussion of the logistical and strategic complexities of so vast a region in *Church in Africa: 1450–1950*, 345–46.

49. F. K. Ekechi, *Missionary Enterprise and Rivalry in Igboland, 1857–1914* (London: Frank Cass, 1972), 60.

50. Ibid., 61.

African missionaries, who generally favored trade as an ally of Christianity. The British traders resented the missionaries' interference and pursued their ruthless capitalism above the protests of the bishop and his men.

After Crowther was disgraced, the *Henry Venn* was taken from under his authority and given over to J. A. Ashcroft, the CMS missionary in charge of finances. Ashcroft had conspired with a British trader, Captain McIntosh of the Niger company, to remove Crowther and make the *Venn* available for commercial use only. McIntosh lied about the activities of Crowther and his associates and aided Ashcroft's plan to seize control. Once Crowther was out of the way, Ashcroft turned over the ship "to trade and profit." Christianity and commerce were to be the key to building a Christian civilization in Africa. Yet commerce was undermining Christianity and threatening the success of the Christian experiment.[51]

Holy Johnson and the aftermath of the Niger incident. Though Crowther had been humiliated by the CMS he lobbied until his death for the establishment of the Niger Delta pastorate to be set up in the new churches along the coast, independent of foreign control just as the native pastorate of Sierra Leone had been. When he died on December 31, 1891, the issue had not been settled. The CMS opposed the idea but independently minded African clergy, aided by the verbal support of E. W. Blyden, pushed ahead in opposition to the CMS.

Most notable among the independent leaders was the Rev. James Johnson. "Holy" Johnson, as he was known, had been born in Sierra Leone and had been a lecturer at Fourah Bay College. After transferring to Nigeria in 1874, Johnson became pastor of the Breadfruit Church in Lagos. In the agitation that followed Crowther's death and the CMS's refusal to grant African Christians the Niger Delta pastorate they demanded, members of Johnson's church left to form the independent "Ethiopian" (Black-controlled) Bethel Church. Everyone expected Johnson to leave the Anglicans and join the new church. He refused. He was a champion of African nationalism but he was not a separatist willing to subvert the forging of international Christian community.

When Johnson addressed a gathering of the Student Volunteer Movement in London in January 1900 (a month before his consecration as the assistant bishop of the Anglican Diocese of Western Equatorial Africa) he subordinated his nationalism for the wider cause of establishing the rule of Christ. "We want evangelists," Johnson declared to the room of White candidates for missions, "young men who will be willing to travel to and fro in the country and proclaim the glad tidings of salvation." While Johnson may have lost enthusiasm for the failed witness of the church, he remained

---

51. See Sanneh's discussion of these events involving Ashcroft in *West African Christianity,* 171ff.

certain that the gospel of the kingdom that the church carried as a treasure in earthen vessels still warranted a community of witness that transcended race and culture.[52] The dream of a kingdom community of love and unity had been battered by nineteenth-century realities but the dream remained alive.

Conclusion: The Failure of Christian Community

The establishment of Freetown and Monrovia at the end of the eighteenth century was to be a sign to American and British evangelicals of the reign of Christ. Soon regenerate hearts would transform the world and hasten the Lord's triumphant return. The gospel of Christianity and commerce would promote this eschatological mission and bring redemption and prosperity to a continent ravaged by disease and slavery.

Such was the expectation. The reality was different. Racism, discord, greed, and self-love undermined the Niger mission and the leadership of Samuel Crowther and divided the church into African-ruled and European-ruled sections.

Many became disillusioned. Blyden never saw the day when "Moham-medans and Pagans, chiefs and people" would join hands with Christians and "march back hand in hand with their returned brethren towards the sun-rise for the regeneration of the continent." Holy Johnson never became a bishop, his appointment denied, he felt, by White prejudice.

Yet the words of Augustine might have comforted the disillusioned. "While the City of God is on pilgrimage in this world," he once wrote, "she has in her midst some who are united with her in participation in the sacra-ments, but who will not join her in the eternal destiny of the saints." The self-love of the City of Man thus lives inside the earthly expression of the City of God—the Christian church. This presence of human greed, lust, and sin within the Christian community is a corrupting presence. Yet no amount of effort will ever perfectly rid the church of this spirit of the second city. "In truth those two cities are interwoven and intermixed in this era," confessed Augustine, "and await separation at the last judgment."[53]

If Augustine's observation is correct, then the church on earth can never be a perfect expression of the kingdom of God. Its witness will always be par-tial and flawed. This realization does not deny either the rule of Jesus Christ over hearts or the need for justice in anticipation of the coming kingdom. What strikes the observer of Christian communities in West Africa is the suc-cess of the Christian movement in spite of its sin and finitude.

52. Tasie, *Christian Missionary Enterprise*, 163.
53. Augustine, *City of God*, Book 1, chap. 35 (New York: Doubleday, 1958), 63–64.

The story of West African Christianity thus points us back to the first aspect of the kingdom—the providential rule of God over all of life for his people. An optimist like Jonathan Edwards, whose postmillennialism pushed him to predict the ultimate triumph of the gospel over all sin before the return of Christ, might have been disappointed with the turn of events in Nigeria or Liberia, but his awareness of the richness of the kingdom would have lifted his spirits. The kingdom of God, wrote Edwards, is like a river with different streams.

> The different streams of this river are apt to appear like mere confusion to us, because we cannot see the whole at once. A man who sees but one of two streams at a time, cannot tell what their course tends to. Their course seems very crooked, and different streams seem to run for a while different and contrary ways: and if we view things at a distance, there seem to be innumerable obstacles and impediments in the way, as rocks and mountains, and the like; to hinder their ever uniting, and coming to the ocean; but yet if we trace them, they all unite at last, all come to the same issue, disgorging themselves in one into the same great ocean.[54]

"They all unite at last." The best witness to the kingdom by West African Christian communities may have been their witness to an unfulfilled but enduring hope.

54. Jonathan Edwards, *Works,* vol. 1 (Edinburgh: Banner of Truth, 1975), 617.

10 A Kingdom Divided

South African Christianity

While West Africa experimented with the limits of Christian community in early-nineteenth-century Africa, South Africa was shaken by a series of Bantu people movements known as the *difaqane* (scattering). Xhosa, Khoi, Tswana, Ndebele, and a number of other tribes scattered in terror across the landscape of southern Africa.

The figure that inspired their terror and drove them to flight was Shaka, king of the Zulu (1787–1828). By 1819 Shaka gained control of a group of tribes in the area between the Drakensburg Mountains and the Indian Ocean and brought them under the hegemony of the previously insignificant Zulu people.[1] He took on the trappings of African sacred kingship and shaped his people into an efficient fighting machine.

Though Shaka's rule lasted only a decade his impact was enduring. He not only gave an identity to the Zulu that would mark them for centuries but he also precipitated the migrations that permanently redrew the map of South Africa. King Mzilikazi migrated north and established a Ndebele kingdom in what would one day be Zimbabwe. In similar ways southern Mozambique and Swaziland were formed by the migrations of the *difaqane*.[2]

One of the kings affected by the Zulu expansion was Moshoeshoe of the Sotho (c. 1785–1870). His people lived in the quiet valleys beyond the mountains of the Dragon (Drakensburg). When other tribes, pressured by the Zulu, invaded their valleys they sought refuge in the mountains. There Moshoeshoe built a stronghold, Thaba-Bosiu, which proved impregnable.

1. The Zulu are a subgroup of the Nguni, which is composed of four other tribes: the North Ndebele, South Ndebele, Swazi, and Xhosa.
2. See the discussion of Shaka and the rise of the Zulus in Kevin Shillington, *A History of Africa* (London: Macmillan, 1989), 259ff.

As Moshoeshoe surveyed the scatterings of kingdoms from his mountain haven he saw more than Bantu kingdoms on the horizon. Moshoeshoe saw the kingdoms of European Christendom, represented by the Boer and the British moving over the land. More perceptively he saw a new religion, Christianity, with its message of the kingdom of God and its ruler Jesus Christ, on the rise, scattering its gospel as widely as Shaka had scattered his spears. While Moshoeshoe had fled the first scattering of kingdoms, he accepted the missionaries and their message of the kingdom of Christ.

The Paris Evangelical Mission Society began work among the Sotho (sometimes called *Basutos*) in 1833. A series of outstanding missionaries, such as Adolphe Mabille and François Coillard (1834–1904), worked among his people with great success, defending them against Boer and Bantu invaders alike.[3] Political advantages came his way as horses and guns began to fill his fortress.

Though he was first drawn to the new faith for economic and political reasons, Moshoeshoe grew to believe the missionary message about the kingdom of Christ. The Sotho king encouraged Christian burial practices and ended traditional initiation. On his deathbed he declared himself a believer in Christ and called for Christian baptism though he died before it could be given to him.[4] Moshoeshoe tied his hopes to the kingdom of Christ and in so doing built one of the most successful and enduring kingdoms in southern Africa.

The fullness of a fragmented witness. Moshoeshoe is a reminder that the clash of kingdoms during the early decades of the nineteenth century involved more than guns and spears. The arrival of the gospel of the kingdom in various forms represented another kind of kingdom clash between traditional concepts of kingship and the new concepts of Christendom and Christ's rule in one's heart. Moshoeshoe saw correctly that the message about heavenly kingdoms had enormous earthly implications.

This chapter surveys how the various witnesses to the kingdom of God spread over South Africa in the nineteenth century and inspired a response among Africans. Approaching the history of nineteenth-century South African Christianity through a kingdom framework sheds light on the story in beneficial ways. In the words of John de Gruchy, "the struggle of the church in South Africa is for the kingdom of God in another segment of world history. Indeed, as we look back on the history of South Africa, and the theologies that have shaped and interpreted that history, the cruciality of the kingdom emerges strongly."[5]

3. Stephen Neill, *A History of Christian Missions* (London: Penguin, 1986), 314–15.

4. Elizabeth Isichei, *A History of Christianity in Africa* (Grand Rapids: Eerdmans, 1995), 120.

5. John de Gruchy, *The Church Struggle in South Africa* (Grand Rapids: Eerdmans, 1979), 199.

In nineteenth-century South Africa, three rival concepts of the kingdom vied for prominence. Afrikaners saw themselves as a chosen people who were commissioned to build a kingdom of divine law on the land of South Africa and offer up a theocratic witness to the rule of Christ. Missionary Christianity emphasized the inwardness of the kingdom and the "absolute surrender" of the soul to the indwelling Jesus. Prophets of the newly emerging social gospel saw the most urgent work of the church as witnessing to God's rule of justice and equality.

The champions of these three understandings of the kingdom seldom cooperated and often clashed, so the kingdom witness of the churches fragmented. But the story of South African Christianity between 1800 and 1900 is not only about this fragmentation. Through the broken witness of a divided church, South African Christianity witnessed to the fullness of the kingdom in surprising ways.

Afrikaner Christianity and the Great Trek: The Kingdom as a Reformed Theocracy

Background of the Great Trek. In 1948 D. F. Malan, a leader of the Afrikaner Nationalist party, pointed to the importance of history to the Afrikaner identity:

> Our history is the greatest masterpiece of the centuries. We hold this nationhood as our due for it was given us by the Architect of the universe. [His] aim was the formation of a new nation among the nations of the world. . . . The last hundred years have witnessed a miracle behind which must lie a divine plan. Indeed, the history of the Afrikaner reveals a will and a determination which makes one feel that Afrikanerdom is not the work of men but the creation of God.[6]

For Malan this special story began "a hundred years" ago. What event triggered this new "creation of God"? Malan was referring to the Great Trek of the 1830s, which witnessed the migration of large numbers of Afrikaners from the Cape to the interior of the continent and led to the creation of the Orange Free State and the Transvaal in the 1850s.

What were the causes of this important migration? British settlers and British missionaries were probably the main reason. England had taken possession of the Cape in 1815 after two previous periods of occupation (1795–1803, 1806–15). South Africa was now a British colony. Though the Dutch Reformed Church still enjoyed special privileges, the British colonial presence meant British settlers and British missionaries. The settlers were easier

---

6. Quoted in Allister Sparks, *The Mind of South Africa* (London: Mandarin, 1990), 31.

to take. Beginning in 1820 with the arrival of 3,500 immigrants from England, British settlement soon created a growing need for more land for the expanding White community.

But land was perhaps secondary to the issue of slavery and emancipation. The Khoisan by the beginning of the nineteenth century had been reduced to servitude. David Livingstone of the London Mission Society had little good to say about the Boers and their treatment of the Africans. He complained that while an African chief like Mzilikazi of the Ndebele was "cruel to his enemies and kind to those he conquered," the Boers "destroyed their enemies, and made slaves of their friends."[7]

Missionaries like John Philip, of whom more will be said later, fought for the freedom of the Khoisan, who were becoming known as the "Coloureds," and in ordinances 49 and 50 the qualified emancipation of the latter was established by law. The antislavery crusade in England led to the liberation of all slaves in British colonies in 1834. This full emancipation as conceived by British evangelicals and other humanitarians meant that Boer and Colored were to be regarded as social equals before the law.

One trekker, Karel Trichardt, declared that the main reason for his emigration from British colonial rule was the equalization of Afrikaner and African.[8] A trekker preacher, Sarel Cilliers, was eager to preach the gospel to all except Blacks because they were "heathen who lived a godless life." But Whites were God's chosen people. In the diaries of a young trekker girl we read that though she was not opposed to the liberation of Blacks, she was opposed to their equalization, which was "contrary to the laws of God and the natural difference in origin and religion."[9] God's kingdom, from an Afrikaner perspective, distinguished between chosen and non-chosen.

The Trek, Blood River, and God's new chosen people. What was needed was a new promised land where the chosen people of South Africa, the Afrikaners in particular, could build the kingdom. One DRC minister, as he contemplated the interior lands that the trekkers proposed to settle, suggested it be called Palestine.[10] To Palestine they went in great numbers. As early as 1825 Boers had moved across the Orange River. The largest migration took place between 1835 and 1840 when some ten thousand trekkers and five thousand Colored servants crossed the eastern frontier of Cape Colony to the interior beyond the Vaal River.

---

7. David Livingstone, *Missionary Travels and Researches in South Africa* (London: John Murray, 1899), 23.

8. Quoted in Hofmeyr and Pillay, eds., *A History of Christianity in South Africa* (Pretoria: Haum Tertiary, 1994), 95.

9. "Strijdig met de wetten van God en het natuurlijk ondershijt van afkomst en geloof." Quoted in Hofmeyr and Pillay, *History of Christianity in South Africa*, 95.

10. Ibid.

These "Voortrekkers" engaged in an adventure that has been viewed in various ways by historians. Some regard the Great Trek as a huge disaster in which Boers "swept like a devastating pestilence through the land, blasting everything in their path."[11] For them the trek marks the moment when the poisonous concept of racial supremacy began its infection of South Africa.[12] Others view the trek as the decisive event in not only establishing Afrikaner identity but also placing "the interior of South Africa within the framework of those European influences already established at the Cape."[13] Whether one views it as a disaster or as a triumph, there can be little debate about its importance.

The central drama of the Great Trek was the battle of Blood River where a group of 530 encircled trekkers defeated a Zulu army under Shaka's successor, Dingane, that numbered about ten thousand on December 16, 1838. The Boer victory was preceded by, as tradition tells it, the "Vow of the Covenant" taken by the outnumbered trekkers just prior to the Zulu attack. In this vow the Afrikaners promised to remember that day forever if God would but grant them victory. Implied in the vow was the idea that victory meant divine approval for taking native land. God was calling them to build a theocratic kingdom on this land just as ancient Israel had been called to build the kingdom on Canaanite land in the Old Testament.

The new churches of the trekkers. The trek was a religious experience for most of the Afrikaners and changed the way they viewed their faith. A conservative group like the Doppers believed that their journey had been prophesied by the biblical prophet Joel and that their destination was the New Jerusalem located somewhere beyond the Vaal River.[14] The mother church back in Cape Colony (properly called the *Nederduitse Gereformeerde Kerk*, or NGK) did not share the sentiments of the Doppers and instead complained bitterly about the trek, arguing that those who emigrated were running away from God and the law.

Tensions mounted that eventually led to the formation of several new denominations. Reverend Van der Hoff established the *Hervormde Kerk* (NHK), arguing in 1853 that "since the Transvaal is politically independent, it must be ecclesiastically as well."[15] When a dispute broke out in the Netherlands over liberalism that led to the formation of the Christian Reformed Church, a similar division occurred in the Transvaal with the formation of the conservative *Gereformeerde Kerk* (GK) in 1859. Though the

11. Dr. Abdul Abdurahman, quoted in Sparks, *Mind*, 109.
12. G. D. J. Duvenage, *Van die Tarka na die Transgariep* (Pretoria: Academia, 1981), 20. Quoted in Hofmeyr and Pillay, *History of Christianity in South Africa*, 93.
13. Hofmeyr and Pillay, *History of Christianity in South Africa*, 93.
14. Isichei, *History of Christianity in Africa*, 111.
15. Hofmeyr and Pillay, *History of Christianity in South Africa*, 114.

original split with the NHK was over the use of evangelical hymns (as opposed to Scripture songs only), there were deeper issues. Central was the degree to which theology and the Bible should be used to support Afrikaner nationalism.

Kuyper, du Toit, and the Afrikaner vision of the kingdom. The Dopper Church (GK) was greatly influenced by a Dutch theologian and statesman, Abraham Kuyper (1837–1920). Kuyper grew up in a Netherlands in ferment over the ideas of the Enlightenment. To stem the rising tide of rationalism and liberalism in the churches, many Dutch Protestants returned to their Calvinistic roots. They saw in Reformation theology a comprehensive world- and lifeview that could arm them against the ideas of modernity.

Kuyper was influenced by the thinking of Groen van Prinsterer (d. 1867). Central to both was the concept that rationalism and egalitarianism destroyed the multifaceted and variegated life that God had made. The quest of the Enlightenment was to reduce the variety to some underlying principle (naturalism, materialism, idealism, etc.) that ultimately distorted the truth and encouraged some form of totalitarianism. Through his political party, the antirevolutionary party (which enabled him to become prime minister in 1901), and through the university he founded in 1880 (the Free University of Amsterdam) Kuyper sought to project a reformational worldview in which a view called "sphere sovereignty" countered Enlightenment reductionism. De Gruchy summarizes Kuyper's views:

> All spheres of life exist by virtue of God's common grace, and therefore each has a sovereignty over its own affairs under God. Education, art, economics, family life, are all spheres through which God operates directly. This common grace, as distinct from saving grace, is built into the structures of creation and provides the basis for Christian nationalism in its various dimensions.[16]

What these ideas translated into politically was a belief that the centralizing of power and blending of distinct cultural heritages was against the laws of creation that God had built into his world. Totalitarianism in all forms was regarded by Kuyper as evil.

As Kuyper's ideas made their way to South Africa they influenced a young Dutch Reformed minister in the Cape named S. J. du Toit (d. 1911). In the early 1870s du Toit and his friends formed the "Society of True Afrikaners." In 1876 they published an Afrikaner magazine called *Die Patriot.*

When the British annexed the Transvaal in 1877, the Cape Colony Afrikaners were as outraged as their Transvaal compatriots. The magazine and

16. De Gruchy, *Church Struggle*, 6.

movement of du Toit became the forum for reawakened Afrikaner rage and religious nationalism. Under du Toit's leadership a new history of the Afrikaner story was written. Its passionate patriotism was hardly concealed.

In the history the British were the villains who had subjugated the Dutch and their cousins, the German people, unfairly. Du Toit made clear that the Afrikaners were God's chosen. No other explanation but God's special providence could account for their survival and success under such harsh and unjust conditions. Du Toit took the ideas of Kuyper and forged them into a concept of Afrikaner nationalism that emphasized that each ethnic group should be given a distinct sphere of operation over which to exercise authority.

Du Toit eventually left the Dutch Reformed Church with which he became impatient. His views influenced the GK and its university in Potchefstroom. Though he preached resistance when the British annexed the Transvaal (1877—though it regained its independence in 1881) he later worked for British-Afrikaner cooperation and opposed the policies of Paul Kruger (d. 1904), president of the Transvaal and champion of the Boer War (1899–1902).

Kuyper would no doubt have repudiated much of what du Toit did with his theology. Calvinism has normally been the enemy of racism and tyranny.[17] Nationalism as an ideology is capable of subverting any form of theology, however noble or sophisticated it might be. Afrikaner neo-Calvinism was modern ethnic nationalism dressed in the clothes of Reformation theology. Whether he subverted Calvinism or merely translated it into the idiom of the Afrikaner experience, S. J. du Toit made a profound impact on South Africa and earned himself the title "father of Afrikaner nationalism."[18] When D. F. Malan, years later, spoke of Afrikaner history as being "the greatest masterpiece of the centuries" he was echoing the voice of S. J. du Toit and his unique but controversial witness to the kingdom.

Missionary Christianity and the Evangelical Vision of the Kingdom

Van der Kemp, John Philip, and the LMS. The nineteenth-century Afrikaner witness to the kingdom did not go unchallenged. One challenge came in the

---

17. It is important to note the views of Irving Hexham. He views Afrikaner religion as an uneasy mixture of two traditions. The "Great Tradition" is Calvinism. The "Little Tradition" is Afrikaner folk religion. Calvinism is not the dominant component in the traditional religion of Afrikaners, argues Hexham. Afrikaner folk religion has been shaped by "European folk beliefs, Malay religion, and indigenous beliefs." The Great Tradition of Calvinism has been eclipsed due to secularization and nationalism by the Little Tradition of Afrikaner folk religion. This folk religion is the source of the Afrikaners' racism and injustice. Cf. "Modernity or Reaction in South Africa: The Case of Afrikaner Religion," in William Nicholls, ed., *Modernity and Religion* (Waterloo, Ont.: Wilfred Laurier, 1987).

18. Cf. Sparks, *Mind*, 117–18.

form of a missionary Christianity that understood the kingdom as the rule of Christ in hearts rather than the rule of the elect on earth. For missionary Christianity, preaching and church planting were the principal means of raising up a twice-born humanity. This missionary movement and its distinctive witness to the kingdom began as a trickle in the early 1800s but then, in contrast to West Africa, developed into a flood. By 1843 David Livingstone wrote that "the number of missionaries of different societies is so large compared to the population it must strike everyone with astonishment."[19] Though the Dutch Reformed Church was part of the missionary movement the contribution of other agencies dominated the century.

Moravian George Schmidt had been the early standard bearer of this alternative witness to the kingdom. He had returned to Herrnhut in 1744 exasperated by Afrikaner opposition to his mission.

In 1792 three Moravian brothers, Hendrik Marsveld, Daniel Schwinn, and Christian Kuhnel, arrived to renew Schmidt's work. They reopened the old settlement of Genadendal and found an early Khoisan convert of Schmidt, old Lena, who welcomed them warmly.[20] It was a sign that the missionary century in South Africa had begun. Afrikanerdom may well have suspected that trouble was on the horizon. With the coming of the London Missionary Society (LMS) and its first representative, J. Van der Kemp, all doubt was removed.

Dr. Johannes Theodore Van der Kemp (1747–1811) arrived in Cape Town in 1799 accompanied by three missionary companions. Van der Kemp was a natural leader who commanded respect. He was fifty when he arrived, having converted to Christianity later in life. He had lived a wild life in the Holland of his youth, rejecting all religion as suspect and accepting the creed of a freethinker. A career as an Army officer and physician led to marriage and a family. The death of his wife and child in a boating accident shook his foundations. In his grief he experienced an evangelical conversion and felt the call to missionary work.[21] The LMS accepted him despite his past and assigned him to South Africa.

His first contacts with the officials at the Cape were cordial. He was permitted to begin his work four hundred miles east of Cape Town on the Xhosa frontier. Within a short time, however, Van der Kemp abandoned the violence of the frontier for a mission among the gentle Khoisan. He founded a Christian village at Bethelsdorp. Van der Kemp identified with the Khoisan closely and became an outspoken critic of Afrikaner injustices against his flock. When Van der Kemp married one of his parishioners, a seventeen-year-old Malagasy girl named Sarah, he became an even larger target of set-

19. Letter to Arthur Tidman, 24 June 1843, *Livingstone's Missionary Correspondence, 1841–1856*, ed. I. Schapera (1961), 44. Quoted in Hastings, *Church in Africa*, 358.

20. Hofmeyr and Pillay, *History of Christianity in South Africa*, 41.

21. Isichei, *History of Christianity in Africa*, 107.

tler scorn. Though the marriage was not a happy one, Johannes, Sarah, and their four children made a strong statement about racial equality.

Van der Kemp has been called "an eccentric, a visionary, and an ideo-logue."[22] He was so hated by the colonists he left a legacy of lasting distrust between the LMS and the Afrikaner community. Yet he left behind more than enmity. The significance of Van der Kemp was his interpretation of the Clapham gospel of Christ and civilization. For many settlers that gospel meant conversion and commerce. For Van der Kemp and his associate, James Read, it meant conversion and justice.[23] When Van der Kemp died in 1811 he left behind a chaotic mission station but a clearer gospel.

It was this gospel that may have influenced one of South Africa's most fa-mous converts. Ntsikana was one of the first Xhosa to embrace Christianity. He did so at a time when hostilities between the Xhosa and the Afrikaners had reached the point of war. He gave up his many wives and withdrew from the traditional dancing in order to worship this new messiah who ruled from heaven. He poured out his worship through hymns that he composed. In the dark days of the Xhosa war of 1818, Ntsikana wrote one of his most endur-ing songs of praise, a song still sung by Xhosa Christians today:

> He is the one who brings together herds which oppose each other; He is the leader who has led us; He is the great blanket which we put on.[24]

As he lay dying in 1821 he insisted on a Christian burial, even rising from his deathbed to take a shovel and begin digging his own grave. He lives in Xhosa memory as a saint.[25] His son Dukwana became a Christian leader as did Tiyo Soga, the son of his disciple and friend old Soga.

Moffat and Livingstone. The death of Van der Kemp and the growing hos-tility of Afrikanerdom did not discourage the LMS. The number of recruits swelled. Among those who attempted to further Van der Kemp's legacy were Robert Moffat and his famous son-in-law, David Livingstone.

Robert Moffat (1795–1883) went from planting gardens in England to planting mission stations in South Africa. His humble background was no deterrent to either his acceptance by the LMS or his brilliant career as a mis-sionary at Kuruman among the Tswana. On his small oasis at the southern edge of the Kalahari desert, Moffat and his converts (about two hundred)[26] built a mission station.

22. Peter Hinchliff, *The Church in South Africa* (London: SPCK, 1968), 24.
23. Hastings, *Church in Africa*, 286.
24. Isichei, *History of Christianity in Africa*, 109.
25. Ibid.
26. K. S. Latourette, *History of the Expansion of Christianity*, vol. 5 (London: Eyre and Spottiswoode, 1943), 345.

His preaching met with only modest success. One particular stumbling block was Moffat's teaching about the kingdom. He found Tswana traditional religion hopelessly deficient.

> They are, I may say, without exception still perfect heathens, and have the most incorrect and corrupt notions of God and Death, which is all that they know anything about. . . . As to Jehovah, a Saviour, Heaven, Hell, the Soul's immortality, and a day of retribution which they hear from the missionaries, [these] are neither understood nor believed by any.[27]

On the important matter of the coming kingdom of God and the resurrection of the dead on that day of his coming, Moffat encountered only disbelief. His conversation with Chief Makaba of the Bamangkhetsi illustrates the communication gap:

> "What!" he exclaimed with astonishment. "What are these words about? The dead, the dead arise!"
> "Yes," was my reply, "all the dead shall arise."
> "Will my father arise?"
> "Yes," I answered, "your father will arise."
> "Will all the slain in battle arise?"
> "Yes" . . .
> "Did ever your ears hear such strange and unheard of news?"[28]

Yet not all rejected Moffat's kingdom witness. His most famous convert was Jager Afrikaner, a Khoisan who had led a band of slaves in an armed insurrection against the Boers. Jager and his band fled north and terrorized the settlers and tribes of Namaqualand.

"At last he was conquered," wrote Gertrude Hance, nineteenth-century missionary to the Zulu, "not by guns or cruelty, but by the influence of Dr. Moffat . . . who taught him of the Great Conquerer of mankind, Jesus Christ."[29] Jager supported the new religion for the remainder of his life.

Despite the highs and lows of mission work among the Khoisan and Tswana, Moffat persevered at Kuruman. Over time the station he founded became a model that would be copied throughout Africa. His primary labor was the translation of the Bible into Tswana. Other than an occasional miscue (translating the phrase "lilies of the field" as "tarantulas of the field"), his translation was a success. His relationship with the local king was a

27. Robert Moffat, *Apprenticeship at Kuruman*, ed. I. Schapera (London: Chatto and Windus, 1951), 56–57.

28. R. Moffat, *Missionary Labours and Scenes in Southern Africa* (1842), 296. Quoted in Hastings, *Church in Africa*, 271.

29. Gertrude Hance, *The Zulu Yesterday and Today* (New York: Negro Universities Press, 1969, orig. 1918), 23.

strong one and a long line of Tswana Christian kings led their people into the twentieth century. When he and his wife Mary retired to England in 1870, he was seventy-five years old and had served with the LMS in Africa for more than fifty years. He was lionized in England as one of her great men.

For all of Moffat's fame, his celebrity was soon overshadowed by that of his son-in-law David Livingstone (d. 1873). Livingstone has been hailed in the past as "one of the greatest and most influential missionaries in the history of mankind."[30] Florence Nightingale regarded him as "the greatest man of his generation."[31]

Yet more modern assessments have noted that "he failed in all he most wished to achieve."[32] As a missionary he made "but one convert, who subsequently lapsed."[33] The two missions that he inspired "ended in fiasco and heavy loss of life."[34] Though his walk across Africa in 1852–56 was a great success, his subsequent search for the source of the Nile ended in failure. Personally, Livingstone was a "failure as a husband and a father."[35] Some who knew Livingstone well found the man to be a puzzle. A contemporary of Livingstone, Dr. John Kirk, wrote, "I can come to no other conclusion than that Dr. Livingstone is out of his mind."[36]

The truth about Livingstone probably lies somewhere between these extremes of opinion. He joined the LMS due to the personal influence of Robert Moffat and arrived in Africa in 1840. Livingstone found relationships with fellow missionaries and local Boers difficult. He found the company of Africans to be the most congenial. After a brief stay at Kuruman, Livingstone struck out on his own, establishing a station at Mobatsa in 1843.

In 1845 he married Moffat's daughter, Mary, and together they planted two additional substations at Chonuane and Koloheng.[37] It was during this time that he made his only known convert, Sechele, king of the Bakuena. Livingstone held African traditional religion in higher regard than did his father-in-law, but like Moffat felt that evangelical eschatology was a key point in the presentation of the gospel. Livingstone described in his journal a crucial conversation with Sechele that centered on the ascended glory of Christ as

---

30. Latourette, *Expansion,* vol. 5, 345.

31. Quoted in Tim Jeal, *Livingstone* (New York: Putnam, 1973), 1. Oliver Ransford's biography *David Livingstone* (New York: St. Martins, 1978) is more appreciative of this "many-sided genius who is still revered as a missionary and emancipator," but Ransford takes a heavily psychological approach to Livingstone, insisting that only by labeling him a Manic-Depressive can we explain "his intrinsic ambivalence, his follies and his sublimities . . . that sometimes . . . verged on the psychotic" (1–2).

32. Ibid.

33. Ibid.

34. Ibid., 2.

35. Ibid.

36. Quoted in Ransford, *David Livingstone,* 4.

37. Livingstone, *Missionary Travels and Researches,* 12.

King. Livingstone described the "scene of the great white throne, and Him who shall sit on it, from whose face the heaven and earth shall flee away."[38] The king was much moved by these words.

"You startle me," Sechele replied. "These words make all my bones to shake."[39] Sechele converted and sought to influence the conversion of his tribe.

Despite the encouraging success of his witness to Sechele, Livingstone soon realized that he was not cut out for conventional missionary work. What he could do best was walk and watch. His famous expedition across southern Africa from 1852 to 1856 gave him firsthand exposure to the horrors and extent of the slave trade. The evangelization of Africa would go forward, he felt, only if the great "open wound" of African slavery was ended. For that to happen a way must be found for trade and commerce to flourish and replace the hated institution.

When he returned to England in 1857 he received a hero's welcome. He decided to leave the LMS and take a position as a special British consul in Africa, which left him free to carry on both his work of exploration as well as his crusade for Christianity and commerce. His visit to Cambridge that year inspired the formation of several mission agencies, including the Universities' Mission to Central Africa (UMCA). He returned to Africa in 1858.

Livingstone spent the rest of his life traveling across southern and central Africa on foot. He logged over thirty thousand miles documenting the extent of the slave trade and searching in vain for navigable waterways that could carry a sufficient flow of Western trade. When he died in 1873 at Mwela Mwape on the shores of Lake Bangweulu, shortly after the famous visit of Henry Stanley, he had not found these highways.

Yet to his companions he was a hero. His body was taken to England by his faithful African assistants, Susi and Chuma. When his remains were finally laid to rest in Westminster Abbey his tomb was inscribed with the words of his last written message: "May heaven's rich blessing come down on every one, American, English, or Turk, who will help to heal this open sore of the world."[40] Despite his failures as a missionary, as an explorer, and as a family man his great legacy was "to revive the commitment both to antislavery and to commerce" in late nineteenth-century missionary work.[41]

Methodists and William Shaw. While the names of Van der Kemp, Moffat, and Livingstone added luster to the reputation of the LMS, the churches they

---

38. Ibid., 14.
39. Ibid.
40. Inscribed on David Livingstone's tomb in Westminster Abbey, London.
41. Hastings, *Church in Africa*, 253.

planted did not thrive. More successful in terms of sheer numbers were the Methodists.[12] Two names stand out in the early story of Methodism in South Africa. The first was Barnabas Shaw (d. 1854). From 1826 to 1854 Shaw worked to establish Methodism in the western Cape. One of the highlights of his work was the establishment of Raithby, a settlement for freed slaves. When he died at Rosebank in 1854 Methodism was firmly rooted in the Cape Town area.[43]

The story of Methodism in the eastern Cape is a story that has as its central character a second Shaw. William Shaw (b. 1798) came to South Africa, not as a missionary, but as a chaplain to a number of Methodist families who settled on the eastern frontier near Grahamstown. But it was soon clear that Shaw's vision could not be limited to the personal needs of his small flock. Shaw developed a growing concern for the salvation of the Xhosa, whose warlike ways made them a challenge to settler and missionary alike. Soon he had a small flock of "natives" that he ministered to in addition to his other duties.

His concept of the kingdom was that of John 3:3: "I tell you the truth, no one can see the kingdom of God unless he is born again." When Shaw asked one of his converts, "How can a man be born again" in the kingdom, he received an answer from his African student that would win the approval of evangelical missionaries from Freetown to Grahamstown. "When a man really believes in God, and prays to him, God sends his Holy Spirit into his heart, by whom his heart is changed, and he is then born again."

Though no mention had been made of Christ or the cross, Shaw exulted upon hearing this response. "There are many pious persons in some of the country parts of England," Shaw wrote in his journal, who "would scarcely be able to give more satisfactory replies than those we frequently receive, on our catechetical occasions, from a people, who but a short time ago knew scarcely any more of God than the brute beasts."[44]

Shaw was more than a typical evangelical missionary preacher, however. He was one of the first missionaries to think strategically about the Christian mission in South Africa. Shaw recognized the need for a chain of mission stations to be systematically built at strategic distances across the span of South Africa and beyond. He worked to bring this vision into reality. By 1860 there were dozens of mission stations, hundreds of Methodist missionaries, and

42. In 1990 Methodists were credited with nearly 6,500 congregations and 3.3 million members and affiliates. The second closest Protestant denomination was the Anglican Church (Church of the Province of South Africa) with 1,200 congregations and 2.5 million members and affiliates. Roman Catholicism in South Africa has 4.3 million members and affiliates. Cf. Patrick Johnstone, *Operation World* (Grand Rapids: Zondervan, 1993), 494.

43. Hofmeyr and Pillay, *History of Christianity in South Africa*, 62.

44. *The Journal of William Shaw*, ed. W. D. Hammond-Tooke (Cape Town: Balkema, 1972), 97.

some five thousand Methodist converts. Methodism was well on its way to becoming the largest of South Africa's Protestant churches.

Christianity was advancing but not always in predictable ways. The spread of Christian ideas among the Xhosa produced results that even the far-seeing Shaw did not anticipate. The frontier wars of the 1840s created thousands of African refugees. The colonial governor, George Grey, developed a "civilizing" program that would resettle these landless people and re-educate them in Western ways. Shaw and his Methodist missionaries cooperated with the building of new settlements and schools but were less than sensitive to the cultural destructiveness of Grey's policy.

Christianized Xhosa felt the prompting of the "Holy Spirit in their hearts" to respond to Grey's ruthless attack on Xhosa culture. In 1850 the Xhosa prophet, Mlanjeni, claimed that "he had been to Heaven and had talked to God who was displeased with the white man for having killed his Son." Because of this "God would help the black man against the white."[45]

Exactly what form this help would take was unclear until 1856, when a sixteen-year-old Xhosa girl, Nonqawuse, and her friend received a message from the ancestors. "Tell them," the ancestors told Nonqawuse in phrases reminiscent of Moffat's conversations with the Tswana kings, "that the whole nation will rise from the dead if all the living cattle are slaughtered because they have been reared with defiled hands, since there are people about who have been practicing witchcraft."[46] Nonqawuse's uncle, a Christian convert, proclaimed this message to the Xhosa tribe. The result was tragic. Four hundred thousand cattle were killed and some forty thousand Xhosa died of starvation.[47]

The Xhosa were a shattered people, their power to resist the Whites broken and their future bleak. Yet agents of hope were found. Tiyo Soga (1829–72) was a Xhosa Christian whose father had sung the hymns of Ntsikana. In 1857 he received ordination as a Presbyterian minister after studying at Glasgow University. Soga returned to the eastern Cape in that year with his Scottish wife, Janet. His aim was to promote Christianity in the Transkei.

Struggling with tuberculosis contracted while in Scotland, Soga sought to rebuild his shattered tribe with the stories of the new faith. He translated the first part of John Bunyan's spiritual classic, *Pilgrim's Progress*, into Xhosa. For eleven years he sought to integrate his faith with his Africanness in the face of cruel prejudice by the White community. Like Blyden of Liberia he wrote about the "value of black people and of Africa" but unlike Blyden, Soga based his arguments more on early North African Christianity than his Bantu experience.[48]

---

45. Isichei, *History of Christianity in Africa*, 110.
46. Ibid.
47. Ibid.
48. Hofmeyr and Pillay, *History of Christianity in South Africa*, 74.

Soga helped change the mission practice of creating Christian villages for converts introduced by the Moravians in the previous century. Instead, Soga counseled Christian Xhosa to stay on tribal lands.[49] This change in policy proved beneficial for both the growth of Christianity and the material well-being of the Xhosa. When he died in 1872, he left a vacuum in the ranks of African Christian leadership that would be difficult to fill.

Scottish Missions and Lovedale. Tiyo Soga was convincing proof that Africans could be capable Christian leaders. What was needed were places that could provide adequate training. One of the first institutions dedicated to this task was Lovedale College, which opened in 1841. William Govan, a missionary with the Glasgow Missionary Society, was the founding principal of this institution located on the site of Lovedale mission station. This seminary began as a rudimentary training school for evangelists and catechists regardless of denomination or race. The first class contained eleven Black and nine White students. Though dormitories and dining halls were segregated by race the college was a place where Africans could receive training. Under the leadership of Dr. James Stewart, the training at Lovedale grew in quality as the century wore on. Stewart would later help found Fort Hare University, an institution that would train many leaders of the African National Congress (ANC).[50]

Robert Gray and Anglicanism. By the 1840s Anglicanism faced a crisis threatening its future. Though the number of churches and adherents had grown steadily since the 1820s, the church had no bishop to confirm new members or ordain clergy. Young people were leaving the Anglican Church to join the DRC, complaining they had no bishop to confirm them.

The answer to this need came in 1848 when Robert Gray was appointed bishop of Cape Town. Gray was a gifted administrator. He set up schools and reorganized the Church of South Africa into three dioceses, each with its own bishop. Gray would remain at Cape Town. Bishop Armstrong was consecrated for the eastern Cape in 1853. In that same year John Colenso was made bishop of Natal. Armstrong worked efficiently and smoothly with Gray. Bishop Colenso, as we shall see, was another case entirely.

Roman Catholic missions. Protestants were not alone in their promotion of a missionary Christianity that presented Christ as King over hearts. Roman Catholicism began its successful work in South Africa in 1837 with the appointment of Fr. Raymond Griffith as the vicar apostolic for South Africa. The locus of the work shifted to Natal, where Catholics remained marginalized until after the Zulu War of 1879. Work among the Zulu and Sotho (un-

---

49. B. A. Pauw, *Christianity and Xhosa Tradition* (Cape Town: Oxford, 1975), 24.
50. Hofmeyr and Pillay, *History of Christianity in South Africa,* 75.

der Fr. Gerard), coupled with a new effort to win the Indian immigrant sugar workers, helped Catholicism make large gains. Bishops Allard and Joliet were far-sighted strategists who made sure that the "Catholic church observed no colour bar."[51]

Andrew Murray and the evangelical vision of the kingdom. Common to most missionary Christianity in nineteenth-century South Africa was an evangelical pietism that regarded personal religion as the "heart of the matter." No figure in South African history exemplifies this pietism better than Andrew Murray Jr. (1828–1917). Though not a missionary himself, Murray was a great promoter of missions and helped found the South Africa General Mission in 1894.[52]

Murray had come from Scotland in 1848 to help remedy a shortage of clergy in the Dutch Reformed Church in South Africa. After a successful pastorate in Bloemfontein in the Transvaal, Murray became pastor of the Reformed Church in Worcester in the West Cape. Soon after his arrival a remarkable awakening broke out within his congregation. Large numbers of churched and unchurched claimed to have an evangelical conversion experience. Some fifty young men dedicated themselves to the ministry.[53]

At first Murray was frightened by the apparent disorder caused by the revival but the evident change in so many lives convinced him that this was a true work of God. He sought ways to preserve the fruits of the revival and decided to write devotional books that could be used by his new converts. The first of these was the most famous. *Abide in Christ* became a religious best-seller all over the English-speaking world and vaulted the young minister to international prominence.

The emphasis on "absolute surrender" to Christ became a feature of what became known as "Keswick" piety, which Murray had no small role in shaping. Keswick piety preached an evangelical perfectionism claiming that through entire consecration one could reach a level of spirituality where the entire focus is on Christ, and the power of sin in the believer is broken.

Though burdened with the responsibilities of his denomination (he served as moderator seven times), Murray devoted his remaining years to fostering a global emphasis on piety and missions. In 1880 he launched a society to promote daily prayer, Bible reading, and meditation.[54] He started missionary training schools and encouraged single women to pursue mis-

---

51. J. B. Brain, *Catholic Beginnings in Natal and Beyond* (Durban: Griggs, 1975), 180–81.
52. Eventually the Africa Evangelical Fellowship (AEF). Cf. James Gray Kallam, "A History of the Africa Evangelical Fellowship from Its Inception to 1917" (unpublished Ph.D. diss., New York University, 1978), 213.
53. Hinchliff, *Church in South Africa*, 80.
54. Ibid., 81.

sionary careers.[55] Murray expressed the essence of his view of true spirituality in a series of addresses he gave in 1900 to the Ecumenical Missionary Conference in New York, later published under the title *The Key to the Missionary Problem*:

> One chief mark of the desire to be truly spiritual is the desire not to sin, to be delivered from the common sins of which the average Christianity is so tolerant. When this desire ripens into faith the soul is brought into an altogether fresh and much clearer consciousness of Christ's power to save—Christ becomes more distinctly the center of all thought and all work, at once the source, the subject, the strength of all our witness— And many have found that what at first was sought for the sake of personal blessing, becomes the power for living to be a blessing to others. *And so the deepening of the Christian life becomes the power of a new devotion to missions and the Kingdom of our Lord [author's emphasis].*[56]

In these words Murray captured the kingdom witness of nineteenth-century missionary Christianity. He also embodied this witness in his life and work. His promotion of mission, revival, and devotion made him "one of the greatest, perhaps the greatest, figure in the Cape church at the time, and that in almost every way he stood for and summed up the principal influences at work in the church."[57]

The situation by the end of the nineteenth century. By the last quarter of the nineteenth century, missionary Christianity was spreading throughout southern Africa. But the churches that were founded remained in White hands. Missionary piety went hand in hand with missionary paternalism in a pattern very different from the one envisioned by Venn at midcentury. All too typical was the judgment of LMS missionary William Ellis who wrote that "the native Churches have not hitherto and do not now contain young men of piety and talent or attainments to render them suitable for becoming students for the Christian ministry."[58] When he penned that comment in 1855 there were no ordained African clergy in South Africa. In contrast, West Africa by 1855 had already witnessed the ordination of Crowther and ten others in the Anglican Church and several more within Methodism. Though Tiyo Soga would be ordained in 1856 eleven years would pass be-

---

55. For a useful discussion of Murray and the role of women in the beginnings of the modern missionary movement in South Africa, see Dana L. Robert, "Mount Holyoke Women and the Dutch Reformed Missionary Movement, 1874–1904," *Missionalia* 21, no. 2 (August 1993): 103–23.

56. Andrew Murray, *The Key to the Missionary Problem* (London: Nisbet, 1901), 90–92.

57. Hinchliff, *Church in South Africa*, 81.

58. Adrian Hastings, *The Church in Africa: 1450–1950* (Oxford: Clarendon Press, 1994), 363.

fore a second African was ordained in the south. Missionary domination fostered the spirit of "Ethiopianism," Black independent churches, which swept over many Black Christians at the turn of the century.

Sincere Christians like Paulo Nzuza (b. 1896) were liberated from this paternalism by visions and dreams. One day in 1916 while standing near the grave of his ancestor, Shaka, the Zulu king, the Spirit of the Lord came upon him, commanding him to throw off the yoke of White supremacy in the church and to found the Church of the Spirit. As we shall see in a later chapter, thousands of leaders like Paulo Nzuza would feel these twin spirits of ancestry and Christian piety and raise up a new witness to the kingdom free from missionary control.[59]

The story thus far has emphasized that the kingdom witness of the church in South Africa was largely theocratic or pietistic in nature. This is not the whole story, for a third witness to the kingdom can be clearly seen in nineteenth-century South African Christianity. To the witness of the kingdom on earth we now turn.

The Kingdom as Justice: John Philip, J. W. Colenso, and John Tengo Jabavu

John Philip. Opposition to Van der Kemp's crusade against Afrikaner injustice reached a point of crisis in the early 1820s. To deal with the situation the LMS recruited a Scottish pastor, appointed him mission superintendent, and sent him to South Africa to help ease the situation. John Philip (1777–1851) proved to be poor at appeasement but powerful at promoting justice and giving added substance to the evangelical kingdom witness at the Cape. Philip supported conventional mission strategy, promoting new mission stations by the LMS as well as other mission societies, but his distinctive legacy was in the area of establishing "native rights."

Philip believed in the full equality of Blacks and Whites. He was even convinced that "the people at our missionary stations are in many instances superior in intelligence to those who look down on them as belonging to an inferior race."[60] Such an attitude, combined with an imperious manner, won Philip many enemies. One nineteenth-century writer lamented that though most missionaries were good people, some of them were "keen politicians and their policy was the same as that of Reverend Dr. Philip—to champion

---

59. The story of Paulo Nzuza is told in Bengt Sundkler, *Zulu Zion* (London: Oxford University Press, 1976), 91–93.

60. Isichei, *History of Christianity in Africa*, 108. The best biography of Philip is Andrew Ross, *John Philip (1775–1851): Missions, Race and Politics in South Africa* (Aberdeen: Aberdeen University Press, 1986).

the cause of the native rulers and native states against those whose motto was South Africa—A White man's country."[61]

The political activities of Philip that brought him under so much criticism centered principally around ordinance 50. In 1826 Philip returned to England to lobby for new laws to protect the right of the Khoisan. He published an influential book in 1828, *Researches in South Africa*, which increased his influence. Ordinance 50 was passed in July of that same year, insuring legal equality for "Hottentots and other free persons of colour."[62]

Philip next went to work to secure protection for the Xhosa on the eastern frontier. He advocated the extension of British rule over the frontier in order to protect the African from the settler. He further championed the "Westernizing" of Africans and encouraged the settlement of Africans on the mission station toward this end. Philip felt—rightly or wrongly—that only educated and Westernized Africans had any chance of competing with White settlers and securing their rights. For these reasons Philip supported the Treaty System of the 1830s by which local tribes would maintain a degree of autonomy while agreeing to come under British law and education. Though Philip believed the system would protect Black autonomy and land ownership, it actually destroyed many of these things as time went on.

Philip's witness to the justice of the kingdom tapered off after the emancipation of the slaves in 1834 and the introduction of the treaty system in 1836. He spent the last years of his life seeking to open new stations. When he died in 1851 at a mission station on the eastern frontier, he was one of South Africa's most vilified and most respected men.

Bishop Colenso. Vilification was a common experience of John Williams Colenso (1814–93), Anglican bishop of Natal. Colenso had been a brilliant student at Cambridge, where he prepared for the Anglican ministry. In 1854 Colenso began his work in Natal with a survey of the diocese.

Upon returning briefly to England he published a report about the Zulu. As interested churchmen read the report, all was well until they got to Colenso's defense of Zulu polygamy. Most were outraged. No sooner had that storm erupted than a new one was added over Colenso's commentary on Romans. Colenso saw Romans as teaching Pelagianism, a humanistic approach to salvation through self-effort that stood in opposition to Augustine's emphasis on human depravity and radical grace.

Colenso was one of the first missionaries to be influenced by the new German theology that attacked the historical reliability of the Bible, the sinfulness of man, and the substitutionary atonement of Christ. Because he believed in universal salvation Colenso felt that the task of the missionary was

61. Hofmeyr and Pillay, *History of Christianity in South Africa*, 55.
62. Ibid.

not to convert the heathen but to enlighten God's estranged children about his love and their inherent nobility in his eyes.

Such theological assumptions led Bishop Colenso to new views about the Bible. In a series of works on the Old Testament Colenso attacked the inspiration and infallibility of Scripture, insisting that the Bible was no more the word of God than the works of "Cicero, Lactantius and the Sikh Gooroos."[63]

All of this was a bit too much for Bishop Gray. He accused Colenso of heresy and demanded that he recant. Colenso refused and in the tangled court cases that followed, found himself retaining his position as a bishop of an independent Anglican diocese that was not answerable to the archbishop of Canterbury or Bishop Gray of Cape Town.

Colenso's last controversies were the most noble and pitted him not against the church but against the colonial government. In 1873 a Zulu king, Langalibalele, was arrested and tried for insubordination, having refused to obey a government order to disarm his tribe. The king was found guilty and condemned to death, though the sentence was changed to exile. Colenso was outraged by what he regarded as an unjust trial. Colenso's protest won better treatment for Langalibalele and led to the resignation of the governor.

Colenso became the advocate of the entire Zulu nation in the Zulu wars of 1878 and 1879. Zulu King Cetshwayo was imprisoned after the war and his Zulu kingdom broken up. Colenso launched a pamphlet war to prove that Cetshwayo had been incited by the British, who desired his removal. Colenso's eloquence was his greatest ally. He used it to good effect in a sermon on Micah 6:8 preached in the Cathedral of St. Peter's in Pietermaritzburg in March 1879. While British troops were systematically slaughtering the Zulu to avenge their humiliating defeat at Isandhlwana, Colenso outlined his understanding of kingdom justice:

> Let those who will, bow down and worship their dumb idols, brute force and proud prestige and crafty policy. But we believe, I trust, in the living God, and, if so, then we are sure that, not His blessing, but His judgment will rest on us, if we are not just and merciful now . . . But if . . . we will go on killing and plundering those who have never harmed us, until we made war upon them . . . treating his message of peace with contempt and neglect, even with ridicule . . . there will be reason to fear that some further great calamity may yet fall on us . . . in what way we cannot tell, but so that we shall know the hand that smites us.[64]

Through public preaching and private intervention Colenso sought to end the war and restore Cetshwayo to his royal office. At last, popular and offi-

63. Hinchliff, *Church in South Africa*, 68.

64. J. W. Colenso, "A sermon preached in the Cathedral Church of St. Peter, Pietermaritzburg" (1879), 9–10. Yale Divinity School Archives.

cial support rallied behind Cetshwayo and he was returned to his kingship. Colenso, however, died before his Zulu friend's final vindication, a lonely but effective voice for the coming kingdom of justice and equality.

Jabavu. A final witness for justice is found in the person of John Tengo Jabavu (1859–1921), founder of the first independent Bantu newspaper in South Africa. Jabavu had been raised by Christian parents and was educated in Methodist mission schools. In 1875 he became a mission school teacher himself but his interests were moving in the direction of journalism and politics. He became the editor of the Lovedale Institute's newspaper in 1881. Jabavu's political concerns soon brought him into conflict with the missionary Christianity of his employers and he left to found his own independent paper, *Imvo Zabantsundu* ("Views of the Bantu People").

As an editor, Jabavu supported a number of changing political causes—from White liberalism to du Toit's Afrikaner Bond Party. In 1909 he went to London to oppose a proposed constitution for South Africa that threatened to revoke the African right to vote. His final years were spent promoting African education. He helped found Fort Hare University College in 1916. Though Jabavu would have agreed with Andrew Murray that the kingdom of Christ conquered hearts, he also agreed with J. W. Colenso that Christ's kingdom required political action. This theme of the kingdom on earth would grow to dominate African Christianity in the latter twentieth century.[65]

Conclusion

A spiritual difaqane: *Christianity's fragmented witness.* When Moshoeshoe built his mountain fortress to protect his people from the Zulu invasion he was in a unique position to see the fragments of conflict swirling around his kingdom. The Xhosa wars of the west and the Zulu wars of the east; the struggle of missionary and settler, of Afrikaner and British, were part of a single whole—a major transformation of South Africa and its future. Wise eyes like Moshoeshoe's could catch the whole in the fragments before him.

This chapter has argued that in nineteenth-century South Africa three rival concepts of the kingdom vied for prominence. Afrikaners who saw themselves as a chosen people commissioned to build a kingdom of divine law in the land of South Africa and to offer up a theocratic witness to the rule of Christ clashed with a missionary Christianity that emphasized the inwardness of the kingdom and the "absolute surrender" of the soul to the in-

---

65. For information about Jabavu, see Mark Lipshutz and R. Kent Rasmussen, *Dictionary of African Historical Biography* (Berkeley: University of California Press, 1989).

dwelling Jesus. Clashing with both were prophets of the social gospel who saw the most urgent work of the church as witnessing to God's rule of justice. But, like Moshoeshoe, the whole arena of conflict taken together yields a unique perspective. Though seldom integrated, these three rival versions of the kingdom did exist side by side. In Augustinian terms, though the sin and self-love of the human agents produced a broken witness to a divided church, glimmers of the unity of the City of God could be seen by those who had eyes to see.

The Violent Kingdom

East African Christianity

Rosine Krapf had never seen such sights: A coral reef that churned the sea into a wall of surf; an Arab city with white-washed mosques.; the ruins of an old Portuguese fort named after her savior. These were but a few of the attractions of the island city of Mombasa. Rosine's missionary husband, Johann, had told her much about exotic Ethiopia, but even he was unprepared for the beauty of Africa's eastern shore.

As she gazed on the beauty of her new surroundings, Rosine thought of her pregnancy. Europe would have been her first choice as a place to have her baby. But now Africa would have to do. No missionary had attempted to reach the people of this vast coast since the Augustinians of the seventeenth century. She regarded it as a privilege to be here with her husband. The baby would be fine. All would be well.

It was May 1844 and Rosine and Johann had moved from Zanzibar to Mombasa. The Sultan of Zanzibar, Sayyid Said, ruler of a vast coastal empire, had taken pity on them. He granted them permission to build a mission station—a tiny outpost of the kingdom of God to be ruled by a young European couple and their baby. The sultan may have acted out of compassion for this young mother-to-be. More likely he sought to strengthen diplomatic ties with England. When Rosine's husband later wrote of the "work which we in our great weakness have commenced in East Africa" he was simply being honest.[1] Compared to the might of the kingdom of Allah represented by the sultan of Zanzibar, the kingdom of Christ looked weak indeed.

Rosine's baby was born in early July. Along with the baby came sickness, however; she, the baby, and her husband were soon racked with malaria. Rosine was not strong enough, after the birth, to fight the fever. She died

---

1. J. Ludwig Krapf, *Travels, Researches and Missionary Labours During an Eighteen Years' Residence in Eastern Africa* (London: Cass, 1968, orig. 1860), 497.

without much struggle. Within a few days the child joined her in the grave. Johann was so ill that he barely realized what had happened. It took all his strength to attend the funeral.

A few days afterwards, Johann wrote to the CMS office in London and grappled with the meaning of Rosine's death. "Tell our friends at home," Johann wrote, "that there is now on the East African coast a lonely missionary grave. This is a sign that you have commenced the struggle. . . . As the victories of the Church are gained by stepping over the graves of her members, you may be more convinced that the hour is at hand when you are summoned to the conversion of Africa from its eastern shore."[2]

Forty-two years later and six hundred miles inland another woman stood contemplating a vast body of water stretched out before her. The waves that lapped upon her shore were not those of the Indian Ocean but of a great inland sea known as Lake Nyanza to the locals and Lake Victoria to the British. The woman was not a missionary but a princess of the royal house of Ganda.

Princess Nalumansi, like Rosine before her, was a new bride in May 1886. Though custom forbade the marriage of a Ganda princess, Nalumansi was no ordinary princess. She had shocked the royal family by becoming a Christian. She was baptized by the White Fathers and took the name Clara. She proved the sincerity of her belief as she took her umbilical cord, religiously preserved by her mother and regarded as a sacred symbol by the Ganda, and cut it into pieces before burning it. Within weeks of her action a persecution of Christians was launched by her king and brother, Mwanga I. Princess Nalumansi would survive this first persecution only to be cut down by a bullet in 1888 when war broke out between Muslims and Christians fighting for control of the kingdom.[3]

Rosine and Nalumansi stand at opposite ends of the near half century that marked the reintroduction of Christianity into East Africa. They share, however, a common testimony. The witness to the kingdom of Christ was sometimes a witness unto death. Rosine's death from disease and Nalumansi's death in martyrdom both point to the price that eastern Africa extorted from kingdom witnesses before the new faith took hold. "The victories of the church are gained," wrote Krapf, "by stepping over the graves of her members."

Christians, however, witnessed to the rule of Christ not only through suffering but also through force. In Ethiopia, Kenya, Tanzania, and Uganda, Christians were killed and engaged in killing to promote the faith. This chap-

---

2. Quoted in William B. Anderson, *The Church in East Africa* (Dodoma: Central Tanganyika Press, 1977).

3. Fragments of the story of Princess Nalumansi are given in Elizabeth Isichei, *A History of Christianity in Africa* (Grand Rapids: Eerdmans, 1995), 148, and Adrian Hastings, *The Church in Africa: 1450–1950* (Oxford: Clarendon, 1994), 379.

ter seeks to tell the story of an East African Christianity that came in meekness and martyrdom only to end in militancy and the maxim gun.

Ethiopia

Ethiopia in the early nineteenth century. East Africa's violent witness to the kingdom begins in Ethiopia. Ethiopia during the reign of Fasilidas (d. 1667) in the seventeenth century had undergone a number of changes. Besides moving the capital to Gondar, Fasilidas expelled the Jesuit missionaries, broke relations with the Portuguese, and initiated a policy of isolation that, in time, withered both church and state. By the early nineteenth century the emperors of Gondar in the central province had maintained their title but lost their power. Real authority in Ethiopia was exercised by rival leaders such as Sahela Sellase in the southern kingdom of Shoa and Webe in the northern kingdom of Tigre.

The one institution that should have been a force for reunification, the Ethiopian church, was riddled with divisions over the doctrine of Christ.[4] Until 1841 the church was without an effective *abun*. Church power was exercised to a lesser degree by the *echege* (or *eccage*), the second highest church officer in Ethiopia.[5] Filpos of Gondar sought to provide leadership to his splintered church but without success. An English traveler wrote that Ethiopian Christianity was in a state of ruin and that "there is reason to fear that, in a short time, the very name of Christ may be lost among them."[6] Into this situation of division and decline came the missionaries.

The Church Missionary Society. In 1830 two CMS missionaries, Samuel Gobat and Christian Kugler, arrived in Ethiopia. These two pioneers were soon joined by a handful of other CMS missionaries enabling the work to fan

4. Donald Crummey describes the three main christological controversies in *Priests and Politicians: Protestant and Catholic Missions in Orthodox Ethiopia, 1830–1868* (Oxford: Clarendon, 1972), 24–25. The three primary theological parties were the Unionists, the Unctionists, and the *Sost Ledat*. The Unionists held the Monophysite view that the perfect union of divine and human in Christ meant that he had but one nature after the incarnation. The Unctionists saw the perfect union of the divine and human to be a work of the Holy Spirit, much to the displeasure of the Unionists, who believed this subordinated Christ to the Spirit. The third party was that of the *Sost Ledat*, or three births party. They regarded Christ as possessing a triple sonship. The first was an eternal one from the begetting by the Father; the second was a temporal sonship from the temporal birth by the Virgin; and the third was the redemptive sonship by an act of the Holy Spirit. These three births and sonships, though an attempt at compromise between the parties, ended in even more division. The *Sost Ledat* was charged with reviving the ancient heresy of adoptionism, which taught that Christ was the Son of God by adoption either at his baptism or later.

5. For a discussion of this term and the significance of this office, see Chris Prouty and Eugene Rosenfeld, *Historical Dictionary of Ethiopia and Eritrea*, 2nd ed. (Metuchen, N.J.: Scarecrow, 1994), 97.

6. Quoted in Crummey, *Priests and Politicians*, 12.

out into Tigre, Gondar, and Shoa. One of the most able was a CMS missionary to Shoa, Johann Ludwig Krapf (1810–87), destined to play a large role
in Kenya's Christian history. His primary desire, however, was to work
among the Galla of the south, whose nomadic kingdom he regarded as "the
Germany of Africa" and the key to the evangelization of eastern Africa.[7] He
feared the spread of Islam in Ethiopia and favored British intervention to prevent Ethiopia from falling further into political factionalism. Krapf's criticism of capricious local rulers and his imprudent call for British meddling
brought his career in Ethiopia to an abrupt halt in 1842 when he was denied
reentry into Shoa. The CMS team in Tigre was expelled in 1843, ostensibly
for their refusal to venerate the Virgin.[8]

The expulsion of 1843 stood in contrast to the CMS experience in the early
1830s when it enjoyed considerable initial favor with the local leaders of Ethiopia, including the *echege* at Gondar who was eager for friendly relations with
Europe. Contributing to this favorable reception was the strategy of reform
adopted by the CMS. The Ethiopian clergy were generally relieved to find that
missionaries like Gobat and Krapf did not intend to plant rival churches.

The CMS vision was to accept the Coptic church as a true church of
Christ and to work within it to purify it of corruptions of doctrine and practice. High on the list of corruptions from a Protestant perspective was prayer
to Mary, the veneration of images, and the grip of monasticism. A purified
Ethiopian church could be the key, felt the missionaries, to the evangelization
of the continent. As the foundation for their work of reform, the Protestants
translated the Scriptures into Amharic and sought to create a movement of
biblical literacy.[9]

In time even this seemingly enlightened policy of the CMS proved unac-
ceptable. The major sticking point was devotion to Mary. The Ethiopian
church finally realized that Protestantism represented "a religious revolution
more radical and more offensive" than they could accept.[10] Gobat left in disgust in 1837. A temporary expulsion of the other CMS missionaries took
place a year later. Krapf was harassed and forced out of Shoa in 1842. A
more permanent expulsion order was given in the north in 1843. Though the
Protestant witness was later restored, its relation with the Ethiopian church
and state was tense. These tensions were increased by the arrival of the
Roman Catholics.

Justin de Jacobis and Catholic missions. It is hard to imagine a more ideal
missionary than Justin de Jacobis (1800–1860). "None ever understood

7. Ibid., 49.
8. John Baur, *2000 Years of African Christianity* (Nairobi: Paulines, 1994), 158.
9. Hastings, *Church in Africa*, 225.
10. Ibid.

Ethiopia better or identified more deeply with its religious tradition," writes Adrian Hastings.[11] De Jacobis came to Ethiopia in 1839 to die as a martyr. His prayer was not granted. He served effectively for twenty years and died of disease and exhaustion.

Ethiopia was without an *abun* when de Jacobis came and many saw him as the spiritual leader the nation lacked. He walked barefoot from village to village living the life of an Ethiopian monk. He sent his disciples out two by two in imitation of Christ and gathered them for periodic instruction. He won converts of unique quality such as Ghebra-Mika'el (a learned Coptic monk), Princess Wayzaro Hirut, and Tekla-Haymanot of Adwa, who wrote a biography of the saintly de Jacobis.[12]

The *echege* and emperor were drawn to the Catholic faith through de Jacobis' witness though they never crossed the line of conversion. De Jacobis started seminaries and converted entire villages. Together with his Catholic colleague, Bishop Massaja, who worked among the Galla, de Jacobis dreamed of a reunion between Rome and Ethiopian Christianity.[13] The early success of his mission seemed to bode well for the future. One major obstacle stood in the way of this dream—the new *abuna* Salama.

In 1841 Salama (d. 1867) became the *abun* of Ethiopia. He had been educated at the CMS boys' school in Cairo and grew up with a bias in favor of Protestantism. When word reached the Catholic missionaries in Ethiopia that Salama was to be appointed as Ethiopian bishop they opposed his nomination, thus winning his permanent enmity. Salama was jealous of the influence of de Jacobis. In an 1854 letter to Queen Victoria he wrote that the Catholics "desire to take possession of our churches."[14] Salama was in no position, however, to act decisively against de Jacobis due to the political disunity in the country. If only he had the backing of a powerful king, he could save his church from the intruders. A year after his letter to the English queen, his prayers were answered.

Reunification under Tewodros II (d. 1868). That answer came in the person of Kasa, governor of Qwara. Beginning in the mid–1840s Kasa conquered the independent kingdoms of Ethiopia. In 1855 his conquests were complete and he was crowned by Abuna Salama as the true "king of kings." He took the name Tewodros II (Theodore) to fulfill the prophecy found in the sixteenth-century *Fakkare Iyasus*, which foretold that at the end of the age a mighty king would emerge "who would do Christ's will, restore the churches, and bring peace."[15] How seriously did Tewodros take this proph-

11. Ibid., 226.
12. Baur, *African Christianity*, 162.
13. For a discussion of Massaja, see Crummey, *Priests and Politicians*, 60–63.
14. Quoted in ibid., 87.
15. Ibid., 230.

ecy? He declared himself to be the elect of God, the true "Son of David and of Solomon."

A British official summarized Tewodros' ambitions under three heads: "reform Abyssinia [Ethiopia], restore the Christian faith, and become the master of the world."[16] He longed for the day when he would liberate Jerusalem from the grip of Islam. Yet for all of his arrogance, Tewodros was a pious emperor, faithful to his barren wife and devoted to the imitation of Christ. The reunification of Ethiopia was met with an enthusiastic reception by the masses and a mixed reaction by the missionaries. It was just the development that Salama had waited for.

Salama now moved aggressively against the Catholics. Their most important Ethiopian leader, Ghebra-Mika'el, was imprisoned and tortured to death in July 1855. De Jacobis was forced into hiding. For nearly five years Salama was able to persecute the Catholics. He rejoiced when de Jacobis died in 1860. But his triumph was short-lived. Salama fell out of favor with the increasingly unstable Tewodros and spent his last years in prison. He died in 1867. By the time of Salama's death it was clear to all that Tewodros was losing his grip and that Ethiopia's relations with England and France were unraveling.

In 1867 matters reached a crisis point. England refused to help the emperor with his internal struggle against rival princes. Tewodros went over the edge. He imprisoned the English missionaries and gathered an army. An English military expedition was sent to free the hostages. On Good Friday, 1868, England dealt Tewodros and his army a humiliating defeat. The emperor's last act as the self-declared Prince of Peace was to kill himself. His violent reign brought no millennium but only decades of devastation.

Yohannes, Menelik, and the Two Invasions. In the wake of Tewodros' fall the imperial office fell first to Yohannes IV (d. 1889) and then Menelik II (d. 1913). Yohannes died defending his country against a new messianic movement from Sudan under Muhammed 'Ahmad, the self-declared *mahdi* ("divinely guided one"). The *mahdi* had gathered an army and reclaimed Khartoum from the British under C. G. Gordon in 1885. His theocratic movement destroyed much of the work of Catholic missions in the Sudan, which had been revived under Fr. Daniel Comboni (1831–81) and his Verona fathers.[17] The *mahdists* destroyed his work completely and took the missionaries into captivity. The death of the *mahdi* in 1885 and the failure of his successors to sustain the movement lessened the threat to Ethiopia's sovereignty.

---

16. Quoted in ibid., 229.

17. For an informed discussion of nineteenth-century missionary work in Sudan and the African reaction, cf. Andrew Wheeler, "Christianity in Sudan," in Zablon Nthamburi, ed., *From Mission to Church* (Nairobi: Uzima, 1991), 37–80.

Menelik faced a greater challenge than the *mahdi* and his messianic kingdom. The kingdoms of Christendom represented by a militant Italy bent on colonial expansion almost destroyed a newly reunited Ethiopia. Italy established itself in Eritrea in 1885 and felt confident, recalling England's easy defeat of Tewodros, that it could soon take possession of the whole kingdom.

Menelik united the nation, however, behind this external threat in a way that Tewodros had been unable to do. The Italian army was soundly defeated at Adowa in 1896, assuring Ethiopia's independence as the new century dawned. The legend of Ethiopianism was enhanced by this decisive victory. Africa's oldest theocratic witness to the kingdom of Christ had begun the nineteenth century in weakness but had ended with a military triumph. A pattern was established that would be repeated by Ethiopia's southern neighbors.

Kenya

Krapf and Rebmann. When missionaries arrived in Ethiopia their purpose was to revive a Christian society in decline. When missionaries came to Africa's eastern shore they found a very different situation. Sultan Sayyid Said of Oman was the lord of a vast trading empire that he ruled, after 1841, from his palace on the island of Zanzibar. England had immediately sent emissaries to court in order to establish relations with the sultan. As mentioned previously these diplomatic ties were important in winning the pragmatic sultan's approval for Krapf's missionary work among the non-Muslim tribes of the coast of Kenya near Mombasa.[18] Christianity needed to be newly planted and the decaying theocratic symbol of Mombasa's Fort Jesus replaced with a personal Christianity in which Christ ruled in hearts.

Rosine's death did not deter Krapf from pursuing this objective. After her death in 1844, Krapf regrouped, pouring his energies into a Swahili grammar and Bible translation as he awaited reinforcements. In 1846 he was joined by Johann Rebmann. J. Erhardt arrived in 1849.

Together with his colleagues, Krapf created a station about fifteen miles inland from Mombasa on a low plateau of scrub land called the *nyika* (bush) and inhabited by a collection of nine tribes contemptuously called the Wanyika (people of the bush). The missionaries located their station at Rabai Mpya and sought to attract one of the Wanyika groups, the Giriama, to a new church they had constructed. The Giriama came and listened to the missionaries. Krapf's message of universal sin and judgment was misunderstood at first. After Krapf clarified the message and added the element of God's

18. Pointing to this pragmatism is Said's comment, "I am nothing but a merchant," quoted in Baur, *African Christianity*, 224.

love, it was rejected. After two decades of work the CMS missionaries could point to only a dozen converts.[19]

But Krapf and his team were hard to discourage. Krapf sustained himself by sketching out a new vision, not of the conversion of the Galla as he had originally dreamed, but of a chain of mission stations stretching from Rabai Mpya across the continent of Africa to the western shore. Krapf knew of the Badagry and Abeokuta and would have agreed with CMS assessments that these were already "two good links" in the chain.[20]

Local Kamba traders near Rabai Mpya told the missionaries of beautiful alpine regions inland and responsive tribes that promised to be similarly good links from the eastern side. Krapf sent some numbers to the CMS. "Now if stations with four missionaries," he told his superiors, "were established at intervals of 100 leagues [about four hundred miles], nine stations and thirty-six missionaries would be needed."[21] As this vision grew in his mind Krapf became militant in his metaphors: "Africa must be conquered by Missions; a chain of Missions must be effected between the east and west though a thousand warriors should fall to the left and ten thousand to the right."[22] Though Krapf's estimate of the number of missionaries needed was unrealistically low, his estimate of the number of lives that would be lost in extending the kingdom was alarmingly accurate.

In pursuit of this grand strategy, Krapf and Rebmann embarked on a number of historic journeys between 1847 and 1851. Rebmann visited Kilimanjaro and wrote back to a skeptical Europe of a glacier-covered mountain on the equator. More important, Rebmann visited the Chagga around Moshi and the Shambaa in Usambara closer to the coast. This latter tribe under the enlightened monarch Kimweri invited Krapf and Rebmann to come and work in their midst. It was an opportunity never seized.[23]

Other opportunities came. Krapf's journey with the Kamba chief, Kivoi, to Ukambani brought him within sight of the snow-capped Mount Kenya. The Kamba seemed responsive to Krapf and open to his message. Krapf was hopeful that a second link in his chain of stations had been found. A work among the Kamba, however, prior to the 1890s was not to be. Krapf and Kivoi were attacked by bandits while exploring near the Tana River in Kitui. Kivoi was killed and Krapf barely escaped with his life. Though the Kamba

19. Anderson, *Church in East Africa*, 2–4.

20. Quoted in C. P. Groves, *The Planting of Christianity in Africa*, vol. 2 (London: Lutterworth, 1954), 110.

21. Ibid., 109.

22. Ibid.

23. Roland Oliver speculates that "Usambara in particular, with its absolute and friendly disposed monarch Kimweri, seemed to offer in miniature all the circumstances which were to prove so advantageous in Buganda." Cf. Roland Oliver, *Missionary Factor in East Africa*, 2nd ed. (London: Longman, 1965), 7.

elders released Krapf of any responsibility in the tragedy, the door was shut for a generation to further missionary work. New links in the chain of stations would have to wait.

Despite these setbacks the CMS supported Krapf's scheme and sent out seven new recruits in 1851. Within months most were dead or incapacitated. Krapf was forced home in 1853, his health broken by disease and hardship. Erhardt returned home in 1855. Only Rebmann remained. For twenty years he and a handful of converts, including Mringe and Abbe Gunja, kept the station at Rabai Mpya alive, a lonely testimony to the coming kingdom of Christ in East Africa. In 1874 Rebmann, his sight nearly gone, returned to Germany to die, closing the first chapter of the CMS story in Kenya.

Though Krapf returned to East Africa in 1862 to assist the Methodist Thomas Wakefield in the founding of a station at Ribe for a work among the Galla,[24] his lasting contribution to the continent was with his pen. His *Travels, Researches and Missionary Labours*, written shortly after his return to Europe in 1853, became one of the great motivational books of the modern missionary enterprise. More important, his work in the Swahili language, producing not only Bible translations but also dictionaries and grammars, proved an immense aid to the later growth of an East African Christianity rooted in the African tongue.

Freretown and kitoro *Christianity.* For all the heroism of these early East African missionaries it was Livingstone and not Krapf and Rebmann who inspired the missionary interest in East Africa in the last quarter of the nineteenth century. Livingstone had reported about the East African slave trade and with his dying words had called down heaven's greatest blessing on any who would help "heal this open sore of the world." When he died in 1873, a year before Rebmann's quiet death in Germany, he had captured the attention of the West and inspired new efforts and agencies.

One of the most significant new efforts inspired by the witness of Livingstone was Freretown. In 1872 Sir Bartle Frere arrived in Zanzibar as Britain's special emissary to Sultan Bargash (1837–88), who had succeeded to power in 1870. Frere's task was to negotiate a treaty with the sultan outlawing the sea-borne slave trade. Frere's timing was impeccable. The previous year a hurricane had destroyed not only the sultan's lucrative clove plantations but most of the island's fleet. Bargash was eager to do business with the British and signed the antislave treaty in 1873. What was needed next was a place to put the recaptives that would result from the provisions of this new treaty. Frere had heard of the work that the Holy Ghost Fathers were doing in Bag-

---

24. For a discussion of the Methodist work on the coast under Thomas Wakefield and Charles New, see R. Elliott Kendall, *Charles New and the East Africa Mission* (Nairobi: Kenya Literature Bureau, 1978).

amoyo and a brief visit there convinced him that just such efforts should be made by Protestant missions.

Frere's view of Christianity was similar to that of Livingstone, who saw no conflict between Christianity and commerce. "I regard the spread of Christianity as practically the same thing as the extinction of both slave-trade and slavery," wrote Frere in a report to the archbishop of Canterbury.[25] To this end Frere proposed that the CMS and other agencies establish colonies for freed slaves modeled along the lines of Bagamoyo. Practical education would be emphasized over purely academic or theological training. He criticized the missions for an overly spiritual approach that failed to prepare the African Christian for practical life in this world.[26]

In response to Frere's report, Freretown was opened in 1874. A school was established for the younger members of the community in 1876, but it slowly moved away from academic preparation and concentrated on the learning of a trade. Swahili rather than English became the language of instruction.[27] Though life within Freretown was restrictive and members of the village were not free to leave (largely for their own safety), other Christian villages were started. In the 1880s runaway slaves streamed into these newly founded Christian villages.

Arab slave owners were outraged by these "cities of refuge" and threatened to "make soup of the missionaries' livers" unless they stopped receiving fugitive slaves. In Ramadhan 1880, Freretown was attacked. To encourage his fearful Christians, the lay superintendent quoted Cromwell: "Trust in God and keep your powder dry."[28] He later confessed that he was ready to signal the slave community in Mombasa to begin a mass riot should the attack turn badly for the Christians.[29] In 1883 a Giriama Christian evangelist and teacher at Fulodoyo, David Koi, was killed by Arabs and beheaded for his witness to *Bwana Isa*. He became Kenya's first martyr.

Koi's courageous Christian witness was not an isolated one. Out of Freretown came a number of notable African Christian leaders and a brand of the faith called *kitoro* (refugee) Christianity. The handful of Christians that Rebmann had left at Rabai when he returned to Europe in 1875 grew to two thousand by 1888. Besides men like Koi, leaders of *kitoro* Christianity included Ismael Semler, George David (called the Crowther of East Africa), John Mgomba, Thomas Mazera, Stephen Kireri, and William Jones.

The case of Jones shows the character of *kitoro* Christianity. Arriving at Rabai in 1865, Jones became the pastor of the two thousand Christians re-

25. Quoted in Anderson, *Church in East Africa*, 9.

26. Ibid.

27. Robert Strayer, *The Making of Mission Communities in East Africa* (London: Heinemann, 1978), 21.

28. Reported in Oliver, *Missionary Factor*, 55–56.

29. Ibid., 56.

siding there by the 1880s. He was ordained in 1895. When Salter Price, the CMS superintendent of Freretown, was ordered in 1888 to stop hiding runaway slaves he quietly complied. Jones, given the same order, refused to obey, declaring that he would turn no one away and would allow no one who had sought refuge to be forcibly removed.[30] Such boldness earned Jones the respect of the *watoro*. They called him "big father" and "looked to him as their great friend and advisor in all their troubles."[31] The reaction of the mission was somewhat different.

What puzzled Jones and many other *kitoro* Christian leaders was the reluctance of the missionary to treat the African Christian as an equal. Paternalism rather than racism seems to have been the root problem.[32]

The mission prohibited African Christian leaders like Jones from wearing Western clothes (encouraging them to dress like Muslims instead) or speaking English. Missionaries argued that they were trying to keep their converts from becoming disenculturated. African Christians saw this as an attempt to keep them from upward mobility. The CMS set the salary of their evangelists and catechists artificially low to discourage materialism though no missionary lived by this policy personally. When Jones protested this double standard he was pressured to resign from the CMS in 1897.[33] Eventually Western dress and the use of English were permitted, but the tensions between missionary Christianity and African Christianity, similar to those in West Africa, became greater.

The leap inward: the Scottish Mission, CMS, AIM, and Roman Catholicism in the 1890s. Kitoro Christianity was not the only version present in late-nineteenth-century Kenya. Various forms of missionary Christianity were alive and well and moving inland. The Church of Scotland Mission (CSM) sent their missionary, James Stewart of Lovedale, inspired by Livingstone, to pioneer a new "industrial" mission in the interior of Kenya in 1891. Kibwezi in Ukambani was the chosen spot. Stewart's safari to Kibwezi was typical of those prerailroad forays into the interior. Two hundred and seventy-three porters were needed to carry the equipment of six missionaries.[34] Later, in 1898, the mission was moved to Kikuyu near Nairobi.

In 1901 the CMS also began inland work in Kikuyuland, centering their work at Kabete. The Methodists followed suit. To preclude competition among the Presbyterians, Methodists, and CMS a comity agreement was drawn up dividing the region into different spheres of influence. A host of other groups took the leap inward in the 1890s, including the Neukirchener

30. Anderson, *Church in East Africa*, 15.
31. Isichei, *History of African Christianity*, 136.
32. In contrast to Isichei's harsher judgment. Ibid.
33. Strayer, *Mission Communities*, 26.
34. Groves, *Planting*, vol. 3, 88.

mission (at Ngao on the Tana River, made famous by Krapf's tragic adventure with Kivoi), the Bavaria Evangelical Mission (Eastern Ukambani), and Africa Inland Mission under the leadership of Peter Cameron Scott (d. 1895).

Scott is an example of the combined influence of Krapf and Livingstone on late-nineteenth-century missions in East Africa. In 1895 Scott and seven missionary associates landed in Mombasa. Their purpose was to fulfill the dream of J. Ludwig Krapf and his plan of a chain of stations across Africa. Born in Scotland but educated in America, Scott had fared badly in an earlier missionary assignment in the Congo where he lost his brother and almost his own life. After a time of convalescence Scott once again pondered the possibility of returning to Africa. A visit to Livingstone's tomb in Westminster Abbey and a reminder that "other sheep I have who are not of this fold" inspired the young Scott to return to Africa a second time.

After arriving in Mombasa, Scott began the arduous trek inland. On December 12, 1895, he arrived in Nzawi in Ukambani and there established the first Africa Inland Church. Within a year, he was dead. All but one of his team was either in the grave or on their way home. Yet the work continued. Kangundo (also in Kamba country) became the center of AIM's work until 1903, when, under the leadership of Charles Hurlburt, the headquarters shifted to Kijabe among the Kikuyu.[35]

The Holy Ghost Fathers pioneered a work at Voi (1891) and Nairobi (1899). It was at their Nairobi mission station, St. Austins, that the fathers introduced a commodity, Arabica coffee (already tried at Bagamoyo), which would impact Kenya's future economy.

The completion of the Uganda Railroad (begun in Mombasa in 1895 and completed in 1901 with the laying of track to the edge of Lake Victoria) meant the end of the old hazards of the safari from the coast (desert, Maasai warriors, and wild animals). The number of missionaries to the interior swelled.

The Imperial British East Africa Company and the end of kitoro *Christianity.* While inland Christianity was growing, coastal Christianity was changing. *Kitoro* Christianity faded away as the traffic in slaves disappeared. Critical to this process was the decision of the newly founded Imperial British East Africa Company (1888) to intervene in the explosive issue of runaway slaves. G. S. Mackenzie, chief administrator of the IBEAC, recognized the potential for violence in the situation. Mackenzie's bold solution was to buy the runaways from their previous masters. On January 1, 1889, almost 1,500 former slaves became freemen and 3,500 pounds sterling was expended to their highly satisfied former owners.[36]

---

35. For the history of AIM, see Dick Anderson, *We Felt Like Grasshoppers: The Story of Africa Inland Mission* (Nottingham, Eng.: Crossway, 1994).

36. Groves, *Planting*, vol. 3, 87.

Within a few years, however, this act of Christian charity became clouded by company blunders. Foremost was the "Mazrui rebellion" in which a company official who had meddled in Muslim clan politics ignited a coastal uprising that took British troops nine months to subdue. The company also engaged the inland Nandi in a war and earned the hostility of the Kikuyu for periodic raids for labor and food. The company was forced to relinquish control to the British government in 1894. The next year Britain declared Kenya a protectorate of the Crown.[37] Soldiers and colonialists soon outnumbered missionaries. The meekness of Rosine's lonely grave was soon forgotten as the flag of a mighty empire was hoisted over a new colony.

Tanzania

The slave trade in Tanzania. The resolution of the slavery question in Tanzania followed a somewhat different course. The main routes of the East African slave trade ran through Tanzania, and great effort would be required to shut those routes down. By the 1850s the blood-red flag of the sultan of Zanzibar was carried by trade caravans past Ujiji on Lake Tanganyika, to the court of Kabaka Mutesa in Kampala, all the way to the upper Congo.[38] The most lucrative of all the commodities that these lines of trade brought to Zanzibar was slaves.

Oliver estimates that the total annual number of slaves reaching the coast each year by midcentury was between fifty thousand and seventy thousand.[39] Most of these would be sold on the auction blocks of Zanzibar, making it the "greatest slave market in the world."[40] From Zanzibar the slaves were taken as far away as America. These slaves arrived in Zanzibar after sailing in dhows for one to three days, stacked like firewood and sustained only by a small portion of water but no food.[41] Before embarking from the mainland the slaves were herded into stockades. Livingstone once saw such a stockade packed with eighty-five captives, most of whom were only about eight years of age.[42]

As Livingstone traveled near the Great Lakes of western Tanzania he witnessed firsthand other evils of the trade. "We passed a woman tied by the neck to a tree and dead," Livingstone wrote in his last journals. "We saw others tied up in a similar manner, and one lying in the path shot or stabbed for

37. Kevin Shillington, *A History of Africa* (London: Macmillan, 1989), 317.
38. Ibid., 2, 93.
39. Oliver, *Missionary Factor*, 3.
40. Baur, *African Christianity*, 226.
41. Kendall, *Charles New*, 160.
42. Ibid.

she was in a pool of blood—We passed village after village, and gardens all deserted."[43]

Equally as cruel was the traffic in ivory. Henry Stanley wrote in 1877, "Slave-raiding becomes innocence when compared with ivory-raiding."[44] Zanzibari Arab traders captured entire villages on the upper Congo to ransom them off for ivory.[45] Western Christendom was again aroused to act.

UMCA. At the very forefront of the fight against the East African slave trade was the Universities Mission to Central Africa, founded in 1857 as a result of an appeal by Livingstone during a visit to Cambridge University. The mission set as its purpose to establish "centres of Christianity and civilization for the promotion of true religion, agriculture, and lawful commerce."[46]

Its first director was Bishop Mackenzie (d. 1863), who in 1861 followed Livingstone to the Shire highlands of Malawi. Though Mackenzie had intended to employ traditional missionary methods he was shocked by the slavery situation he found. A work begun among the Manganja was jeopardized by the slave raiding of the neighboring Yao.[47] Mackenzie and Livingstone decided to raid the Yao and liberate the slaves. Their surprise attack enabled them to accomplish their purpose without the firing of a shot or the loss of a single life. Ninety Manganja were liberated. With these ex-slaves Mackenzie sought to establish a Christian village in the Shire valley. The possibility of Yao reprisals made the experiment risky. Within a few months Mackenzie was dead. The maintenance of the Christian village became untenable and the mission entered a year of uncertainty.[48]

In 1864 the new director, Bishop Tozer, decided to abandon the militant mission to Malawi and move the operation to Zanzibar. It proved to be the right decision. In Zanzibar the UMCA founded East Africa's first theological college in 1869. St. Andrews College at Kiungani promoted Swahili language study and translation work and laid the foundations for a learned Anglican clergy in East Africa.

In 1873 the selling of slaves became illegal in Zanzibar. The UMCA purchased the site where thousands had been tortured and erected a cathedral. The move to the Tanzanian mainland came in 1875 when a Christian village modeled after Bagamoyo was opened in Magila. In 1876 many of the liber-

---

43. David Livingstone, *The Last Journals: David Livingstone in Central Africa,* vol. 1 (Westport, Conn.: Greenwood, orig. 1874, reprint 1970), 56, 62, 64.

44. Stanley's report to the Emin Relief Expedition, quoted in Oliver, *Missionary Factor,* 100.

45. Ibid.

46. Ibid., 13.

47. Henry Rowley, *The Story of the Universities' Mission to Central Africa* (New York: Negro Universities Press, orig. 1867, reprint 1969), 183.

48. Ibid., 226.

ated slaves from Malawi who had been aided and instructed by the UMCA missionaries in Zanzibar and Magila migrated back home. While en route they traveled through the kingdom of the Yao chief Matola of Masasi in southern Tanzania. The *Watoro* asked permission to settle in Matola's pleasant land. The king agreed. Christianity soon took root among these warlike people. Before the century ended the UMCA became one of the largest agencies working in Tanzania.

Bagamoyo. For all of the success of the UMCA in Magila no place is more famous in East African church history than Bagamoyo. In 1868 the Holy Ghost Fathers under Father Horner, the first superintendent, established this Christian village on the Tanzanian coast just opposite Zanzibar. Bagamoyo was the collecting point for slaves awaiting the passage to Zanzibar. Sultan Bargash granted Horner eighty acres of land in Bagamoyo and the community was soon underway with over three hundred freed slaves, most of whom had been handed over to the Fathers by the British consul in Zanzibar.[49]

What guided the Holy Ghost Fathers in their construction of Bagamoyo? The concept of the Christian village was not original with them. In a general way, the experiment at Freetown in West Africa was an inspiration. More structured was the experiment of John Eliot (d. 1690), a New England Puritan missionary to the Nipmucs of Massachusetts. Eliot gathered his converts into "praying villages" to protect them from White racism and worldly distractions. Similarly, the Jesuits in seventeenth-century Paraguay built their famous *Reductions* to provide safe havens for newly converted Indians. Though Bagamoyo was not original it was effective for nearly a generation.

Central to Bagamoyo's philosophy was *labora et ora* (work and prayer). The former seems to have been emphasized more than the latter. "The value of work and the love for work," reads a Bagamoyo diary entry of May 1880, "was an essential factor in the moral education of the people."[50] Eleven hours of the day was split equally between school and manual work. An additional two or three hours was given to religious exercises.[51] Through rigorous discipline and an unselfconscious socialism, the freed-slave colony became self-supporting. Coconuts and coffee were cultivated as cash crops. When couples married they were given a plot of land to farm as their own. An African Eden seemed to have been regained.

Even paradise, however, can have its problems. Bagamoyo was no exception. The problem was freedom. Initial enthusiasm for the gospel was followed by suspicions that Christianity would lead to the strict curbing of private freedoms. The refuge of Bagamoyo became a prison for its inhabitants

49. Oliver, *Missionary Factor*, 21.
50. Baur, *African Christianity*, 232.
51. Oliver, *Missionary Factor*, 22.

and an obstacle to its neighbors. The strict curfews, law courts, mandatory work, and required worship became too burdensome a way of life.[52] By 1880 many former residents had run away. Bagamoyo faded into obscurity as the colonial era and its new opportunities dawned.

Though the work at Bagamoyo declined, the mission of the Holy Ghost Fathers expanded. From the very beginning, the Fathers intended to launch a mission to the interior. Soon after the founding of Bagamoyo new Christian centers were planted along the coast and inland among the Chagga of Kilimanjaro. Catechists from Bagamoyo were the key agents of this outreach.

A Mandara mission was begun under Fr. Picarda. He distinguished himself by his opposition to the widespread practice of infanticide. Any natural disaster seemed to be an occasion to kill a child in order to appease an angry spirit. Picarda and other missionaries were instrumental in educating the conscience of their African constituencies and ending infanticide.[53]

The Holy Ghost Fathers were not alone in introducing Catholic Christianity into Tanzania. The White Fathers of Cardinal Lavigerie arrived at Lake Tanganyika in 1879. Like their brother order they gathered free slaves into Christian communities. But the White Fathers were more militant than the Holy Ghost Fathers. Arab slave trading around the lakes reached new peaks in the 1880s and mission stations feared Arab attacks. Cardinal Lavigerie sent out a contingent of French soldiers under Captain Joubert to teach the Fathers how to defend themselves. They became so proficient with their weapons that they soon joined Joubert's attacks on Arab caravans. Like Mackenzie in Malawi the White Fathers found guns strangely compatible with the gospel in the mission to East Africa.[54] From their position on the lakes the White Fathers expanded into Uganda, Burundi, and Rwanda.

The London Missionary Society. The LMS had preceded the arrival of the White Fathers at Lake Tanganyika by two years, commencing their work in Ujiji in 1877. Additional stations were opened at Urambo, Kavala Island, and Mtowa. A unique aspect of the LMS ministry on the lake was their use of a steamer. Livingstone's search for inland waterways to serve the cause of Christianity and commerce had inspired the British philanthropist, Robert Arthington of Leeds, to contribute £5000 for the purchase of a steamer for Lake Tanganyika. By 1882 the steamer was in operation on the lake, having been carried piece by piece by African porters over the two hundred miles separating Lake Nyasa from Tanganyika.

Through the expert leadership of missionary mariners such as E. C. Hore and A. J. Swan, the prospects of Christianity and commerce replacing the

52. Anderson, *Church in East Africa*, 13.
53. Ibid., 52–53.
54. Ibid., 14.

cvils of the slave trade in the Lake District of Eastern Africa looked bright.[55] Yet success was denied. By 1893 the steamer was sold, the missionaries were gone, and the stations were abandoned. What had happened? The answer lies in the hostilities directed against the Christian missions by two Arab slave traders.

Tippu Tib, Rumaliza, and the Arab War of 1887–91. The LMS made every effort to maintain good relations with the Arab traders they found in the region. By 1884, however, relations broke down. Tippu Tib and Rumaliza decided to rid the area of Christians once and for all. Tippu Tib was already fighting the Belgians in Zaire, where his Muslim trading empire was challenged by King Leopold's declaration of the Congo Free State. The intrusion of Carl Peters and the German East Africa Company in 1885 on his eastern flank was the final straw.

The armies of Tippu Tib and Rumaliza launched a series of raids that decimated mission stations throughout western Tanzania. By 1891 the tide had turned. German forces under Hermann Wissman crushed the Arab attackers and destroyed the inland slave trade. Germany declared a protectorate in that same year.[56] Though the LMS abandoned East Africa, a host of new missionaries and African evangelists resumed their quiet work after the guns were silenced.

Uganda

Buganda before Stanley: the impact of Islam. In 1856 Mutesa I (d. 1884) became *kabaka* of Buganda. From his thatched palace that still stands atop one of Kampala's seven hills, he ruled a kingdom that extended back to the fifteenth century. A *kattikiro*, or prime minister, was at his right hand to do his every bidding. Ten *bakungu*, or royal governors, ruled the counties and clans assisted by military officers, the *batangole*. Hundreds of pages served at court.

Standing atop this political pyramid was the *kabaka*, who like the ancient pharaohs of Egypt, was regarded more as a god than a man. When the *kabaka* died he became one of the *balubaale*, or hero gods, which ruled Buganda and protected the royal family. The *kabaka* was regarded as greater than the traditional religion, and loyalty to him was more important than loyalty to the ancestors. Worship of the creator god *Katonga* had already been eclipsed by the *Balubaale* cult. From time to time, Kabaka Mutesa plundered the temples of the traditional religion just to remind the onlookers in

55. Oliver, *Missionary Factor*, 42–44.
56. Peter Falk, *Growth of the Church in Africa* (Grand Rapids: Zondervan, 1979), 238.

heaven and on earth who was in charge.[57] The king had the right to order human sacrifices to the royal cult whenever he wished. Mutesa I was reverently called by his people, "cause of tears."[58]

Early in Mutesa's twenty-eight-year reign, a new religion came to court. As a divine king, Mutesa could change the nation's religion at will, but prudence was needed lest the foundations of his sacred kingship be undermined. The new religion that courted the king's favor was Islam.

Mutesa was impressed by stories of the sultan of Zanzibar's vast wealth and power. To share the same faith might be useful. For ten years the king was instructed in the Quran and observed Ramadhan. Many at court were attracted to this learned religion and its lofty monotheism. As one subject of the king noted, "it looked as if the whole country was going to embrace the religion."[59] At this critical juncture the explorer Henry Stanley arrived in Buganda.

Mutesa, Stanley, and Alexander Mackay. In April 1875 Stanley visited Kabaka Mutesa. His message to his king was the superiority of Christianity to Islam. Stanley argued that if the power of the sultan of Zanzibar was attributable to his religion then the superior power of the European should be attributed to Christianity. The king called his chiefs together and challenged them to choose either Christianity or Islam. Reading the *kabaka*'s mood they chose Christianity.

Stanley felt that a great triumph had been won. He sent a letter to London's *Daily Telegraph* in November 1875 urging England to send missionaries to Buganda. If missionaries would but seize this opportunity, said Stanley, he could guarantee that "in one year you will have more converts than all other missions united can muster."[60] To prepare for the coming of the missionaries, Stanley left behind Dallington Muftaa to translate portions of the Bible into Luganda.[61]

Ganda Muslims at court were critical of Mutesa's religious switch and dared to challenge him on the issue. His reaction was bloody. Seventy chiefs were burned and a kingdom-wide persecution led to a thousand deaths. The Ugandan martyrs of Allah, a decade before those of Christ, bore witness to earthly rulers that a transcendent King existed before whom earthly kings must bow. Such a message was not always well received by Africa's sacred kings.[62]

57. Ibid., 20.
58. Isichei, *History of African Christianity*, 145.
59. Quoted in John Vernon Taylor, *Growth of the Church in Buganda* (London: SCM, 1958), 26.
60. Quoted in J. F. Faupel, *African Holocaust: The Story of the Uganda Martyrs* (New York: Kennedy and Sons, 1962), 11.
61. Baur, *African Christianity*, 234.
62. Cf. Baur's appropriate comments. Ibid.

The CMS was the first to respond to Stanley's appeal for missionaries. A large anonymous donation was received (later disclosed as a gift from Robert Arthington of Lake Tanganyika steamer fame) to underwrite the Uganda mission. On June 30, 1877, the first two CMS missionaries arrived. Shergold Smith and C. T. Wilson were warmly received by the king. Wilson preached at court and the king himself translated for his chiefs. Mutesa appeared moved by the gospel that Wilson proclaimed, remarking "Isa, Isa, was there ever anyone like him."[63] Tragedy soon struck, however. An Arab trader quarreled with Smith and killed him. Wilson was alone and requested help. The replacement that the CMS sent in 1878 was destined to make a lasting impression on Bugandan Christianity.

Alexander Mackay (d. 1890) was an unlikely missionary. Born in a Free Church minister's home in Aberdeenshire, Scotland, in 1849, Mackay determined on a career in engineering. After graduating from Edinburgh University he took a position with a large Berlin engineering firm. He had an aptitude for language, becoming fluent in German in a very short time. His passion, however, was not machines but missions.

In 1875 Mackay applied to the CMS for a position in Mombasa. The opening was filled by another. When the need for new recruits for the Uganda mission was publicized the following year, he jumped at the opportunity, turning down a lucrative job offer. He joined Wilson in November 1878 and immediately began translating the Scriptures into Swahili, having learned the language on the safari from Mombasa.

Mackay wasted no time in getting to the point with the *kabaka*. Islam was the religion of "the false prophet, Muhammad." Slavery was a great evil in which no man or king had the right to engage. The *Lubaale* cult was wrong, he declared, and on one occasion to prove his point threw a *lubaale* charm into the fire to the gasps from his terrified audience. When no evil befell him for such a scandalous act, many began to take seriously his message. His skill with his hands made him a popular advisor to the *kabaka*.

Central to Mackay's Christianity was his kingdom theology. In a letter to his father he applauded the new ideas of the kingdom that were beginning to circulate in the Scottish churches. "Christ should rule Individual, Social, and National life," he wrote. "He is Lord, and the more we recognize this fact, and yield our hearts to it in all things, the more truly will His kingdom come, and His will be done on earth."[64] For Mackay, this meant that a Christian revolution was needed in Uganda that would transform the religion, politics, and economics of the Ganda kingdom. Everything he wrote, preached, or taught to the young boys who entered his school contributed to this coming

63. Quoted in Anderson, *Church in East Africa*, 22.
64. J. W. H. MacKay, *A. M. MacKay: Pioneer Missionary* (London: Frank Cass, reprint 1970, orig. 1890), 282.

revolution. The revolution was progressing and the king seemed daily closer to the kingdom of God.

The White Fathers. Other Christian voices demanded a hearing at the palace of the king. In 1879 the White Fathers entered Uganda and offered the king a rival version of Christianity. Simeon Lourdel represented the Catholics. His methods were as blunt as Mackay's. He presented the king with guns and denounced Mackay as a heretic.[65]

The battle was underway. Side by side, Lourdel and Mackay debated Reformation issues before the king and his ministers. The court was delighted by the display of theological logic.[66] After a few months the king asked to be baptized by both the Protestants and the Catholics. Each group refused on the grounds of the king's polygamy. A noticeable cooling in the *kabaka*'s zeal came in the aftermath of this rejection. Mutesa separated himself completely from the missionaries and their new religion and returned to the *Balubaale* cult. Suspicions sowed by Muslim advisors that the missionaries were agents of British imperialism were given weight by the British attack on Egypt in 1882. When Mutesa died in 1884, he was still a traditionalist.

Christian conversions. Though the king turned away, the faith found a foothold among the members of the *kabaka*'s court. Protestantism appealed to those who were connected with the ministry of the treasury under Chief Kulugu while Catholicism made inroads among the pages at the palace. From these early converts came the *basomi* (readers), whose studies in the Bible led to the first baptisms in 1881. The new *kabaka*, Mwanga, at first was favorable to the faith. The White Fathers built an orphanage and began a community for freed slaves. Mackay and his colleagues continued their school and began a printing press. As more and more conversions were made by both Anglicans and Roman Catholics, MacKay's Christian revolution seemed immanent.

Catholic withdrawal. Just when it looked like the White Fathers were pulling ahead in the race for the Ganda soul, they withdrew from the country. Moral corruption at court may have been a contributing cause. The new king had been introduced to homosexuality by the Arab traders who frequented the court. The royal pages were expected to submit to the king's will in this matter. Removal to a safe distance with their converts seemed to be the best policy to avoid a direct confrontation with the new king.

Mwanga and martyrdom. But just such a direct confrontation occurred. Though favorable at first, the eighteen-year-old Mwanga revealed his true

65. Groves, *Planting*, vol. 2, 328.
66. According to Kevin Ward, "A History of Christianity in Uganda," in Zablon Nthamburi, ed., *From Mission to Church* (Nairobi: Uzima, 1991), 84.

colors soon after his coronation. He was openly skeptical of religion in general and Christianity in particular. His soldiers brutally murdered Bishop Hannington and his party in 1885 simply because they had entered Uganda from the wrong side.[67] Mwanga's homosexual practices only deepened the disapproval he sensed from the missionaries. After his sexual advances were rejected by a Christian page, Mwanga went on a savage rampage.

On June 3, 1886, soot-smeared executioners rounded up Catholics and Protestants and took them to Namugongo, the site of religious sacrifice. Thirty-one Christians, both Catholic and Protestant, were burned alive bearing joyful testimony of their assurance of heaven.[68] The martyrs fueled the cause of Christianity. They sang. They preached. They testified. Though sporadic persecutions broke out in different parts of the kingdom, Christianity was not exterminated.

The wars of religion and the Christian revolution. Mwanga never recovered from the consequences of his rage. In 1888 Christian, Muslim, and Catholic militia units acting in concert overthrew the tyrant. The Muslims seized power, ousted the Christians, and declared Buganda a Muslim state. The kingdom of Allah seemed once again to have triumphed. Yet by 1889 a second coup had brought the Christians back into power, thanks to the timely intervention of an IBEAC agent, Captain Lugard, and his maxim gun.

Mackay died in 1890 and did not live to see the third and final coup of 1892 that brought the Protestants (again with the support of Lugard) into permanent leadership. Mwanga became the puppet king. In 1894 Buganda was declared a protectorate. Mackay finally got his Christian revolution. The rule of Christ now governed "Individual, Social, and National life" or so it seemed. As the gospel spread to the surrounding kingdoms of Toro, Ankole, Busoga, Teso, and Acholi through African evangelists like Apolo Kivebulaya, the conquest of East Africa that Krapf had written about seemed complete though the cost had been high.

Conclusion

When CMS missionary to Uganda, George Pilkington, lay dying in 1893, a bullet having severed his femoral artery, his African associate, Aloni, warned him that death was near. Pilkington agreed and responded, "Yes, my child, it is as you say." Aloni tried to comfort the bleeding missionary. "Sebo, he that believeth in Christ, although he die yet shall he live." With his last breaths, Pilkington affirmed the truth of Aloni's words.

67. Cf. E. C. Dawson, *James Hannington* (London: Seeley, 1887), 446ff.
68. Faupel, *African Holocaust*, 198.

The death of Rosine Krapf, Princess Nalumansi, Ghebra Mika'el, David Koi, and the Ugandan martyrs bore a violent witness to the kingdom of Christ in nineteenth-century East Africa. Theirs was the witness described by Tertullian when he said that the blood of martyrs was seed.

More troubling was the violent witness of the Lugards, Mackenzies, Tewodroses, and Wissmans. They bore witness to European Christendom and its imperialism. Missionaries and African Christians were caught between the violent extremes of martyrdom and militancy in their attempt to establish the rule of Christ in East Africa. Much good was done. Much genuine Christianity was planted.

Yet the warnings of Krapf went unheeded. "Expect nothing, or very little, from political changes in Eastern Africa. As soon as you begin to anticipate much good for missionary labor from politics, you will be in danger of mixing yourself up with them," he wrote in 1860, having learned the hard way in Ethiopia. "Banish the thought that Europe must spread her protecting wings over Eastern Africa, if missionary work is to prosper in that land of outer darkness."[69]

Few of those who witnessed to the rule of Christ shared Krapf's gloomy forecast. The missionary ambassadors of the kingdom who flooded all parts of Africa in the colonial decades were more optimistic that militancy rather than meekness would inherit the earth. "Committed to expanding the Kingdom of God," observed Crummey, "they also furthered the Kingdom of Man."[70]

69. Krapf, *Travels, Researches and Missionary Labours*, 512–13.
70. Crummey, *Priests and Politicians*, 151.

Part **4**

The Kingdom on Earth

African Christianity
in the Twentieth Century

Ambassadors of the Kingdom

The Missionary Factor in Colonial Africa

As Carl Bender sailed up the Cameroon River to the Baptist mission station at Duala to begin his missionary career, his mind was filled with ideas about the kingdom. Just a few months before, in 1899, Bender had graduated from Rochester Seminary in New York. He had studied under a number of gifted teachers, many of whom had doubtless influenced his ideas about missions.

Principal among those who had an influence on Bender was Walter Rauschenbusch. Rauschenbusch believed in missions. "Missions," declared Rauschenbusch, is "another constructive influence in the advance of the social conception of the Kingdom."[1] This great proponent of the social gospel had himself desired to go to India as a missionary. The Rauschenbusch that Bender knew in the classroom was warmly evangelical, revivalistic, and mission-oriented. At the same time Rauschenbusch, with no apparent sense of conflict, held to a concept of the kingdom of God that called for the reform and redemption of social structures and political systems.

Bender's own theology of mission blended evangelistic preaching and social action in an attempt to build the kingdom of God. Bender's convictions about the kingdom were not uncommon for nineteenth-century evangelicals but it was not the only view. Different views of the kingdom and consequently of missions were being voiced in evangelical ranks.

Across the continent in British East Africa, Charles Hurlburt, Africa Inland Mission's director, stood on the edge of the Rift Valley on a windy June day surrounded by a gathering of missionaries, settlers, and government officials to dedicate Rift Valley Academy, a new boarding school for missionary children.

---

1. Quoted in Charles Weber, *International Influences and Baptist Mission in West Cameroon* (Leiden: E. J. Brill, 1993). The life and work of Bender are discussed in chap. 2.

Hurlburt was a tall reed of a man. In 1895, after twelve years in YMCA work, Hurlburt had become the founding president of the Pennsylvania Bible Institute, a school that was soon caught up in two powerful movements. One was the new wave of premillennial teaching sweeping through evangelical circles in the 1890s. The other was the Student Volunteer Movement started a decade earlier at D. L. Moody's Mount Hermon conference in Northfield, Massachusetts. This movement redirected the lives of tens of thousands of young people toward the mission field. Dozens of Bible institutes like PBI had started to train these young missionary recruits.

In that same year, 1895, Hurlburt became a board member of the newly founded AIM. The first director, Peter Cameron Scott, had died in 1896 establishing some mission stations in Kenya. Hurlburt had been appointed as AIM's second director and had come to Kenya in 1901.

Though Hurlburt's first few letters emphasized the need for teachers and tradesmen to come and civilize savage Africa, he rejected the idea that missions was building the kingdom. As he stood before the stone structure of the school's first building, the only divine kingdom he recognized was the "upper kingdom" where Christ dwelt and from where he sends his Spirit to redeem the lost. The proper way to witness to the kingdom of God, for missionaries like Hurlburt, was through preaching and evangelism.[2]

Standing next to Charles Hurlburt at the dedication of Rift Valley Academy was the former president of the United States, Colonel Teddy Roosevelt. Having lost his bid for reelection a few years earlier, he had come to Kenya upon Hurlburt's invitation and had cordially agreed to make a few appropriate remarks at the dedication ceremony. After congratulating both missionaries and settlers for their civilizing work and encouraging both groups to "work together," Roosevelt offered his own vision of the coming kingdom in a short speech punctuated by laughter and applause from the audience. "If you give me a chance," Roosevelt shouted above the wind, "in London or anywhere else, I will talk just as straight as I can . . . that this is destined to be a White man's land."[3]

Though he would not have denied the kingdom visions of Bender or Hurlburt, the vision that most gripped Roosevelt was the colonial vision of empire. This blunt witness to the kingdom of Western civilization and its colonizing mission was no doubt endorsed by many in the crowd that had gathered that June day in 1909.

2. Cf. AIM's early promotional publication, *Hearing and Doing* 6, nos. 11–12 (November–December 1902). Hurlburt's first impressions of Africa and his call for a civilizing mission are found in *Hearing and Doing* 5, no. 8 (December 1901). As time goes on, this more holistic approach seems to have faded somewhat in Hurlburt's thinking.

3. The text of the Roosevelt speech can be found in the AIM Kenya Branch archives, Nairobi, Kenya.

Among the Africans who may have heard the words of Hurlburt and Roosevelt on that day of dedication perhaps one or two later heard the whispered legend that would make the rounds of the Kikuyu community. An African messiah was coming who would free the Kikuyu people from the yoke of the missionary and the colonial administrator. By 1916 the rumor was widespread.

A native evangelist named John reported, "I find it very hard to preach to the people these days because their god is coming soon." John was told that an old person had gone into a trance and received a message from above. The message was one of hope that "their god would come and be their king and the white people would all leave and they would have everything their own way and be always happy." John complained that "they do not want to hear my words, for their own king is coming and they do not wish another." The coming kingdom of African liberation and prosperity was yet another version of the kingdom to compete with the visions of Bender, Hurlburt, and Roosevelt.[4]

Criticisms of colonial missions. The colonial era in Africa can be dated from 1885, the year of the Berlin Conference that initiated the scramble for Africa, to 1960, the great year of independence when more than fourteen new African nations were born, including Zaire and Nigeria. This era coincided with one of the most remarkable stories of church growth in the annals of church history.

In 1900 there were an estimated 4 million Christians on the continent (compared to about 60 million Muslims). By 1914 the number of professing Christians stood at 7 million. By 1930 we read of an estimated 16 million Christians. By the autumn of colonialism in 1950, the number of African Christians had reached 34 million. This remarkable pattern of growth coincided with a great influx of Western missionaries in the early twentieth century who "were thicker upon the ground than colonial officials."[5]

For the missionaries that came to Africa from Paris, London, or New York these imperial decades had a single overriding purpose: to advance the kingdom of God. For most of these missionaries this meant the "restoration of mankind to a right relationship to its creator." Such a restoration "would be achieved through the realization of the lordship of Christ over the kingdoms of this world."[6]

If there was a key text for the missionary vision in Africa it was Revelation 11:15: "The kingdoms of this world are become the kingdoms of our

4. *Hearing and Doing* 21, no. 3 (July–December 1916): 14.
5. Roland Oliver, *The African Experience* (San Francisco: HarperCollins, 1991), 207.
6. Brian Stanley, *The Bible and the Flag: Protestant Missions and British Imperialism in the Nineteenth and Twentieth Centuries* (Leicester: Apollos, 1990), 63.

Lord, and of his Christ" (KJV). Yet this kingdom mission faced stiff competition. In the seventy-five-year history of colonialism in Africa the kingdom visions of missionaries, colonialists, Arabs, and Africans collided. This collision of views and values created confusion as to the true motive and message of the missionaries. Which model of the kingdom were they really witnessing to? How closely allied with the colonial vision did they become?

This chapter tells the story of the missionary impact on Africa between the scramble and the dawn of independence and explores the relationship between Christianity and colonialism. Yet telling this story has become more difficult than it once was due to a growing negative consensus that colonial era missions was simply "imperialism at prayer."

Yale missiologist Lamin Sanneh laments that "the forces pitted against a fair understanding of mission in the late twentieth century are formidable."[7] Stephen Neill went as far as saying that the condemnation of Christian missions for their complicity with colonialism "has been the standing argument of the critics and opponents of missions for more than a century."[8] For many, notes English historian Brian Stanley, the "belief that 'the Bible and the flag' went hand in hand in the history of Western imperial expansion is fast becoming established as one of the unquestioned orthodoxies of general historical knowledge."[9]

Collaboration with government. Four major criticisms stand out above the many that are leveled against the missionary enterprise in the age of imperialism. The first charge is that the missionary and the colonial powers were allies in oppression. A. J. Temu suggests that, "politically, the missions became an adjunct of the administration."[10] The missionary was guilty of aiding and abetting the enemy. The doctrine of providence is sometimes fingered as an underlying ideological cause of this complicity. If God in his sovereignty gave success to the imperialists then God must be on the side of the invaders. A play performed at the Fifth Assembly of the World Council of Churches in Nairobi in 1975 "was a ruthless portrayal of the exploitation of Africa by outsiders: Arab slave-traders, European colonialists, and Christian missionaries." The colonialists and the missionaries were thus partners in the crime of imperialism.

Cultural and religious imperialism. Second, closely related to this charge of collaboration is the charge of religious imperialism and intolerance of African culture and religion. The missionary was so blinded by the doctrine of

---

7. Lamin Sanneh, *Translating the Message: The Missionary Impact on Culture* (Maryknoll: Orbis, 1989), 88.
8. Stephen Neill, *Christianity and Colonialism* (New York: McGraw-Hill, 1966), 13.
9. Stanley, *Bible and Flag*, 12.
10. A. J. Temu, *British Protestant Missions* (London: Longman, 1972), 9.

Christ's uniqueness and supremacy as Lord and the assumption of Western cultural superiority that he was "almost incapable of seeing anything positive and valuable in the life and culture of the African."[11] Temu adds that "almost all the Protestant missionaries to Kenya viewed all native customs and tradition with abhorrence."[12] "To be Christian meant to be 'civilized,'" reports Kenyan professor J. N. K. Mugambi, and that "meant abandoning African life which was described as 'primitive' and 'savage.'"[13]

Sociologist T. O. Beidelman argues that the combination of contempt for African culture and religion with a conviction of the superiority of Western civilization led to a crusade of aggressive evangelism that did irreparable damage to African tradition. "The most poignant and destructive aspect of evangelism in Africa," notes Beidelman, "was the missionaries' failure . . . to appreciate fully the integrated quality of traditional African life."[14] Thus missionary Christianity, in the mind of certain critics, was indeed "imperialism at prayer."

Paternalism in the church. The third charge is paternalism. Beidelman calls missions "'greedy institutions' demanding total control." Because missionaries "aimed at . . . a colonization of heart and mind" they "demonstrated a more radical and morally intense commitment to rule than political administrators or business men."[15] This "morally intense commitment to rule" led to the missionary becoming the "undisputed ruler" in the church.

The Christian understanding of disciplemaking found in the Great Commission of Matthew 28:19 may have been the rationalization for the tendency to turn the convert into a lifetime apprentice. An authoritarian style became normal even when Africans were capable of assuming leadership because "Europeans [meaning any expatriate] were reluctant to give up their roles as pastors after evangelism bore fruit."[16] New missionaries to the field south of the Zambezi were told that "here we do not shake hands with Africans."[17] The African was the "child" who must be brought to maturity under the tutelage of the missionary parent.

Indoctrination in education: narrow pietism and social anemia. To the charges of collaboration, cultural imperialism, and condescending paternalism can be added the fourth charge of narrow pietism. The missionaries

---

11. Geoffrey Moorhouse, *The Missionaries* (Philadelphia: Lippincott, 1973), 322.

12. Temu, *British Protestant Missions*, 155.

13. J. N. K. Mugambi, *Critiques of Christianity in African Literature* (Nairobi: EAEP, 1992), 25.

14. T. O. Beidelman, *Colonial Evangelism* (Bloomington: University of Indiana Press, 1982), 25.

15. Ibid., 6.

16. Ibid., 21.

17. Reported in John Baur, *2000 Years of Christianity in Africa* (Nairobi: Paulines, 1994), 281.

and the education they offered did not prepare the African for the complex world of colonial society and the social, political, and economic issues that it raised for the African. Fueling this narrow view of life was a doctrine of the kingdom of God that emphasized the spiritual and inward aspects of the kingdom to the neglect of the political and social aspects emphasized by others.

Such a narrow understanding of the kingdom had a political agenda of its own: submission to the status quo. "Essentially," says Temu, "the missions taught and demanded submission and total obedience, neither of which could be reconciled with the rising nationalism of the Africans, led by the mission graduates."[18] Langat contends that "for the missionaries, education was seen as an instrument to convert and influence the would-be leaders of Africa."[19] So narrow was the pietism of the missionaries that some objected to running schools for the converts. Missionary strategist Roland Allen opposed involving missionaries in education at all. "To him, anything that distracted missionaries from evangelism was to be dismissed."[20] Though schools were built and staffed by missionaries in great numbers, the suspicion still lingers that a confining biblicism dominated the curriculum. Only by rejecting such spiritual indoctrination has the African been able to advance.[21]

How true are these charges? What role did the doctrines of providence, Christology, discipleship, and kingdom play in shaping missionary behavior? Which kingdom did the missionary ultimately serve, that of Christ or Caesar? This chapter seeks to answer such questions.

The story moves through the three periods of colonial history: the scramble to World War I; the end of World War I to 1945; and finally the end of World War II to 1960. The picture of missionary Christianity that will emerge from this story is that of a movement that bore a flawed but surprisingly effective witness to the kingdom of Christ.

Missions between the Scramble and the End of World War I: The Happy Accident

The scramble for Africa. From the 1870s on, various European powers laid claim to sizable pieces of Africa. Leopold II of Belgium circled the Congo

---

18. Temu, *British Protestant Missions*, 9.
19. Robert Langat, "Western Evangelical Missionary Influence on East African Culture" (Ph.D. diss., Iliff School of Theology and University of Denver, 1991), 81.
20. Beidelman, *Colonial Evangelism*, 121.
21. Cf. Temu's discussion of the independent schools and churches of Kikuyuland in Kenya in the 1920s. These schools and not those of the mission "became ideological centres for the training of the Kikuyu who came to wage the nationalist struggle to regain Kenya's independence" (*British Protestant Missions*, 9).

basin for years waiting to strike. Portugal effectively annexed Mozambique by 1880. England occupied Egypt in 1882.

But these casual and sporadic intrusions into Africa were replaced by a swift and systematic campaign of conquest after 1885. The Berlin Conference, held between November 1884 and February 1885, laid down the "rules to be observed in future with regard to the occupation of territory on the coasts of Africa."[22] Not only did Berlin base colonial rights on "spheres of influence" but it declared that spheres of influence were determined by "effective occupation." The policy of effective occupation initiated a period of military intervention and conquest in Africa that would not cool until nearly the entire continent was in European hands, a condition reached by 1902.[23]

The scramble for souls had begun much earlier than the scramble for colonies. Missionary presence was established in Africa a century before Berlin. But a different era in Africa missions dawned in 1885. New features are visible in African Christianity, beginning with the colonial occupation of the continent to the end of the First World War. Specifically there was new growth in the number of converts, a new level of cooperation between mission and colonial power, and a new kind of missionary recruit and convert.

Church growth and the "colonial principle." First, African Christianity grew in unprecedented ways during this first period of the colonial era. We may explain the growth of missionaries and converts in the decades prior to World War I as "the colonial principle." Stated simply, from 1885 to 1914 Christianity grew wherever a colonial power was perceived to exercise effective and beneficial control. The growth of the church throughout the continent was remarkable. The CMS recorded 11,000 baptisms in 1914 alone, the most successful year since their founding in 1799.[24] But the CMS was not alone in producing impressive numbers.

West and Central Africa witnessed dramatic church growth wherever colonial control extended. In *Nigeria* Britain had proclaimed a protectorate over the coast in 1888. Northern Nigeria with its Muslim majority did not come under British control until 1900. The twelve-year gap between colonial control of the coast and the north partly explains why by 1914 out of 51,750 baptized converts, only 499 came from the north where the colonial impact was weaker, more recent, and consequently more dominated by Islam.

22. A. Adu Boahen, ed., *Africa under Colonial Domination: General History of Africa,* vol. 7 (Paris: UNESCO, 1990), 15.

23. The story of the scramble has been recently retold by Thomas Pakenham, *The Scramble for Africa* (New York: Random House, 1991).

24. K. S. Latourette, *A History of the Expansion of Christianity,* vol. 5 (New York: Harper and Row, 1943), 221.

The Roman Catholic numbers for this same period are slightly smaller but reflect the same pattern.[25] Faith missions such as SIM (Sudan Interior Mission) and SUM (Sudan United Mission) began their work during this period aided by the protectorate.

In *Ghana* the Ashanti war in 1896 that ended with a British victory was a turning point in church growth. Little numeric success had been seen in Ghana prior to this date. The Wesleyan Methodist mission started to work among the defeated Ashanti soon after the tribal war. By 1913 they had baptized 26,000 members. The Basel mission had been at work in Ghana since 1828 experiencing early frustration. After the Ashanti war and beginning of the British protectorate in 1899 matters changed. By 1913 the mission could point to nearly 25,000 converts. The Roman Catholic Church, which had begun only in 1880, boasted 11,000 members in Ghana by the time of the First World War.

Southern Africa was experiencing new church growth. The Union of *South Africa* in 1910 brought together the three major regions of the country (Cape Colony, Transvaal, Orange Free State). This helped heal the divisions created by the South Africa (Boer) War of 1899–1902. Mission activity on behalf of the non-White majorities of the nation increased. The South African General Missionary Society (established in 1904 but conceived by Andrew Murray Jr., in the 1880s) spurred much of this growth.[26] And the growth was nothing less than phenomenal. The estimated seventy thousand Christians in 1870 grew to the 1.5 million Christians recorded in the census of 1911.

In *Malawi* (then called Nyasaland) colonial protection also acted like a magic wand in spurring conversions. The Livingstonia Mission, founded in 1874 (a month after the funeral of Livingstone) and led by the capable Robert Laws, could only point to 15 converts in 1890. The next year British rule was extended over the area. In the next 13 years 49 new missionaries and 9,500 communicants were added in addition to 900 schools, 1,600 teachers, and 57,000 students. Similar reports could be drawn from Namibia, Zimbabwe, and Zambia.[27]

Missions in *eastern Africa* enjoyed major successes. In *Uganda*, the CMS had less than 200 baptized converts in 1894, the year Britain established a protectorate. By 1914 the Protestant community had 98,777 and the Roman Catholics numbered 136,000. This "Christian Revolution" saw converts (most often Bugandan Protestants) sweep into the colonial civil service prior to World War 1.

25. Ibid., 438.
26. Falk, *Growth of the Church in Africa*, 181–82.
27. Cf. ibid., 185ff.

The presence of a colonial power did not guarantee church growth. *Angola* illustrates the possibility of colonial rule undermining the work of missions. Due to the injustices of the Portuguese regime, which supported "rum and gun" slave traders and their exploits, the number of professing Christians dropped sharply from an estimated 250,000 to 29,200 between 1885 and 1914. This illuminates an important corollary to the colonial principle of church growth. Where missionaries were perceived as helpful mediators between the indigenous people and a potentially beneficial foreign power, local response to the missionary message was generally favorable. When the colonial power was perceived to be weak or sinister, church growth was damaged. The character of the colonial regime made a difference in missionary success.

Missionaries and colonialists: the happy accident. The second feature of early colonial missions was the high degree of cooperation between mission agency and colonial administration. Not since the Portuguese mission of the fifteenth and sixteenth centuries had missionaries worked so closely with the colonial power. This cooperation is seen all over the continent and is the basis for the charge that the missionary and the colonial administrator were playing on the same team. Latourette seems to lump colonialist and missionary together when he identifies the dominant factor in missionary success the "penetration of Africa and the partition of the continent by the Whites."[28] But there are two sides to every story.

One side of the story is the fact of complicity. All over the continent missionaries welcomed, invited, and sometimes pressured the colonial power to take control of their area. The voices of welcome were the most common. Though missionaries were at work in Africa long before colonialism, they entered new areas of the continent, particularly inland areas, which had been opened by the colonial presence and were happy for the stability and logistical support that this meant. An example of this is AIM in the Ukambani region of *Kenya*. A British administration was erected in the Kamba town of Machakos in the 1890s making it opportune for the entrance of missionaries who wanted to benefit from the protection and security that could be expected from the colonial power. AIM began in various locations in Ukambani but flourished in Machakos under the cooperative eye of British colonial officers.

George Grenfell, pioneer leader of the Baptist Mission Society in *Zaire* (Congo), wrote enthusiastically of the advent of colonial rule. Though he could "claim to know better than a great many what is meant by native rule" he had after ten years seen enough of it and was "grateful beyond measure" when he learned that "King Leopold of Belgium was taking on his shoulders

28. Latourette, *Expansion*, vol. 5, 460.

the burdens involved by the administration of the Congo territory. A marvelous change, during the second decade of my African life, came over the distracted country I had previously known under the chaotic sway of hundreds of independent chiefs."[29]

But other mission voices were even more strident in their support of imperialism. In 1888 Cardinal Lavigerie, director of the White Fathers, "threw the weight of his influence into the imperialist scale."[30] He lobbied the powers of Europe to take every measure possible to end the dreaded slave trade along Africa's eastern shore.

In *Malawi* Scottish missionaries who had labored in the shire highlands to promote Christianity and legitimate commerce (the ivory trade) found their plan blocked by slave-trading Arabs and land-greedy Portuguese. They openly called for a British protectorate. Cecil Rhodes, icon of British imperialism, supported the missionary plan and promised his support. After a tense period of uncertainty Malawi became a protectorate in 1891. Yet what has sometimes been overlooked was the true nature of the missionary motive in this episode. Missionary representative Horace Waller clarified their position to Lord Salisbury in a memo of March 1887: "The object of the missionaries was not to gain protection from personal danger or to be able to rely on military force against native barbarism; on the contrary their sole desire was to save the settled tribes among whom they were settled from the vice of demoralization which must result if the Portuguese were to push on to the lake."[31]

Sometimes the missionary's role was more sinister. In 1888 an LMS missionary named Rev. Helm deliberately cheated the Ndebele king, Lobengula, out of his land by mistranslating a document from a group of South African businessmen. Though he undoubtedly felt that his work would have a better chance for success under Cecil Rhodes than under an African king, Helm's action represents a damning piece of evidence for the charge that missionaries were agents of imperialism. Though the episodes of such "holy" treachery were few they are but extreme expressions of a general enthusiasm that the missionary felt for the coming of colonial protection.

But there is a second side of the story. On the islands of *São Tomé and Príncipe,* Portuguese treatment of cocoa plantation workers led missionaries to complain to British authorities. The plantation system was modified as a result though Portuguese dislike of missionaries increased.[32] Bishop Tucker of Uganda complained about the German administration policies in Tanzania.[33]

29. Oliver, *African Experience*, 207.
30. Oliver, *Missionary Factor*, 117.
31. McCracken, *John, Politics and Christianity in Malawi (1875–1940)* (Cambridge: Cambridge University Press, 1977).
32. Falk, *Growth of the Church in Africa*, 369.
33. Beidelman, *Colonial Evangelism*, 93.

In *northern Nigeria* CMS missionary Walter Miller "was directly responsible for encouraging the founding of a political organization, the Northern People's Congress, to advance African political aims against British authorities."[34] In *Kenya*, AIM missionary John Stauffacher opposed Lord Delamere's treatment of the Maasai.

In *Togo*, Rev. Zahn protested the occupation of the country by his native Germany, fearing that "the people's confidence . . . can easily be lost, when the missionaries belong to the ruling nation." He warned his fellow missionaries "to remain neutral."[35]

What can we conclude about the partnership between missionary and colonialist prior to World War I? Cooperation can be demonstrated but significant differences also appear. Mission work benefited from the "law and order" brought by European conquest but often bristled when perceived injustices were done to themselves or to their converts. Oliver is right that "the cynic would . . . be wrong to label the missionary enterprise for the years 1884–1904 as merely an auxiliary arm of the imperialist expansion." Whatever common interests they shared were not part of a sinister conspiracy but rather more like "a happy accident."[36] Missionaries and administrators cooperated not because they worked for the same cause but because their differing causes coincidentally benefited through their unofficial partnership.

White missionaries and Black Christians: the new aggressiveness. The final feature of early colonial missions was the emergence of a new kind of missionary and a new kind of African convert. A new aggressiveness characterized both the missionary recruit and the newly won African believer. This aggressiveness was most visible in a new level of evangelistic activity and a new concern for holiness that characterized both the young missionaries from American Bible institutes and British universities as well as the converts who joined the swelling ranks of African evangelists. Additionally, this aggressiveness promoted new struggles for leadership between missionary and convert.

The aggressive recruit. Never before had Africa seen the waves of new missionary recruits that began pouring into the continent after 1885. In 1890 only nine hundred Americans were working overseas compared to a consid-

---

34. Sanneh, *Translating the Message,* 118. Further colonial administrators like Lord Lugard opposed the attempts of missions to evangelize among the Muslim groups of northern Nigeria. This policy "created an unhappy relation between the administration and missions," according to Yusufu Turaki in his study, "The Institutionalization of the Inferior Status and Socio-political Role of the non-Muslim Groups in the Colonial Hierarchical Structure of the Northern Region of Nigeria" (Ph.D. diss., Boston University, 1982), 143.

35. Hans Debrunner, *A Church Between the Colonial Powers* (London: Lutterworth, 1965), 105.

36. Oliver, *Missionary Factor,* 179.

erably higher number of British missionaries. By 1900 the totals had risen to five thousand and by World War I that figure had doubled, with many of the new recruits heading for African destinations.[37] Led by missions statesman John R. Mott, the Student Volunteer Movement helped swell the ranks.

The boats that landed in Durban, Lagos, or Mombasa disgorged hosts of young and inexperienced Westerners who would effect what one historian has called "a dramatic change in missionary attitudes."[38] The older strategy of CMS's visionary secretary Henry Venn (d. 1873) called for the creation of self-governing, -supporting, and -propagating churches and the subsequent euthanasia of mission in an area. The new strategy, while calling for the full utilization of native evangelists, preferred to keep leadership in missionary hands. Why this new attitude?

Some of the explanation lies in new views of the kingdom that were emerging in England and North America at the close of the nineteenth century. Josiah Strong, secretary of the Evangelical Alliance for the USA, spoke for many when he proclaimed that "America was called by providence to join Britain in spreading Christianity and Anglo-Saxon civilization throughout the globe." This evangelical version of the "White man's burden" suggested that the mantle of leadership had been draped by the hand of an all-knowing Providence upon the shoulders of Westerners. This view of the kingdom was often postmillennial, envisioning the triumph of the global church and Christian civilization around the world as a way to usher in the return of Christ.

Other views of the kingdom were gaining momentum. Dispensational premillennialism, popularized by J. N. Darby (d. 1882), was much less optimistic about the triumph of Western civilization but was increasingly zealous about "the evangelization of the world in this generation" (the slogan of the Student Volunteer Movement), largely due to its belief that the only precondition for the return of Christ was the evangelization of the world. Given this urgent task there was no time to build civilizations. The immediate and all-compelling task was to evangelize the lost.

Through the network of Bible institutes, prophecy conferences, and student missionary movements the job of rescuing the perishing for the upper kingdom began to replace the task of transforming Africa into a kingdom of God on earth. Though older evangelical mission supporters such as Rauschenbusch opposed this premillennial version of kingdom missions he was helpless to stem the tide.[39]

---

37. Langat, "Western Evangelical Missionary Influence," 88.
38. C. G. Baâta, ed., *Christianity in Tropical Africa* (Oxford: Oxford University Press, 1968), 17.
39. Patterson, "Kingdom and Great Commission," 93.

Fired by one or more of these rival eschatologies men and women, often with very little formal training or social status, came to an Africa disoriented by the flood of change. To their surprise they found a new status on the field that they could never hope to find at home.

Women played a crucial role. Before 1880, the CMS had employed only eighty-seven women out of a total missionary force of nearly one thousand. In 1915 women (including wives and single women) constituted over half of all CMS missionaries.[40]

The new missionary to Africa, sniffed White hunter Sir John Willoughby, "has only to go to school for a year or two and learn a certain amount of medicine and carpentry, flavored with a little theology, and he is turned out a full-blown missionary and orthodox deacon by the local bishop." If the whisper of such criticism and contempt reached missionary ears they could always reply that because of Keswick holiness with its emphasis on "rebirth, complete surrender, holy living and constant victory over sin" they had a moral right to rule.[41]

More surprising than the background of kingdom theology, Keswick piety, and modest pedigree that the new missionaries brought with them to Africa is the astonishing amount of work they accomplished. The church growth statistics attest to the energy these young missionaries brought to a wide range of tasks.

Like Peter Cameron Scott of AIM, who died only eighteen months after arriving in Kenya, they built mission stations. Like Alfred Tucker, who served in Uganda as bishop from 1890 to 1911, they built schools and organized denominations often with a progressive vision for the leadership potential of the African convert. Like Roland Bingham, founder of Sudan Interior Mission, they often buried their colleagues and kept going. Like Bruno Gutman of Tanzania, they sometimes experimented with innovative missionary strategy and sought to indigenize as much as possible.

Like George Grenfell of the Baptist Mission Society in Congo, they were tireless explorers and enemies of the slave trade. Like P. A. Bennett, acting secretary of the CMS in Nigeria, they were sometimes incorrigible racists. But like Archdeacon Dennis, also of the CMS in Nigeria, they more often opposed racism with equal vigor.[42] And, perhaps most important of all, like Carl Christian Reindorf of Ghana, they mastered the vernacular languages of the people and, like George Pilkington of Uganda, they translated the Scriptures and trained native evangelists.[43]

---

40. Elizabeth Isichei, *A History of Christianity in Africa* (Grand Rapids: Eerdmans, 1995), 80.

41. Tasie, *Christian Missionary Enterprise*, 106.

42. F. K. Ekechi, *Missionary Enterprise and Rivalry in Igboland, 1857–1914* (London: Frank Cass, 1972), 220.

43. On Pilkington, see Oliver, *Missionary Factor*, 184ff.

The aggressive convert. The African "readers" and evangelists that emerged between the scramble and World War I matched the missionaries in terms of energy, accomplishment, and in many cases independence of spirit. "The main lesson of African ecclesiastical history," observes Roland Oliver, "is that the core message tended to run far ahead of its expatriate preachers. Most African societies first received the gospel from fellow Africans."[44]

Central to this new zeal and independence was the role of the vernacular. "Local Christians acquired from the vernacular translations confidence in the indigenous cause," contends Lamin Sanneh. "Local Christians" were "able to respond to colonial events in light of vernacular self-understanding."[45] That the King of kings would choose one's own vernacular to speak his very word gave a new dignity and power to vernacular culture that transcended the insults of imperialism.

Armed with this new self-confidence inspired by a vernacular Christianity, the new converts worked for the kingdom. Some worked side by side with the missionary, like Pilkington's eighty Ugandan evangelists, "who went out two and two from Mengo, carrying Gospels and reading-sheets, to the principal places of the land" and effected the Ugandan revolution. Others like Liberian William Wade Harris struck out on their own armed only with the message that they had heard in the vernacular. The movement that he founded in Ivory Coast and Ghana between 1913 and 1915 claimed over one hundred thousand adherents.

This new aggressiveness is also seen in Lesotho, where believers sent African missionaries on their own initiative to Zambia,[46] and in Mozambique, where a national brought the gospel to the city of Lourenco Marques in advance of the Methodist missionaries who built on his work later. Other new converts broke from mission ranks and formed new churches. Still others fought for national independence. The seed of vernacular Christianity produced a hardy and prolific native plant.

The career of the Rev. James Johnson, mentioned in a previous chapter, is a further example of this new aggressiveness. Known as "Holy Johnson" in Lagos, Johnson was consecrated as the assistant bishop of Western Equatorial Africa by the archbishop of Canterbury in January 1900.

Johnson had lived through the tragic humiliation of Bishop Samuel Crowther, the great missionary to the Niger River Delta, who had been hounded by younger missionary critics and was forced to resign his position. He had also seen the subsequent overthrow of the Venn policies by the CMS as the new recruits from Britain sought more control over the West African church. Though he worked within the church for most of his career and "ac-

44. Oliver, *African Experience*, 204.
45. Sanneh, *Translating the Message*, 123.
46. Falk, *Growth of the Church in Africa*, 198.

cepted missionary partnership" he nonetheless "encouraged the delta churches to strive for self-reliance."[47] Though he opposed the independent churches that were emerging around the prophet figures of the Niger Delta he also spoke against colonialism, "European manners, customs, and dress." Johnson's own statement of his position captures well the spirit of new aggressiveness:

> Christianity is a Religion intended for and is suitable for every Race and Tribe of people on the face of the Globe. Acceptance of it was never intended by its Founder to denationalize any people and it is indeed its glory that every race of people may profess and practice it and imprint upon it its own native characteristics, giving it a peculiar type among themselves without its losing anything of its virtue. And why should not there be an African Christianity as there has been a European and an Asiatic Christianity?[48]

Why not indeed? Johnson's words underscore the radical pluralism of the Christian faith with its "translatability," its power to become vernacular without losing its universal and transcendent message. As Johnson entered into his new duties shortly after his consecration his new views got him into trouble with CMS authorities. Not only was he thrown out of his position but his belongings were dumped into a street in Lagos.

This shameful treatment led to the formation of an independent church and the "Bethelite" movement in Nigeria. The leaders of this movement "resolved to overtake the CMS in Yoruba country and create an alternative to Anglicanism."[49] Kingdom missions from the West were beginning the long struggle with the African vision of the liberating rule of Christ.

Johnson was not the only example of what the new African convert was like. Other African converts reacted even more militantly against White domination in both church and state. When Charles Domingo joined the Church of Scotland mission at Livingstonia he was regarded as a very promising future leader. In 1908, after a clash with missionary Donald Fraser, Domingo withdrew from the mission and came under the influence of the missionary radical Joseph Booth and his Seventh-day Baptist church. Domingo's Ethiopianism found full expression. In a famous letter Domingo critiqued European Christianity and its concept of the kingdom:

> There is too much failure among all Europeans in Nyasaland. The Three Combined Bodies: Missionaries, government—and Companies or Gainers of money do form the same rule to look on the Native with mockery eyes. It sometimes startles us to see that the Three combined bodies are from Europe

47. Sanneh, *Translating the Message,* 144.
48. Quoted in ibid.
49. Ibid., 145.

and along with them is a title 'CHRISTENDOM'. And to compare or make a comparison between the MASTER of the title and His Servants it pushes any African away from believing the Master of the title. If we had power enough to communicate ourselves to Europe, we would have advised them not to call themselves 'CHRISTENDOM' but 'Europeandom'. We see that the title 'CHRISTENDOM' does not belong to Europe but to future BRIDE. Therefore the life of the Three Combined bodies is altogether too cheaty, too thefty, too mockery.[50]

Domingo's critical assessment of the European view of the kingdom shared, he felt, by missionaries, colonial officials, and traders alike, did not lead him to reject Christianity but rather to reform it. He was convinced that behind the "mockery eyes" of the Westerner was a defective kingdom theology which needed serious revision.

Domingo's aggressiveness as an African Christian is mild compared with the case of John Chilembwe. Chilembwe illustrates how explosive the issue of the kingdom of God could become for African Christians. He first appears as a cook to Joseph Booth and his Zambezi Industrial Mission in the Shire highlands of Malawi. Booth helped him to go to America in 1897 where he received training at a Baptist College. He returned to Malawi in 1900 and began the Providence Industrial Mission with help from his African-American friends. His work was a great success, showing steady growth right up to the eve of World War I.

The years 1913–14 proved to be a turning point for Chilembwe. Three events brought about a radical transformation in his life. The first was White settler injustice. The nearby settler farm at Magomero was managed by William Jervis Livingstone, a descendant of the great missionary. Livingstone had treated harshly members of Chilembwe's church who were squatters on the estates, on one occasion even burning their houses and churches. Chilembwe was outraged.

The second event was the outbreak of world war. Malawi was the scene of severe fighting between German and English forces. Many Africans lost their lives. When recruits ran short the colonial government seized Africans by force. Chilembwe protested this injustice in a letter to the *Nyasaland Times* in November 1914. His mild protest never reached his intended audience. That issue of the paper was confiscated by the government. The frustration mounted.

The third event was the preaching of Watch Tower millennialism in Malawi by Eliot Kamwana. Kamwana proclaimed the end of the world and the return of Christ in 1914. All earthly authorities, he insisted, were enemies of the kingdom of God. When the kingdom comes all rival kingdoms will be

---

50. *Letters of Charles Domingo*, ed. H. Langworthy (Zomba, 1983), quoted in Adrian Hastings, *The Church in Africa: 1450–1950* (Oxford: Clarendon Press, 1994), 484.

destroyed. How much of Kamwana's radical millennialism Chilembwe imbibed is not known for certain. What is known is that on January 23, 1915, Chilembwe and a group of his followers attacked the settler homes at Magomero. They decapitated William Jervis Livingstone and murdered several other Europeans. Chilembwe bore the head of Livingstone back to his church. Government forces broke the rebellion and killed Chilembwe when he attempted to escape to Mozambique. Though Chilembwe became a famous symbol of African nationalism he remains an enigma—an African Christian leader whose Ethiopianism was transformed into a violent rage in an attempt, perhaps, to usher in the kingdom.[51]

Missions between the End of World War I and the End of World War II: The Uneasy Partnership

Changing attitudes. World War I ended this first period of colonial Christianity with its new growth, close collaborations with colonial power, and aggressive recruits and converts. The extent to which the war disrupted the work of missionaries and native evangelists varied.

Actual fighting between German and English military took place in East Africa. Churches were disrupted when missionaries and church members joined the war effort and left their parishes depleted. Missionaries were cut off from their lines of support and new agencies were formed to care for those thus stranded. German missionaries in Tanzania, Namibia, Togo, and the Cameroons (including Carl Bender) were put into internment camps and their work transferred to non-German mission societies. One AIM official described the conditions in Kenya in late 1914: "The situation in Africa is very serious—the British Protectorate is under martial law, the German residents are being arrested and placed in custody."[52]

The remarkable fact is that African Christianity bounced back from the impact of war in stunning ways. The thirty years from 1914 to 1944 "constituted one of the greatest periods in [Christianity's] long history" in Africa. The estimated 724,000 African Roman Catholics became 4.6 million by 1933 served by approximately 10,000 missionaries. Protestants numbered 556,000 in 1911 and 2.1 million in 1936 with the figure of 7,500 missionaries for 1936.

However disturbed actual mission work was by World War I, colonialism and the overseas missions agencies who had ridden its coattails experi-

---

51. For a discussion of the Chilembwe case, cf. Hastings, *Church in Africa: 1450–1950,* 484–86.

52. Letter of Rev. Palmer to C. F. Johnston, October 1914, Billy Graham Archives, 81.22.8.

enced an identity crisis. To all appearances the control of Africa by colonist and missionary grew in size and scope between 1918 and 1945. This was "the time when all important initiatives in Africa were taken by Europeans. During this period there were hardly any Africans in positions of real responsibility in their own countries. . . . Everywhere colonial governments were at the zenith of their power."[53]

Yet this flurry of activity and appearance of control were deceptive. What Roland Oliver said of African Christianity in the 1950s was true of colonial ideology and Western church triumphalism in the period between the wars: it was expanding at the circumference while collapsing at the center.

The First World War "shattered the faith of Europe in the moral values which it had inherited from the nineteenth century, and gravely injured the churches which seemed to be so closely connected with those values." Consequently, "imperialism in general and missions in particular fell sharply in the esteem of a public opinion which no longer felt that western civilization had incalculable benefits to confer upon inferior races."[54]

Fundamentalists with their spiritual and future view of the kingdom became increasing disturbed by liberals with their earthbound visions of social justice. Similarly, representatives of Teddy Roosevelt's vision of White domination grew nervous while Africans, who had risen to the challenge as soldiers and church leaders, enjoyed a surge of new confidence. This was seen on the international scene. The presence of non-European Christians at the great missions gathering in Edinburgh in 1910 was small. The number had increased by the Jerusalem conference of 1928. By the Madras meeting of 1938 non-Europeans were in the majority.

Missionaries began to doubt the wisdom of colonial partnership. When the German missionaries who had been expelled from their fields during the war returned in the 1920s to resume their work (a provision guaranteed by the Treaty of Versailles) their relationship with the new colonial management was often difficult.[55] The happy accident of mission and colonial cooperation between 1885 and 1914 became the uneasy partnership in the thirty years before the end of World War II. The work of translation, medicine, evangelism, and church planting went on at record pace but the issue that dominates these decades is education.

Education and missions. Colonialism after the folly of World War I needed a "justifying policy."[56] The deliberations of the newly formed League of Na-

53. Roland Oliver and J. D. Fage, *A Short History of Africa*, 6th ed. (London: Penguin, 1988), 190.

54. Oliver, *Missionary Factor,* 231.

55. For an authoritative discussion of German missions in the colonial era, cf. Marcia Wright, *German Missions in Tanganyika: 1892–1941* (Oxford: Clarendon, 1971).

56. Oliver and Fage, *Short History of Africa,* 184.

tions provided the colonial powers with just such a policy. Instead of following Teddy Roosevelt's vision of Africa as a "White man's country," the new vision was more benevolent. The colonial powers would remain in charge of Africa until the Africans themselves were able to "stand on their own feet in the arduous conditions of the modern world."[57]

This new vision of colonialism as tutor was expressed in the new crusade to educate the African. Missions had always seen this as part of their job. A religion of the Book such as Christianity required a literate audience. Bush schools were as much a fixture of African Christianity as the mission station itself. But the new colonial vision went beyond the need for literacy. The new educational task required training the African to govern.

It was with this idea in mind that the Phelps-Stokes Commission was established and dispatched to Africa to determine how this new approach to education might be accomplished. Two commissions came. The first commission visited West, Central, and South Africa from 1920 to 1921. The second commission toured East Africa three years later.

The two commissions discovered that the mission schools were everywhere and immediately sensed a way to save government money and still "lift the native." Though the mission schools were, in the eyes of the commission, "little nothings" with a Western-oriented curriculum that had little relevance to African culture or needs, the report encouraged the Colonial Office to use the mission school network in order to achieve the goal of African empowerment. In 1925 the colonial governors of the colonies were summoned to a continent-wide conference, where "a practicable and far-reaching education policy was agreed whereby colonial governments would spend their limited funds in subsidizing, inspecting and improving schools already operated by the Christian missions."[58]

Initially most missions responded to this new initiative in education with enthusiasm. J. H. Oldham, secretary of the International Missionary Council in London that represented a number of British and North American boards, saw this joint venture in education as the key to the liberation of the African from colonial attitudes and control. As he looked at Lord Northey's repressive labor laws in Kenya and General Smuts' attitude of White supremacy in South Africa, Oldham saw education as liberation. "Will the dominant white race," Oldham asked, "look on [Africans] primarily as instruments of its own economic advantage or recognize that its duty and responsibility is to guide and assist them to the highest development of which they are capable?" The answer to his own question Oldham knew was the schoolhouse.

How did the missionary in the field look at this push to educate? The working missionary had seen that the impact of colonialism was the "rapid

57. Ibid.
58. Ibid., 187.

disintegration of the old patterns of African life." To augment evangelism and church planting with a new thrust in the area of education would help provide the "spiritual basis of a fresh society on the ruins of the old."[59]

They began this work with relish. Oliver writes of the "thin superstructure of schools for the Christian elite" that were set up by the various mission organizations, "prestigious boarding schools for the children of the African middle class, like Mfantsepim in Uganda, the Alliance High Schools in Kenya, Livingstonia in Nyasaland, Lovedale in the eastern Cape; and everywhere some higher schooling for the training of primary school teachers." In Africa south of the Sahara "until the middle of the 1920s Christian missions did all these things on their own initiative and at their own expense."[60]

These schools erected what Richard Gray has described as a "narrow and precarious ladder, up which a few persistent and fortunate individuals could climb towards a position from which they could claim to challenge the whites' claim to superiority."[61]

The price that missions had to pay for this partnership with the colonial regime in education was not a small one. The building of the school rather than the building of the church became first priority. The position expressed by Francis Hindsley, cardinal archbishop of Westminster, was representative of most Catholic and Protestant agencies: "Collaborate with all your power; and when it is impossible for you to carry on both the immediate task of evangelism and your educational work, neglect your churches in order to perfect your schools."[62] Though convinced of the essential rightness of the new educational policy, many missionaries were exhausted by the demands of running schools and frustrated by the government's constant pressure.

Developments in West and Central Africa. In West Africa mission initiatives in education were widespread. *Nigeria* saw new developments all over the country but none as remarkable as the "school miracle" of Father Shanahan. Bishop Joseph Shanahan arrived in Nigeria in 1902, the first Irish missionary to the country. Long before the Phelps-Stokes Commission he had reached the conclusion that schools were the key to the Christianizing of Africa.

"The school-children," predicted Shanahan, "would open every home to the missionary; they would be 'tiny apostles' gradually converting their parents."[63] He traveled by bicycle and by foot over Igboland in eastern Nigeria. He praised the intelligence of the young Africans he met, and felt that Igbo culture needed "transformation rather than destruction."

59. Latourette, *Expansion*, vol. 6, 217.
60. Oliver, *African Experience*, 210.
61. Quoted in ibid.
62. Ibid., 211.
63. Baur, *2000 Years of African Christianity*, 150.

To accomplish this transformation he needed schools. He recruited priests and sisters to staff the growing number of schools that he founded. Under his leadership the number of Catholics "doubled nearly every third year." When Shanahan left Nigeria in 1931 (eventually dying in Nairobi in 1943) he left behind 33,000 students in the Catholic mission schools of Igboland. And Shanahan was right. These students were "tiny apostles" who brought their parents to the church, for the number of catechumens in 1931 was 85,000.

In *Togo* the Presbyterian Church had picked up the work left by expelled German missionaries. The Basel Mission had left such a well-trained African leadership behind that the synod was soon dominated by capable Africans. By 1931 the synod "took full financial control for its extensive schools."[64]

In *Ghana* the work of church and school was so successful that by 1936, though Islam was spreading, it "was no longer a pagan country, that fetish house and small temples had largely vanished, that the sorcerer and the old wild dances were passing and that many non-Christians participated in Christian festivals, read the Bible, joined in Christian Prayers, and regarded themselves as belonging to the Christian community."[65]

In *Cameroon* Baptist missions were moving ahead on the two fronts of church and school. Carl Bender returned to West Cameroon after the war and saw his Soppo church grow from 38 to 1,400 members. Central to the success of the work were outstanding native evangelists such as Robert Jam and Joseph Mamadu. But equally significant was the progress of the schools, which by 1944 were 24 in number with over 21,000 students. By as early as 1938 nationals had gone through the mission schools and government training centers and were joining the staffs as trained teachers.

The role played by single women missionaries in staffing the schools and guiding them to success was as significant here as it was throughout the continent.[66] But frustration with the colonial powers was also rising. In 1944 George Dunger, one of Bender's successors, wrote with anger and concern of the disruption caused by World War II and the British expulsion of German missions. The entire work of the Cameroon Baptist Mission was threatened by the discord between the colonial powers.

The government of independent *Liberia*, in contrast to colonial countries in West Africa like Cameroon, did not invest in education in the interior. "The deliberate policy of the American Negro bureaucracy," writes Groves, "in intimidating the interior tribes naturally deprived these of all opportunity for progress." The one ray of hope according to the Christy Commission of 1933 were the places where "a few missionaries are in-

64. Latourette, *Expansion*, vol. 6, 247.
65. Ibid., 248.
66. Weber, *International Influences and Baptist Mission*, 127.

stalled."[67] Independent Liberia was a reminder that colonialism had no monopoly on injustice.

Zaire recovered slowly from World War I. Though Belgium had fallen to Germany the colonial administration continued. After the war the government supported the rise and development of Catholic schools. Protestants jumped on the educational bandwagon.

Tensions soon mounted between Protestant missions and the colonial government when a pattern of prejudice and discrimination against Protestantism became apparent with the closing of some schools and the government's intimidation of chiefs who were regarded as "pro-Protestant."[68]

Additionally, some evangelical missions in Zaire such as the Conservative Baptist Foreign Mission Society (which entered in 1946) resented the concept of a "civilizing mission" because "the term carried a liberal 'Social Gospel' connotation for the conservative minded Baptist missionaries." Though they approved of medical missions, which were growing everywhere in Africa during this second phase of colonialism, conservative evangelicals were reluctant to overextend themselves in building the kind of educational system their African churches demanded.[69]

Tensions in southern Africa. In *South Africa* Christianity was undergoing transformation during this second era of colonialism. The union of South Africa in 1910 had meant effective independence for White South Africans from direct British rule though several territories within South Africa still remained under the Union Jack.

Christianity seemed to flourish under these conditions. By 1936, 99 percent of all White South Africans claimed some kind of church affiliation. Among non-Whites 50 percent were numbered as Christians. Yet these large numbers veiled struggles within the church over issues such as urbanization, industrialization, and racism. The latter issue gave the church particular concern.

Though colonialism was ending in South Africa as a political system it was still alive as a way of thinking. The Color Bar legislation of 1926 excluded non-Whites from industrial jobs. This was opposed by most of the churches. A student Christian conference in the 1920s composed of Whites and non-Whites testified to the power of Christian faith to overcome colonial attitudes of White supremacy. What was needed in addition to churches and primary schools were Christian universities where Africans could be prepared, as the Phelps-Stokes Commission had stated, to "stand on their own feet in the arduous conditions of the modern world."

67. Groves, *Planting of the Church in Africa*, vol. 4, 182.
68. Latourette, *Expansion*, vol. 6, 241.
69. Jack E. Nelson, "Christian Missionizing and Social Transformation" (Ph.D. diss., Temple University, 1989), 9.

The Paris Evangelical Mission Society continued in Basutoland, increasing its emphasis on the training of indigenous leaders. More significant was the decision of Sir George Grey in 1916 to found the University College of Fort Hare for the Black population of South Africa. In 1942 the Christian Council of South Africa chose Fort Hare as the venue for their conference on the task of the church in "Christian Reconstruction" after the war ended. The need for Christian higher education would become more critical as the church in South Africa faced the National Party's victory in the aftermath of the Second World War.

East Africa. These were momentous decades for eastern Africa. *Ethiopia* was conquered by Italy in 1936 and began a short but devastating period under the colonial yoke affecting not only the Coptic church but also the important work of the Presbyterians, the Sudan Interior Mission, and the CMS. Yet it was just south of Ethiopia in *Kenya* that the uneasy partnership of church and mission was most visible.

As was the case all over the continent Christianity was growing numerically in Kenya between the wars. Among Protestants, there were 47,078 adherents in 1924; 77,537 in 1936. On the Catholic side, there were 8,556 adherents in 1921; 60,505 in 1936.

AIM missionary W. J. Guilding wrote to the home office in New York of the growth of the church in Machakos. "The new church seating between 600 and 700 has an average attendance at the Sunday Gospel Service of 550." In addition "the catechumen class now numbers over 300."[70] While African churches were growing, African land was shrinking. After the First World War the indigenous population of 3 million watched a steady stream of retired British soldiers move to the hospitable climate and rich farmland of the highlands that ran from Mount Kenya on the equator south toward the Rift Valley and Kilimanjaro.

Both the colonial government and the Kenyans themselves looked to education as the salvation from this impending takeover by White settlers. Both groups put pressure on the mission agencies to increase their educational work. Schools multiplied. New missionaries were recruited and deployed as full-time staff and part-time church workers. By 1928 the strain was showing.

C. F. Johnston grumbled that in spite of increased efforts in education, "the Christian natives are no longer satisfied with what we have been and are doing for them and their children."[71] Missionary Clara Guilding, faced with additional pressure from supporters in the States whose vision of kingdom missions did not include education, wrote with exasperation that

70. W. J. Guilding, letter of June 10, 1925, Billy Graham Archives, 81.21.3
71. Letter of May 14, 1928, Billy Graham Archives, 81.22.9.

Mrs. Hotchell's Bible class expressed their wish to undertake my full support on the field. They are very anxious that their missionary should do only evangelistic work. It is useless to tell them that all our work is of that character. They are opposed to school and girls work. People who have not been on the field just cannot realize conditions.[72]

The conditions that Clara Guilding referred to included not only tension between mission and government but also tension between mission and African national. The Kikuyu circumcision crisis of 1929 was one expression of this tension. Because African children were now expected to be in school any absences would be noticed. When large numbers of Kikuyu girls were absent from their schools during the time of traditional circumcision, the missions (primarily the Church of Scotland mission, AIM, and the GMS) began a crusade fully approved by the colonial government to stamp the practice out.

The Kikuyu tribe reacted to this attack on their culture. The height of the crisis was reached with the brutal murder of an AIM missionary and several Africans loyal to the mission. When CMS missionary John Comely took a strong stand in 1931 against the practice of female circumcision, school attendance plummeted from 1,734 to 346. Baptisms fell from 107 in 1930 to 14 in 1932. "Wherever the missions took a hard line against," writes Brian Stanley, "dissident Kikuyu Christians took the lead in establishing independent schools, and, in some cases, in forming Kenya's first independent churches."[73]

For the first time on any significant scale the resentment that had been previously reserved for the government was now directed at Christian missions. This anti-mission attitude would also mean that the "Christianity as cultural imperialism" argument would become a familiar part of the Kikuyu and nationalistic critique of missions. Though the immediate conflict died down in the 1930s the missionary had to wonder if the partnership between government and mission was taking a toll on its relationship with the churches it had founded. This uneasy partnership would face even more severe tests in the final phase of the colonial era.

Missions between the End of World War II and Independence: The Long Goodbye

New winds of independence. The rise and fall of Nazism and fascism on the European Continent severely tested the missionary enterprise during World War II. For a small but vocal coterie of German missionaries and Afrikaner

---

72. Clara Guilding, letter of June 11, 1926, Billy Graham Archives, 81.21.3.
73. Stanley, *Bible and Flag*, 152.

nationalists Hitler was a messianic figure building a kingdom of glory and greatness that would transform the world. The more innocent rhetoric of a Josiah Strong or a Teddy Roosevelt about the divine destiny and supremacy of the Anglo-Saxon race became a force of mass destruction in the propaganda of the National Socialists.

Two men stand as telling icons of the last era of colonialism. The first is a symbol of liberation; the second, a symbol of repression.

By 1950 the king of kings, the Conquering Lion of Judah, was ruling his beloved African kingdom. Emperor Haile Selassie, bearer of these sacred names, had overthrown, with the help of the Allied powers, the colonial intruder Italy. Once again, as had been the case so often in Africa's past, Ethiopia's kingdom symbolism made credible by her new independence inspired the continent. Many other Africans who had returned in triumph from the Second World War felt this new confidence in their own souls. Such inspiration was needed. The 1950s saw colonial powers and White supremacists tighten their grip on an Africa that was rich in raw materials like uranium, cobalt, and copper needed by the West.

In 1950 Dr. Hendrik Verwoerd, son of a missionary and the leading theorist of apartheid in South Africa, became minister of native affairs and began to implement his views driven by "an almost messianic conviction of both the justice of his policies and his own divine mission to bring them to realization."[74] These symbols of liberation and oppression fueled the drive for independence in church and state. And independence and leadership were the dominant issues in African Christianity in the 1940s and 1950s.

These winds of independence blew through the churches of the humble as well as the state houses of the great. In the highlands of Kenya a group of Kikuyu elders gathered in November 1947 to demand that the Africa Inland Mission leave the area because of the poor quality of their schools and the mission's lack of interest in development: "After all these years we have been with you we have *thought* and *understood that we shall never get anywhere* under this mission leadership. We Agikuyu have a saying equivalent to English saying that 'Leadership is Everything.' Now, the church members of *Githumu District* ask you very *anxiously to leave Githumu District for good.*"[75]

"Leadership is Everything." No three words better summarize the fifteen years between the end of the Second World War and the dawn of independence. When AIM resisted the request from Githumu they were taken to court and lost the judgment. Many of the plaintiffs in the case went on to start an independent church, African Christian Churches and Schools, to in-

74. Adrian Hastings, *History of African Christianity: 1950–1975* (Cambridge: Cambridge University Press, 1979), 9.
75. Letter of the Githumu Elders, November 24, 1947, Billy Graham Archives, 81.12.38.

sure that they would be properly prepared for leadership. "Leadership," after all, "is everything."[76]

Broad, continent-wide forces were at work in this local case in Githumu, though few of the elders would have known it at the time. Political, cultural, and ecclesiastical developments across Africa contributed to this drive for leadership and through leadership, independence.

Political developments promoting independence. In 1957 the colony of Gold Coast became the independent nation of *Ghana*. Kwame Nkrumah, Ghana's first prime minister, was the dynamic visionary who after years of imprisonment and political agitation saw his kingdom vision realized. "Seek first the political kingdom," Nkrumah once said, "and all other things will be added unto you." He took the title "black messiah" and tried to earn it by promoting Pan-Africanism, a movement of liberation and solidarity for all of oppressed Africa.

In 1958 Nkrumah hosted in his capital of Accra the All-African Peoples Conference. Five hundred delegates from all over the continent gathered and heard the chairman, Tom Mboya of Kenya, sound the theme not only of the conference but also of the decade: "We meet here in Africa to announce African unity and solidarity, to tell the colonial nations—your time is past, Africa must be free."[77]

In that same year France, her confidence shaken by her defeat in Vietnam in 1954, offered her African colonies the independence of which Mboya spoke. In 1960 a dozen new French-speaking nations were born.

In *Kenya* the violent but militarily unsuccessful Mau Mau rebellion of the mid-1950s, nearly as anti-missionary as it was anti-colonialist, impressed the British government sufficiently to begin the quick march toward independence there. Mission-educated Jomo Kenyatta, imprisoned for his involvement in the Mau Mau rebellion for much of the 1950s, would become the new nation's president in 1962.

Cultural developments promoting independence. This climate of independence was furthered by literary and cultural movements that were distinctly African. Just as the spirit of secularism threatened to cut off Europe and North America from their religious and cultural roots, African poets and writers rediscovered the value of their own religious and cultural roots. Capturing the spirit of African identity and independence in their poetry was the *négritude* movement of Leopold Senghor, Aime Cesaire, and Leon Coutran Damas.

76. For an in-depth case study of a mission and church relationship during the colonial era, and particularly the trying decade of the 1950s, see John Gration, "The Relationship of the Africa Inland Mission and its National Church in Kenya between 1895 and 1971" (Ph.D. diss., New York University, 1973).

77. Hastings, *History of African Christianity: 1950–1975*, 94.

Under the influence of such eloquence, Europeans and Africans were forced to look with new appreciation and respect at African culture. African clergy and catechumens could not help but feel the force of this movement throughout the continent. One missionary, Franciscan F. Placide Tempels, had anticipated some of this cultural rediscovery as early as 1945 with the publication of his *Bantu Philosophy,* which reflected a new appreciation for the uniqueness of African religion and culture. "It is amazing," wrote a Dahomean priest after reading Tempels, "how this Father who knew only a few Bantu tribes was able to express the deepest feelings of our souls."[78]

But Tempels was the exception and not the rule. Missionaries were reluctant to engage in any serious indigenization of Christian faith and doctrine until after independence but at least some were pointing to the future. Soon African Christian youth, echoing the desire of James Johnson of Nigeria decades earlier, would insist on a distinctively African Christianity.

Church growth and emerging autonomy. Throughout the war years and into the 1950s Africa went to church. By 1950 the number of African Christians had reached 34 million. Fueling some of this growth in *Tanzania, Uganda,* and *Kenya* was the East Africa Revival, which began in the late 1920s but reached its climax in the 1950s. Church members were revitalized and their new enthusiasm for their faith attracted others. The continued rise in adherents put pressure on the missionary establishment to train pastors for the growing flock.

Who would lead this burgeoning church? Cautious steps were made to make African churches more capable of caring for the new members. Church leadership was still in the hands of missionaries in 1950 but constitutional changes occurred in the decade before independence that gave many of the mission-founded churches legal autonomy. This was a major step to the self-governing principle that most missions officially endorsed.

Anglican churches in West Africa and Central Africa became autonomous from Canterbury in the early 1950s. East Africa Anglicanism became a "province" church in 1960 and 1961. Catholic hierarchies shifted more power to their national churches in British West Africa in 1950, South Africa in 1951, East Africa in 1953, and French Africa in 1955.[79]

Presbyterianism became locally autonomous in Ghana in 1950 and East Africa in 1943. Sudan Interior Mission agreed to a separate constitution for the Evangelical Churches of West Africa in 1956–57. The creation of churches that were now legally autonomous from their parent churches or agencies was a long stride toward a self-governing church but, as Hastings notes, however, "change did not normally bring with it the effective commencement of black responsibility for church leadership."[80]

78. Quoted in Baur, *2000 Years of African Christianity,* 284.
79. Hastings, *History of African Christianity: 1950–1975,* 112.
80. Ibid.

The key to church independence: leadership development. It was clear to both missionaries and African Christians in the historic churches that the pressures for self-government would not go away. Both sides agreed that well-trained and qualified leaders was the best way to insure a smooth transition from mission to church. The number of trained leaders in the 1950s was inadequate to care for the number of parishioners.

In the words of Adrian Hastings, "when the missionary Mother Hubbard went to her cupboard to get a 'black bishop,' the cupboard would prove all too bare of men with experience and education."[81] When Bishop Neill did his 1950 study to respond to this scarcity of leaders he concluded that "while the churches had worked hard since the 1920s on the development of schools and hospitals—they had done strangely little in most places to train a local clergy" who could replace the missionaries.

Theological departments were started at major universities and united theological colleges such as St. Paul's in Limuru, Kenya, were founded (1955). Of significance for the whole continent was the establishment of the theological faculty of Lovanium University in Kinshasa, Zaire, in the 1950s, regarded as the birthplace of African theology.[82]

The point that should not be missed in this survey of the 1950s is that White missionary and Black priest were both beginning to realize that the future lay with an independent church intellectually capable of shaping an authentic Christianity that avoided the secularism of the West or the syncretism of the East. This realization pointed to highly trained clergy lest the church on one side be "spurned and ignored by the educated minority" who would lead the new nations or on the other side be corrupted by a christo-paganism from below that would cause the church to "disintegrate at the centre while it is still expanding at the circumference."

Writing shortly after independence, Roland Oliver predicted that "the decisive act of the missionary drama lies . . . in the theological colleges, in the secondary schools and above all in the impact of European Christianity upon visiting students from Africa." The education question still determines what the "legacy of the missionary factor" in Africa will be.[83]

The end of the missionary era. The colonial era had begun with a scramble and ended with the rush to independence in 1960. By that time mission and church relationships were tense everywhere.

One Sunday in November 1960 Paul Hurlburt, the son of Charles Hurlburt of AIM, tried to take his customary place in the pulpit of the Baptist

---

81. Ibid.
82. On the significance of the Catholic faculty of Kinshasa, see Gordon Molyneux, "The Contribution to African Theology of the Faculte de Theologie Catholique in Kinshasa, Zaire," *Africa Journal of Evangelical Theology* 11, no. 2 (1992): 58–89.
83. Oliver, *Missionary Factor in East Africa,* 291–92.

church in Katwa mission in Zaire. Paul had labored in Zaire since 1929 and had seen the country move through the various periods of colonial rule to independence, which had been won earlier in 1960. The African pastor of the church, Gabriel Kulala, protested the old missionary's presence. The missionary and the African began fighting for the pulpit. Suddenly the young people in the congregation rushed forward and told Hurlburt to leave. As he left he was shoved and kicked. After leaving the building Hurlburt and his party were peppered with stones hurled by an angry group of youth who yelled, "The day of mercy is over." Soldiers arrived and after an ugly and violent clash, restored order.

The clash at Katwa mission was a sad but certain sign that missions in the colonial era had ended. Angry Africans and other independents would no longer take second place in the church of Africa. They had been downtrodden by the White presence long enough. Africa belonged to the African again and the African church should follow suit. The day of mercy was over.[84]

Evaluating the Mission Impact

The missionary factor in Africa during the colonial era that stretched roughly from 1885 to 1960 was critical in once again reestablishing Christianity, one of Africa's oldest religions, throughout the continent. But at what price? Which kingdom did the missionary witness to? Bender's postmillennial kingdom? Hurlburt's spiritual and heavenly kingdom? Roosevelt's "bully" kingdom of White supremacy? The Kikuyu kingdom of liberation?

We conclude this chapter with an evaluation of the four criticisms of the missionary enterprise in the age of imperialism. A series of paradoxes in the missionary witness to the kingdom appear.

The paradox of collaboration with the government. First, the same belief in divine sovereignty that permitted missionaries to welcome and exploit the evangelistic opportunities afforded by colonialism enabled them to criticize it and its abuses.

Colonialism was not an unmixed blessing for missions. Though the "colonial principle" seemed to advance the gospel in the earliest phase of colonialism, "the explosive growth of new churches since independence in the twentieth century is enough of a hint that colonialism had inhibited the gospel in many parts."[85] Even while the missionaries cooperated with the forces of imperialism they also relished their role as leading critics of colonialism.

84. Reported in Nelson, "Christian Missionizing and Social Transformation," 1–2.
85. Sanneh, *Translating the Message*, 112.

The missionaries preached about One who "had been unjustly judged and crucified by the cynical representative of a colonial power."[86]

Frequently the missionaries were from countries other than that of the ruling colonial power and therefore felt no "patriotic duty" to support the new overlords. AIM's John Stauffacher was an ardent advocate of Maasai rights and a continual thorn in Lord Delamere's side in the 1920s. Missionary Walter Miller opposed British rule in northern Nigeria. The excesses of King Leopold's rule in Congo were first brought to the world's attention by missionaries critical of any form of ruthless colonialism and protective of the rights of their flock. Alexander Mackay of Uganda the year before his death in 1890 summed up his reaction to the colonial intrusion into East Africa by remarking, "In former years the universal aim was to steal the African from Africa. Today the determination of Europe is to steal Africa from the African."

This missionary "double mindedness" cannot be understood apart from the Christian doctrine of God's sovereignty in history. This doctrine of providence has two sides. While God's sovereign will directs the rise, fall, and expansion of nations, the believer's response to God's sovereign initiatives must always be within the boundaries of God's moral will. In other words, the doctrine of providence taught missionaries to accept the intrusions of colonialism as an opportunity while simultaneously alerting them to watch for any violation of God's standards of justice and righteousness.

While missions was never as consistent as it should have been in responding to both sides of the doctrine of providence it is nonetheless this "Christian belief in divine providence," writes Brian Stanley, "that goes a long way towards explaining why most missionaries and their supporters accepted imperialism as a general historical process, but the converse of their belief in providence was their unrelenting insistence on moral and spiritual responsibility to challenge and criticize the reality of imperial policy on the field."[87] The kingly rule of God, as most missionaries perceived it, seldom produced revolutionaries but it frequently produced reformers.

Cultural and religious imperialism. Second, the same belief in the redemptive lordship of Christ that led missionaries to disrupt African culture and oppose African religion also helped produce the renewal of African culture and planted the seeds of a radical religious pluralism. The missionary is accused of cultural imperialism and intolerance because of the uncompromising emphasis on the supremacy of Christ, an emphasis that seems somewhat arrogant and intolerant at the present time when the value of other third world cultures and religions is being rediscovered. The history of missions in Africa

86. Oliver, *African Experience*, 204.
87. Stanley, *Bible and Flag*, 70.

is full of cultural insensitivity, petty denominational rivalry, arrogant attitudes, and unfair attacks against African tradition.

Yet there is more to the missionary impact on African culture than arrogance or disruption. Three observations need to be made. First, the missionary often softened the blow of cultural disruption brought on by colonialism by being a buffer and bridge between the world of the West and the world of African tradition, making what could have been a harsher process of change less damaging. "With a foot in both worlds," observes Robert Strayer, "mission communities represented an important arena for the making of a new African culture."[88]

Second, most Africans became Christians because they wanted to. "African Christianity," writes Richard Gray, "is not the result of brainwashing by foreign missionaries." Rather, it was embraced freely and enthusiastically by thousands of Africans "because this faith was seen to meet . . . some of the long-standing needs and demands of African societies."[89]

Third, the historical record also shows that the missionary generally had a higher view of the African and the culture than did the colonial administrator. One evidence of this is the fact that missionaries devoted years of study "to languages spoken by as few as ten thousand people."[90]

Because missionaries believed in the message of the redemptive lordship of Christ as the greatest gift that could be given to another culture they learned the vernacular languages in order to preach and translate the message. The work of the missionary in vernacular translations of the Bible had a transforming impact on African culture.

Lamin Sanneh argues persuasively in his *Translating the Message* that vernacular translations gave tribal cultures their first written literature and increased the value of the culture by the fact that the very words of God and of his divine Son were now contained in the language of the tribe. Indigenous cultures were revitalized by this revolutionary act. "In their vernacular work, Christian missions helped nurse the sentiments for the national cause, which mother tongues crystallized and incited."

What this accomplished over time was stunning. Through the vernacular translation of the message of Christ "were sown the seeds of vernacular renewal."[91]

One might think that a narrow view of the uniqueness of Christ and a strong emphasis on his saving lordship would oppose pluralism. Yet the very lordship of Christ so strongly held by conservative Catholics and Protestants

88. Strayer, *Making of Mission Communities*, 159.
89. Richard Gray, *Black Christians and White Missionaries* (New Haven: Yale University Press, 1990), 83–84.
90. Oliver, *Missionary Factor*, 181.
91. Sanneh, *Translating the Message*, 124.

also led them to study the traditional worldview of African traditional religion in order to extend Christ's lordship over the African mind. These were years when African traditional religion was "rediscovered" by missionaries. Placides Tempels' 1945 study, *The Bantu Philosophy*, is the breakthrough study that opened the way for a new appreciation of African religious concepts. The scientific study of African religions and philosophies was promoted, in many cases, by those who seemed most convinced of Christian uniqueness. Thus, "the Christian missionary impact has created a worldwide pluralist movement distinguished by the forces of radical pluralism and social destigmatization."[92]

Paternalism in church affairs. Third, the Christian belief in discipleship introduced an initial paternalism and authoritarian pattern into African Christianity even while it fostered and empowered African leadership. There is sufficient documentary evidence to show that the racism and superiority attitude that is so often associated with colonialism was sometimes shared by the missionary. The new missionary type that came to Africa in the wake of the Crowther disgrace was less willing to hand over power and take second place to the African Christian.

The missionaries of the colonial era came with a new attitude of authoritarianism. Venn's policy of partnership until a national church can stand on its own was replaced by a new paternalism in the late nineteenth and early twentieth centuries. This is most clearly seen in the case of Samuel Crowther, who was pressured by the new waves of missionaries coming from Britain into relinquishing financial control to them. The rapid promotion of African Christians to positions of leadership slows down and does not regain momentum until the end of the colonial era.

This shift in attitude does not denote a decline in piety or zeal on the part of the missionary. Perhaps more significant was a shifting paradigm of the kingdom. The early-nineteenth-century model of the kingdom—Christ's direct rule over hearts that would transform individuals and cultures—underwent a significant modification. The establishment of that rule required European leadership and tutelage for a longer period than previously thought. The hard nut of African traditional culture and religion was found to be harder to crack than had been realized. An apprenticeship of several decades under the European master would be necessary.

Yet side by side with this pragmatic reading of the situation the missionary's own self-understanding as a disciple of Christ and a maker of disciples in Christ forced abandonment of this paternalism over time and empowerment of the African to lead. Significantly, the commitment of missions to education and the dependence on nationals for evangelism and discipleship

92. Ibid., 234.

would hasten the respect and confidence in African leadership that would re-place this disappointing paternalism. Missionaries were dependent upon Af-rican evangelistic zeal and expertise in the growth of Christianity. From the ranks of these faithful evangelists would come not only the future leaders of the African church but also the indisputable evidence of African competence that would eventually explode the myths of Western superiority and vindi-cate the Christian belief in the centrality of disciplemaking.

Indoctrination in education: narrow pietism and social anemia. Finally, the missionary's belief in the coming kingdom of God on earth produced a nar-row pietism and biblicism in education that led paradoxically to a growing secularism and political activism. Many missionary critics have pointed to the irony that the education found in the mission schools, though dominated by the pietism and biblicism of evangelical missionaries like Hurlburt and to a lesser degree Bender, led to a kind of secularism. Ali Mazrui has stated bluntly, "the carriers of Christianity into Africa were also the carriers of western secular education."[93] The missionary teacher and African colleague in the school preached that the kingdom of God was spiritual in nature yet was "somehow integrally connected with literacy, Western medicine, and such technological wonders as guns and textiles."[94]

One CMS missionary went as far as saying that "modern thought was es-sentially a Christian product."[95] Beidelman points out that when the mis-sionary taught the Old Testament to her African students she was teaching a manual of nationalism and cultural independence from foreign powers.

Geoffrey Moorhouse observes that within the narrow confines of the missionary school came the great leaders of Africa's first wave of indepen-dence such as Kenneth Kaunda of Zambia, Julius Nyerere of Tanzania, Hastings Banda of Malawi, Jomo Kenyatta of Kenya, and Kwame Nkrumah of Ghana. What surprises him is that missionaries unwittingly taught con-cepts that "meant the end of European supremacy on the once Dark conti-nent." Additionally their teaching meant "the beginning of the freedom to control one's own life, to stand up in the congress of nations with the right to speak as an equal upon the affairs of the whole world." Moorhouse con-cludes that through a strange paradox "the missionaries were the agents of that freedom."[96]

How do we explain this paradox? One factor that must not be over-looked is the hidden implications of the missionary belief in the coming king-dom of Christ. In light of the coming kingdom no earthly government or cul-

---

93. Ali Mazrui, *The African Condition* (London: Cambridge University Press, 1980), 50.
94. Beidelman, *Colonial Evangelism*, 27.
95. Ibid.
96. Geoffrey Moorhouse, *The Missionaries* (Philadelphia: Lippincott, 1973), 335.

ture was absolute. Neither the British Empire nor the traditional tribal culture could be equated with the kingdom of God. This was the Protestant principle that had functioned fitfully and sporadically throughout Western culture since the Reformation—no earthly structures are eternal. These "doctrines and the sacred scriptures of which the missionaries had of necessity been the purveyors, were in themselves revolutionary and egalitarian influences within the colonial context."[97]

John de Gruchy makes this paradoxical impact of the coming kingdom clearer: "God's eschatological purpose is to transform this world and so make all things new through his Spirit." Thus "the promised kingdom judges our clinging to the past, or our attachment to the present status quo and, in Gilkey's words 'lures us in to the future,' making us dissatisfied with anything less than God's righteousness, justice and peace in the world."[98]

In a way no missionary fully appreciated, a strong biblicism coupled with a transcendent view of the coming kingdom led to a kind of secularism (a concern for the things of this world) that was coupled with a strong desire for change (no earthly structure is final or permanent). The supposedly narrow and Westernized views of the kingdom borne by Carl Bender and to a greater degree by Charles Hurlburt actually provided a transcendent reference point by which the status quo could be judged and even changed. In spite of the faults and inconsistencies of the missionaries themselves, the message of the kingdom was a leaven that transformed the colonial era from within.

Conclusion

The missionary factor in Africa between 1885 and 1960 was both profound and paradoxical. The missionaries planted churches, evangelized the lost, made disciples, built schools and hospitals, translated the message, and bore witness to Christ in ways that often went beyond their intentions. They were not heroic angels but neither were they imperialistic devils. In the eyes of many they were fools, fools who bore a witness in a way they did not fully understand to a kingdom whose meaning they seemed never fully to grasp. Sometimes they were plain fools stumbling through African culture or blindly sharing the values of imperialism. More often than not, however, they were fools of Christ, who works in paradoxical ways in the world and uses foolish things to confound the wise.

---

97. Oliver, *African Experience*, 204.
98. De Gruchy, *Church Struggle in South Africa*, 198–99.

Cities of Zion

Independent Christian Movements before 1960

In the heart of Zaire lies the holy city of Nkamba. In this city lies the body of Simon Kimbangu, prophet and founder of the Church of Jesus Christ on Earth through the prophet Simon Kimbangu (EJCSK). For several decades the guardian of this holy city was Dialungana K. Salomon, the second son of the dead prophet.

To honor his father and to exalt the city of Nkamba, Salomon wrote a Kimbanguist hymn, *Zolanga Yelusalemi dia Mpia*, "Being Loyal to the New Jerusalem." The hymn speaks of how the humiliation and suffering of Africans ("the most dishonoured of all races whom God created in this earth") came from the "hill of Satan" but that God had sent his prophet, Simon Kimbangu, to convert hearts, perform miracles, teach the Bible, and lift the people up from their suffering and humiliation. Kimbangu had done these things at Nkamba. Nkamba was thus the sacred place where "God our Father and his Son Jesus Christ are returned to us." Though other prophets had their Zions, only Nkamba was the true Jerusalem.[1]

In the sixty years before independence, convictions as powerful as those captured by Salomon gave rise to thousands of African independent churches and new religious movements like the East Africa Revival.[2] David Barrett es-

---

1. W. MacGaffey, "The Beloved City: Commentary on a Kimbanguist Text," *Journal of Religion in Africa* 2 (1969): 129–47.

2. Perhaps we need a new term to replace the standard term, "African independent (or initiated) churches." A term like "African independent Christian movements" (AICM), though clumsy, may be better than the traditional terminology although other terms may serve just as well, such as David Barrett's "African religious initiatives" or Harold Turner's "independent religious movements." The point here is that the term "African independent churches" is showing signs of strain. First, contemporary discussion of independent churches in the 1990s has raised questions about the adequacy of the older terminology (cf. Paul Gifford, ed., *New Dimensions in African Christianity* [Nairobi: AACC, 1992], 5). The proliferation of new charismatic/

timated the number of independent churches at five thousand in 1970 with about 13 million members.[3] South Africa led all countries with some three thousand groups. Nigeria was second with seven hundred. Kenya numbered about one hundred and fifty. John Baur estimates the total number of groups at eight thousand by 1990 with 30 million adherents.[4]

Reasons for the rise of independency are many. Some point to the Protestant practice of separatism as the principal cause. Others stress missionary authoritarianism. A desire to preserve something of the African religious heritage and ritual is a possible third cause.[5] A more fundamental cause, however, lies behind these others. Whether they spoke of sacred places on the land as did Salomon, or sacred places in the soul as did the Revival brethren, a common concern for all independents was the problem of evil and ways of deliverance.

The problem of evil was seen differently by African Christians than by Westerners. For centuries European and North American Christianity pondered the philosophical problem of a good God and the existence of evil. The African looked at the problem more functionally. For the African Christian there were three faces of evil, each requiring a different response. All three appear in the Zimbanguist hymn, "Being Loyal to the New Jerusalem."

The first face of evil was humiliation or shame. To treat someone who was deserving of honor with disrespect or contempt was a great evil. For many Africans the words of Salomon rung true: Africans were "the most dishonoured of all races whom God created in this earth." The contempt of co-

---

Pentecostal churches and the success of itinerant evangelists such as Reinhard Bonnke and his crusade evangelism indicate the need for new terminology for the current situation. Better categories to describe the current scene may also be more appropriate to describe developments before 1960. Second, African responses to the gospel before 1960 did not always mean forming new churches as the case of the East African Revival illustrates. The new terminology thus seems to be more inclusive of a diversity of independent Christian responses. In 1968 Barrett used terms such as independent church movements. We may want to consider such designations. For a fuller discussion of this question, cf. Janet Hodgson, "'Don't Fence Me In': Some Problems in the Classification of African Religious Movements," in Walls and Schenk, eds., *Exploring New Religious Movements* (Elkhart, Ind.: Mission Focus Publications, 1990), 83–94.

3. David B. Barrett, *Schism and Renewal in Africa* (Nairobi: Oxford University Press, 1968), 64.

4. John Baur, *2000 Years of African Christianity* (Paulines: Nairobi, 1994), 353.

5. In his *History of African Christianity: 1950–1975* (Cambridge: Cambridge University Press, 1979), Adrian Hastings lists six reasons for the rise of independent churches and movements: (1) the Protestant tradition of dissent; (2) missionary authoritarianism and discrimination; (3) desire to preserve African tradition; (4) Old Testament emphasis on extraordinary revelation; (5) not enough ritual in low church Protestantism; (6) desire for sacred places ("no theme is more vital to African independency," 72). John Baur's list of causes is shorter: "Colonialism and Protestantism were the root causes for the separatist protest movements of 'Ethiopian' and 'African' churches; the religious and social African heritage was the main source that gave birth to the prophetic-charismatic movement, the 'Spirit,' 'prayer' (Aladura), or 'healing' (Zionist) churches." Cf. Baur, *African Christianity*, 352.

lonialist and missionary inspired a number of reactions to deal with this evil. Church splits were one. These became the so-called Ethiopian type churches, not so very different in doctrine or in practice from the missionary churches from which they separated.[6] Their contribution, as Richard Gray has written, was to challenge "racial discrimination and white domination in church and state."[7]

The second face of evil came not from the society of humankind but rather from the mysterious world of the spirits. This was the evil that "detracts or destroys life."[8] Such things as "illness, infertility, pestilence, famine, and sudden or inexplicable death" have more than natural explanations to those who believe in this second evil. Ancestral and demonic spirits are the underlying cause of these things. Witchcraft was a religious industry in Africa built around the existence of this second evil and the widespread fear it generated. Christianity appealed to traditional African society partly because it gave a name to this second evil—Satan—and partly because it proclaimed a power greater than the demonic—the power of the kingdom of God.[9]

A second kind of independent Christian church, sometimes called "Spirit" or "prophet" churches, appropriated this aspect of the Christian message and proclaimed the existence of sacred places like Nkamba in Zaire or Isaiah Shembe's Ekuphakameni ("high and elevated place") where the kingdom of God had come on earth. When the Kimbanguists sang about being loyal to the New Jerusalem of Nkamba it was because it was a place of miracles and healing. The kingdom was thus conceived by such churches as a spiritual power to overcome the power of Satan, the ancestors, and the demonic.

The third face of evil was that of alienation. In Salomon's hymn he writes of how "God our Father and his Son Jesus Christ are returned to us." Such language assumes an earlier alienation when the people were estranged from the Father and the Son. For many independent movements alienation was the least of the three evils that plagued them. For adherents of the East Africa Revival this third evil was the most deadly one.

Alienation refers to the feeling of being a stranger, of not belonging or of being separated from the source of blessing and fullness. Christ's question from the cross, "My God, my God, why have you forsaken me?" captures the anguished essence of the alienated. If one feels separated from the kingdom of God, the source of all blessing, more may be required than founding

6. The designations "Ethiopian type" and "prophet or Spirit type" churches stems originally from the classic study by Bengt Sundkler, *Bantu Prophets in South Africa,* 2nd ed. (Oxford: Oxford University Press/IAI, 1961).

7. Richard Gray, *Black Christians and White Missionaries* (New Haven: Yale University Press, 1990), 99.

8. Ibid., 101.

9. Gray mentions that "a contrasting referent to Satan in the New Testament is the Kingdom of God" (ibid., 104).

a new denomination or conducting a pilgrimage to the sacred place. We are alienated from the power of God not by geography or ritual but by attitudes like spiritual coldness and deadness.

For many Africans the shedding of blood is necessary to deal with the evil of alienation and bring the distant God near. In the East Africa Revival the blood of Christ was the central symbol and the source of power and efficacy. Though the most famous revival hymn was *Tukutendereza Yesu* ("We Praise You, Jesus"), a close second was the song, "What Can Wash Away My Sin, Nothing but the Blood of Jesus."

One Anglican missionary became so concerned about the emphasis on the blood of Christ that he requested revival leaders to cease using this chorus.[10] But for those seeking to conquer the evil of alienation, the symbolism of a sacrificial death was too crucial to ignore. Through a new awareness of the power of the blood one can be awakened from spiritual slumber and find the internal Jerusalem of spiritual blessing. By joining the ranks of the "saved ones" the evil of unbelief and indifference to spiritual things can be broken and one can "walk in the light" of the kingdom of God. For tens of thousands of African Christians in the 1940s and 1950s, the path from alienation to the kingdom led through the experience of becoming *zukuka* ("awake").

This chapter looks at these varied African responses to the Western ambassadors of the kingdom discussed in the previous chapter. Ethiopian, prophet, and revival type movements interacted with Western Christianity and, more profoundly, with the three evils that the gospel sought to oppose. These independent movements rose from 1890 to 1950 and then reached their height during the 1950s and early 1960s. Though different from the social gospel that characterized many mainline churches in post-independence Africa, these religious movements stressed the inbreaking in current time and space of the kingdom of God in power and glory. This intensification of the motif of the kingdom on earth anticipated the dominant witness of the churches in the decades after political independence. For all three types of African independent Christian movements, "release from the power of evil wherever it is encountered, involves yet another metaphor: the coming of the kingdom."[11]

The Rise of Independent Movements, 1890–1950

Three waves of independency occurred between 1890 and 1950.[12] The first wave occurred between 1890 and 1910, the earliest years of colonialism. Ethiopianism was the characteristic independent response of African Christians.

---

10. Reported in Kevin Ward, "'Tukutendereza Yesu,' The Balokole Revival in Uganda," in Zablon Nthamburi, *From Mission to Church* (Nairobi: Uzima, 1991), 130.
11. Richard Gray, *Black Christians*, 105.
12. The periodization is suggested by Hastings, *History of African Christianity*, 67.

Ethiopianism. Nigeria provides the first example. In 1888 the Native Baptist Church was founded in Lagos by D. B. Vincent, who eventually shed his Western name to become Mojola Agbebi.[13] Born in 1860 in an Anglican Yoruba home, Agbebi eventually joined the Baptist church in Lagos. The church was resonant with revival in the early 1880s, hiding a problem that became only too real by the late 1880s. Agbebi ran into disagreement with the White American missionary that led the Baptist work. With a group of disaffected Baptist laity, Agbebi separated.

By 1894 he had africanized his name and rejected European dress. In a sermon of 1902 he rejected "hymn-books, harmoniums, dedications, pew constructions, surpliced choir, the white man's names, the white man's dress, so many non-essentials, so many props and crutches affecting the religious manhood of the Christian Africans."[14]

Other churches took heed of his cry for dignity in the face of White domination in church and state. In 1913 he became the first president of the African Communion of Independent Churches. When he died in 1917 he was known internationally as "an unsuppressible propagandist for a non-missionary version of African Christianity."[15] By 1920 nearly a third of all Yoruba Christians belonged to an independent church.[16]

The first independent church of southern Africa was the Tembu National Church of Nehemiah Tile. It was founded in 1884, anticipating Agbebi's Nigerian church by four years.[17] This was just the beginning. In 1892 a former Wesleyan minister, Mangena Mokone, founded the Ethiopian Church of South Africa. Exposure to the African Methodist Episcopal Church (AME) in the United States led Mokone and his friend James Dwane to join in 1894. The AME in South Africa took on the character of an Ethiopian church, growing to 18,000 members by 1916.[18] Other denominations experienced similar internal crises. Major Presbyterian splits occurred in 1898. Congregationalists lost large numbers to independency in secessions that took place in 1890 and 1896.[19]

These churches of protest could be easily dismissed as little more than reactionary churches fueled by resentment. Yet there is more behind these initial expressions of independency. Most notable is a certain vision of the king-

---

13. A fuller account of the case of Mojola Agbebi can be found in Hastings, *The Church in Africa: 1450–1950* (Oxford: Clarendon, 1994), 493ff.

14. Quoted in Hastings, *Church in Africa*, 495.

15. Ibid., 494.

16. Ibid., 497.

17. J. W. Hofmeyr, and Gerald Pillay, eds., *A History of Christianity in South Africa*, vol. 1 (Pretoria: Haum Tertiary, 1994), 209.

18. J. Mutero Chirenje, *Ethiopianism and Afro-Americans in Southern Africa, 1883–1916* (Baton Rouge: Louisiana State University Press, 1987), 164–65.

19. Hastings, *Church in Africa*, 498.

dom. "The basic underlying thought [of Ethiopianism]," writes Peter Falk, "was the conversion of Africans and the establishment of a Christian theocracy that would embrace all of Africa."[20]

Perhaps more to the point, Ethiopianism looked for the presence of the kingdom in terms of a true racial justice. Psalm 68:31 prophesied that Ethiopia would rise to greatness. The African nation of Ethiopia, with her defeat of the Italian invaders in 1896, triggered hope that Scripture was about to be fulfilled. Fired by the example of Ethiopia and an eschatology of hope, "Ethiopian church leaders took up the cause of African liberation and some played a role in connection with the formation of the African Native Congress in 1912."[21] Their theology of the kingdom on earth anticipated the Black theology movement of the 1960s and provides an indigenous source for what many have seen as an American phenomenon.[22]

After 1910 Ethiopianism expanded around the continent. The increasingly political nature of these churches was more obvious than in the earlier period.

In 1929 Reuben Spartas founded the African Greek Orthodox Church just outside Kampala. Four years earlier he had tried unsuccessfully to found a nationalist organization, the African Progressive Society. Spartas had been influenced by the ideas of Marcus Garvey, a Jamaican who promoted Pan-Africanism.

There was more than one path to progress, however. The new church could serve the cause of nationalism just as well. By 1946 Spartas had visited Alexandria and was appointed the patriarch's vicar general in Africa. Success seemed imminent. His church had grown to around ten thousand. He had received international recognition from the patriarch of Alexandria. Spartas saw a unique opportunity to advance his cause further in 1949 by supporting the *Bataka* (clan heads) movement. Spartas was arrested and imprisoned in 1950. He was released in 1953 and continued to work for Ugandan independence, a clear reminder of the political implications of Ethiopianism.

In neighboring Kenya a burst of Ethiopian independency occurred in the 1930s and 1940s. A branch of the African Orthodox Church was formed in Kikuyuland. At the same time the African Independent Pentecostal Church was founded. In 1947 the African Christian Churches and Schools broke away from Africa Inland Mission.

But in the foothills of the Abedare Mountains another voice of independency could be heard. The Arathi prophets under their founding prophet, Jo-

---

20. Peter Falk, *The Growth of the Church in Africa* (Grand Rapids: Zondervan, 1979), 455. Cf. similar comments by E. A. Ayandele, *The Missionary Impact on Modern Nigeria, 1842–1914* (London: Longman, 1966), 178.

21. G. C. Oosthuizen, *The Birth of Christian Zionism in South Africa* (KwaDlangezwa: University of Zululand, 1987), 11.

22. Hofmeyr, *Christianity in South Africa*, 211.

seph Ng'ang'a, called impoverished Christian Kikuyu out of the worldly society of colonial Kenya to a more ritually pure existence as the people of God following a code derived partly from the Old Testament and partly from Kikuyu custom.

The manner of his calling to prophethood is important. One night in a drunken stupor, Ng'ang'a had a dream. In his dream God called him to leave his drunkenness, receive salvation, be baptized, and then "pray for his people that they might be liberated from their rulers."[23] Ng'ang'a obeyed the heavenly word and founded a movement that continued on the fringes of Kenyan Christianity for decades. While echoing many of the themes of Ethiopian Christianity, this new form of independency was also unique and pointed to a new development occurring across Africa—the rise of prophet churches.

Prophet churches. Prophet churches form around a charismatic figure who promises to "help people in their need by solving conflicts, taking personal interest in the sick, especially those who have problems with illnesses related to the African cosmology like sorcery and witchcraft—diseases which are associated with the activities of evil spirits."[24] The prophet does not derive this power to heal from ordination or education. His power "has at its source a metaphysical force."[25]

Among Zionist churches of South Africa the healing role of the prophet is paramount. "The majority implicitly believed in *complete healing,*" writes M. L. Daneel, "effected through the aiding powers of these Zionist prophets." For followers of these new churches that proliferated after World War I, the future age described in the closing chapters of Revelation when there will be no more tears and no more death can break into the present through the mediation of a charismatic prophet.

All across the continent the spell of the prophet was cast. Among those upon whom the spell fell with particular power were Isaiah Shembe in South Africa, W. Wade Harris in Ivory Coast, Simon Kimbangu in Zaire, and Garrick Braide and the Aladura prophets of Nigeria.

Isaiah Shembe (1870–1935) of the Amanazaretha Church (Church of the Nazarite) was one of the most famous and most controversial of the Zionist prophets of South Africa. Shembe's spiritual roots can actually be traced back to two White religious leaders, J. A. Dowie and P. L. Le Roux.

It is one of the paradoxes of Zulu Zionism that this most African form of Christianity was originally inspired by a radical American pentecostal preacher. J. Alexander Dowie (d. 1907) was the founder of a new Jerusalem

23. Jocelyn Murray, "Kikuyu Spirit Churches," *Journal of Religion in Africa* 5 (1973): 202–3.

24. G. C. Oosthuizen, *The Healer-Prophet in Afro-Christian Churches* (Leiden: E. J. Brill, 1992), 19.

25. Ibid.

just outside Chicago, Illinois, that he called Zion City, where healing and miracles were regular occurrences at the Zion tabernacle of his Christian Catholic Apostolic Church. In 1901 Dowie declared himself "Elijah the Restorer" and sought to spread the word through his publication, *Leaves of Healing*. His hope for public recognition as the last of the prophets before the coming of the messiah was never realized. He died in 1907, a frustrated visionary whom many dismissed as insane.[26]

The message of Dowie, however, was taken with extreme seriousness by at least one missionary in South Africa. P. L. Le Roux was a Dutch Reformed missionary to the Zulus who left his Afrikaner church in 1903 to join a South African chapter of Dowie's Christian Catholic Apostolic Church.[27] Closely linked with a number of key Zulu Christians, Le Roux's call "to reinvent Jerusalem in one's own land"[28] met with enormous response and triggered a movement that by 1990 claimed some two thousand or more Black churches in South Africa with an estimated membership of 4 million (31% of the population).[29] Shembe's Amanazaretha Church was one example of those who heeded the call.

Shembe appropriated much in this prophetic heritage but was not restricted by it. He had been a member of the breakaway African National Baptist Church (1906) but his spiritual restlessness led in 1911 to the founding of the Nazarite Church. A few years later a series of visions moved him to build the holy city of Ekuphakameni eighteen miles north of Durban. In Nazarite worship Ekuphakameni ("high and elevated place") became the New Jerusalem and Shembe became its new David, a Black messiah.

"I remember Ekuphakameni," proclaims a hymn composed by Shembe, "Where the springs are, Springs of living water, lasting forever."[30] In another hymn Shembe makes clear that Ekuphakameni is heaven on earth:

> We are all standing before thee,
> Gates of Ekuphakameni.
> All the generations of Heaven
> jubilate because of thee, Ekuphakameni.[31]

"The Book of Revelation," writes Sundkler, "has kindled in the heart of the Zionist prophet a longing to enter the heavenly Jerusalem."[32] This cli-

---

26. A fairly complete summary of the life of J. A. Dowies can be found in G. C. Oosthuizen, *Birth of Christian Zionism*, 1–9.
27. Hastings, *Church in Africa*, 499–500.
28. Ibid., 500.
29. Baur, *African Christianity*, 353.
30. Quoted in Sundkler, *Bantu Prophets*, 292.
31. Ibid.
32. Ibid., 293.

mate of the Book of Revelation that surrounds the Nazarites shapes their view of their founder. Shembe is more than a prophet; he is the Christ. He referred to himself as the "Promised One" and in the official theology of the church he rose from the dead in 1935 and wrote hymns for the church confirming his messianic status.[33]

Sundkler concludes that in Amanazaretha "there is no room for the Son in the creed and life of the believers" for "His place had been usurped by another."[34] The pattern of the deification of the self, so visible in Egyptian Gnostic Christianity of the early centuries, resurfaces.[35] After Shembe's death, the prophet's son was declared the new leader of the church and the movement continued to grow, numbering about seventy thousand in 1970.

In sharp contrast to Shembe stands the West African prophet, W. Wade Harris (c. 1865–1929). As a young Grebo Anglican catechist and political activist in Liberia he had been jailed for antigovernment activity on two different occasions. In 1910 during his second imprisonment his wife died. His political dreams dashed, his wife dead, and his six children destitute, Harris looked for answers.

The Angel Gabriel came to him in a vision, calling "him to be a prophet, to preach a gospel of repentance, to destroy 'fetish' worship, and to baptize those who obeyed." After his release from prison he recruited two female companions who accompanied him as he traveled throughout Ivory Coast and Ghana (then the Gold Coast) healing and proclaiming the message given to him by Gabriel that "Jesus Christ must reign" and that "I am his prophet."[36] Some one hundred thousand believed.

Soon opposition by French authorities forced Harris back to Liberia in 1915 where he preached with less success until his death in 1929. Though the French attempted to destroy his movement, Harris had told his followers to wait for the "White preacher" to come. In 1923 a Methodist missionary, W. J. Platt, arrived and organized the scattered masses into a church.[37]

---

33. Ibid., 286.

34. Ibid., 283.

35. Shembe's Gnostic-like attitudes and ideas may have been more than accidental. He may have had some link with the theosophical teaching of P. G. Bowen. For a discussion of this, cf. Oosthuizan and Hexham, eds., *Afro Christian Religion at the Grassroots in Southern Africa* (Lewiston: Edwin Mellen, 1991), 366ff. If this is the case, then there may be a real link between various forms of New Age religion and certain older African independent movements like Shembe's.

36. The best recent source for Harris's life and theology is David Shank, *Prophet Harris, the 'Black Elijah' of West Africa*, abridged by Jocelyn Murray (Leiden: E. J. Brill, 1994). Valuable additional studies include Gordon Haliburton, *The Prophet Harris* (New York: Oxford University Press, 1973) and Sheila Walker, *The Religious Revolution in the Ivory Coast: The Prophet Harris and the Harrist Church* (Chapel Hill: University of North Carolina Press, 1983).

37. Hastings, *Church in Africa*, 506.

The message Harris proclaimed was heavy with eschatology. Harris believed that "he was the final prophet who was to precede the Christ at the coming of the eschatological reign about to be established on earth."[38] He no longer preached the politics of Grebo nationalism but instead proclaimed a new political vision of "bringing all nations under the political, peaceful rule on the earth of the messiah Jesus of Nazareth." Harris saw himself as a prophet of that heavenly kingdom soon to come to earth.

The power of this message in the minds of his hearers lay in the promise of the conquest of the demonic evil that daily tormented their lives. Harris was not the apolitical preacher that some have interpreted him to be but was rather a "subversive character" who adopted a position, perhaps similar to Ghandi's, of "revolutionary subordination."[39] The political kingdom that he sought to subvert was that of Satan, the source of sickness and death. His spiritual pilgrimage led him beyond missionary Christianity to a stage that focused on the "coming kingdom of God, demonstrated in the personalized gifts and potential in the service of peace, justice, healing, and reconciliation of the new creation."[40] Eschatological faith was the prophetic breakthrough that ignited Harris's proclamation.

When he died in 1929 Harris had his final earthly vision of the coming kingdom. Though frail and bed-ridden, he called on those gathered around his bed "to look at the heavens to see the appearance of Christ who was reaching out his hand to them."[41]

Simon Kimbangu (1889–1951) is a third prophet figure whose story bears resemblance to that of the reluctant biblical prophet, Jonah. Kimbangu was born in the village of Nkamba not far from a Baptist mission station. At twenty-six years of age he along with his wife was baptized into the Baptist Church. In a dream Kimbangu heard the call of God to preach.

Though he was accepted as a lay evangelist in 1918 the dreams demanded more. To escape the dreams he went to Kinshasa to work. Within a matter of months he was home again, unable to resist God's troubling call. By March he was preaching to vast crowds that streamed into Nkamba and was healing many of the sick.[42]

His message was clearly Christian. Like Harris, he strongly emphasized millennialism. Such teaching "was at least as potentially explosive here as anywhere."[43] The local Baptist elders gave Kimbangu their blessing but

38. Shank, *Prophet Harris*, 145.
39. Ibid., 290.
40. David Shank, "African Christian Religious Itinerary," in A. F. Walls and Wilbert Shenk, eds., *Exploring New Religious Movements* (Elkhart, Ind.: Mission Focus, 1990), 152.
41. Ibid., 153.
42. Hastings provides a good account of Kimbangu's life and work in *Church in Africa*, 508ff.
43. Ibid., 511.

Catholic clerics and White settlers called on the government to suppress the movement. In September 1921 Kimbangu was arrested. In October he was condemned to death but an appeal by the Baptist community to King Albert changed the sentence to life imprisonment.

From jail, Kimbangu continued to be the spiritual inspiration of the movement. Hymns were written that not only spoke of the sacredness of Nkamba but also spoke of Kimbangu as the "Apostle whom God sent in order to fulfill the promises made by Jesus to the Blacks."[44] His following continued to grow during his long imprisonment and even after his death in 1951. The parallels between the sufferings of Christ and the sufferings of Kimbangu were drawn in sermons and songs. Though Kimbangu's body was entombed in Nkamba, hymns of resurrection appeared:

> Risen, he is risen! Risen, he is risen!
> Let us praise Almighty God for having raised him
> from the dead—
> Our prophet has risen! Our prophet has risen!
> Let us praise the Lord Jesus for having raised him from the dead.[45]

This apparent contradiction between a buried prophet and an affirmation of his resurrection is resolved by appealing to Congo cosmology, where "the noble dead are more alive than the living and consequently, the grave is not a cul-de-sac, but a gateway to the world of spirit."[46] Such a prophet, powerful in life and risen from death, insured that pilgrims would continue to crowd the pathways into Nkamba and that the Church of Jesus Christ on Earth through the Prophet Simon Kimbangu (EJCSK) would flourish.

Our final examples of prophetic independency come from Nigeria and center around the Aladura movement and its cluster of founding prophets. The background to the Aladura churches is found in the ministry of Garrick Braide (d. 1918). A disaffected Anglican, Braide had broken both with the Native pastorate as well as with moderates like Holy Johnson and, following the path of Agbebi, founded his own church, Christ Army Church, in 1915 as World War I was raging in Europe.

The war years were a politically volatile time. When Braide began to threaten the colonial government with the judgment of God, his movement was suppressed by Talbot, the colonial district officer. Braide was arrested on charges of sedition but released on bail. He returned, like Kimbangu would do a few years later, to his home village. There Braide allegedly preached that he was "the king of the world, before whom the king of En-

---

44. Quoted in K. Gordon Molyneux, *African Christian Theology: The Quest for Selfhood* (San Francisco: Mellen Research University Press, 1993), 175.
45. Ibid., 177.
46. Ibid.

gland would come and kneel."[47] Braide died soon after and his eight thousand followers became restless for another word from the Lord.

For many that further word came through Moses Orimolade, the Baba Aladura. Orimolade was a contemporary of Braide who had an established reputation as a preacher. Also from an Anglican background, he joined with others such as Joseph Sadare and Isaac Akinyele and sought a purer church life. After years of drifting through various pentecostal churches, Orimolade founded the Cherubim and Seraphim on the basis of a vision by a prophetess.

Akinyele founded the Christ Apostolic Church (1941) among the Yoruba. The emphasis was upon prayer and healing, and the growing throngs who filled the various branch tabernacles became known as "Aladura" (praying people).[48] They rejected Western medicine and looked to God alone for healing through prayer.

These early Aladura churches became widespread in the 1930s due to the "revival" preaching of Jospeh Babalola (b. 1904). Babalola preached against idols, fetishes, and juju (ritual dolls). God was to be their only god. A mass movement began that hastened the spread of Aladura throughout Yorubaland.[49] Babalola eventually joined with Akinyele in founding the Christ Apostolic Church. One last founding prophet, Josiah Oshitelu, who had been affected by the preaching of Babalola, established the Church of the Lord (Aladura), which unlike the other Aladura churches permitted polygamy.[50]

While major differences can be noted among Shembe, Harris, Kimbangu, and the prophets of Aladura, what ties them together is their prophetic/charismatic attack on supernatural evil and their emphasis on a holistic healing that can rid the African of such a curse.

The East African Revival. For a growing number of Anglicans and other Protestants in the 1920s and 1930s, the problems of White supremacy and Black magic took a back seat to the problems of alienation and nominalism in the church. Spiritual dryness and deadness became the focus of a group of religious innovators who are often given the name "revivalists." Such were the Ugandan preachers who led the most famous of all such African movements, known variously as the *Balokole* ("saved ones") Revival or the East Africa Revival.[51]

47. Quoted in Harold Turner, *Religious Innovation in Africa* (Boston: G. K. Hall, 1979), 141.

48. Hastings, *Church in Africa*, 514.

49. Ibid., 516.

50. Ibid., 517.

51. For a list of relevant sources for the East Africa Revival, cf. Jocelyn Murray, "A Bibliography of the East African Revival Movement," *Journal of Religion in Africa*, 8 (1976): 144–47. Updated information is found in Kevin Ward, "'Tukutendereza Jesu': The Balokole Revival in Kenya," in *From Mission to Church*, 113–44.

The pioneer figure of the revival was a Bagandan named Simeoni Nsibambi. While a clerk in the administration of the *kabaka* in the early 1920s, Nsibambi underwent a powerful religious experience. In a vision from God Nsibambi, frustrated over his failure to obtain a scholarship to study abroad, was told that such things meant little when compared with the Pearl of Great Price, the gospel of salvation. Nsibambi, both humbled and inspired by this vision, began to preach a message of repentance and renewal.

He found a kindred spirit in Dr. Joe Church, a young missionary working at the Rwanda Mission's Gahini hospital. The Rwanda Mission of the CMS tended to be staffed by Anglican evangelicals critical of the spiritual state of the Church of Uganda. Yet Church found himself in a state of spiritual depression due to overwork and exhaustion. He met Nsibambi in Namirembe and found that the young preacher was as hungry for spiritual renewal as he was. Church engaged in several days of intensive Bible study and prayer with Nsibambi and eventually returned to Gahini, according to his diary, "in the power of Pentecost."[52] Nsibambi stayed at Namirembe making disciples.

Nsibambi's younger brother, Blasio Kigozi, was one such disciple. Kigozi was sent to Gahini to work with Church in 1931 and began to preach a message of total surrender to Christ. After initial rejection of this message a number of hospital workers, most notably Yosiya Kinuka, repented, confessing their "Laodicean" or lukewarm Christianity.

At a church convention at Gahini in 1933–34, a mass revival broke out. Participants were soon called the *abaka*, those on fire, and teams of evangelists spread the flame to various locations in Rwanda and Southwest Uganda. At a convention held in Kabale, Uganda, in 1935, Church, Kigozi, and Kinuka preached the message of the revival. The result was widespread "confession of sin, restitutions, apologies," and a new zeal for evangelism.[53] Kigozi then traveled to Kampala, where he made an impassioned appeal to the "sleeping" church of Uganda to *zukuka* (awake). Within days Kigozi was dead from fever but the revival continued.

Church officials began to take notice of the movement. Bishop Stuart of Uganda was sympathetic. He hoped that the Diamond Jubilee in 1937 would further the revival. But the results of revival activity in 1937 were disappointing. Instead of arousing revival the movement aroused critics.

And there were things to criticize. The Keswick emphasis on the second blessing experience that gave one complete power and victory over sin led to some extremes of perfectionism. In the late 1930s at Nsibambi's home outside of Kampala a small group of men and women declared themselves free of sexual lust and impervious to sexual temptation. To prove their victory

---

52. Joe Church, *Quest for the Highest: An Autobiographical Account of the East Africa Revival* (Exeter: Paternoster, 1981), 68.
53. Ward, "Tukutendereza," 116.

over temptation they walked about naked during their meetings and claimed the power to sleep side by side with the opposite sex without falling into sin. Nsibambi successfully opposed this extremist group before it completely discredited the movement.

One legacy of this episode was the rejection by mainstream *balokole* of the doctrine of *okufuba*, or striving. This doctrine taught that one should seek or strive for a second blessing experience that would usher the recipient into a state of near sinlessness. Early leaders like Church had taught this view, which came out of Keswick piety and could be found in the notes of the widely read Scofield Bible.

Leaders of the revival rejected the concept of *okufuba*, largely on the grounds that it obscured the greatest blessing of the Christian, the cross of Christ, and the experience of being washed, spiritually and by faith alone, in the blood of Christ. Temptations needed to be fought each day, taught the revival leadership. We will never reach a stage of perfection in this life that would permit us to drop our guard. This correction in the theology and spirituality of the revival was an important one, but criticisms of the movement as a whole still mounted.[54]

William Nagenda and the Mukono Incident of 1941. Among the leading critics of the *balokole* movement was the warden of Bishop Tucker Theological College at Mukono. John Jones was not at all happy that by 1941 a group of about forty students (out of 120) were gathering to pray for revival, vocally condemning the sins they saw on campus such as theft, immorality, theological liberalism, and high church worship. Jones recognized that he was the personal target of the last two criticisms and reacted by banning the prayer meetings and barring revival preaching.[55]

The leader of the pro-revival group was a student, William Nagenda, brother-in-law to both Nsibambi and Kigozi. He refused to accept these regulations of the college. Jones promptly dismissed Nagenda and twenty-nine others, including the college chaplain.[56] The *balokole* were declared to be *bajeemu* (rebels). The *balokole* responded to this charge by issuing a memorandum in December 1941 that insisted on the rightness of their position and rejected the modernist spirit at Mukono which, in their view, "minimizes sin, and the substitutionary death of Christ on the Cross, and mocks at the ideal of separation from the world to a holy and victorious life."[57]

54. Ibid., 126–27.
55. Ibid., 119.
56. For a complete list of those dismissed and more information on the crisis itself, cf. Kevin Ward, "'Obedient Rebels'—The Relationship between the Early 'Balokole' and the Church of Uganda: The Mukono Crisis of 1941," *Journal of Religion in Africa* 19, no. 3 (1989): 194–222.
57. Quoted in Ward, "Tukutendereza," 120.

By 1943 the impending split between the *balokole* and the church was avoided largely through Bishop Stuart's fourteen guidelines for unity, which he published as *The New Way*.[58] Reluctantly, pro- and antirevival factions accepted the plan and division was averted. The easing of tensions led to a new outburst of evangelism. The movement spread widely throughout Uganda, bringing renewal in its wake. Thousands testified that the revival had conquered a great evil in their lives and in their churches—the evil of apathy and the alienation from God's blessing that such apathy produces. The *balokole* revival entered the 1950s, as did the Ethiopian and prophetic movements continent-wide, with great optimism that the best was yet to be.

The Height of Independency, 1950–60

Adrian Hastings has called the 1950s the golden age of independency. "Almost everywhere numbers grew rapidly, and if there had been 800 independent churches in South Africa in 1948, there were 2200 by 1960."[59] It was also the decade of the internationalization of independency.

The Cherubim and Seraphim of Nigeria spread to Ghana. The Church of the Lord (Aladura) spread to Sierra Leone and Ghana. Groups like the Nigerian Christ Apostolic Church showed signs of maturity by opening a theological college in 1956. Movements like Kimbanguism were enjoying new government recognition by 1957. New groups like the Legio Maria in Kenya (1963) proliferated, and *balokole* revivalist Matthew Ajuoga's Churches of Christ of Africa broke off from Anglicanism in western Kenya in 1958. Theological concerns about Simeon Ondeto's Legio Maria and Kimbanguist Separatist Simon Mpadi's Church of the Blacks in Zaire with its mandatory polygamy raised questions about the Christian content of new prophetic movements, but the growing number of adherents argued for their continuing appeal and relevance.

Along with growth came new challenges. No greater challenge faced independency than that of the new nationalism that was emerging everywhere. New aspirations for political independency—for a kingdom on earth of justice and equality—often clashed with the sacred places and visions of prophets and revivalists. All longed for the coming kingdom to conquer evil but not all agreed as to what the real evil was. Ethiopianism with its sense that the primary evil was racism and inequality saw African nationalism as the primary hope. Both prophetic and revivalist forms of independency, which insisted that spiritual evil (whether demons or dullness) was the true source

58. Ibid., 122.
59. Hastings, *History of African Christianity*, 121.

of trouble, demanded spiritual solutions. The 1950s and early 1960s saw independency navigating its way through these dangerous waters of a rising nationalism.

Women prophets and the challenge of nationalism. The 1950s and early 1960s were also the decade of women prophets like Alice Lenshina (Lumpa Church of Zambia), Gaudencio Aoko (Legio Maria, Kenya), Mia Chaza (Zimbabwe), Miriam Ragot, Ma Nku, Ma Mbele (South Africa), and Captain Abiodun (Nigeria). Yet these new prophetic movements found that African nationalists could be as unfriendly to their visions as European colonialists had been.

Consider the case of Alice Lenshina (1920–78). The turning point in her life came when she was thirty-three. Alice had contracted cerebral malaria in September 1953 and slipped into a deep coma. Family and friends began to prepare for her burial in the village of Kasomo.

To the surprise of all, Alice recovered. Even more startling were her stories of a heavenly encounter with Jesus Christ, who called her to be a prophetess and to live up to the meaning of her name, Lenshina (queen).[60] A revival gathered around her as she shared her testimony. She became baptized at the local Presbyterian church and enjoyed the fellowship of several missionaries. By 1955 the character of Lenshina's revival had changed. Its most outstanding feature was no longer the call to repentance but the eradication of witches and a strong emphasis on millennialism.

Her movement organized itself into an independent church called *Lumpa*. Her home village of Kasomo was declared a new Zion. The movement grew to one hundred thousand adherents by 1961. Alice reminded her followers repeatedly, "Do not look for the things of this world."[61] To be faithful to their heavenly King Jesus, her followers were gathered into Lumpa villages where they became "a body politic of their own; a sort of independent theocratic peasant state."[62]

When Zambia achieved its independence in 1964 this "independent theocratic state" was perceived as a threat. Lenshina's former primary school classmate, President Kenneth Kaunda, eventually ordered his police to destroy these kingdom villages. Seven hundred people were killed. Alice was imprisoned. Her church was banned. It would be a mistake to read this conflict as a clash between heavenly-minded African Zionists and a secular-minded nationalist government. To say that it was a conflict between rival versions of the kingdom on earth would be closer to the truth.

---

60. The story of Alice's near-death experience is retold in Hugo Hinfelaar, "Women's Revolt: The Lumpa Church of Lenshina Mulenga in the 1950s," *Journal of Religion in Africa* 21, no. 2 (1991): 121ff.

61. Quoted in Hastings, *History of African Christianity*, 156.

62. Ibid., 156.

Revival and nationalistic conflict in Kenya. The impact of the *balokole* revival in various African countries (including South Africa and Angola) as well as in England, India, Brazil, and North America was a notable development in the 1950s.[63] Kenya became one of the centers of the movement where the Revival Brethren faced the challenge of African nationalism in the form of the Mau Mau movement. The *balokole* movement had made a powerful impact on the mainline churches of Kenya although the Africa Inland Church stayed notably aloof. By the 1950s regular Revival conventions were held to stoke the fires of religious zeal and extend the reach of the *balokole.*

Parallel with the rise of the Revival in Kenya was the nationalistic movement of Mau Mau. Beginning in 1949 and continuing into the 1950s an oathing movement spread among the Kikuyu which involved the repudiation of Christianity and the pledge to overthrow the British at all costs. Members of the Revival refused to take the oath and many paid with their lives. Max Warren writes of the brutal slaughter of a Kikuyu Christian named Ganthon and his wife Rebekah merely for serving tea to some thirsty British police officers.[64] Heshbon Mwangi, one of the outstanding leaders of the Revival in Kenya, was beaten and left for dead for refusing to take the oath.[65] The deeply internalized sense of the kingdom that marked the Revival movement clashed with the rival aspirations of African nationalism.

New partnerships with nationalism. Conflict between independency and the spirit of nationalism was not, however, always the case. Many prophetic movements were able to accommodate themselves to the demands of African nationalism.

In Ghana the Musama Disco Christo Church was founded in the 1920 by Joseph Appiah, the *Akaboha* (king), and the female prophet Nathalomea. Appiah and his queen were treated like traditional Akan royalty, complete with drummers and ceremonial umbrellas.[66] As the decades passed the movement "rose gradually in the social scale" numbering heads of state and politicians among its adherents.[67] Similarly in Swaziland, the Swazi Zionist Churches have become a virtual state religion supporting the Swazi monarchy and enjoying special status in exchange for their support. Little distinction is made between doing God's work and the king's work.[68]

What could be said generally about independency by the early 1960s, whether opposed or courted by the forces of African nationalism, is that it was a significant and enduring part of African Christianity.

63. Church, *Quest,* 250.
64. Max Warren, *Revival: An Enquiry* (London: SCM, 1954), 5.
65. Church, *Quest,* 250.
66. Isichei, *History of Christianity in Africa,* 289–90.
67. Ibid., 290.
68. J. B. Mzizi, "Swazi Zionism and the Royal Politics of the Kingdom," in Oosthuizen, Kitshoff, and Dube, eds., *Afro-Christianity at the Grassroots* (Leiden: E. J. Brill, 1994), 64.

Conclusion

Though Adrian Hastings has stated that events since political independence "have brought to a close the age of independency as a major ecclesiastical phenomenon in African Christianity," recent research into the new religious movements in African urban areas contradicts this judgment.[69]

The Ethiopian, prophetic, and revivalist movements that made up African Christian independency from 1890 to 1950 reached their height during the 1950s and early 1960s. They addressed a wide range of evils and sought to find in Christ the solution to these evils. In their ardent supernaturalism they opposed a more secularized political Christianity that would characterize mainline churches in the years after independence.

Yet in remarkable ways these religious movements anticipated the same *realized* eschatology of political Christianity in their stress on the inbreaking of the kingdom of God in power and glory. This chapter has sought to establish that independency's intensification of the motif of the kingdom on earth anticipated the dominant witness of the churches in the decades after political independence.

What do we make then of the witness to the kingdom offered by the Reuben Spartases, the Isaiah Shembes, and the Alice Lenshinas?

First, the witness of many independent movements was a contradiction of the kingdom. Jesus Christ, the embodiment and essence of the kingdom and its rule, according to historic African Christianity, was often obscured by independency. All too often, Isaiah Shembe or Simon Kimbangu become the focus of faith rather than Christ.

The syncretism of many movements caused a similar shift away from the historic Christ. Augustine's warning about the City of Man and its self-love is relevant here. African Zions, whether of the Ethiopian, prophetic, or revival type, were all subject to the temptation to turn their witness for Christ into a promotion of themselves. Such a man-centered witness was deeply inconsistent with the church's historic purpose of pointing away from herself to her risen and ascended Christ as the Lord of all.

Second, the witness of independency also spoke of the countercultural character of the kingdom. Like the ancient Egyptian Coptic church, the world-denying aspects of the Lumpa church and its theocratic alternative to nationalism, the New Jerusalems that dot the African continent as a rebuke to the standing order, or the *balokole* criticism of nominalism, all point in imperfect ways to a longing for a world order that is to come, a place to truly feel at home, not just for time but for eternity. A witness to the coming kingdom of justice and righteousness is thus found within these African initiatives in religion.

69. Cf. Paul Gifford, ed., *New Dimensions in African Christianity* (Nairobi: AACC, 1992).

Third, the witness of the independent Christian movements of colonial Africa pointed to the nature of the churches' spiritual warfare. For all three types of African independent Christian movements, "release from the power of evil wherever it is encountered, involves yet another metaphor: the coming of the kingdom."[70] The inbreaking of the kingdom is best seen not in elaborate cathedrals or complicated theologies but in the power of the cross producing a people opposed to evil and its faces of racism, demonism, and nominalism.[71] Though the Kimbanguist sang of loyalty to Nkamba and the *balokole* sang their *Tukutendereza Yesu* in their native Bugandan, their songs were songs for all of Africa.

---

70. Richard Gray, *Black Christians*, 105.

71. The relationship of the *Christus Victor* understanding of the atonement and African expressions of Christianity has been explored by Paul Omieka Ebhomielen, "Gustaf Aulen's Christus Victor View of the Atonement as It Relates to the Demonic in Africa" (unpublished Ph.D. diss., Baylor University, 1982).

Kingdom on Earth 14

Christianity in Independent Africa

He was Ghana's gift to the freedom struggle. In ways reminiscent of a Kimbangu or a Shembe, Kwame Nkrumah (1909–72), liberator, Pan-Africanist, Christian, and Marxist, was hailed as a Black messiah.

His path to power had been rocky. Nkrumah grew up in the mission schools of the Gold Coast, becoming a teacher after his graduation. In the 1940s he went first to the United States and then to England for further studies. His contact with the African intellectual diaspora drew him into politics. In 1945 he helped found the Pan-African Congress.

After returning to Ghana in 1947 Nkrumah resumed his political involvement and flirted with Marxism. In 1949 he founded the Convention People's Party (CPP). He was imprisoned for his work stoppage campaigns and nonviolent protests. When his party swept the election of 1951 Nkrumah was released from jail to lead the new government. In 1957 he guided Ghana to independence from Britain and began a new era in African history.

Nkrumah became the leader of a continent. In 1963 he was a key player in the formation of the Organization of African Unity. When trouble began at home, he tightened his grip on power. In 1964 he abolished all political parties but his own and declared himself president for life.

Nkrumah interpreted his rule in kingdom terms. He was so fond of quoting his parody of Matthew 6:33 that the words were inscribed on his statue in Accra: "Seek first the political kingdom and all other things will be added unto you."

Charles Weber has noted that though "this linking of Nkrumah with Christ and a secularizing and politicizing of Christ's teaching stirred continual negative reaction from missions—Nkrumah never retracted the statement."[1]

---

1. Charles Weber, "The Role of Churches in the Decolonization Movements of West Africa," unpublished paper given at the Fifth Yale–Edinburgh Meeting on the Missionary Movement, June 1995, 14.

He encouraged a messianic personality cult. The youth wing of his party responded with a revision of the Apostles' Creed:

> I believe in the Convention People's Party, the opportune savior of Ghana and in Kwame Nkrumah, its founder and leader; who is endowed with the Ghana spirit, born as true Ghanaian for Ghana; suffering under victimization, was vilified, threatened with deportation; he disentangled himself from the clutches of the UGCC; and the same day he rose victorious with the 'verandah boys'; ascended the political heights; and sitteth at the Supreme head of the CPP.[2]

Nkrumah, the Black messiah, was deposed by the military in 1966 and lived most of his remaining years in exile in Sekou Toure's Guinea, eventually dying in Romania in 1972. Nkrumah's legacy was a new political theology. His gospel proclaimed that the kingdom had come to earth as the messianic nation-state before whom all must bow their knees.

Desmond Tutu. In 1960, three years after Nkrumah led Ghana to independence, an obscure Black priest was ordained to Anglican orders in South Africa. With that ordination, Desmond Mpilo Tutu (1931–) began his ascent up the church hierarchy, becoming dean of Johannesburg in 1975 and bishop of Lesotho in 1977. In 1978 he became the first Black head of the South African Council of Churches (SACC). Many wondered whether this small and unremarkable bishop would be an "Uncle Tom."

Within a short time it was clear that Desmond Tutu was a vocal advocate of a kingdom politics that rejected racism and injustice as incompatible with a truly Christian society. "He attacked the homeland policy, supported the ordination of women and the right to conscientious objection, and hotly defended the banned Christian Institute against Minister of Police Jimmy Kruger's charge that it favored violent revolution."[3] He justified the WCC's controversial Program to Combat Racism.

Yet Tutu was more than a Christian activist. He was also a man of deep piety who spent several hours a day in prayer. In 1984 Tutu was awarded the Nobel Peace Prize in recognition of "the courage and heroism shown by black South Africans in their use of peaceful methods in the struggle against apartheid." His appointment as archbishop of Cape Town in 1986 gave him added clout in his ongoing protest of racism and injustice. When the walls of apartheid came tumbling down in the early 1990s, Tutu led the cheers.

He was an advocate of nationalism as much as Nkrumah, but not a messianic nationalism that stood above the demands of justice. When a government minister wrote to Tutu in 1988 asking "whether you are acting on be-

2. Quoted in John Pobee, *Religion and Politics in Ghana* (Accra: Asempa, 1991), 119.
3. Marjorie Hope and James Young, T*he South African Churches in a Revolutionary Situation* (Maryknoll: Orbis, 1981), 109.

half of the kingdom of God, or the kingdom promised by the ANC," Tutu was incensed. "My theological position derives from the Bible and from the Church."[4]

Tutu later elaborated on his view of the kingdom. "Our God is not a God who sanctifies the *status quo*. He is a God of surprises, uprooting the powerful and unjust to establish His kingdom."[5] The coming kingdom established standards of social righteousness against which the new nations of Africa could be measured. To Tutu, "the God of Exodus is a liberator God who leads His people out of every kind of bondage, spiritual, political, social, and economic."[6]

W. F. Kumuyi. If nationalism was an idol for Nkrumah and a prophetic challenge for Tutu, it turned into an empty dream for William Folorunso Kumuyi (1941–). Kumuyi, the eldest of five children, was born to Yoruba parents in the Nigerian village of Orunwa. Kumuyi's early training was remarkable for its modernism. The Mayflower School that he entered in 1958 was founded by Dr. Tai Salarin, noted for his atheism and his belief in the power of man to bring about a future of peace and prosperity.[7] The school was dedicated to this creed of humanism.

Kumuyi drew close to Salarin but broke from his humanism in 1964 when he underwent a "born again" experience. Though a product of an Anglican upbringing Kumuyi found the preaching of the Apostolic Faith Church, Ikenne, irresistible. Despite this religious change Salarin sponsored Kumuyi at the University of Ibadan in 1967. Kumuyi returned to Mayflower School as a teacher after his graduation. In 1972 he left to take a position at the University of Lagos. He attempted without success to combine doctoral work with his growing ministry as a Bible teacher and evangelist. By 1973 his Bible study had grown so large that it was forced to meet in a larger auditorium off campus.

In 1975 Kumuyi was expelled from the Apostolic Faith Church for teaching and preaching without ordination. Kumuyi organized his Bible study into the Deeper Life Bible Church. He left the university in 1983 to devote himself full-time to his church. Thousands responded to his vision of a life beyond a secular utopia: "Was your plan before conversion to build houses, buy cars, have many children, or visit European capitals . . . ? You cannot cling to your pet ambitions and profess to be committed to evangelism."[8]

Kumuyi appealed to young people in a troubled Nigeria to seek the kingdom of God as their highest treasure. In addition to an emphasis on personal holiness Kumuyi's church promised health, wealth, and healing to those who

4. Quoted in Allister Sparks, *The Mind of South Africa* (London: Mandarin, 1990), 280.
5. Ibid., 292.
6. Quoted in ibid., 291.
7. Matthews Ojo, "Deeper Life Bible Church of Nigeria," in Paul Gifford, ed., *New Dimensions in African Christianity* (Nairobi: All Africa Conference of Churches, 1992), 137.
8. Ibid., 146.

put God first: "It does not take God one hour to heal a person. It does not take God one whole month to make a barren woman pregnant. It does not take God a long time to give a job to the jobless, or to give prosperity to the poor. It is sin that delays our blessing."[9]

Kumuyi publicly promised that "if you are blind, sick, lame, barren, jobless, tired, and dead spiritually, hear and believe the word of God as it is coming forth from my mouth and the power of God will touch you."[10] By the 1990s Deeper Life Bible Churches had spread across Nigeria and beyond to several African and Western nations, their vision of the kingdom decidedly less political than the visions of either Nkrumah or Tutu.

Despite all of their obvious differences, the contrast among Nkrumah, Tutu, and Kumuyi should not be overdrawn. From one perspective they each represent different sides of a central concern of modern African Christianity: realizing the presence of the kingdom on earth.

For Nkrumah, as for many secularized Christians among Africa's educated elite, African nationalism became the path to realizing the kingdom. For Tutu the promise of nationalism was compromised by political injustice. Combating racism and economic discrimination was the proper path to the kingdom. A Christian prophetic stance was the only credible Christian witness. For Kumuyi, the nation-state experiment was a failure. Independence did not bring about an earthly utopia, but war, poverty, and disillusionment. The kingdom as earthly utopia would be realized only through a spiritual community where healing and holiness descended from heaven to earth.

This chapter explores the kingdom emphasis that has dominated African Christianity in the twentieth century. Whether in its political, prophetic, or pentecostal expressions the modern African church's central witness to the kingdom emphasized the coming of the kingdom on earth. This note was struck at the WCC-sponsored Melbourne Conference on World Mission and Evangelism in 1980 which concluded that to pray for Christ's kingdom to come is "to ask therefore to work for the end of the powers which are the ordered structures of society and the spiritual powers which lie behind them and undergird religious structures, intellectual structures, moral structures, political structures, etc."[11] The African church's move toward this model of the kingdom on earth has plunged her into a struggle to choose among political idolatry, political activism, and political escapism.

The ancient church once described its witness to the kingdom in terms of four "marks"—oneness, holiness, catholicity, and apostolicity. What was meant by these terms? Oneness meant the forging of bonds of unity and co-

---

9. Quoted in ibid.
10. Quoted in ibid., 147.
11. *Your Kingdom Come: Report of the Melbourne Conference on World Mission and Evangelism, 1980* (Geneva: WCC, 1980), 3.

operation on the basis of the gospel in a deeply divided world. Holiness meant treasuring God more than the world and its idols. Catholicity meant that the church was open to all (as opposed to the elitism of the heretics). This third mark spoke of the church's mission to the world and commitment to evangelism. Apostolicity meant preaching, teaching, and confessing Christ as Lord on the basis of the Scriptures.

As the witness to the threefold kingdom of God (sovereign rule, redemptive reign, and earthly justice) shifted to the latter aspect of the kingdom in the modern period, the meaning of the four marks was affected. Questions of justice and wholeness in politically chaotic times dominated the theology, mission, lifestyle, and fellowship of the churches of Africa in ways that recalled the ancient church in the centuries of persecution. The challenge of African Christianity in its attempt to be one, holy, catholic, and apostolic in modern times was the challenge presented by the Christian martyrs, who saw in Christ a higher Lord than Caesar. Whose kingdom do we witness to? That of Caesar or of Christ?

This chapter surveys the four marks of the African church's witness to the kingdom since independence. We begin with the mark of holiness and the crucible within which that mark faced its greatest test—the struggle between church and state.

Church and State (Holy)

The year 1960 was "the year of Africa."[12] In that year fourteen African nations achieved selfhood. A decade earlier only four countries were independent of colonial rule. But by the early 1960s the situation was completely reversed, with all but a handful of former colonies independent, though Zimbabwe and South Africa were under White rule.

In 1963 the Organization of African Unity (OAU) was formed in Addis Ababa. African novelists such as the Nigerians Wole Soyinka and Chinua Achebe and the Kenyan, Ngugi Wa'Thiongo, were finding their way into print. A new renaissance of African culture and life was unfolding under the smiling oversight of the nation-state. There was widespread agreement on that point. The nation-state, despite its colonial boundaries and languages, was the structure that would restore the dignity and respect of the African after colonialism. Independence would demonstrate "the ability of the Black man to build a strong, progressive, and prosperous modern nation," declared General Gowon of Nigeria, and "ensure respect, dignity, and equality in the community of nations for our prosperity."[13]

12. Adrian Hastings' phrase in his *History of African Christianity: 1950–1975* (Cambridge: Cambridge University Press, 1977), 132.

13. Quoted in Kevin Shillington, *History of Africa* (London: Macmillan, 1989), 409.

Yet the era of hope was short-lived. The overarching fact of modern African life since the late 1960s has been widespread disillusionment with the nation-state. The new ruling elite, many educated in mission schools and Western universities, had moved into the state houses and limousines of the departing colonial governors in the early 1960s and had made magnificent promises to their eager and expectant constituencies. But by the mid-1960s the state houses were mobbed with the president's relatives, the limousines had multiplied, and the promises remained unfulfilled.

"Before independence," bemoaned a villager in Kwilu, Tanzania, "we dreamed that it would bring us masses of marvelous things. All of that was to descend upon us from the sky . . . Deliverance and Salvation. . . . On the contrary our life is more difficult; we are more poor than before."[14]

For the Kwame Nkrumahs of Africa this growing dissatisfaction with African rule meant tightening control, increasing repression, and promoting a messianic nationalism that would restore the political faith of the masses. Inevitably such measures ended in military coups, assassinated or exiled leaders, and often, as a prelude to violence, conflict with the church.

Such conflict was not a foregone conclusion in 1960. The church's response to the new nationalism was generally enthusiastic. But as the structures of a participatory democracy were dismantled in country after country the church found itself the only independent voice left. The church had historically functioned as the conscience of the state with varying degrees of integrity and success. The injustices of the new governments in the early 1960s and the growing messiah complex of their leaders brought about the first stages of a conflict that would continue into the 1970s and 1980s and reach a new climax in Africa's so-called second independence in the early 1990s.[15]

In some cases, such as Rwanda, the church was implicated in the violence. In most other cases, she was violence's victim. The church's response in each case moved between the poles represented by Tutu and Kumuyi, the poles of protest or escapism. A few case studies may help us picture the church's responses to messianic nationalism under its guises, varying from African authenticity campaigns and socialism/Marxism to Muslim theocracies and regimes of racism.

Liberia and Zaire. Modern African Christianity has often been puzzled by the politics of African authenticity. Some independent regimes, staggering under official corruption and misrule, have sought to silence dissent by labeling critics "unpatriotic" or motivated by "foreign ideologies." While a Hastings Banda of Malawi, an Eyadema of Togo, or a Macias Nguema of Equa-

---

14. Quoted in Hastings, *History of African Christianity: 1950–1975,* 150.
15. An overview of the second independence is given in Paul Gifford, "Recent Developments in African Christianity," *African Affairs* (1994): 93, 513–34.

torial Guinea would be equally sinister examples of African tyranny, Doe's Liberia and Mobutu's Zaire deserve a closer look.

Modern Liberia's nearly 3 million citizens have been ruled by descendants of freed slaves, who represent less than 5 percent of the population. In the 1920s Liberia's economy was dominated by multinational corporations such as Firestone, who struck deals with the ruling elite accustomed to squandering public resources on private ends. President William Tubman (served 1944–71) consolidated power through an extensive patronage system as well as through a cult of the presidency. Opponents were eliminated. Every institution in the country was bent toward solidifying the president's power and personal prestige. More money was spent on the president's yacht than on the country's justice system.[16]

Tubman's successor, William Tolbert, continued this system of misrule until confronted with the protests of the late 1970s. When Tolbert announced in 1979 that the price of rice would be raised (in order to pay for a new convention center) riots broke out that were severely repressed by the police.

In April 1980 a group of army officers under Sgt. Samuel K. Doe (1951–93) seized power, killing Tolbert and a number of government leaders. Doe's initial popularity was soon squandered by the new leader's arbitrary actions. Elections were held in 1985 but were manipulated by Doe and his Liberian Action Party. African authenticity was used to discredit and disqualify Doe's leading rivals, who were accused of importing "foreign ideologies." Newspapers and radio stations were closed by presidential whim, and the country sank into economic ruin. Bribery was rampant throughout the civil service.

The church's response to Doe's misrule was mixed. Some were vocal in their protest. Archbishop Michael Francis, Baptist leader Walter Richard, and independent church leader Abba Karnga condemned the corruption and lawlessness that characterized Doe's regime. A more typical Christian response was that of a spokesman for the Mt. Calvary United Holy Church, who urged church leaders "to stop using the pulpit to express their political views and instead strive to win more souls to Christ." Charismatic preachers and evangelists avoided any confrontation with the Doe regime by blaming poverty and injustice on territorial demons that hovered above Liberia. There was a "prince of Liberia," declared a Ghanaian evangelist in Monrovia, who was responsible for all the political and economic problems. "We do not war against men—our enemies are not earthly powers."[17]

For many evangelicals and charismatics, demons caused all personal and social sins. There was even a demon of rice shortages. "Where poverty and

16. Gifford, *New Dimensions*, 35.
17. From a sermon given in June 1989 at Jesus Festival '89. Quoted in Paul Gifford, *Church and State in Doe's Liberia* (Cambridge: Cambridge University Press, 1993), 117.

sickness are attributed to evil spirits," notes historian Paul Gifford, "there is, of course, no need to find economic or political causes for them, and the remedy becomes prayer, not social or political activity."[18]

There is a paradox to this position, however. To spiritualize evil by relegating it exclusively to the kingdom of darkness was itself a political act. "It was a solid vote for the status quo, an unfailing support for the beneficiaries of the system."[19] This was just the kind of piety Doe could use.

In 1990 Doe was assassinated and Liberia descended into civil war and anarchy. Churches attempted to ameliorate the suffering of many through a wide variety of social and spiritual services. Church growth occurred even as the country collapsed.

Yet despite the contribution of Christianity in the midst of chaos, the churches bore some responsibility for allowing the chaos to occur. By spiritualizing and demonizing social injustice in the 1980s when reform was still possible, "Christianity facilitated Liberia's spiral to total destruction."[20]

The case of Liberia was instructive for those churches dealing with government corruption and the abuse of power such as Zambia and Kenya in the 1980s and 1990s.[21] To insist that the kingdom of God is only spiritual is to promote the status quo.

Zaire. In 1965 Zaire's Mobutu Sese Seko (1930–) came to power in a bloodless coup. His military government ended officially in 1967 with the adoption of a new constitution and Mobutu's appointment as president. All political power was put into the hands of the president and his *Mouvement Populaire de la Révolution* (MPR) Party.

In 1970 Mobutu began his authenticity campaign banning foreign names, renaming Congo "Zaire," barring foreign clothing (neckties) and ideologies. When Cardinal Malula opposed Mobutu's policies, the president attacked the church, banning all religious youth movements, closing down religious newspapers and radio stations, barring the meeting of its bishops, nationalizing the Catholic University of Lovanium in Kinshasa, and sending Cardinal Malula into exile. Mobutu justified his suppression of the church in the name of a new religion, "Mobutuism." The credo of this new religion was summarized in a government statement of June 1974:

> God has sent us a great prophet, our wondrous Mobutu Sese Seko. This prophet is shaking us out of our torpor. He has delivered us from our mental alienation. He is teaching us how to love each other. This prophet is our lib-

18. Ibid.
19. Ibid., 142.
20. Gifford, *New Dimensions*, 52.
21. For a discussion of church–state tensions in Kenya, see David Gitari, "Church and Politics in Kenya," *Transformation* (July–September 1991): 7–17.

erator, our messiah, the one who has come to make all things new in Zaire. Jesus is the prophet of the Hebrews. He is dead. Christ is no longer alive. He called himself God. Mobutu is not a god and he does not call himself God. He too will die but he is leading his people towards a better life. How can honour and veneration be refused to the one who had founded the new Church of Zaire? Our church is the Popular Movement of the Revolution [MPR].[22]

The church adopted a low profile for the remainder of the decade. By the late 1970s Mobutu had backed away from his messianic vision. Cardinal Malula was reinstated. In the early 1990s chaos once again descended upon Zaire. Mobutu retained a tenuous hold on power while a Catholic bishop acted as prime minister and ran the nation. The autonomy of the church during the decades of totalitarianism made it the only credible institution left to manage the transition to true democracy. Unlike Liberia, the characteristic Christian attitude in Zaire toward the state was prudent concern and shrewd involvement rather than overspiritualization and escapism.

Islam. The *mahdi* movement in nineteenth-century Sudan was a reminder of the messianic impulse within Islam. That impulse continued into the late twentieth century. Nigeria and Uganda are both witnesses to its resurgence.

Nigeria. Nigeria is Africa's most populous country, with an estimated population of somewhere around 120 million.[23] One reason for the vagueness of this statistic is the lack of a reliable census. Tribalism and religious rivalry between the predominantly Muslim north and the Christian south stand behind the ongoing census debate.

Independence in 1960 saw Nigeria divided into three states. The Northern Region was dominated by Hausa-speaking groups and tended to be Muslim though there were significant minorities of Protestant Christians mostly associated with the ECWA churches of SIM (Sudan Interior Mission, now SIM International) or the TEKAN churches of SUM (Sudan United Mission). The most powerful political figure in the north was Sarduana of Sokoto, who talked openly of a jihad against the Christian south.

The two remaining states were the Yoruba-dominated Western Region and the predominantly Igbo Eastern Region. Due to a long history of Christian influence and Western education the Igbo spread rapidly throughout Nigeria, particularly in the north, finding ready employment in both the public and private sectors. The rivalry among these three regions led to a military coup in 1966 led by Igbo army officers. When atrocities broke out against Igbo living in the north, one of the officers, General Ojukwu, declared inde-

---

22. Quoted in Hastings, *History of African Christianity: 1950–1975*, 193.
23. J. Ramsay, ed., *Global Studies: Africa* (Guilford, Conn.: Dushkin, 1991), 48.

pendence for the Eastern Region. General Gowon, a Christian from the north, championed the cause of a united Nigeria and a civil war ensued lasting from July 1967 to January 1970.

Ojukwu propagandized the Biafran cause as that of "a non-Muslim island in a raging Islamic sea."[24] The federal blockade reduced the Igbo to starvation and disease. Some eight thousand relief trips were flown by church charities to alleviate rebel suffering and indirectly support the "Christian cause."[25]

The rebels finally succumbed in 1970. Catholic missionaries were put on trial for their role in the war and expelled. Reconciliation was surprisingly swift in the aftermath of the conflict aided by the new prosperity brought on by the oil boom and by the fact that the conflict was not at heart a religious war. The war had, according to one observer, "more the smell of petrol than of incense."[26]

The Muslim–Christian tension became more pronounced in the last decades of the twentieth century. Muslim-backed military governments dominated Nigerian politics in the 1980s and 1990s. In 1982 a Muslim crowd in Kano burned a number of churches.[27] In 1986 suspicions were high that Nigeria had secretly joined the Islamic Conference Organization and that Muslim law, the *sharia*, would be imposed on the nation. Christians were on alert against an aggressive Islam. Nigerian believers increasingly identified with the situation faced by Christian contemporaries in southern Sudan as well as their Christian ancestors in medieval Nubia, North Africa, Ethiopia, and Egypt.

Uganda. The church struggle in Uganda was also a struggle against an aggressive Islam. After Uganda's independence in 1962, Milton Obote's United People's Party (UPC) shared power with Mutesa II's Royalist Party. In 1966 when Obote and his ally, Colonel Idi Amin, were under investigation for misappropriation of funds, Obote suspended the constitution, exiled the king, and promoted Amin as head of his military forces.

Obote's dictatorial rule came to an end in 1971 when Amin seized power, had himself declared president, and abolished the Parliament. His expulsion of the forty thousand-member Asian community was seen as a popular gesture that proved to be economically disastrous.

Though at first appearing friendly to the Christian community, Amin, a Muslim, soon launched a campaign to promote Islam by moving against the church. In September 1972 he killed a leading Christian political leader, Be-

24. Quoted in Hastings, *History of African Christianity: 1950–1975*, 198.

25. The eight thousand figure is used by Baur, *2000 Years of African Christianity*, 383, versus the five thousand estimated by Hastings, *History of African Christianity: 1950–1975*, 199.

26. The phrase belongs to Glélé. Quoted in Baur, *2000 Years of African Christianity*, 383.

27. Elizabeth Isichei, *A History of Christianity in Africa* (Grand Rapids: Eerdmans, 1995), 342.

nidicto Kiwanuka. In October, Amin revealed plans to "Ugandanize the churches." Fifty-five Catholic priests were expelled from the country. Father Clement Kiggundo, editor of the Catholic daily, *Munno*, was killed. The pro-revival Anglican archbishop Janani Luwum was murdered. By 1978 Amin's reign of terror had eliminated nearly five hundred thousand Ugandans, most of them Christians. His invasion of Tanzania in 1978 proved to be Amin's downfall. He was overthrown in 1979, fleeing first to Libya and later to Saudi Arabia.

Obote's return to power proved to be almost as violent as the Amin years. He was overthrown in 1985. In 1986 Yoweri Museveni and his National Re-sistance Movement (NRM) gained power and sought to return the country to normalcy. "The worst thing for Christian Uganda," writes John Baur, "was that the value of human life had become so cheap, that killing was prac-ticed for much lower aims than the ancient gods once had demanded."[28]

Most of the Christians who made up the majority of Uganda's population were ready to put the years of suffering and bloodshed behind them. A wide-spread sentiment among the majority was that they had become too politi-cized in the years following independence. Other Christians, however, disil-lusioned with the secular visions of the kingdom on earth sought more radical solutions.

In 1987 Alice Lekwana ("Messenger") a young female prophet from northern Uganda, envisioned the establishment of a truly Christian kingdom on earth. She raised an army and concocted magic potions to protect them from bullets. Models of helicopters, tanks, and artillery were made in order to magically render real ones impotent.

Alice's father, who declared himself God the Father, promised to raise the dead. Another man, Joseph Kony, claimed to be the Holy Spirit. Tens of thousands joined her movement of Holy Spirit Rebels. They marched on Kampala singing Christian hymns. They fought their way to within sixty-two miles of the city. Museveni's troops finally inflicted upon this army of the Lord a crippling defeat. Thousands of followers were killed though Alice es-caped into exile.[29] By 1995 a splinter group, the Lord's Resistance Army (LRA), had added rocket-propelled grenades to their magic and their prayers and were still fighting for the heaven on earth that modern politics had failed to realize.[30]

The movement of Alice Lekwana was evidence that Christian eschatol-ogy was becoming politicized even at the grassroots level. The prevalence of such violent visions of the kingdom created concern about future stability in an already shaken nation.

28. Baur, *2000 Years of African Christianity*, 488.
29. J. Ramsay, ed., *Global Studies: Africa*, 129.
30. Reuters News Service, April 21.

Racism and Reconciliation in South Africa. The struggle of the church in places like South Africa, Rwanda, Burundi, and Zimbabwe had more to do with racial hatred than dictatorship, corruption, or rival religion. Zimbabwe had successfully made the transition to majority rule in the 1980s, and the church had thrived in the new atmosphere. Less successful were the countries of Rwanda and Burundi. Brutal genocide between Hutu and Tutsi in Burundi and Rwanda broke out in 1994 (as it had done before). Nearly a million lives were lost in Rwanda alone. That both countries contained a Christian majority increased the dimensions of the tragedy.

The outbreak of violent racial hatred between Tutsi and Hutu by the western shores of Lake Victoria in 1994 was, however, overshadowed in that same year by an equally dramatic outbreak of racial reconciliation. In that year, more than four decades of racist rule by the Afrikaner Nationalist government of South Africa ended.

Since the early 1950s the policy of apartheid had aroused a spirited Christian protest from various segments of South Africa's churches. The Bantu Education Act of 1954 was one of the earliest expressions of apartheid. Schools that were formerly in church hands were nationalized. Z. K. Matthews, principal of Fort Hare College and an outstanding graduate of the school, was forced to resign. Many missions closed their schools rather than hand them over to the government.

After the nationalizing of the schools, standards dropped in the non-White schools as government expenditure on education of Blacks dropped. Ninety percent of the education budget was spent on White schools; 10 percent on those of the Blacks.[31] The 1950s were also a time when older ANC leaders, such as Albert Luthuli, passed the torch to more radical younger leaders such as Nelson Mandela and Oliver Tambo. These older leaders believed that "the road to freedom was via the cross" and that "Christianity is not the 'opiate for the people' but the hope of the future."[32] Yet their protests of apartheid seemed to fall on the deaf ears of both the government and the wider Christian community.

In time White Christians took notice of the Black church struggle. Alan Paton penned his moving novel, *Cry, Beloved Country*, in sympathy with their suffering. In 1955 Trevor Huddleston, an Anglican priest in Johannesburg who had published criticisms of apartheid, was sent back to England by his conservative archbishop, Geoffrey Clayton. Huddleston subsequently published one of the most effective anti-apartheid books of the decade, *Naught for Your Comfort,* a firsthand account of the slums of Johannesburg and the evils of South African racism.

31. Baur, *2000 Years of African Christianity,* 409.
32. John de Gruchy, *The Church Struggle in South Africa* (Grand Rapids: Eerdmans, 1979), 51.

The Sharpville massacre of March 21, 1960, was a turning point for many. The sudden and unprovoked government killing of hundreds of Black protesters shocked Christian consciences. In the wake of Sharpville, Black political parties were banned and ANC leader Nelson Mandela was imprisoned. One positive result of Sharpville was the Cottesloe Consultation in which a number of South African church leaders declared apartheid to be contrary to the Word of God.

In response to Cottesloe, Beyers Naudé, a Dutch Reformed minister, launched the Christian Institute in 1963. Through study groups and publications the Institute labored for racial equality and justice in the name of Christ. Naudé suffered much for his witness to justice. His ordination was revoked by the Dutch Reformed Church. In 1977 he was arrested and banned. The Christian Institute was dissolved.

By 1985, however, the ban was lifted and Naudé was back in action. He succeeded Desmond Tutu as the general secretary of the SACC. Under his leadership the SACC produced a landmark document in the churches' growing protest against apartheid—the Kairos Document of 1985. Joined by Allan Boesak of the Dutch Reformed Mission Church, Wolfgang Kistner of the SACC, and Desmond Tutu, Naudé called the Kairos Document "a challenge to the church." The document condemned a "church theology" that supported the idolatry of the state and insisted that reconciliation is unbiblical if not built on justice. Apartheid was evil and unreformable. Majority rule was the only way forward.[33]

While the Dutch Reformed Church rejected the Kairos Document on the grounds that it represented "a revolutionary liberation ideology in which Christ's salvation was made a political liberation,"[34] many Christians responded to the declaration with enthusiasm. South African evangelicals produced an important statement called *Evangelical Witness in South Africa: A Critique of Evangelical Theology by Evangelicals Themselves.*[35] Calling themselves "concerned evangelicals," the drafters of this document repented of evangelical indifference and escapism in matters of justice and pledged to work on the side of the oppressed. Pentecostals responded with *Pentecostal Witness in South Africa* (1986).

With the release of Nelson Mandela from prison in February 1990, political justice seemed close at hand. Sensing that the political winds had

33. For a discussion of the Kairos Document and its impact, see J. W. Hofmeyr and G. J. Pillay, eds., *A History of Christianity in South Africa* (Haum Tertiary, 1994), 288–89.
34. Ibid., 289.
35. Concerned Evangelicals, *Evangelical Witness in South Africa: A Critique of Evangelical Theology by Evangelicals Themselves* (Dobsonville, RSA: Concerned Evangelicals, 1986). For a study of this movement, see David Walker, "'Radical Evangelicalism': An Expression of Evangelical Social Concern Relevant to South Africa," *Journal of Theology for Southern Africa* (March 1990).

shifted, Prime Minister F. W. de Klerk dismantled the structures of apartheid and moved the country toward majority rule. Christian teaching and prophetic preaching against apartheid contributed both to the sweeping away of racist legislation in the early 1990s and to the success of the April elections of 1994, which brought Mandela and the ANC to power. Mandela called for a government of reconciliation. The church in South Africa, after decades of damning silence and complicity, mounted their finest witness to the coming kingdom in the closing years of the century.[36]

Socialism and Marxism. The fourth form of church–state tension came from the political Left. Socialism in both mild and extreme forms dreamed of a society ruled by a simple utopian maxim: "From each according to his ability, to each according to his need." It was, however, a maxim easier to say than to do. Yet several African leaders reached toward this ideal. Kaunda's Zambia and Nyerere's Tanzania represented the moderate face of socialism. Mengistu's Ethiopia took socialism's more extreme form—Marxism. This fourth form of church–state tensions produced some of the most severe persecutions of the church. It also produced some of the most dramatic political reversals and Christian resurgence in modern African history.

Kenneth Kaunda's attempt at "scientific socialism" was an abysmal failure in Zambia. For twenty-seven years Kaunda, a Methodist layman, had professed personal faith in Christ and a growing political faith in leftist ideology. Churches were harassed and intimidated into cooperating with Kaunda's socialism. Jehovah Witnesses were violently suppressed for their "disloyalty" to the government. Kaunda's heavy-handed tactics inspired a growing movement of protest that eventually led to the first multiparty elections on the continent in 1991 and began Africa's second independence.

Francis Chiluba, a jailed trade union leader who converted to Pentecostal Christianity during his imprisonment, ran for the presidency after his release and defeated Kaunda and his socialist policies. Pentecostal churches, in contrast to the escapist tendencies displayed in Liberia, actively supported the new president. For Zambians, Africa's second independence meant free elections, free enterprise, and fervent charismatic faith.[37]

---

36. Reports have circulated of the role played by Dr. Okumu of Kenya in bringing the Inkatha leader, Buthelezi, into the April 1994 elections after the latter staged an eleventh-hour walkout. As part of the negotiating team Okumu had appealed to Buthelezi to continue the dialogue on the basis of "Christian fellowship." Buthelezi spurned Okumu's final appeal and departed in his plane, only to return minutes later due to engine trouble. "God has turned my plane around," Buthelezi reportedly told Okumu. "I was like Jonah and like Jonah, God has brought me back." In the talks that followed, the three major parties reconciled and the Zulus entered the elections (based on statements made by Buthelezi at a live TV broadcast reported by Dr. Stewart Snook in a letter of June 1994).

37. Cf. "Chiluba Claims Africa for Christ," *Charisma* (April 1995): 55–56.

Tanzania. In 1967 Julius Nyerere (1922–) issued the Arusha declaration, which instituted the policy of *Ujamaa* (from *jamaa*, Swahili for "family"). *Ujamaa* as a form of African socialism was based on Nyerere's understanding of African history. In traditional Africa, villagers worked together for the common good. This value would be restored. To form a unified and egalitarian society in a nation with 140 tribes and significant Muslim and Christian tensions, Nyerere relied on an aggressive villagization program that relocated millions of Tanzanians into government-created "villages." Private *dukas* (Swahili, "store") were closed and only poorly stocked government stores were permitted.

Nyerere as a committed Catholic Christian, perhaps recalling the experiment of Bagamoyo, expected the church to support his socialism. To his disappointment the Christian community seemed reluctant to follow the *Mwalimu*'s lead. Many church leaders feared that Nyerere's turn to the Left would eventually mean an embrace of atheistic communism and church persecution. Nyerere courted the churches rather than opposing them. By 1972 the Christian community was supportive of *Ujamaa,* seeing in the "other-orientation" of socialism a reflection of the gospel's emphasis on unselfish love.[38]

By 1985, though socialism had won a number of social and cultural victories in unifying Tanzania's divided society, *Ujamaa* had failed economically. Disillusioned, Nyerere resigned as president. His hand-picked successor, Ali Hasan Mwinyi, moved the country in the direction of a free market economy and the churches began their adjustment to yet another economic system. New challenges also arose. When Zanzibar unilaterally joined the Islamic Conference Organization in the early 1990s and threatened succession from Tanzania if the nation did not join the African Organization of Islamic States, it became apparent that the new church–state tension would be provided not by socialism but by a newly aggressive Islam.[39]

Ethiopia. Tanzanian Christians learned to embrace socialism as an ally. Ethiopian Christians found Marxism to be an implacable enemy. In 1974 Emperor Haile Selassie, who had ruled Ethiopia since 1916 (except for the years of Italian occupation, 1936–41), was overthrown by the military. A Provisional Military Administrative Council or *Derg* (Amharic, "committee") oversaw the affairs of state.

In 1977 Colonel Mengistu Haile Mariam (1937–) seized power from the factious *Derg* and began the transformation of Ethiopia from a medieval feudal state into a Marxist nation. Soviet aid and Cuban soldiers filled the

---

38. Cf. Jospeh Bitangisake Kalem'Imana, "Christianity and Socialism in Tanzania" (unpublished Ph.D. diss., Drew University, 1986), 260–63.
39. Baur, *2000 Years of African Christianity*, 497.

countryside. Atheism was declared the official creed of the country. The Holy Trinity Cathedral of Addis Ababa was closed. The patriarch of the Ethiopian Orthodox Church and eight bishops were deposed. Protestant and Catholic churches were harassed. Pastors and priests were imprisoned, property was seized and nationalized, and Christian radio stations were converted to state use. Though thousands suffered for their faith, Christianity grew during these years of repression, civil war, and famine. In 1991 Mengistu was overthrown by a coalition of secessionist groups and freedom of religion was restored.[40] Christianity in Ethiopia experienced a new resurgence of life.

Racism, totalitarianism, Islam, and socialism/Marxism have each challenged the church in Africa since independence. The response of the church has varied along the spectrum represented by Tutu and Kumuyi. Because of these church–state tensions, African Christians welcomed the continent's second independence movement in the early 1990s. The church's support for this new wave of multiparty democracy was born out of a deep disillusionment with the failed promise of the African nation-state. Basil Davidson captured this sense of disillusionment when he called the African nation-state "the Black man's burden."[41]

Such despair, however, should not be surprising. The burden that modernity has put upon the nation is more than it can bear. The shift of emphasis from the kingdom of God as a transcendent reality to its secularized version as an earthly utopia has contributed to both the idolizing of the state and the demonizing of it.

Lesslie Newbigin has argued that since the Enlightenment era of the late eighteenth century, the primary emphasis of modernity has become the "rights of man." Chief among those rights is the right to earthly happiness. Since the reality of the supernatural in general and the existence of heaven in particular were denied by Enlightenment rationalism, happiness needed to be achieved on earth. "If the right of every person to life, liberty, and the pursuit of happiness is asserted, . . ." asks Newbigin, "who is under obligation to honor the claim?"[42]

The answer that the modern world gave to this question was the nation-state. "The nation-state replaces the holy church and the holy empire as the centerpiece in the post-Enlightenment ordering of society." More dramatically "the nation-state has taken the place of God as the source to which we look for happiness, health, and welfare."[43] No earthly structure can bear the strain of such utopian expectations.

40. Ibid., 401.
41. Basil Davidson, *Black Man's Burden* (Nairobi: EAEP, 1992).
42. Lesslie Newbigin, *Foolishness to the Greeks* (Grand Rapids: Eerdmans, 1986), 27.
43. Ibid.

In its struggle to be holy the African church has wrestled with the claims of such a messianic nationalism. Its greatest legacy to modern Africa may come from a return to Augustine's theology of the two cities. Such a theology may help her desacralize the earthly city of the state and restore the vigor of her witness to the treasures of an eternal city not made with hands and to a sane reform of earthly powers purged of utopian delusions.

African Christian Theology (Apostolic)

Theology has been one way in which African Christianity has responded to African nationalism. Theology represents the church's historic effort to be apostolic. While the statistics of African Christianity have borne testimony to the church's growth in size, the emergence of an African Christian theology in the decades since independence has been a notable testimony to her growing depth. Four major expressions of African Christian theology dominate these decades.

African theology. Cardinal Joseph Ratzinger has dismissed African theology as more a "project than a reality."[44] The number of theologians at work in this area and the degree to which their ideas are percolating down into Africa's eight hundred theological schools and shaping the next generation of Africa church leaders argues against such an easy dismissal. African theology is a movement with deep roots and wide reach. In general, African theology has sought to demonstrate the value of the African religious heritage and to build bridges between that heritage and Christian faith.

The first seeds of contemporary African theology were sown in the 1950s. Indigenization and inculturation were the watchwords of that decade. Fr. Placide Tempels wrote the pioneering study, *Bantu Philosophy* (French publication 1945, English translation 1955), which set the terms of discussion for years thereafter. Tempels argued that the essence of African thought was the "life-force" (*la force vitale*). In light of Tempels' searching study of the African mind, Bénézet Bujo has called Tempels the "father of African Theology."

Inspired by Tempels' ideas, the Christian Council of Ghana sponsored a conference in 1955 that "defended the continuity between African culture and Christianity." More radical was the challenge to the church issued by this conference to "use African culture as the only language to proclaim the gospel in Africa."[45]

Francophone Africa took up this issue in 1960. Tharcisse Tshibangu, a theology student at the University of Lovanium, Kinshasa (and later the rec-

---

44. Mentioned in Isichei, *History of Christianity in Africa*, 330.
45. Baur, *2000 Years of African Christianity*, 291.

tor of the university), argued that African religion and philosophy could provide the seeds of an authentic African Christian theology.

J. A. Vanneste, dean of the faculty, responded to Tshibangu's assertions by insisting that theology should be transcultural and international. He wondered how the "primitive and magical concepts" that make up African religion could be the basis of African Christian theology. Tshibangu's position won the most support with Vincent Mulago taking up this cause in the late 1960s.[46] Vanneste later modified his own views in favor of a more pluralist approach to Christian theology.[47] Other Francophone voices in the development of African theology included Englebert Mveng, Nginud Mushete, Anselme Sanon, Eboussi Boulaga, and Bénézet Bujo.[48]

In the same year that Tshibangu and Vanneste had debated about the necessity of African theology within a Catholic context, Lutheran Bishop Bengt Sundkler called for a new initiative among African Protestants in his *Christian Ministry in Africa*. This initiative was seen in 1966 in Ibadan, Nigeria, when a theological consultation was held which included Kwesi Dickson, Bolaji Idowu, John Mbiti, and Harry Sawyer. Their deliberations were published in *Biblical Revelation and African Beliefs*, one of the first Anglophone publications on African theology. In the 1970s and 1980s these early voices of African theology were joined by writers such as Edward Fasholé-Luke, John Pobee, Charles Nyamiti, Jesse Mugambi, Laurenti Magesa, and Ukachukwu Chris Manus.

The common note beneath the surface diversity of African theology was the positive valuation of African culture. Bénézet Bujo of Zaire summarized the project of African theology: "To restore the liberating dimension of African religion, we need to rediscover some basic elements which have been buried under the combined weight of colonialism, missionary proselytism, and modern technical culture. The balance of African culture has been profoundly disturbed, and many Africans know virtually nothing of their traditions, however much they may continue to be unconsciously influenced by them."[49]

The spirit of nationalism in these words should not be missed. Just as independence from the West politically asserted itself in the early 1960s, so independence theologically followed suit. The great value of this African theology was to build a number of useful bridges between the gospel and African culture (e.g., Nyamiti's Christ as Ancestor, Chris Manus's Christ as an African king).

46. V. Mulago, *Une Visage africaine du Christianisme* (Paris, 1965).
47. For a discussion of this debate and an assessment of Lovanium's contribution to African theological development, see Gordon Molyneux, "The Contribution to African Theology of the Faculte de Theologie, Kinshasa, Zaire," *Africa Journal of Evangelical Theology* 11, no. 2 (1992): 3ff.
48. Baur provides a useful survey of these thinkers in *2000 Years of African Christianity*, 298–300.
49. Bénézet Bujo, *African Theology in its Social Context* (Maryknoll: Orbis, 1992), 130.

By the late 1970s tensions between the African church and African states mounted. African theology tended to support the political status quo of the new nationalism and seemed increasingly remote from the real conditions of post-independence Africa. John Mbiti, a Kenyan who was the most prolific of all of the early figures of African theology, symbolized this remoteness by his relocation in 1972 to Geneva to assume the directorship of Bossey Ecumenical Institute. A more critical theology, rooted not in a nostalgia over Africa's past but in a more relevant concern for real African political and economic issues, was needed.

Liberation theology. Two events in the mid-1970s nudged African Christianity from questions of cultural continuity to questions of political and economic justice. The first event was the Fifth General Assembly of the World Council of Churches in Nairobi (1975). The strong endorsement of the WCC's controversial "Program to Combat Racism" by the 750 delegates (including the 116 African representatives) made clear that a new emphasis on racial justice was being added to the earlier emphasis on culture.[50]

The second meeting was the initial conference of Third World Theologians in Dar es Salaam (1976) spearheaded by Chilean liberation theologian Sergio Torres. The delegates at Dar defined the purpose of theology as the creation of "a new world order, which is founded on justice, brotherhood, and freedom."[51] Christians are to participate in the struggle for this new world order, the kingdom of God in history.[52] This struggle for the kingdom necessitated a struggle not only with the colonial past but also with the new African ruling class who were exploiting the poor. Out of this conference came the Ecumenical Association of Third World Theologians (EATWoT), which has promoted this new theological agenda globally.

Jean-Marc Ela was a leading voice of African liberation theology. A Cameroonian theologian who has worked among the poor in North Cameroon, Ela argued that "liberation of the oppressed must be the primary condition for any authentic inculturation of the Christian message."[53] The true theology of the cross for Ela opens us "to this brutal fact: Africa today is crucified."[54]

The theology that Africa needs is a theology that begins with the need of the poor and gives to them the hope of the coming kingdom. "In assuming the condition of the people, the Servant battles for the liberation of the human being and the coming of the Reign of God."[55] Such a theology of the

50. See Hastings, *History of African Christianity*, 233.
51. Quoted in P. Beyerhaus, *The Kingdom of God and the Utopian Error* (Wheaton: Crossway, 1992), 121.
52. Ibid., 122.
53. Jean-Marc Ela, *My Faith as an African* (Maryknoll: Orbis, 1988), xvi.
54. Ibid., 146.
55. Ibid.

kingdom can give hope to those who "live in a continent marked by supposedly inescapable unhappiness, a continent where poverty alone seems to have a prosperous future."[56]

African feminist theologians such as Mercy Amba Oduyoye of Ghana have found in liberation theology the idiom with which to address their own grievances and express their hope for a larger role in Africa's future.[57]

Black theology. Coupled with the rise of liberation theology has been the related movement of Black theology. Partly inspired by the writings of African American James Cone, Black theology has found its most responsive followers in South Africa. Allan Boesak, a Colored Reformed pastor, and Manas Buthelezi, Lutheran bishop and former president of the SACC, were two of the leading writers of Black theology.[58] Archbishop Desmond Tutu is one of the movement's major promoters.

Black theology was directly relevant to the Black Consciousness Movement (BCM) that heavily influenced the direction of the South African Students Organization (SASO) founded in 1969 by Steve Biko. According to Biko, "Black theology seeks to relate God and Christ once more to the Black man and his daily problems. It wants to describe Christ as a fighting God and not a passive God. . . . In time we shall be able to bestow upon South Africa the greatest gift possible—a more human face."[59]

The Kairos Document of 1985 represented a culminating expression of Black theology. There can be no doubt that such a theology contributed to the struggle for racial equality in South Africa. Whether this theology can survive the collapse of apartheid remains to be seen. Ali Mazrui is one observer who feels that it will. Black theology's continuing role, argues Mazrui, is in the "re-masculation of Christianity, a readiness to invoke the macho values of militant combat in defense of justice."[60]

Evangelical theology. A final face of African Christian theology is provided by African evangelicalism. The founding father of modern African evangelical theology was Byang Kato (d. 1975) of Nigeria, noted for his hostility to African theology's overly optimistic view of African traditional religion. Kato's death by drowning in 1975 silenced a promising theological voice.

Among the leading recent contributors are Tite Tienou (Burkina Faso), Kwame Bediako (Ghana), O. Imasogie (Nigeria), Cornelius Olowala (Nige-

56. Ibid., 182.

57. Her main work is *Hearing and Knowing: Theological Reflections on Christianity in Africa* (Maryknoll: Orbis, 1986).

58. Cf. Allan Boesak, *Farewell to Innocence* (Maryknoll: Orbis, 1977) and Manas Buthelezi's essay in H. J. Becken, ed., *Relevant Theology for Africa* (Durban: Lutheran Publishing House, 1973).

59. Quoted in Hofmeyr and Pillay, *History of Christianity in South Africa*, 279.

60. Ali Mazrui, *The African Condition* (London: Cambridge University Press, 1980), 52.

ria), and Tokunboh Adeyemo (Nigeria, General Secretary of the Association of evangelicals of Africa). Many of their contributions have been published in the *Africa Journal of Evangelical Theology*, founded in 1982. Yet in light of the large number of evangelicals in Africa, evangelical theology has been in many ways an underachiever compared to her sister theological movements. Serious academic theology by African evangelicals has been hard to find. Profound interaction with current African issues has also been lacking in the monographs thus far produced.[61]

Yet despite these past disappointments, African evangelical theology showed signs of new life in the closing years of the twentieth century. An impetus to this renewal was the Lausanne Conference in 1974 in which several thousand evangelicals from around the world gathered in Switzerland to strategize for global evangelism. Scores of African representatives led by Byang Kato attended Lausanne. One of the enduring fruits of Lausanne was the Lausanne Covenant. This document was a modern restatement of evangelical theology that preserved historic distinctives while responding to modern questions.

The impact of the Lausanne Covenant on Africa was profound. It affected African evangelicalism in ways that paralleled the impact of Vatican II on African Catholicism. Three theological developments within African evangelical theology can be traced directly or indirectly to Lausanne: (1) the growth of national fellowships of evangelicals committed to the uniqueness of Christ; (2) the emergence of the Gospel and Culture seminars in Zaire; and (3) the reassertion of a futurist and Christ-centered view of the kingdom of God.

A number of evangelical national fellowships sprang up after Lausanne. Zambia, Kenya, and Nigeria are but three examples of a wider trend. With the formation of these national fellowships, the question of theological agreement became central. Joint theological statements were produced in a number of countries and, in some instances, fresh restatements of African evangelical faith emerged.

An example of such a restatement is the Declaration of Nigeria Evangelicals (1975), which attempted to forge a middle way between African theology and liberation theology.[62]

---

61. On the underdevelopment of African evangelical theology, see the important essay by Tite Tienou, *The Theological Task of the Church in Africa* (Ghana: Africa Christian Press, 1992).

62. "We declare that as Christians we should be involved in the political, economic, and social life of our nation as its worthy citizens. In our involvement, however, we must not fall into the mould of the sinful world system so manifest in our nation in the form of bribery, corruption, nepotism, tribalism, ostentatious living, and the like. On the contrary, we must influence society through our changed lives." Statement of Nigerian Evangelicals, 1976, printed as an appendix in S. de la Haye, *Byang Kato: Ambassador for Christ* (Ghana: Africa Christian Press, 1986).

Nigerian evangelicals, like their counterparts in other parts of Africa, were concerned to keep Christ central to Christianity. "The call to salvation is the call for men to be reconciled to God through Jesus Christ. This is Nigeria's greatest need. We further affirm that wherever this occurs, it should have a wholesome effect on the political, economic, and social life of the community."[63] Both the individualism of evangelicalism (society is changed by transformed individuals) and its high Christology are seen in this statement.

This stress on the uniqueness of Christ ran against the grain of late-twentieth-century religious pluralism, which reckoned all (or most) religions as equally valid paths to God. Nigerian evangelicalism, following the lead of Byang Kato and Lausanne, reaffirmed the uniqueness of Christ in uncompromising ways: "While it is true that Jesus Christ loved all men, even false religious leaders and had discourses with them, He categorically declared 'I am the way, and the truth, and the life; no one comes to the Father but by me' (John 14:6). We affirm, therefore, that only through Jesus Christ can anyone be saved."[64]

A second development from Lausanne that affected African evangelical theology was a new emphasis on the positive relationship between gospel and culture. This had been a theme of Byang Kato but the dialogue tended to be defensive and at times reactionary. A more positive and less defensive thrust in this area were the Gospel and Culture seminars in Zaire and Kenya. After the Lausanne Conference of 1974 a follow-up conference, the Willowbank Consultation on the Gospel and Culture, was held in 1978 to deal with this critical issue.

One participant of both Lausanne and Willowbank, American missionary John Gration, visited his former African colleagues in Zaire in 1981 to discover ways that the church at the grassroots level could exploit some of the new understandings about gospel and culture. As a result of these preliminary discussions, Gration designed and facilitated a number of seminars with church leaders. African leaders later confessed to Gration that these seminars provided a forum for the examination of issues that they had never before discussed with missionaries "because they would laugh at us."[65] Gration employed adult learning principles and stayed very much in the background in order not to "set the agenda" but merely to stimulate the thinking of the participants.[66] New understanding of the gospel and of the role of the church in Zaire emerged from these discussions. Twenty-

63. Ibid.
64. Ibid.
65. Quoted in Gordon Molyneux, *African Christian Theology: The Quest for Selfhood* (San Francisco: Mellen Research University Press, 1993), 275.
66. Ibid., 299.

nine topics for further discussion by African-led groups emerged from these seminars, setting an agenda that guided the CECA churches for years to come.

A similar movement in Kenya, the Theological Advisory Group (TAG) of the Africa Inland Church, built a theology from below through stimulating interactions among African pastors, theological educators, and lay leaders.[67] Though often accused of excessive individualism, evangelical theology in Africa was finding a new group orientation.

The third theological development in Africa traceable to Lausanne was the reassertion of a futurist and Christ-centered view of the kingdom of God. While evangelical views of the kingdom were regarded by critics as too inward or otherworldly to be relevant to the struggle for justice, that picture was changing by the 1990s. Evangelicals in South Africa found a new social conscience as demonstrated by the "concerned evangelicals" of South Africa. Evangelicals all over the continent witnessed to the power of their futurist eschatology.

In contrast, African Christianity since independence emphasized the kingdom as "here and now." So strong was this emphasis that African theology was in danger of losing the transcendent and the future aspects of the kingdom. African theology in its various forms was also in danger of identifying the kingdom with various political or economic ideologies rather than with the personal rule of Christ. When those political or economic ideologies failed, many Christians became disillusioned.

Lausanne reasserted a strongly futurist and christological understanding of the kingdom that impressed African evangelicals. The final paragraph of the Lausanne Covenant reads:

> We believe that Jesus Christ will return personally and visibly, in power and glory, to consummate his salvation and his judgment. The promise of his coming is a further spur to our evangelism, for we remember his words that the Gospel must first be preached to all nations. We believe that the interim period between Christ's ascension and return is to be filled with the mission of the people of God, who have no liberty to stop before the end.[68]

The Declaration of Nigerian Evangelicals echoes this conviction: "In the light of the imminent return of our Lord Jesus Christ who says, 'Surely I am coming soon' (Revelation 22:20), we see evangelism as an urgent task for the Church."[69] What does such a futurist and Christ-centered eschatology offer to Africa? David Bosch explains:

---

67. Key leaders of the TAG movment in Kenya have been Titus Kivunzi, Joseph Ndebe, Jacob Kibor, and Richard Gehman, faculty members of Scott Theological College.

68. Lausanne Covenant, paragraph 15.

69. Declaration of Nigerian Evangelicals, in De La Haye, *Byang Kato*, 126.

By nature, we are all romantics and Pelagians . . . confident that we have both the will and the power to usher in a new world. We too easily identify God's will and power with ours. . . . It belongs to the essence of Christian teleology that it doubts that the eschatological vision can be fully realized in history. . . . The ultimate triumph remains uniquely God's gift. . . . If we turn off the lighthouse of eschatology we can only grope in darkness and despair.[70]

By preaching a concept of the kingdom that refused to be identified with human ideologies or programs calculated "to usher in a new world order," evangelicalism is a return to the gospel asserting that Jesus Christ is the hope of the world. "Perhaps the most significant contribution that Evangelicalism can make to the future of Christianity," argues Alister McGrath, "is to force others to realize that the liberal experiment has failed and the future of Christianity lies in returning to the New Testament and rediscovering the appeal of biblical Christianity."[71]

While Paul Gifford has pointed out that a passive evangelicalism served the cause of the unjust status quo in Liberia, he also notes that this has not been the case with evangelicalism in South Africa, Latin America, and North America.[72] Admittedly, African evangelicalism had within itself, particularly in its charismatic wing, the seeds of both an escapist view of the kingdom and/or an overrealized eschatology of the kingdom (perfect healing, perfect holiness, personal ecstasy).

Evangelicalism's kingdom vision, however, does not have to be escapist or capitulate to some form of charismatic overrealized eschatology. To the degree that it remains centered on the risen Christ and looks to the end of time, African evangelical theology can provide the foundation for a critique of messianic nationalism with its pretensions about building the kingdom on earth. Such an eschatology can be a useful reminder that all human structures are fallen and limited. A rediscovery of the lordship of the risen and returning Christ of orthodoxy over the political and intellectual Caesars of our time may be a force for the renewal of African Christianity in the third millennium.

Ecumenism and Church Growth (Oneness and Catholicity)

Two final marks of African Christianity since independence deserve mention—the pursuit of oneness and catholicity. The first mark has pushed the fractured church of Africa toward ecumenism and new forms of unity repre-

---

70. David Bosch, *Transforming Mission* (Maryknoll: Orbis, 1991), 509.
71. Alister McGrath, *Evangelicalism and the Future of Christianity* (Downers Grove, Ill.: InterVarsity, 1995), 186.
72. Gifford, *Doe's Liberia*, 144–45.

sented by small Christian communities and parachurch agencies. The pursuit of the mark of catholicity has led from the debate about a moratorium on missions to the resurgence of missions and charismatic church growth in the 1980s and 1990s.

Bengt Sundkler once dreamed that the church in Africa would learn from the culture and build an ecclesiology of the Great Family.[73] The critical observer of African Christianity might be tempted to describe the church on the continent more like a fractured family.

Despite the great diversity of Christian groups in Africa, signs of oneness exist. The most notable development in oneness has been the conciliar movement in Africa since 1960. This conciliar movement has affected Roman Catholics, mainline Protestants, and evangelicals in a number of ways. A central benefit has been improved communication and cooperation among Christians separated by history, geography, and economic resources.

The pioneer body was the All Africa Conference of Churches (AACC) founded in 1963 in Kampala. Under the outstanding leadership of Canon Burgess Carr of Liberia, the AACC, from its Nairobi headquarters, promoted justice and worked as an agent of reconciliation (particularly in Sudan) in the 1970s and 1980s. Its periodic assemblies have dealt with critical issues facing the church such as selfhood (1963) and moratorium (Lusaka, 1974).

The evangelical movement has been unified by the Association of Evangelicals of Africa. Like their AACC counterparts they have their headquarters in Nairobi. Their General Assemblies have focused on aspects of evangelism and witness, a central evangelical concern. In December 1994 a Pan African Christian Leadership Assembly (PACLA) was held in Nairobi with the AACC and AEA cooperating as respectful partners in the dialogue about evangelism and justice.

Catholic Christianity in Africa rejoiced in the special African Synod of Bishops held in Rome in April 1994. This synod marked a new level of recognition by the Roman Catholic Church of the strength and value of African Catholic Christianity.

Independent churches have also formed their own associations and several leading groups, such as the Kimbanguists, are part of the World Council of Churches.

Oneness in the church means more, however, than formal associations. On another level the church of Africa has been discovering the oneness of mutual ministry and shared lives. Roman Catholicism has seen an explosion of SCCs (Small Christian Communities) in the closing decades of the century. In 1977 a Roman Bishops Synod concluded that "the ideal way of renewing a

---

73. Bengt Sundkler, *The Christian Ministry in Africa* (London: SCM, 1962), 109.

parish is by making it a community of communities."[74] Episcopal support has been given to the proliferation of these SCCs. Inspired by small group movements within Latin American Catholicism and within African independent churches, Catholicism has promoted such groups throughout the continent.

These groups function on three levels. First is the basic level of prayer and Bible study. Groups experience the oneness of mutual ministry and building each other up in Christ. The second level is that of pastoral activities, such as visiting the sick and even performing the sacraments. The third level is that of mission. Groups can engage meaningfully in witness, social action, and ecumenical activities.[75] Though resistance to SCCs continues in some areas, their promise remains great. Protestant and charismatic group life could benefit from more interaction with the SCCs within Catholicism.

Parachurch agencies have fostered new opportunities for cooperation. Among theological schools the Accrediting Council for Theological Education in Africa (ACTEA) has labored not only to upgrade standards for many of the eight hundred theological schools in Africa but also to provide forums for the exchange of ideas and mutual encouragement. The 1992 ACTEA conference for theological educators, held in Limuru, Kenya, was a step of progress in providing a new unity on this level of church life.

Groups such as World Vision, World Relief, Tear Fund, MAP International, and numerous Catholic relief agencies have been agents of cooperation knitting different churches together for the common cause of development and relief. Bible translation projects have also been arenas of unity for the church. Baur notes that in 1977 alone there were seventy-eight ecumenical Bible translation projects underway.[76] So prevalent are these parachurch agencies that some observers speak of the NGO-ization of the historic churches.[77]

Challenges to oneness remain. More evangelical-Catholic dialogue is needed. Progress in this area has occurred in the West but little has been seen in Africa.[78] The role of women in the church remains unresolved.[79] The rise of charismatic Christianity has caused some strains. In August 1993 the United Church of Zambia split over the issue of charismatic practices.[80]

Messiah complexes and big egos continue to threaten unity as much as doctrinal deterioration and the proliferation of new religious movements.

74. Baur, *2000 Years of African Christianity,* 319.
75. Ibid.
76. Ibid., 361.
77. Gifford, "Recent Developments," 521.
78. One thinks of ERCDOM (Evangelical–Roman Catholic Dialogue on Mission) in 1984 and the 1992 document "Evangelicals and Catholics Together" produced by representatives of both sides in the United States.
79. The WCC sponsored a decade for women's issues, "Churches in Solidarity with Women: 1988–1998." As part of this, the AACC sponsored an all-women's conference in 1989.
80. Gifford, "Recent Developments," 521.

Paul Gifford links this "Big Man" model of leadership with the political model many churches witness in their nations.[81] Churches of every theological stripe have witnessed abuses of power and money by such church leaders. Movement toward oneness can be seen in African Christianity, but sectarianism and abusive leadership cast an unwelcome shadow over this mark.

Catholicity. The mark of catholicity speaks of the mission of the church. Christianity is not just a cultural religion of the West but a truly global faith open and responsive to all. Irenaus of Lyons in the second century used the term to describe the true church as the church in all lands, open to all, in contrast to the heretical groups such as Gnosticism, which tended to be geographically limited to Egypt and closed to all but an elite.

This mark has undergone a number of twists and turns since independence. In the 1970s a number of African leaders issued a call for moratorium on missions from the West. John Gatu was the first to sound this note. Speaking at a 1971 missions festival in Milwaukee, Wisconsin, the moderator of the Presbyterian Church of Kenya stunned his audience by claiming that "the continuation of the present missionary movement is a hindrance to the selfhood of the church" in Africa.[82]

The AACC at its Third General Assembly in Lusaka in 1974 approved an "option" supported by the Secretary General Burgess Carr calling for a temporary moratorium "on external assistance in money and personnel."[83] Catholic theologian Eboussi Boulaga joined the call for moratorium in 1974, arguing that the West was still the real master of African Christianity and that what was needed was the "de-missionization" of the church.

Reactions to this call for moratorium were swift and varied. A number of groups changed their policies to comply with the new call. The United Presbyterian Church reduced the number of its missionaries. The Basel Mission restricted its missionaries to short-term and specialized service. The London Missionary Society created mutual teams of African and Western missionaries serving in partnership.

Other groups, however, rejected the call for moratorium. In 1974 in Rome at the Synod of Bishops, the Catholic Church insisted that "there was still an urgent need" for missionaries and rejected the call for moratorium as "contrary to the Gospel."[84] In that same year the Evangelical Congress on World Evangelization in Lausanne also rejected the call for moratorium on the same grounds as that of the Vatican and pledged to send one hundred thousand new missionaries to fulfill the Great Commission of Matthew

81. Ibid., 520.
82. Baur, *2000 Years of African Christianity*, 312.
83. Ibid.
84. Ibid., 314.

28:19 by the year 2000. Even the AACC was having second thoughts. Burgess Carr, faced with an unfinished headquarters in Nairobi, withdrew the earlier call for moratorium on financial assistance.

Though mainline missionaries decreased from 5,000 in 1959 to 3,000 in 1971, evangelical missionaries from largely independent faith missions increased from 11,000 to 16,000. In a number of African countries the Protestant missionary presence (mostly North Americans) has grown. Expatriate Protestant missionaries in Kenya have increased from 1,150 in 1978 to 2,321 in 1993. In Zaire the numbers have jumped from 1,000 in 1978 to 1,406 in 1993. Zimbabwe has gone from 250 foreign Christian workers in the late 1970s to 630 in 1993. Nigeria has seen a net decline probably due to the government's reluctance to grant missionary visas due to Muslim–Christian tensions.[85]

Though their numbers have fallen slightly, Catholic missionaries still outnumber Protestant missionaries in Africa (1993 statistics: 4,366 to 1,406 in Zaire; 3,210 to 2,321 in Kenya; 1,640 to 689 in Cameroon).[86] These numbers were justified on the basis of new challenges facing the church in the modern world.

Urbanization, secularization, and the resurgence of Islam are but a few of these new challenges causing churches of Africa to forge new partnerships with the churches of the West. Along with the increase of Western missions has been the growth in African mission agencies such as that of the ECWA churches of Nigeria with nearly five hundred national missionaries under the able leadership of Panya Baba.

The real story of church growth and expansion of African Christianity in the closing decades of the century, however, goes beyond the story of foreign or national missionaries. It is a story of largely indigenous African efforts of a revival type (see chapter 13) that have resulted in the explosion of Pentecostal/charismatic churches. Gifford summarizes:

> In the last decade an important development has occurred in African Christianity. This is the proliferation of new religious groups, churches, and ministers, nearly all of them Pentecostal. These initiatives are evident particularly in major cities like Nairobi, Kinshasa, or Lagos, but are increasingly obvious in rural areas, too. This Christianity is promoted through literature, workshops, Bible colleges, revivals, and crusades, which are now such a feature of so many African cities.[87]

As a revival-type religious movement the major problem it addresses is that of alienation from modern life and from relational intimacy with God.

85. Gifford, "Recent Developments," 519.
86. Ibid., 522.
87. Gifford, *New Dimensions,* 1.

Unlike previous revival-type movements one of the striking features of this new charismatic African Christianity is its emphasis on the kingdom as present now in healing and prosperity for believers. This new emphasis has enabled new charismatic movements to steal some of the thunder of the older African independent churches. "The faith gospel of health and wealth is central to many, probably most," observes Paul Gifford.[88]

Dealing with spirits is a second standard feature. Both of these issues reflect an indigenous African concern with evil as that which threatens physical and material well-being. Benson Idahosa of Nigeria is the founder of a church that addresses these issues in charismatic ways. His Church of God Mission International with its one thousand branches has made him one of Africa's new religious leaders. At a charismatic "Fire" conference in Harare in 1986 he revealed the theology to which he credits his success. By the power of signs and wonders, "the church can stop Marxism, communism, and bad politicians."[89] Charismatic power can make heaven on earth.

The rhetoric of Idahosa is a kingdom rhetoric that has characterized the pentecostal movement from its inception. Harvey Cox explains: "Not only did the early Pentecostals believe that the kingdom of God was coming soon, they also believed they themselves were the evidence of its arrival."[90] For charismatic preachers and their audience, "Healings and tongues and prophecies were seen as certain signs of the imminent arrival of the reign of Christ the King."[91]

But Cox notes a change in the kingdom witness of modern charismatic churches. "In most churches today the message centers on the immediate presence and compassionate availability of the Spirit of Jesus Christ as helper, healer, and companion." The eschatological note of Christ's second coming "has been muted."[92] Consequently the movement seems to have settled down with the current status quo and has lost much of its prophetic edge and refining fire. The private experience of the self becomes the new utopia, the kingdom on earth. The worlds of the nation-state, culture, and ideas are irrelevant to the world of the insulated self.

One of the central unanswered questions about these new religious movements is whether they will move beyond the collapsing of the kingdom vision into the self and rediscover the transcendent and future reality of the coming kingdom that shaped classic Pentecostalism. Such a renewed kingdom vision may enable them to be more effective agents of a wider reform and renewal of African Christianity and African cultural and political life. True catholic-

88. Gifford, "Recent Developments," 516.
89. Quoted in Isichei, *History of Christianity in Africa*, 336.
90. Harvey Cox, *Fire from Heaven: The Rise of Pentecostal Spirituality and the Reshaping of Religion in the Twenty-first Century* (Reading, Mass.: Addison-Wesley, 1995), 317.
91. Ibid.
92. Ibid.

ity happens when the church becomes "a redeemed and reconciling community among the nations; in this way the church becomes a sign that the kingdom of God has broken through." Just as "freedom to the slave was a nineteenth-century sign of the presence of the kingdom" so, too, working for "desert control, home industries development, urban housing, and energy conservation programmes" are signs of the kingdom today.[93]

Conclusion

The witness of Speratus of Carthage. When Speratus and his eleven Christian compatriots were arrested by the proconsul Saturnus of Carthage in A.D. 180, they were offered their freedom if they would only renounce the kingdom of God and pledge their loyalty to Caesar and the empire of Rome. Speratus, speaking for the twelve in chains, flatly refused the proconsul's offer. He renounced the "empire of this world" in favor of him who is the "emperor of kings and of all nations." Speratus and the Scillian martyrs were then killed.[94]

The struggle of the ancient church, the struggle between the lordship of Christ and Caesar, continued to challenge the church in modern Africa. What had changed in the intervening centuries was the understanding of the kingdom. For Speratus the kingdom of God and the kingdoms of this world were diametrically opposed. In contemporary Africa the church expected to find the presence of the kingdom within the kingdoms of this world. As we asserted at the beginning of this chapter: whether in its political, prophetic, or pentecostal expressions the modern African church's central witness to the kingdom emphasized the coming of the kingdom on earth.

What Speratus knew so well the modern church needs to relearn. "The state is not the kingdom of God nor is it run by saints," writes John de Gruchy. "Therefore the church has to keep awake, recognizing the ambiguities of politics, the dilemmas of power, and especially the pretenses of politicians."[95] The challenge of the church is whether it "can become national without being at the same time 'nationalized.'"[96] The church must confess that "neither the theocratic government of the Puritans nor the social gospel of this century, neither the liberation struggles of the oppressed nor world evangelism, has the ability to usher in utopia."[97]

Even while the church must repent of her pretensions about building the kingdom and of believing in ideologies that promise the same, she must reas-

93. David Schenk, *Peace and Reconciliation in Africa* (Nairobi: Uzima, 1983), 112–13.
94. W. H. C. Frend, *The Rise of Christianity* (Philadelphia: Fortress, 1984), 290.
95. De Gruchy, *Church Struggle*, 226.
96. Charles Forman, *The Nation and the Kingdom* (New York: Friendship Press, 1964), 171.
97. De Gruchy, *Church Struggle*, 229.

sert her witness to the true kingdom of Jesus Christ. In the days of Speratus, Roman society permitted private religious societies (*cultus privatus*) as long as they worshiped the lordship of Caesar, which was regarded as the only legitimate public religion (*cultus publicus*). Rome refused to permit Christianity to become a public religion—one that might shape political loyalties and behavior. Christianity refused to become anything less.

Lesslie Newbigin has spoken of the need to reconnect the concept of the kingdom of God to the person of Jesus Christ. "The kingdom now has a name and a face, the name and the face of Jesus."[98]

Because this Jesus is also the universal Lord, Christianity cannot be content to be a private religion in a world dominated by the public religions of Enlightenment humanism with its ideologies of capitalism, communism, and messianic nationalism. "The Church can be a sign of the kingdom insofar as it follows Jesus in steadfastly challenging the powers of evil in the life of the world accepting total solidarity with those who are the victims of those powers."[99]

African Christianity, the churches poised between Tutu and Kumuyi, must follow the witness of Speratus. Only as she lives a life that is one, holy, catholic, and apostolic among the new nations of Africa can she hope to draw the world to him who is "emperor of kings and of all nations."

---

98. Lesslie Newbigin, *Sign of the Kingdom* (Grand Rapids: Eerdmans, 1981), 18.
99. Ibid., 51.

The Presence of the Kingdom

Lessons from the African Story

It was front-page news in Nairobi's *Daily Nation*. The kingdom was coming. Mozambique, a country often ranked as the poorest country in the world, ravaged by years of civil war and misrule, was to become the location of the kingdom of God on earth. President Chissano invited in the Dutch-based "Heaven on Earth Development Co." owned by the Maharishi Mahesh Yogi, best known as the Beatles' former guru.

The agreement permits the guru's company to pursue a development project officially named "Project Paradise on Earth." Though not yet approved by the full cabinet of ministers, said the article, the president had given the go-ahead on the project. His reasons? He was convinced that the 1992 peace agreement between the government and Renamo rebels as well as the end of a devastating drought were the results of transcendental meditation.[1]

There is an element of humor in this story. The idea that one can build heaven on earth as if it were an amusement park is certainly laughable. But there is a serious side to this story. "Project Paradise" is a revealing glimpse into the soul of Africa. Building eternity in the midst of poverty and dreaming of heaven resting among the ruins of a broken nation are appropriate metaphors for African Christianity. As this history of African Christianity has shown, a longing for the kingdom is one of the most dominant features of African Christianity.

Like the parable of the buried treasure that Christ told in Matthew 13, the African church is a vast and troubled field where the seeds of nominalism, syncretism, racism, and warfare can produce a Rwanda, a nation declared to be 80 percent Christian, where Christian raised machete against Christian until nearly a million were dead. It is a field full of sometimes bizarre churches

---

1. *Daily Nation*, June 10, 1994, 1.

that mingle magic with the Messiah. It is a field where mainline churches are often more interested in politics than prayer. It is a field where charismatic churches cast out demons while their nation goes to the devil. It is a field where within a very few years one out of every five believers in the world will be found.

In this troubled field lies a buried treasure—the pearl of the gospel of the kingdom. This treasure, however, is hidden inside a box—the broken box of African Christianity's kingdom witness. The African church really is a "Heaven on Earth Development Company," which has proclaimed and struggled with the presence of the threefold kingdom of God throughout her two-thousand-year history.

In this final chapter we review the ways in which African Christianity has witnessed to the presence of the kingdom and suggest some lessons that can be learned from that long and troubled witness.

The Anatomy of a Witness

Ogbu Kalu has suggested that "the basic assumption of church history is that the Kingdom of God is here among men." Charting the presence of the kingdom is a task that historians of African Christianity must not ignore. As Howard Snyder reminds us: "One cannot understand Church History without grasping the role the kingdom concept has played."[2] How can we map the signs of the kingdom in the African past? This study has followed the suggestion of H. R. Niebuhr. Niebuhr believed that awareness of the tripartite pattern of the kingdom was the key to seeing its presence in history:

> The Christian faith in the kingdom of God is a threefold thing. Its first element is confidence in the divine sovereignty which, however hidden, is still the reality behind and in all realities. A second element is the conviction that in Jesus Christ the hidden kingdom was not only revealed in a convincing fashion but also began a special and new career among men, who had rebelled against the true law of their nature. The third element is the direction of life to the coming of the kingdom in power.[3]

In what ways has the African church made visible these three aspects of the kingdom? These three aspects have been understood in a variety of ways. Howard Snyder's *Models of the Kingdom* talks of eight primary models that the church has used throughout history to reflect the presence of the kingdom.[4] It must be noted that these models are not mutually exclusive and that

2. Howard Snyder, *Models of the Kingdom* (Nashville: Abingdon, 1991), 22.
3. H. R. Niebuhr, *The Kingdom of God in America* (New York: Harper and Row, 1937), 88.
4. I have adapted Snyder's scheme somewhat but follow his basic outline.

some individuals and groups within African church history embraced several at once. The following chart relates Snyder's models to the threefold nature of the kingdom:

The Kingdom of God as the totality of the Trinity's work of creation, judgment, redemption and consummation								
Sovereign Rule of God: institutional emphasis on God's law (judaistic aspect of the kingdom)			Redemptive Reign of Christ: relational emphasis on reconcilation with God (evangelical aspect of the kingdom)			Coming Kingdom of Peace and Justice: social emphasis on human liberation and fulfillment (egalitarian or hellenistic aspect of the kingdom)		
Theocratic model: Christian political state	Churchly model: Kingdom as the institutional Church	Transformation model: Kingdom as Christianized Society	Inner Model: Kingdom as inner spiritual experience	Heavenly model: Kingdom as mystical communion	Subversive model: Kingdom as counter culture	Utopia model: Kingdom as just society or earthly paradise	Future model: Kingdom as future hope
Byzantium, Ethiopia, Nubia, Portugal, Afrikanerdom	Cyprian, Donatism, Augustine, Roman Catholicism before Vatican II, Zionist Churches, Ethiopian Churches	Augustine, Livingstone, Christianity and commerce, Clapham sect	Gnosticism, Revival brethren, Andrew Murray, New Religious Movements (Kumuyi)	Monasticism, liturgical churches	St. Antony, Circumcellions, Coptics, Alice Lenshina, Alice Lekwana, Liberation theology	WCC, AACC, Zionism, Health and wealth gospel, Messianic nationalism, Nkrumah	Tertullian, dispensationalism, some independent churches, Old Pentecostalism

The kingdom as sovereign reign of God. In the first fifteen hundred years of African Christianity the dominant witness to the kingdom was through theocratic institutions of church and state. The assumption of the theocratic model is that the presence of God's rule is experienced through the institutionalizing of divine law. This type of witness found two primary expressions. The theocratic model seen in Constantine's Rome, Justinian's Byzantium, Zara-Yaqob's Ethiopia, or Prince Henry's Portugal was that of the Christian political state dominating all areas of life for the glory of God. In more recent years the civil religion of Afrikanerdom reflected this witness to the kingdom. A second version of this theocratic witness is found in the churchly model that identifies the institutional church with the City of God. Augustine is one example of this. Modern-day prophets in Africa such as Isaiah Shembe have done the same.

The strength of such models is found in their passion for divine law. Like the Psalmist, the theocratic witness "delights in the law of God." Without a framework of divine law, human society could not exist. Basic values and norms that create the foundation for successful civilizations and institutions are provided by such witnesses. The negative aspect of the theocratic witnesses to the kingdom is found in their subordination of Christ, personal redemption, and social justice to the demands of the institutional state or church and to the rule of law. Coercion through the sword replaces persuasion by the Word in this model. The element of grace and humanitarianism, what the Bible would call love, is often sacrificed by the proponents of a theocratic witness.

The kingdom as the redemptive rule of Christ. The second aspect of the kingdom has inspired an even greater cloud of witnesses than the first.

Three primary models to the redeeming power of the kingdom can be seen in the African past. The transformational model witnesses to the kingdom through the building of Christianized societies. While similar in goals to the theocratic model, the transformational model rejects coercion and promotes revivalism, evangelism, persuasion, and education as the primary methods of witness. Legislation is regarded as an important but secondary means. The antislavery campaign in England, the nineteenth-century missionary gospel of Christianity and commerce, and Krio Christianity in West Africa are examples of this witness.

Another version of the redemptive witness to the kingdom is the inner model, which stresses the presence of the kingdom as a profound psychological and spiritual experience. The inwardness of the kingdom was seen in St. Antony of Egypt who spent his days fighting the demons within his own soul. It was also seen in such diverse movements as Gnosticism in ancient Egypt with its secret salvific knowledge; the Revival movement of Uganda with its emphasis on the new birth; Andrew Murray's piety of "Absolute Surrender"; and the charismatic Christianity of W. F. Kumuyi's Deeper Life Bible Church of Nigeria.

The third model of kingdom witness to the redemptive rule of Christ is the "heavenly" model, which emphasizes not the individual piety of the soul but the spiritual communion of the church on earth with the church in heaven through prayer and the sacraments. This model is distinctively African in that the monasticism that champions it began on African soil. Ethiopian monks and Jesuit missionaries sometimes embraced this model. Liturgical churches in Africa that emphasize the Eucharist bear witness to the heavenly rule of the Redeemer by focusing on his ascended glory.

The strength of these three witnesses to the kingdom lies chiefly in the emphasis on salvation from sin. The profound diagnosis of the human condition inherent in this model is that humanity is dead in trespasses and sins. Human effort alone cannot save. Christ's death has done what no human achievement could do—atone for sins and reconcile us with God.

If the theocratic model emphasized law, the redemptive models emphasized grace. Where these three versions differ, however, is on the extent to which redemption in Christ can transform us and the world around us. The nineteenth-century missionary model of the Clapham sect, Livingstone, and Samuel Crowther was quite optimistic about the social power of the gospel. Gnosticism, charismatic Christianity, and Zionism in general tend to be more escapist. The inwardness of this model makes possible the touch of the kingdom in the heart. Too much inwardness and the kingdom of God collapses into the kingdom of the self.

The kingdom as coming utopia of justice. The final aspect of the kingdom, the coming kingdom of peace and justice, has also inspired its cluster of witnesses in African church history. Common to each variant is the emphasis on the kingdom as bringing about human liberation and human fulfillment within time.

The most controversial of the three models of the coming kingdom may be the subversive model. According to this model, a radical cleavage exists between the coming kingdom of God and all human kingdoms. The task of the church is to oppose the standing order and create a counterculture that better reflects the values of the heavenly reign. Circumcellions in the days of Augustine, Alice Lenshina's *Lumpa* church in Zambia, and a host of liberation movements have given expression to these convictions in the past.

More positive has been the utopian model. While sharing some of the dissatisfaction of those in the subversive model, advocates of this view are more optimistic about "a new world order" being established through the efforts of sincere and committed Christians. Some forms of liberation theology, leaders such as Beyers Naudé and Desmond Tutu, some groups within the ecumenical orbit, a number of Zionist groups, and (in secularized form) a host of messianic nationalist leaders like Nkrumah or messianic ideologues like Mengistu of Ethiopia and Machel of Mozambique bear witness to this approach.

A third group emphasizes the future character of the coming kingdom. Tertullian, conservative evangelical groups associated with Lausanne, and older Pentecostal theology are examples of this third model of the coming kingdom.

The strength of these witnesses to the coming is the degree to which they refuse to accept the status quo as the norm. Those who emphasize either the theocratic nature of the kingdom or the redemptive aspect of the kingdom can accommodate themselves to the status quo more easily than those whose focus is on the kingdom to come. The liability of this third group of witnesses is the temptation to Pelagianism, the emphasis on human effort and human goodness in bringing the kingdom down. This human effort can take the form of either destroying the current order (subversive model); transforming the current order (utopian model); or evangelizing the current order (future model). With David Bosch, African Christianity must reaffirm that "the ultimate triumph remains uniquely God's gift."[5]

Lessons from Africa's Broken Witness

What are we to make of these eight models of the kingdom? If the story of African church history is a story of an abundant but broken witness to the

5. David Bosch, *Transforming Mission* (Maryknoll: Orbis, 1991), 509.

threefold kingdom of God, what significance does that have for the contemporary church? As the world prepares for the coming of what Walbert Bühlmann has called the Third Church (a dominant Third World church in the third millennium after Christ), the message of African Christianity takes on new importance. Consider four lessons that can be gleaned from the story of African Christianity.

First, no one group or denomination or tradition comprises an adequate expression of the total vision of the kingdom of God. The kingdom of God according to the Scriptures is a threefold reality that includes the sovereign reign of God over all things through his providence, the redemptive reign of Jesus Christ over those who believe, and the coming kingdom of justice when Christ returns. Each of these three emphases on its own is an incomplete understanding of the kingdom of God. Yet churches and individuals tend to stress one aspect to the neglect of the others. This gives us a basis for criticism of every expression of the church. We are not obligated to put "halos" over the head of any individual or denomination.

The early kingdoms of Africa sensed the presence of God's sovereign rule in a way that now seems strange to us just as our inward and individualistic Christianity today would, perhaps, seem strange to them. The lack of an integrated witness to the kingdom is one of the most surprising features of the African Christian story.

Second, every expression of Christianity in Africa has a place in the witness to the kingdom. Newbigin has emphasized that the church is the hermeneutic of the kingdom. By this he means that the community of God's people have as their central task to make clear and credible to the world the existence and rule of the risen and coming King, Jesus Christ. By its oneness, holiness, catholicity, and apostolicity, the church bears witness to the presence of the kingdom. Its very life in the world proclaims the presence of the kingdom.

The church, however, has had trouble keeping the threefold nature of the kingdom in full view. Balance has been a problem. This lack of balanced witness to the fullness of the kingdom has produced tensions and even rival factions in the church. Sad as these divisions may be they can be seen as part of God's providential rule keeping each of the three emphases of the kingdom alive.

From this perspective, every expression of the church has value in witnessing to the kingdom of God. Protest movements against missionary churches take their rightful place alongside churches that were little more than clones of their Western counterparts. Liberals as well as evangelicals have their place in the complicated task of bearing witness to the kingdom. From a kingdom perspective even Islam and African traditional religion have had their role in influencing the church's understanding of the kingdom. The

Christian may hesitate to say that rival religions are ways of salvation but they may be seen as ways of witness pointing to the nonredemptive aspects of God's rule such as his providence and his passion for justice. If an observer stands back far enough and surveys the whole, the splintered pieces of Africa's witness begin to form a unity that reminds us of the invisible hand that has shaped the story. The kingdom is equidistant from us all.

Third, the distinctive contribution of the evangelical impulse in Africa is to bear witness to the redemptive heart of the kingdom. The evangelical impulse in Africa is central to the full understanding of the kingdom. This is not because evangelicalism has been balanced or three-dimensional in its witness. The reason why the evangelical witness is so crucial to the African church story is because it points to the redemptive heart of the rule of God in a way that is not true of other emphases. The kingdom is not primarily about power (the theocratic understanding) though it is powerful. The kingdom is not primarily about justice and human happiness (the social justice understanding of the kingdom) though it is the greatest hope for human justice and happiness in the world.

The church must bear primary witness to the fact that the kingdom message is primarily about salvation from sin and death and that this salvation is through Jesus Christ and his death for us. God's kingdom of power and justice has its center in this salvation through Christ. This is the great contribution of the evangelical witness in Africa. Whether this witness was carried on in protest against White Christianity or in cooperation with White Christianity; whether this evangelical witness was borne by a Catholic, a charismatic, or a Coptic matters little. The evangelical impulse, wherever it appears in the story, is nonetheless central to the church's witness to the kingdom in a way that is not true of the utopian and theocratic aspects of the reign of God. This impulse reminds us that the true sign of the kingdom is the risen and coming redeemer Jesus Christ. As Howard Snyder reminds us: "The kingdom of God is to be interpreted in the light of Jesus Christ."[6]

Fourth, the pattern of African church history is the pattern of Good Friday and Easter Sunday. Though the church's struggle to bear a balanced witness to the kingdom has consistently failed, God has taken the defeat of the church and in surprising and gracious ways raised up to life a three-dimensional witness to the kingdom in spite of his people's failures. The cross is not just the place of our salvation; it is a pattern of the church's life in the world. The apparent defeat of Good Friday becomes the astonishing victory of Easter Sunday. God may bring his kingdom witnesses low but it is only to raise them high once again. The church is thus "God's fool" who bears an effective

6. Snyder, *Models*, 128.

witness to the kingdom in an unexpected way through a weakness which permits God's strength to shine through (2 Cor. 12:10). This is the "theology of the cross" that is the key to the real meaning of history.

For an ex-slave like Crowther, to be the first bearer of freedom in Christ to West Africa; for a humble village Christian to create a movement as powerful as Kimbanguism after only months of ministry and years in jail; for colonialism and culturally insensitive foreign missionaries to be used to plant a Christianity that quickly became indigenous; for broken reeds and smoking wicks to become tall trees and blazing torches of witness; for good to come out of evil as it does time and again in the annals of African Christian history—all this points to the One who through death brought life and calls his followers to walk that same path.

This pattern of the cross that bisects the African story is a reminder to worldly churches that enjoy moments of proud success that God will bring them low. At the same time the pattern of the cross is a word of hope to the suffering churches of the continent who live by faith. God brings them low only to lift them high. That is the pattern of the cross and the pattern of this paradoxical kingdom that justifies sinners, empowers the weak, and produces life from death.

Conclusion

The Mahareshi Yogi is building heaven on earth in Mozambique. The sentiment must seem silly to sensible people but it is very characteristic of the African story. President Chissano's party, Frelimo, wanted to build the kingdom on earth through Marxism. Zulu Zions and New Jerusalems dot the African time and space proclaiming similar aspirations.

Just as Jacob wrestled through the night with the Angel of the Lord and just as Achebe's Okonkwo once wrestled Amalinze the Cat, so Africa has wrestled for centuries with rival concepts of Christ and his kingdom. Throughout this long struggle African Christians have discovered that reflecting the rule of Christ and his kingdom is often an elusive ideal never perfectly achieved by any of the real world institutions that bear his name. Though the church's real life imitation and obedience of Christ their King is always flawed and often unfaithful, she continues to wrestle on. This ongoing struggle of African Christianity to bridge the gap between kingdom ideals and African church reality reminds us that the story of the kingdom of God in Africa is a story for the world.

Appendix *Maps*

MAP 1
Early African Christianity: Egypt, Nubia, and Ethiopia

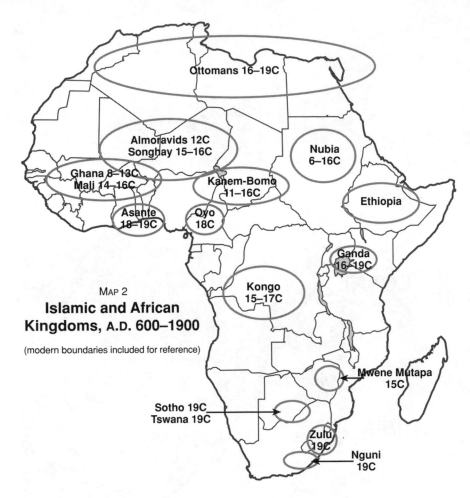

Ottomans 16–19C

Almoravids 12C
Songhay 15–16C

Nubia
6–16C

Ghana 8–13C
Mali 14–16C

Kanem-Bornu
11–16C

Ethiopia

Asante
18–19C

Oyo
18C

Ganda
16–19C

Map 2

**Islamic and African
Kingdoms, A.D. 600–1900**

(modern boundaries included for reference)

Kongo
15–17C

Mwene Mutapa
15C

Sotho 19C
Tswana 19C

Zulu
19C

Nguni
19C

MAP 3

**The European Discovery
of Africa, 1450–1700**

(modern boundaries included for reference)

Key
Da = Danish
Du = Dutch
E = English
F = French
P = Portuguese
S = Spanish

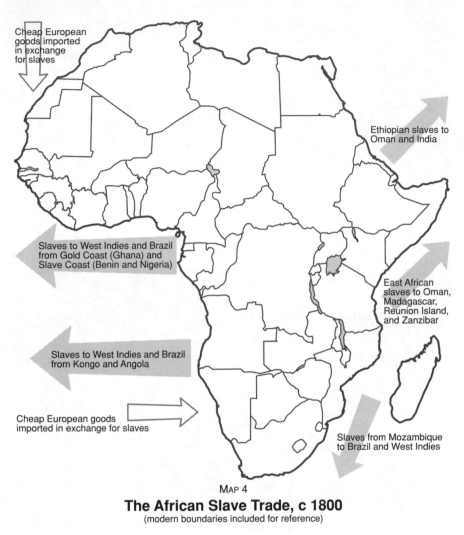

Cheap European goods imported in exchange for slaves

Ethiopian slaves to Oman and India

Slaves to West Indies and Brazil from Gold Coast (Ghana) and Slave Coast (Benin and Nigeria)

East African slaves to Oman, Madagascar, Reunion Island, and Zanzibar

Slaves to West Indies and Brazil from Kongo and Angola

Cheap European goods imported in exchange for slaves

Slaves from Mozambique to Brazil and West Indies

MAP 4

The African Slave Trade, c 1800
(modern boundaries included for reference)

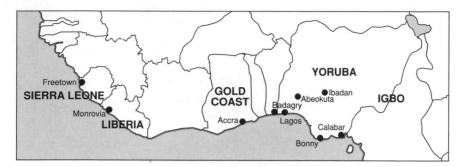

Map 5
West Africa in the Nineteenth Century
(modern boundaries given for reference)

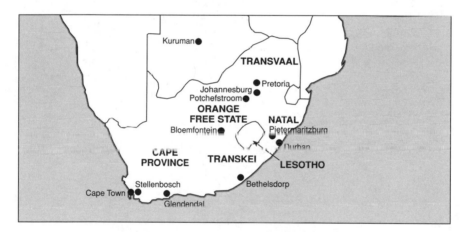

Map 6
South Africa in the Nineteenth Century
(modern boundaries given for reference)

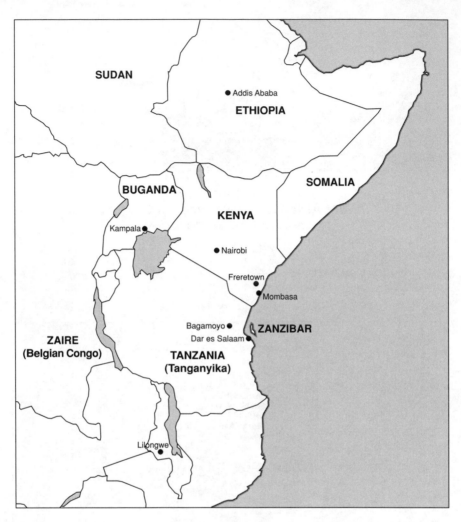

MAP 7
East Africa in the Nineteenth Century
(modern boundaries given for reference)

Mauritania	Morocco	Mali	Algeria	Niger	Libya	Tunisia	Chad	Sudan	Egypt
PM 1870	NAM 1883 OFM 1908	WF 1895	OCR 1843 WF 1872	CSSp 1884	WF 1879 OFM 1913	NAM 1881	CSSp 1883	FSCI 1872 WF 1099 CMS 1899 PRES(US) 1900 SIM 1920	Origin of African Christianity OFM 1623 CMS 1825 PRES(US) 1854 SMA 1877 SJ 1879 NAM 1892

Northern Africa

Western Africa

Eastern Africa

Southern Africa

Senegal	CSSp 1846, PEMS 1862
Gambia	WMS 1821, CSSp 1849
Guinea-Bissau	RC since 16th C, OFM 1940
Sierra Leone	BMS 1792, LMS 1795, GS 1796, WMS 1796, CMS 1804, UBC 1855, SMA 1859, CSSp 1864
Benin	OFM(C) 17th C, CSSp 1860, SMA 1861
CAR	CSSp 1883
Liberia	ME 1811, PRES(US) 1833, ABC 1833, PEC 1835, CSSp 1842
Nigeria	WMS 1841, CMS 1842, CSM 1846, SB 1852, SMA 1861, CSSp 1885, PM 1893, SIM 1873, SUM 1906, MH 1922, OP 1928, SSP 1934
Ivory Coast	SMA 1895, OFM 1957
Congo	CSSp 1865, LIM 1878
Zaire	WF 1878, LIM 1883, CICM 1887, PB 1888, CSSp 1890, PRES(US) 1891, SJ 1891, BMS 1895, AIM 1912
Ghana	DRC 1742, MB 1751, SPG 1765, BM 1828, VMS 1834, SVD 1893
Cameroon	BMS 1845, SMS 1846, CSSp 1848, PRES(US) 1879, BM 1897

Somalia	Trin 1904, IMC 1924, OFM(C) 1930, OFM 1930
Ethiopia	SJ 1554, CMS 1830, OMI 1846, OFM(C) 1846, SIM 1927
Kenya	OSA 16th C, CMS 1844, CSSp 1883, CSM 1898, AIM 1895, IMC 1902, MH 1925, SSP 1953, OFM 1983
Uganda	CMS 1877, WF 1879, MH 1894, FSCI 1910, OFM 1983
Tanzania	UMCA 1869, CSSp, 1868, CMS 1876, WF 1878, B.III 1886, IMC 1902, LM 1893, B.I 1903, CP 1935, SDS 1955
Malawi	UMCA 1861, FC 1875, CSM 1876, WF 1897
Zimbabwe	LMS 1801, PEMS 1877, OBC 1891, ME 1897

Angola	Namibia	South Africa	Botswana	Lesotho	Zambia	Madagascar
SJ 1861	NMS 1876	MB 1736	LMS 1802	PEMS 1829	LMS 1859	LMS 1818
WF 1879	LMS 1801	WMS 1823	PEMS 1829	HM 1857	PEMS 1877	SJ 1861
BMS 1879	WMS 1816	OMI 1851		OMI 1862	PB 1882	NMS 1876
ABC 1881	RM 1824	PEMS 1883			SJ 1879	
CSSp 1883	FMS 1875	SAGM 1895				
ME 1895						

MAP 8
The Missionary Factor in Africa
Based on data in Freeman-Grenville, *The New Atlas of African History*
(New York: Simon and Schuster, 1991)

Protestant Missions

AIM	Africa Inland Mission	PEMS	Paris Evangelical Mission Society
ABC	American Board of Commissioners	PM	Primitive Methodist Missionary Society
B.I	Berlin Missionary Society	PRES	Presbyterian Church of USA
B.III	Bethel bei Bielfeld Mission	RM	Rhenish Missionary Society
BM	Basel Mission	SAGM	South Africa General Mission
BMS	Baptist Missionary Society	SB	Southern Baptist Convention USA
CMS	Church Missionary Society	SMS	Swedish Missionary Society
CSM	Church of Scotland Mission	SPG	Society for the Propagation of the Gospel
DRC	Dutch Reformed Church	SIM	Sudan Inland Mission
FC	Free Church of Scotland	SUM	Sudan United Mission
FM	Free Methodist (USA)	UBC	United Brethren in Christ (USA)
FMS	Finnish Missionary Society	UMCA	Universities Mission to Central Africa
GS	Glasgow Missionary Society	WMS	Wesleyan Methodist Missionary Society
HAM	Heart of Africa Mission		
HM	Hermannsburg Mission		
PB	Plymouth Brethren		
PEC	Protestant Episcopal Church		

Roman Catholic Missions

CICM	Scheut Frs.	OMI	Oblates of Mary
CM	Lazarist Frs.	OP	Dominicans
CP	Passionist Frs.	OSA	Augustinians
CSSp	Holy Ghost Frs.	OSB	Benedictines
FMC	Friars Minor Conventual	SAC	Pallotine Frs.
FSCI	Verona Frs.	SDS	Salvatorian Frs.
IC	Rosminian Frs.	SJ	Jesuits
IMC	Consolata Frs.	SMA	African Missionary Society, Lyons
MH	Mill Hill Frs.	SMM	Montfort Marist Frs.
MM	Maryknoll Frs.	SSP	Kiltegan Frs.
ODC	Discalced Carmelites	SVD	Divine Word Frs.
OCR	Trappists	SX	Xaverian Frs.
OFM	Order of Friars Minor	TRIN	Trinitarian Frs.
OFM(C)	Capuchins		

Tunisia (1956)
7.2m (T 0.1, C 0.1, M 99)

Morocco (1956)
21.9m (C 0.1, M 99)

Algeria (1962)
3.25m (T 0.2, C 0.4, M 99.4)

Libya (1951)
3.8m (T 0.5, C 3, M 96)

Egypt (1922)
49m (T 1, C 14, M 85)

Mauritania (1960) (FWA)
1.9m (T 0.1, C 0.5, M 99)

Senegal (1960) (FWA)
6.5m (T 2, C 6, M 92)

Gambia (1965)
0.7m (T 10, C 2, M 88)

Guinea-Bissau (1958)
(Portuguese Guinea)
6m (T 49, C 11, M 40)

Mali (1960) (FWA)
8.2m (T 15, C 3, M 82)

Niger (1960) (FWA)
6.5m (T 10, C 0.5, M 90)

Chad (1960) (FWA)
5m (T 20, C 35, M 45)

Sudan (1957)
(Anglo-Egyptian Sudan)
21.5m (T 10, C 20, M 70)

Eritrea (1994)
3.3m (T 3, C 46, M 51)

Djibouti (1977)
(French Somaliland)
0.4m (C 5, M 95)

Burkina-Faso (1960) (FWA)
8.9m (T 35, C 15, M 50)

Nigeria (1960)
100m (T 8, C 47, M 45)

Central Africa
Republic (1960) (FEA)
2.6m (T 13, C 84, M 3)

Ethiopia (1941)
43m (T 7, C 58, M 35)

Somalia (1960)
(divided into British and
Italian Somaliland)
5.8m (C 0.05, M 99.5)

Sierra Leone (1961)
3.1m (T 49, C 9, M 41)

Liberia (1847)
1.5m (T 39 C 37, M 23)

Ivory Coast (1960) (FWA)
10m (T 39, C 35, M 26)

Ghana (1957)
(Gold Coast)
12.2m (T 35, C 49, M 16)

Togo (1960)
3m (T 36, C 43, M 21)

Benin (1960)
3.9m (T 55, C 28. M 17)

Cameroon (1960)
(French Cameroon, British
Cameroon)
10.1m (T 36, C 43, M 20)

Equatorial Guinea
(1968) (Spanish Guinea)
0.4m (T 6, C 93, M 1)

Gabon (1960)
1.2m (T 9, C 87, M 4)

Congo (1960) (FEA)
1.7m (T 12, C 86, M 2)

Uganda (1962)
16.5m (T 8, C 84, M 8)

Kenya (1963)
20.3m (T 12,
C 82, M 6)

Zaire (1960)
(Belgian Congo)
34.7m (T 3, C 96, M 1)

Tanzania (1961)
(Tanganyika)
21.7m (T 14, C 51, M 35)

Rwanda (1962)
(Ruanda-Urundi)
6.1m (T 10, C 80, M 10)

Burundi (1962)
4.7m (T 7, C 92, M 1)

Malawi (1964)
(Nyasaland)
7.1m (T 5, C 81, M 14)

Angola (1975)
8.8m (T 14, C 85)

Zambia (1989)
(Northern Rhodesia)
6.7m (T 24, C 75, M 1)

Mozambique (1975)
14m (T 45, C 42, M 13)

Zimbabwe (1979)
(Southern Rhodesia)
8.7m (T 36, C 62, M 2)

Madagascar (1960)
10m (T 44, C 53, M 2)

Namibia (1990)
(South-West Africa)
1.2m (T 9, C 91)

Botswana (1966)
(Bechuanaland)
1.1m (T 37, C 62, M 1)

Swaziland (1967)
0.6m (T 19, C 81, M 1)

Lesotho (1966)
(Basutoland)
1.4m (T 7, C 93)

Republic of South Africa (1931)
(Union of South Africa)
28.5m (T 26, C 73, M 1)

MAP 9
Africa in the 1990s: Politics and Religion

Key
(1956) = date of independence
(Basutoland) = pre-independence name
m = millions
T = percentage of traditional or other religions
C = percentage of Christians
M = percentage of Muslims
FWA = French West Africa
FEA = French Equatorial Africa

Bibliography of Works Cited

The following list gives the majority of sources cited in the notes. For an extensive bibliography on African church history the reader is referred to Adrian Hastings, *The Church in Africa: 1450–1950* (Oxford: Clarendon, 1994).

Achebe, Chinua. *Things Fall Apart*. London: Heinemann, 1959.

Adams, William. *Nubia: Corridor to Africa*. Princeton: Princeton University Press, 1977.

Adeolu, E. A. "A Research Proposal." *The Ecumenical Review* 32, no. 2 (April 1980).

Ajayi, J. F. A. "Henry Venn and the Policy of Development." In *The History of Christianity in West Africa*, ed. Ogbu Kalu. London: Longman, 1980.

Al-Sayid, Abdul Malik. *Social Ethics of Islam*. New York: Vantage, 1982.

Anderson, Dick. *We Felt Like Grasshoppers: The Story of Africa Inland Mission*. Nottingham, Eng.: Crossway, 1994.

Anderson, William B. *The Church in East Africa*. Dodoma: Central Tanganyika Press, 1977.

Augustine. *The City of God*. Garden City: Doubleday, 1958.

Ayandele, E. A. *The Mission Impact on Modern Nigeria, 1842–1914*. London: Longman, 1966.

Baëta, C. G., ed. *Christianity in Tropical Africa*. Oxford. Oxford University Press, 1968.

Barrett, David B. *Schism and Renewal in Africa*. Nairobi: Oxford University Press, 1968.

Bates, Robert, V. Y. Mudimbe, and Jean O'Barr. *Africa and the Disciplines*. Chicago: University of Chicago Press, 1993.

Battenhouse, Roy, ed. *A Companion to the Study of Augustine*. Grand Rapids: Baker, 1955.

Baur, W. *Orthodoxy and Heresy in Earliest Christianity*. Trans. and ed. R. A. Kraft. Philadelphia: Fortress, 1977.

Baur, John. *2000 Years of Christianity in Africa*. Nairobi: Paulines, 1994.

Bebbington, David. *Evangelicalism in Modern Britain*. London: Unwin Hyman, 1989.

Becken, H. J., ed. *Relevant Theology for Africa*. Durban: Lutheran Publishing House, 1973.

Bediako, Kwame. "Cry Jesus! Christian Theology and Presence in Modern Africa." *Vox Evangelica* 23 (1993).

Beidelman, T. O. *Colonial Evangelism*. Bloomington: University of Indiana Press, 1982.

Beyerhaus, P. *The Kingdom of God and the Utopian Error.* Wheaton: Crossway, 1992.

Blyden, E. W. *Christianity, Islam and the Negro Race.* Edinburgh: University Press, 1967, orig. 1887.

Boahen, A. Adu, ed. *Africa under Colonial Domination.* Vol. 7, *General History of Africa.* Paris: UNESCO, 1990.

Boesak, Allan. *Farewell to Innocence.* Maryknoll: Orbis, 1977.

Bosch, David. *Transforming Mission.* Maryknoll: Orbis, 1991.

Bowers, Paul. "Nubian Christianity: The Neglected Heritage." *East Africa Journal of Evangelical Theology* [now *Africa Journal of Evangelical Theology*] 4, no. 1 (1985): 3–23.

Brain, J. B. *Catholic Beginnings in Natal and Beyond.* Durban: Griggs, 1975.

Braukämper, Ulrich. "Aspects of Religious Syncretism in Southern Ethiopia." *Journal of Religion in Africa* 22, fasc. 3 (August 1992): 197.

Bravmann, Rene. *Islam and Tribal Art in West Africa.* Cambridge: Cambridge University Press, 1974.

Bray, Gerald. *Holiness and the Will of God: Perspectives on the Theology of Tertullian.* Atlanta: John Knox, 1979.

Brown, Ford K. *Fathers of the Victorians.* Cambridge: Cambridge University Press, 1961.

Brown, Peter. *Augustine of Hippo.* London: Faber, 1967.

Bujo, Bénézet. *African Theology in Its Social Context.* Maryknoll: Orbis, 1992.

Buxton, Thomas. *The African Slave Trade and Its Remedy.* London: Cass and Ltd., 1967, orig. 1839.

Carpenter, Joel. "Propagating the Faith Once Delivered: The Fundamentalist Missionary Enterprise, 1920–1945." In *Earthen Vessels: American Evangelicals and Foreign Missions: 1880–1980,* ed. J. Carpenter and W. Schenk. Grand Rapids: Eerdmans, 1990.

Chadwick, Henry. *Augustine.* Oxford: Oxford University Press, 1986.

Chirenje, J. Mutero. *Ethiopianism and Afro-Americans in Southern Africa, 1883–1916.* Baton Rouge: Louisiana State University Press, 1987.

Church, Joe. *Quest for the Highest: An Autobiographical Account of the East Africa Revival.* Exeter: Paternoster, 1981.

Clark, J. D., ed. *Cambridge History of Africa.* Vol. 1. Cambridge: Cambridge University Press, 1982.

Colenso, J. W. "A Sermon Preached in the Cathedral Church of St. Peter, Pietermaritzburg" (1879). Yale Divinity School Archives.

Concerned Evangelicals. *Evangelical Witness in South Africa: A Critique of Evangelical Theology by Evangelicals Themselves.* Dobsonville, RSA: Concerned Evangelicals, 1986.

Cox, Harvey. *Fire from Heaven: The Rise of Pentecostal Spirituality and the Reshaping of Religion in the Twenty-First Century.* Reading, Mass.: Addison-Wesley, 1995.

Crummey, Donald. *Priests and Politicians: Protestant and Catholic Missions in Orthodox Ethiopia, 1830–1868.* Oxford: Clarendon, 1972.

Daniel, Robin. *Holy Seed.* Harpendon, Eng.: Tamarisk, 1992.

Davidson, Basil. *Africa in History.* London: Granada, 1984, rev. ed.

Davidson, Basil. *The African Past: Chronicles from Antiquity to Modern Times.* Boston: Little, Brown, 1964.

Davidson, Basil. *Black Man's Burden.* Nairobi: EAEP, 1992.

De Gruchy, John. *The Church Struggle in South Africa.* Grand Rapids: Eerdmans, 1979.

De la Haye, S. *Byang Kato: Ambassador for Christ.* Ghana: Africa Christian Press, 1986.

Debrunner, Hans. *A Church Between the Colonial Powers.* London: Lutterworth, 1965.

Diffie, Bailey, and George Winius. *Foundations of the Portuguese Empire, 1450–1580.* Minneapolis: University of Minnesota Press, 1977.

Ebhomielen, Paul Omieka. "Gustaf Aulen's Christus Victor View of the Atonement as It Relates to the Demonic in Africa." Unpublished Ph.D. diss., Baylor University, 1982.

Edwards, Jonathan. *The Works of Jonathan Edwards.* Vol. 1. Edinburgh: Banner of Truth, 1974.

Edwards, Jonathan. *The Great Awakening.* Vol. 4 of *The Works of Jonathan Edwards.* New Haven: Yale University Press, 1972.

Edwards, Jonathan. *Apocalyptic Writings.* Vol. 5 of *The Works of Jonathan Edwards.* New Haven: Yale University Press, 1977.

Ejofodomi, Luckson. "The Missionary Career of Alexander Crummell in Liberia: 1853–1873." Unpublished Ph.D. diss., Boston University, 1974.

Ekechi, F. K. *Missionary Enterprise and Rivalry in Igboland, 1857–1914.* London: Frank Cass, 1972.

Ela, Jean-Marc. *My Faith as an African.* Maryknoll: Orbis, 1988.

Elphick, Richard. *KhoiKhoi and the Founding of White South Africa.* Johannesburg: Ravan, 1985.

Eusebius. *Ecclesiastical History.* Nicene and Post-Nicene Fathers. 2nd series, vol. 1. Grand Rapids. Baker, 1955.

Fage, J. D., and Roland Oliver, eds. *The Cambridge History of Africa.* 8 vols. Cambridge: Cambridge University Press, 1975–86.

Falk, Peter. *The Growth of the Church in Africa.* Grand Rapids: Zondervan, 1979.

Faupel, J. F. *African Holocaust: The Story of the Uganda Martyrs.* New York: Kennedy and Sons, 1962.

Ferguson, McHugh, and Norris, eds. *Encyclopedia of Early Christianity.* New York: Garland, 1990.

Fitts, Leroy. *Lott Carey: First Black Missionary to Africa.* Valley Forge: Judson, 1978.

Forman, Charles. *The Nation and the Kingdom.* New York: Friendship Press, 1964.

Frend, W. H. C. *The Donatist Church.* Oxford: Clarendon, 1952.

Frend, W. H. C. *The Rise of Christianity.* Philadelphia: Fortress, 1984.

Fyfe, Christopher. *A History of Sierra Leone.* London: Oxford University Press, 1962.

Gehman, Richard. *African Traditional Religion in Biblical Perspective.* Kijabe: Kesho, 1989.

Gifford, Paul. "Recent Developments in African Christianity." *African Affairs* (1994): 93, 513–34.

Gifford, Paul. *Church and State in Doe's Liberia.* Cambridge: Cambridge University Press, 1993.

Gifford, Paul, ed. *New Dimensions in African Christianity.* Nairobi: All Africa Conference of Churches, 1992.

Gitari, David. "Church and Politics in Kenya." *Transformation* (July–September, 1991): 7–17.

Gration, John. "The Relationship of the Africa Inland Mission and Its National Church in Kenya between 1895 and 1971." Unpublished Ph.D. diss., New York University, 1973.

Gray, Richard. *Black Christians and White Missionaries.* New Haven: Yale University Press, 1990.

Green, Henry. "The Socio-Economic Background of Christianity in Egypt." In *The Roots of Egyptian Christianity,* ed. Pearson and Goering. Philadelphia: Fortress, 1986.

Greenslade, S. L., ed. *Early Latin Theology.* Vol. 5, Library of Christian Classics. Philadelphia: Westminster, 1956.

Gregg, Robert C., trans. *Athanasius: Life of Antony and the Letter to Marcellinus.* New York: Paulist, 1980.

Groves, C. P. *The Planting of Christianity in Africa.* 4 vols. London: Lutterworth, 1948–58.

Guillaume, Alfred. *Islam.* London: Penguin, 1956.

Haberland, Eike. *Altes Christentum in Süd Äthiopien.* Wiesbaden: Franz Steiner Verlag, 1976.

Haliburton, Gordon. *The Prophet Harris.* New York: Oxford University Press, 1973.

Hammond-Tooke, W. D., ed. *The Journal of William Shaw.* Cape Town: Balkema, 1972.

Hance, Gertrude. *The Zulu Yesterday and Today.* New York: Negro Universities Press, 1969, orig. 1918.

Harnack, Adolf. *The Expansion of Christianity in the First Three Centuries.* Vol. 2. New York: G. P. Putnam, 1905.

Harnack, Adolf. *History of Dogma.* 7 vols. Boston: Roberts, 1896–99.

Hastings, Adrian. *The Church in Africa: 1450–1950.* Oxford: Clarendon, 1994.

Hastings, Adrian. *A History of African Christianity: 1950–1975.* Cambridge: Cambridge University Press, 1979.

Henderson, Richard. *The King in Every Man: Evolutionary Trends in Onitsha Ibo Society and Culture.* New Haven: Yale University Press, 1972.

Hexham, Irving. "Modernity or Reaction in South Africa: The Case of Afrikaner Religion." In *Modernity and Religion,* ed. William Nicholls. Waterloo, Ont.: Wilfred Laurier, 1987.

Hilton, Anne. *Kingdom of Kongo.* Oxford: Clarendon, 1985.

Hilton, Boyd. *The Age of Atonement: The Influence of Evangelicalism on Social and Economic Thought, 1795–1865.* Oxford: Clarendon, 1988.

Hinchliff, Peter. *The Church in South Africa.* London: SPCK, 1968.

Hinchliff, Peter. *Cyprian of Carthage.* London: Geoffrey Chapman, 1974.

Hinfelaar, Hugo. "Women's Revolt: The Lumpa Church of Lenshina Mulenga in the 1950s." *Journal of Religion in Africa* 21, no. 2 (1991).

Hofmeyr, J. W., and G. J. Pillay, eds. *A History of Christianity in South Africa.* Haum Tertiary, 1994.

Hogan, Edmund M. *Catholic Missionaries and Liberia: A Study of Christian Enterprise in West Africa, 1842–1950.* Cork: Cork University Press, 1981.

Hope, Marjorie, and James Young. *The South African Church in a Revolutionary Situation.* Maryknoll: Orbis, 1981.

Howse, Ernest. *Saints in Politics: The "Clapham Sect" and the Growth of Freedom.* Toronto: Toronto University Press, 1952.

Hutchison, William. *Errand to the World: American Protestant Thought and Foreign Missions.* Chicago: University of Chicago Press, 1987.

Ikenga-Metuh, Emefie. "Religious Concepts in West African Cosmogonies." *Journal of Religion in Africa* 12, no. 1 (1982): 11–23.

Isichei, Elizabeth, *A History of Christianity in Africa.* Grand Rapids: Eerdmans, 1995.

Isichei, Elizabeth, ed. *Varieties of Christian Experience in Nigeria.* London: Macmillan, 1982.

Jeal, Tim. *Livingstone.* New York: Putnam, 1973.

Jonas, Hans. *The Gnostic Religion.* 2nd ed. Boston: Beacon, 1963.

Kalem'Imana, J. Bitangisake. "Christianity and Socialism in Tanzania." Unpublished Ph.D. diss., Drew University, 1986.

Kallam, James Gray. "A History of the Africa Evangelical Fellowship from Its Inception to 1917." Unpublished Ph.D. diss., New York University, 1978.

Kalu, Ogbu. "Doing Church History." Unpublished lecture, Yale Divinity School Archives, n.d.

Kalu, Ogbu. "African Church Historiography: An Ecumenical Perspective." In *African Church Historiography: an Ecumenical Perspective,* ed. Ogbu Kalu. Bern: Lukas Vischer, 1988.

Kalu, Ogbu, ed. *The History of Christianity in West Africa.* London: Longman, 1980.

Kamil, Jill. *Coptic Egypt.* Cairo: American University Press, 1987.

Kaplan, Steven. "Ezana's Conversion Reconsidered." *Journal of Religion in Africa* 13, no. 2 (1982).

Kaplan, Steven. *The Monastic Holy Man and the Christianization of Early Solomonic Ethiopia.* Wiesbaden: Franz Steiner Verlag, 1984.

Kee, Howard Clark, et al. *Christianity: A Social and Cultural History.* New York: Macmillan, 1991.

Kendall, R. Elliott. *Charles New and the East Africa Mission.* Nairobi: Kenya Literature Bureau, 1978.

Klingberg, Frank. *The Anti-Slavery Movement in England.* Hamden: Archon, 1968.

Krapf, J. Ludwig. *Travels, Researches and Missionary Labours During an Eighteen Years' Residence in Eastern Africa.* London: Frank Cass, 1968, orig. 1860.

Langat, Robert. "Western Evangelical Missionary Influence on East African Culture." Unpublished Ph.D. diss., Iliff School of Theology and University of Denver, 1991.

Latourette, Kenneth Scott. *A History of the Expansion of Christianity.* Vol. 5. London: Eyre and Spottiswoode, 1943.

Lean, Garth. *God's Politician.* London: Darton, Longman & Todd, 1980.

Lewis, I. M. *Islam in Tropical Africa.* International African Institute and Indiana State University, 1980.

Lipshutz, Mark, and R. Kent Rasmussen. *Dictionary of African Historical Biography.* Berkeley: University of California Press, 1989.

Livingstone, David. *The Last Journals: David Livingstone in Central Africa.* Vol. 1. Westport, Conn.: Greenwood, reprint 1970, orig. 1874.

Livingstone, David. *Missionary Travels and Researches in South Africa.* London: John Murray, 1899.

Lynch, Hollis. "The Native Pastorate Controversy and Cultural Ethnocentrism in Sierra Leone 1871–4." In *The History of Christianity in West Africa,* ed. Ogbu Kalu. London: Longman, 1980.

MacGaffey, W. "The Beloved City: Commentary on a Kimbanguist Test." *Journal of Religion in Africa* 2 (1969): 129–47.

Mackay, J. W. H. *A. M. Mackay: Pioneer Missionary.* London: Frank Cass, 1970, orig. 1890.

Manus, Ukachukwu Chris. *Christ the African King.* Frankfurt: Peter Lang, 1993.

Mazrui, Ali. *The African Condition.* London: Cambridge University Press, 1980.

Mazrui, Ali. *The Africans.* Boston: Little, Brown, 1986.

Mazrui, Ali, and Michael Tidy. *Nationalism and New States in Africa.* London: Heinemann, 1984.

Mbiti, John. *African Religions and Philosophy.* London: SPCK, 1969.

McCracken, John. *Politics and Christianity in Malawi (1875–1940).* Cambridge: Cambridge University Press, 1977.

McGloughlin, W. *Revivals Awakenings, and Reform.* Chicago: University of Chicago Press, 1978.

McGrath, Alister. *Evangelicalism and the Future of Christianity.* Downers Grove, Ill.: InterVarsity, 1995.

McManners, John, ed. *The Oxford Illustrated History of Christianity.* Oxford: Oxford University Press, 1990.

Moffat, Robert. *Apprenticeship at Kuruman,* ed. I. Schapera. London: Chatto and Windus, 1951.

Mokhtar, G., ed. *Ancient Civilizations in Africa.* Vol. 2 of *General History of Africa.* Paris: UNESCO, 1990.

Molyneux, Gordon. "The Contribution to African Theology of the Faculte de Theologie Catholique in Kinshasa, Zaire." *Africa Journal of Evangelical Theology* 11, no. 2 (1992).

Molyneux, Gordon. *African Christian Theology: The Quest for Selfhood.* San Francisco: Mellen Research University Press, 1993.

Moorhouse, Geoffrey. *The Missionaries.* Philadelphia: Lippincott, 1973.

Moscati, Sabatino. *The Face of the Ancient Orient.* Garden City, N.Y.: Doubleday, 1962.

Mugambi, J. N. K. *Critiques of Christianity in African Literature.* Nairobi: EAEP, 1992.

Mulago, V. *Une Visage Africaine du Christianisme.* Paris, 1965.

Murray, Andrew. *The Key to the Missionary Problem.* London: Nisbet, 1901.

Murray, Iain. *The Puritan Hope.* Edinburgh: Banner of Truth Trust, 1971.

Murray, Jocelyn. "Kikuyu Spirit Churches." *Journal of Religion in Africa* 5 (1973): 202–3.

Mzizi, J. B. "Swazi Zionism and the Royal Politics of the Kingdom." In *Afro-Christianity at the Grassroots,* ed. Oosthuizen, Kitshoff, and Dube. Leiden: E. J. Brill, 1994.

Neill, Stephen. *Christianity and Colonialism.* New York: McGraw-Hill, 1966.

Neill, Stephen. *A History of Christian Missions.* 2nd ed. London: Penguin, 1986.

Neill, Stephen. *Jesus Through Many Eyes.* Philadelphia: Fortress, 1976.

Nelson, Jack E. "Christian Missionizing and Social Transformation." Ph.D. diss., Temple University, 1989.

Newbigin, Lesslie. *Foolishness to the Greeks.* Grand Rapids: Eerdmans, 1986.

Newbigin, Lesslie. *Sign of the Kingdom.* Grand Rapids: Eerdmans, 1981.

Niebuhr, H. R. *The Kingdom of God in America.* New York: Harper and Row, 1937.

Noshy, Ibrahim. *The Coptic Church.* Washington: Sloan Associates, 1955.

Nthamburi, Zablon, ed. *From Mission to Church.* Nairobi: Uzima, 1991.

Nyamiti, Charles. *Christ as Our Ancestor.* Gweru, Zimbabwe: Mambo Press, 1984.

Nygren, Andyrs. *Agape and Eros.* Chicago: University of Chicago Press, 1982.

Oliver, Roland. *The African Experience.* San Francisco: HarperCollins, 1991.

Oliver, Roland, *Missionary Factor in East Africa.* 2nd ed. London: Longman, 1965.

Oliver, Roland, and J. D. Fage. *A Short History of Africa.* 6th ed. London: Penguin, 1988.

Onyeidu, Samuel. "The African Lay Agents of the Church Missionary Society in West Africa: 1810–1850." Unpublished M.Litt. thesis, University of Aberdeen, 1978.

Oosthuizen, G. C. *The Birth of Christian Zionism in South Africa.* KwaDlangezwa: University of Zululand, 1987.

Oosthuizen, G. C. *The Healer-Prophet in Afro-Christian Churches.* Leiden: E. J. Brill, 1992.

Oosthuizen, G. C., and Irving Hexham, eds. *Afro-Christian Religion at the Grassroots in Southern Africa.* Lewiston: Edwin Mellen, 1991.

Oosthuizen, G. C., M. C. Kitshoff, and S. W. D. Dube, eds. *Afro-Christianity at the Grassroots.* Leiden: E. J. Brill, 1994.

Outler, Albert, ed. *Augustine's Confessions.* Vol. 7. Library of Christian Classics. Philadelphia: Westminster, 1955.

Packer, J. I. *A Quest for Godliness.* Wheaton: Crossway, 1990.

Page, Jesse. *The Black Bishop.* London, 1908.

Pakenham, Thomas. *The Scramble for Africa.* New York: Random House, 1991.

Pannenberg, Wolfhart. *Theology and the Kingdom of God.* Philadelphia: Westminster, 1969.

Patterson, James. "The Kingdom and the Great Commission: Social Gospel Impulses and American Protestant Missionary Leaders: 1890–1920." *Fides et Historia* 25, no. 1 (Winter–Spring 1993).

Pauw, B. A. *Christianity and Xhosa Tradition.* Cape Town: Oxford, 1975.

Pearson, Birger. "Earliest Christianity in Egypt." In *The Roots of Egyptian Christianity,* ed. Pearson and Goering. Philadelphia: Fortress, 1986.

Phillips, William, Jr. *Slavery from Roman Times to the Early Transatlantic Trade.* Minneapolis: University of Minnesota Press, 1985.

Pobee, John. *Religion and Politics in Ghana.* Accra: Asempa Publishers, 1991.

Prouty, Chris, and Eugene Rosenfeld. *Historical Dictionary of Ethiopia and Eritrea.* 2nd ed. Metuchen, N.J.: Scarecrow, 1994.

Ramsay, J., ed. *Global Studies: Africa.* Guilford, Conn.: Dushkin, 1991.

Ransford, Oliver. *David Livingstone.* New York: St. Martins, 1978.

Ridderbos, Herman. *The Coming of the Kingdom.* Phillipsburg, N.J.: Presbyterian and Reformed, 1962.

Robert, Dana. "'The Crisis of Missions': Premillennial Mission Theory and the Origins of Independent Evangelical Missions." In *Earthen Vessels: American Evangelicals and Foreign Missions: 1880–1980,* ed. J. Carpenter and W. Schenk. Grand Rapids: Eerdmans, 1990.

Robert, Dana L. "Mount Holyoke Women and the Dutch Reformed Missionary Movement, 1874–1904." *Missionalia* 21, no. 2 (August 1993).

Roberts, Colin. *Manuscript, Society, and Belief in Early Christian Egypt.* London: Oxford University Press, 1979.

Rodney, Walter. "Africa in Europe and the Americas." In *Cambridge History of Africa,* vol. 4, ed. Richard Gray. Cambridge: Cambridge University Press, 1975.

Ross, Andrew. *John Philip (1775–1851): Missions, Race and Politics in South Africa.* Aberdeen: Aberdeen University Press, 1986.

Rowley, Henry. *The Story of the Universities' Mission to Central Africa.* New York: Negro Universities Press, reprint 1969, orig. 1867.

Sanneh, Lamin. *Encountering the West: Christianity and the Global Cultural Process.* Maryknoll: Orbis, 1993.

Sanneh, Lamin. *Translating the Message: The Missionary Impact on Culture.* Maryknoll: Orbis, 1989.

Sanneh, Lamin. *West African Christianity: The Religious Impact.* Maryknoll: Orbis, 1983.

Sanneh, Lamin. "World Christianity and the Teaching of History." Unpublished paper, Yale–Edinburgh Conference, 1994.

Schama, Simon. *The Embarrassment of Riches: An Interpretation of Dutch Culture in the Golden Age.* New York: Knopf, 1988.

Schenk, David. *Peace and Reconciliation in Africa.* Nairobi: Uzima, 1983.

Scholasticus, Socrates. *Ecclesiastical History.* Nicene and Post-Nicene Fathers, 2nd series, vol. 2, ed. Shaff and Wace. Grand Rapids: Eerdmans, 1978.

Shank, David. "African Christian Religious Itinerary." In *Exploring New Religious Movements,* ed. A. F. Walls and Wilbert Shenk. Elkhart, Ind.: Mission Focus, 1990.

Shank, David. *Prophet Harris, the 'Black Elijah' of West Africa,* abridged by Jocelyn Murray. Leiden: E. J. Brill, 1994.

Shepherd, Arthur P. *Tucker of Uganda, Artist and Apostle, 1849–1914.* London: Student Christian Movement, 1929.

Shillington, Kevin. *A History of Africa*. London: Macmillan, 1989.

Smith, Morton. *Clement of Alexandria and a Secret Gospel of Mark*. Cambridge, Mass.: Harvard University Press, 1973.

Snyder, Howard. *Models of the Kingdom*. Nashville: Abingdon, 1991.

Snyder, Howard. "Models of the Kingdom." *Transformation* 10, no. 1 (January–April, 1993).

Sparks, Allister. *The Mind of South Africa*. London: Mandarin, 1990.

Stanley, Brian. *The Bible and the Flag: Protestant Missions and British Imperialism in the Nineteenth and Twentieth Centuries*. Leicester: Apollos, 1990.

Strandes, Justus. *The Portuguese Period in East Africa*. Nairobi: East African Literature Bureau, 1968, orig. 1899.

Strayer, Robert. *The Making of Mission Communities in East Africa: Anglicans and Africans in Colonial Kenya, 1875–1935*. London: Heinemann, 1978.

Sundkler, Bengt. *Bantu Prophets in South Africa*. 2nd ed. Oxford University Press/International African Institute, 1961.

Sundkler, Bengt. *The Christian Ministry in Africa*. London: SCM, 1962.

Sundkler, Bengt. *Zulu Zion and some Swazi Zionists*. London: Oxford University Press, 1976.

Swanstrom, Roy. *History in the Making*. Downers Grove, Ill.: InterVarsity, 1978.

Tamrat, Tadesse. *Church and State in Ethiopia: 1270–1527*. Oxford: Clarendon, 1972.

Tamrat, Tadesse. "Ethiopia, the Red Sea and the Horn." In *Cambridge History of Africa*, vol. 3, ed. Roland Oliver. Cambridge: Cambridge University Press, 1977.

Tasie, G. O. M. *Christian Missionary Enterprise in the Niger Delta: 1864–1918*. Leiden: E. J. Brill, 1978.

Taylor, John Vernon. *Growth of the Church in Buganda*. London: SCM, 1958.

Temperley, Howard. *British Antislavery: 1833–1870*. Columbia: University of South Carolina Press, 1972.

Temu, A. J. *British Protestant Missions*. London: Longman, 1972.

Tienou, Tite. *The Theological Task of the Church in Africa*. Ghana: Africa Christian Press, 1992.

Trimingham, J. Spencer. *The Influence of Islam upon Africa*. 2nd ed. London: Longman, 1980.

Trimingham, J. Spencer. *Islam in East Africa*. Oxford: Clarendon, 1964.

Turaki, Yusufu. "The Institutionalization of the Inferior Status and Socio-Political Role of the Non-Muslim Groups in the Colonial Hierarchical Structure of the Northern Region of Nigeria." Unpublished Ph.D. diss., Boston University, 1982.

Turner, Harold. *Religious Innovation in Africa*. Boston: G. K. Hall, 1979.

Vantini, Giovanni. *Christianity in the Sudan*. Bologna: EMI, 1981.

Walker, David. "'Radical Evangelicalism': An Expression of Evangelical Social Concern Relevant to South Africa." *Journal of Theology for Southern Africa* (March 1990).

Walker, Sheila. *The Religious Revolution in the Ivory Coast: The Prophet Harris and the Harrist Church*. Chapel Hill: University of North Carolina Press, 1983.

Walls, A. F. "Africa's Place in Christian History." In *Religion in a Pluralist Society*, ed. John Pobee. Leiden: E. J. Brill, 1976.

Walls, A. F. "The Significance of Christianity in Africa." The St. Colm's Lecture, 1989, Edinburgh, unpublished.

Walls, A. F., and Wilbert Shenk, eds. *Exploring New Religious Movements*. Elkhart, Ind.: Mission Focus, 1990.

Walvin, James. *Black Ivory: A History of British Slavery*. London: Fontana, 1993.

Walvin, James. *England, Slaves and Freedom, 1776–1838*. Jackson: University Press of Mississippi, 1986.

Ward, Kevin. "'Obedient Rebels'—The Relationship Between the Early *'Balokole'* and the Church of Uganda: The Mukono Crisis of 1941." *Journal of Religion in Africa* 19, no. 3 (1989): 194–222.

Ward, Kevin. "Tukutendereza Yesu: The *Balokole* Revival Movement in Uganda." In *From Mission to Church: A Handbook of Christianity in East Africa*, ed. Zablon Nthamburi. Nairobi: Uzima, 1991.

Warren, Max. *Revival: An Enquiry*. London: SCM, 1954.

Weber, Charles. "The Role of Churches in the Decolonization Movements of West Africa." Unpublished paper given at the Fifth Yale–Edinburgh Meetings on the Missionary Movement, June 1995.

Weber, Charles. *International Influences and Baptist Mission in West Cameroon*. Leiden: E. J. Brill, 1993.

Wells, Ronald. *History Through the Eyes of Faith: Western Civilization and the Kingdom of God*. San Francisco: Harper and Row, 1989.

Wright, Marcia. *German Missions in Tanganyika: 1892–1941*. Oxford: Clarendon, 1971.

Your Kingdom Come: Report of the Melbourne Conference on World Mission and Evangelism, 1980. Geneva: WCC, 1980.

Index